D1480502

DATE DUE

JAPANESE BUSINESS

JAPANESE BUSINESS

Cultural Perspectives

Edited by
Subhash Durlabhji
and
Norton E. Marks

with assistance from
Scott Roach

WITHDRAWN

STATE UNIVERSITY OF NEW YORK PRESS

Production by Ruth Fisher
Marketing by Dana Yanulavich

Published by
State University of New York Press, Albany

For information, address State University of New York
Press, State University Plaza, Albany, NY 12246

Library of Congress Cataloging-in-Publication Data

Japanese business : cultural perspectives / edited by Subhash
    Durlabhji and Norton E. Marks ; with assistance from Scott Roach.
        p.   cm.
      ISBN 0–7914–1251–2 (CH : Acid-free) : — ISBN 0–7914–1252–0 (PB :
    Acid-free)
        1. Industrial management —Japan. 2. Corporate culture—Japan.
    3. National characteristics, Japanese. I. Durlabhji, Subhash.
    1947– . II. Marks, Norton E. III. Roach, Scott.
    HD 70.J3J393   1993
    302.3'5'0952—dc20
                                                                91–42663
                                                                CIP

10 9 8 7 6 5 4 3 2 1

Dedicated to
Raehan Kher Durlabhji
Kile Evans Marks
and
Katie Nicole Roach

Who will inherit a world
which we hope will contain
the understanding and compassion
that we seek to promote through this book

CONTENTS

FOREWORD

The number of media reports as well as academic studies available on Japanese management, organizations, and society in English has grown enormously over the past decade. This has had at least two effects: First, knowledge of the Japanese people has diffused greatly throughout the world, creating more appreciation for and understanding of them, as well as encouraging some people to believe they are experts on Japan even though they have never visited or intensively studied the Japanese. In general, however, this diffusion of information benefits everyone, including the Japanese. Second, it has become impossible for anyone to keep up with all this material, which means that many articles and books are published in a variety of places that even professional observers of Japan miss. Therefore, the need is great for anthologies, and I hope to see more of them in the future centered around various themes of relevance to Japanese management.

This volume presents a useful collection of materials on cultural, social, and interpersonal aspects of Japanese behavior and society that apply to Japanese business. Some of the articles also treat institutions that have supported business in Japan, such as the national government and the educational system. Specific management techniques embedded in Japanese organizations and corporate group relationships that have promoted efficiency and flexibility in operations, such as for manufacturing and supplier management, marketing, and accounting are also covered.

My own work on Japanese manufacturing innovations in the automobile industry and, more recently, on Japanese software factories[1] is representative of a portion of the work on Japan that does not emphasize culture explicitly. Rather, this research seeks to understand the general historical and market contexts of managerial innovations in distinct industries and then to examine the specific strategies, tools, and techniques, as well as the organizational forms, that have enabled certain Japanese firms to perform so well in domestic and international competition.

I have long felt that telling American managers that Japanese workers and managers, or manufacturers and suppliers, cooperate so well because they have had, for example, a 2,000-year tradition of rice-paddy cultivation is not as useful as describing, specifically and in detail, how this cooperation takes place today, why it continues, and with what results. There are also many practices that have evolved in the twentieth century, some even after World War II, that need not be related back to past traditions. In addition, Japanese firms have succeeded in adapting their manufacturing and management techniques to workers and suppliers in other countries, such as the United States; this tells us that Japanese management is not restricted to Japanese people and the Japanese culture as it exists in Japan.

Yet no individual, company, or nation operates without a cultural or, to use a broader term, a historical setting. Whatever Japanese people claim to believe today, they are inevitably influenced to some degree by their common heritage and language and their common experiences, such as the Meiji Restoration and the defeat of World War II, or the shortage of land and resources in contemporary Japan. Both the general and the specific elements of this common experience are important to understand for foreigners contemplating the Japanese or competing with them. Collecting studies such as these into one volume reminds us of how clever the Japanese have been as managers and workers as well as how complex they are as individuals and as a society.

Michael A. Cusumano
Mitsubishi Career Development Professor
Massachusetts Institute of Technology
Cambridge, Massachusetts

ACKNOWLEDGMENTS

This book would not have been possible without the assistance of a number of people. First and foremost, of course, are all the contributing authors, without whose scholarly efforts this book would not even have been conceived. Neelam Kher Durlabhji and Leslie Marks made many sacrifices to make it possible for us to devote time to this project and generally provided the support without which we would have given the project up in despair. Our special thanks to them. Northwestern State University provided a Summer Fellowship to one of us for this project. The administrative support we received from both Northwestern State University and California State University–San Bernadino is appreciated. Special thanks also go to Jacque Collingsworth and Cassie Renz, who typed the manuscript in record time. We are grateful to the publishers for their cooperation and to the anonymous reviewers of the manuscript, whose comments resulted in considerable improvement in the book.

INTRODUCTION

Only twenty years ago, books and articles about Japan were the exclusive province of a handful of Japanologists—and about as numerous. Much of this literature was esoteric and of little use to businesses and individuals interested in establishing some kind of relationship with the Japanese. Japan was an "exotic" culture, and the Japanese were "inscrutable"—this was the sum of the knowledge the intelligent business person or the curious MBA student could garner from a thorough survey of the English language material on Japan then available.

Today, the pendulum has swung in the opposite direction. The current flood of books and articles about Japan and the Japanese has left those seeking to prepare themselves for commercial interaction with the Japanese, whether as suppliers, partners, or customers, with an unmanageable and frustrating task. There are the inevitable pieces in newspapers and magazines, almost mandatory in every issue, with a periodic special issue devoted to the Pacific Century or some such "buzz phrase." Numerous articles in many journals analyze Japanese business from various perspectives. There are hundreds of books, ranging from *The Real Art of Japanese Management: The Book of Five Rings* to *The False Promise of The Japanese Miracle*. Most books deal with specific techniques of Japanese management, especially manufacturing management, such as quality circles or just-in-time inventory control, and these are generally useful for those managers and executives who plan to apply these techniques to their own operations. Many other books are either too specialized or promote a particular point of view and are thus unsuitable for the reader seeking a broad, unbiased understanding of Japanese business culture.

The need for such an understanding is clear. Japan is the world's second most powerful economy. More important, America's

trade deficit with Japan is intolerably vast and by far larger than
its deficit with any other country. Only one solution to this problem will take these two strategically crucial countries towards
equilibrium and harmony: increased American presence in the
Japanese market.

The substantial and rapidly increasing direct investment by
the Japanese in the United States further guarantees that few
American businesses will be able to avoid involvement with the
Japanese. Direct competition with Japanese companies will be
increasingly widespread. Direct involvement even by small businesses is becoming more frequent, as managers of Japanese owned
businesses seek suppliers for parts and dealers for their products.
Although many Japanese executives attempt to adapt themselves
to the American ways, they have deeply held views and attitudes
that they are not able or willing to give up.

The collection of readings presented in this volume makes
available, in a single source, a broad introduction to the most significant aspects of Japanese business. The articles included here
were selected to fit the needs of those individuals who are now, or
soon will be, involved in commercial interactions with Japanese
individuals and businesses. Those who expect to sell to, buy from,
collaborate with, or work for the Japanese will be well served by a
careful reading of this volume. Students at the undergraduate and
graduate levels who envisage a similar role for themselves in the
future—an increasingly likely prospect—will also find this book to
be an invaluable resource.

One other reality guided the selections included in this volume. There is little doubt today of the economic and strategic
importance of Japan to the United States, an importance that will
certainly continue well into the twenty-first century. The U.S.-
Japan trade relationship has been contentious and often nerve-
racking. Some of the "bickering" and alleged Japan-bashing has
left bitter residues that will continue to fester, but overall the
pressure has resulted in considerable leveling of the playing field.
Government-created as well as structural trade barriers have been
reduced and are on the way to being eliminated. If success in competing with the Japanese, at home or in Japan, continues to elude
American businesses, the reasons will henceforth increasingly
have to be found in our inadequate comprehension of, and sensitivity to, the *cultural* imperatives of Japan.

The selections presented in this book provide this important
cultural perspective. Articles have been included that incorporate
cultural explanations for Japanese business practices. We have not

limited our selections to mainstream "business" journals, but have included materials that will contribute to the reader's understanding of Japanese business, regardless of the source. This cultural perspective is vital in providing the foundation for a long-lasting and productive relationship.

This book was conceived with the vision that it should serve as a *foundation* for anyone who expects to have commercial interaction with the Japanese. For a deeper understanding of a particular aspect of Japanese business and society, as may be required, for example, by a "specialist" in Japanese consumer behavior, further study and research may be required. We believe that the broad cultural understanding that this book makes available will greatly enhance the return from effort devoted to more specialized reading.

Culture Contrast

As contrasts go, there are few other pairs of culture as distinct from each other as the Japanese and the American. Japan's many centuries of history and especially its Buddhist heritage has given the Japanese an attitude of repose—the best course is to let it be: When the time is ripe, things will work out by themselves. America, on the other hand, is just a few centuries old and displays an almost volcanic vitality and restlessness. For the Japanese, social harmony has a prior claim in every circumstance; for the American, harmony is the *result* of the rational interaction of free and fair-minded people. One does not lightly deviate from traditions in Japan, many of which are centuries old; in the United States, the habits and attitudes of even one's parent's generation are suspect.

Every culture, through its legal and institutional arrangements, embodies the society's resolution of some basic human problems. These can provide a useful framework for the analysis of cultural differences. Organizations also face the same problems and usually take their cue from the prevailing culture in designing solutions to these problems. This suggests that the perspective provided by viewing culture through the framework of these problems will be useful for organizational analysis as well. The following sections present a discussion of such a framework in the context of the contrast between Japan and the United States. Before this is presented, however, we must alert the reader that the differences are stated here as being sharper than they may be in reality. On each of the dimensions discussed later, there is naturally considerable variation within each culture, so that examples demonstrating a cultural reality opposite to the one described in this book can be found readily. Thus, the following discussion should be viewed in the perspective in which it is presented, as generalizations and tendencies rather than as absolutes.

Freedom versus Order

"The distinctive modern problem," wrote Frank Knight, "is to have freedom (enough and of the right kind) for change and progress, without having so much (and of the wrong kind) as to bring chaos or to destroy itself."[1] We will refer to this as the *freedom versus order* theme. Certainly, both Japan and the United States seek to maximize the freedom available to individuals. Yet, as the selections that follow will demonstrate, the Japanese quest for freedom for individuals is subordinate to a far greater emphasis on order and harmony that prevails throughout the society. Constraints on individual freedom that the Japanese are subject to would horrify most Americans; the Japanese, on the other hand, are disturbed by the apparent mayhem and disorder in American life. Japanese culture considers checks on egoistic impulses to be fundamentally necessary for civilized life; American culture considers the opportunity to pursue egoistic impulses without restraint to be the fundamental goal served by social and political arrangements.

This priority of order over freedom leads to the much more "intrusive" role government is expected to have in Japan, not as much in the lives of individuals as in the functioning of organizations. Here too, unrestrained pursuit of "egoistic" impulses by corporations is viewed as damaging to the social fabric. Fierce competition between companies certainly exists, but is expected to remain within the context of harmony and national interest. Government is viewed by the Japanese people as having the responsibility to ensure that companies operate within this context. In the United States, the role of government in the regulation of corporate behavior is much more narrowly proscribed. Whereas regulation has increased in recent years, a substantial group of intellectuals and business executives remain firmly convinced that government should not interfere with corporations. The paradigm at the foundation of the American economic system provides little room for businesses to incorporate considerations of "national interest" in their decision making and even less for government to monitor or impose such considerations.

Within organizations everywhere, the same tension between freedom and order prevails. The need for order is even greater within the organization, since patterned action is the essence of organized effort. At the same time, to survive in a changing environment organizations must change and grow. Organizations must thus provide employees with the freedom to initiate change and challenge established patterns of action. Through their choice of structure and process, organizations provide employees with environments containing a specific resolution of the freedom versus order problem, a resolution that is, however, consistent with the norms and values of the culture. Order and harmony take precedence in Japanese organizations: the individual's behavior, not only within the organization but even outside it, is specified in great detail. A high level of conformity to specified patterns of behavior is expected, in everything from punctuality to exchanging greetings to seating and speaking order. Even after work hours, employees are expected to conform to standards of public conduct consistent with their membership and position in the organization.

The American organization limits its regulation of employee behavior to the minimum necessary for achievement of narrowly specified organizational goals. Work rules must be observed, and basic standards of reasonable interpersonal conduct maintained. Beyond that, however, few American organizations venture to impose order, nor could they without inviting criticism and even legal action. The ideology of individual freedom prevailing outside the company presses heavily upon the organization. Unless a work rule can be shown to be specifically necessary for the performance of the work, it is probably a violation of the rights of the individual, and therefore subject to challenge in court.

Individual versus Society

In many ways, the *freedom versus order* theme just discussed is a subset of the larger issue of the balance between individual and social interests. But freedom is not the only demand that individuals make, nor order the only requirement of a civilized society. In fact, freedom is largely academic to someone who does not know where his next meal is coming from, or who does not have adequate shelter. People want access to a livelihood, a secure environment, human warmth. The pursuit of these must nonetheless be tempered with some consideration of other people's needs. To what extent does the culture encourage, or insist upon, the inclusion of other people's interests in essentially personal decision making? Japanese culture predisposes the average Japanese individual to be much more inclusive in his or her decision making than the American culture. For example, a Japanese individual is likely to consider his or her family's viewpoint when making a decision as intensely personal as whom to marry or whether to seek divorce. Even the implications of the decision for his or her company are likely to have an impact on the decision.

For various historical and cultural reasons, as some of the selections in this book point out, the Japanese are considerably more group oriented than Americans. Individualism, a cardinal principle of American culture, is largely equated with selfishness in Japan and considered undesirable. The Japanese find themselves tightly bound up in a web of obligations and debts that affects their every action. To be born and raised in Japan is to be forever in debt to parents who made many sacrifices to nurture you and provide you with opportunities. The debt extends to all who have done you any "favor," from teachers who educated you to society in general for creating and providing the infrastructure from which all the amenities of life flow. The Japanese take these debts very seriously indeed and cannot act without considering the implications of their actions on all those who have been so kind to them. "Duty is duty," the Japanese say, and by this they mean that there is no avoiding the obligations they have incurred.

Japan's emphasis on obligations and duties is matched in the United States by an equally strident emphasis on rights. From birth onward, each individual is an autonomous being endowed with certain inalienable rights. These rights do not depend on family or community: They are *entitlements*, not favors. Parents are obligated, by law if not by any innate predisposition, to provide you with adequate care. This attitude of entitlement affects education and employment as well. One does not have to feel obligated to anyone for what one receives as a matter of right. Certainly, many Americans are endowed with a deep sense of obligation and gratitude towards those who have nurtured them, but the underlying paradigm of American life emphasizes rights rather than obligations.

Whereas success for the Japanese individual is viewed as flowing from the kindness and cooperation of many other people, American culture attributes success to the individual's drive, ambition, effort, and talent. You stand on your own two feet—or you fall. You have to look out for yourself, and you should not expect anybody else to look out for you. Raised under this ideology,

Americans tend to make limited reference to others in their decision making. Japanese culture predisposes the Japanese to ask, in
every situation, "What do others expect of me?" American culture
predisposes Americans to ask "What do I want?"

The individual versus society theme is found in organizations
also, where the problem presents itself as *individual versus organization*. No organization can survive if it does not succeed in
motivating employees to look out for organizational interests.
Organizations have to structure themselves to ensure that individual and organizational interests are roughly aligned.

The difficulty of aligning individual and organizational goals
in a company populated by employees who strive to maximize their
own interests "above all else" is immense. The upheaval in management thinking over the past two decades in the United States,
fueled by the proposition that individual interests and organizational interests are basically incompatible, is one indication of this
difficulty. The American manager has an uphill task motivating
employees to ask "What is good for the organization?" instead of
(or at least in addition to) "What is good for me?" Japanese
employees, on the other hand, are already predisposed to view
their interests as being aligned with the interests of their group.
Reflecting these differences, we find American organizations
devoting considerable attention to the design of compensation and
reward policies that ensure that organizationally beneficial behavior results in the achievement of personal goals as well. Japanese
organizations, in contrast, devote their energy to furthering the
perception that individual well-being rests on organizational well-
being.

Equality versus Differentiation

"All men are created equal" may or may not be true, but it is certain that great differences among people exist, and are recognized
to exist, at all levels and in all societies. It is neither possible nor
perhaps even desirable to eliminate differentiation from human
life. Equality of opportunity and equality under law are certainly
worthwhile and morally necessary goals for any society, and they
are pursued vigorously by both Japan and the United States.
Nonetheless, differentiation and stratification exist, and will continue to exist, in all societies. Distributions of power and influence,
reward and punishment, and respect and status are far from uniform in human life anywhere.

Societies differ in the nature of the balance they seek
between equality and differentiation and in the institutional
arrangements they make to operationalize their vision of equality.
The American vision rejects all bases for differentiation except
merit. Yet, in real life merit turns out to be difficult to assess, and
a great many other criteria creep into the processes by which
power, privilege, and respect get distributed. The struggle to eliminate differentiation on the basis of race, ethnic background, and
sex continues on many fronts and is far from over. In the mundane
world of everyday interaction, the American vision of equality displays considerable vitality. The use of first names, regardless of
age, sex, or relationship, is perhaps the most visible symbol of the
American ideal of equality.

The Confucian ideal of family and society, on the other hand,
considers hierarchy to be natural and unavoidable. Japanese culture does not set out to eliminate differentiation but to legitimize
it. Acceptance of and respect for the hierarchical order of society is
fundamental to the Confucian strategy for achieving harmony, and
no goal is greater than harmony. The Japanese thus do not share
the American vision of equality. In fact, differences of rank are
among the most pervasive social realities in Japan. Every social
encounter requires knowledge of the relative ranks of the parties
to the encounter: everything, from the proper form of greeting to
the appropriateness of the content of the interaction, depends on
rank. Far from eliminating the identification of differences in
everyday speech, Japanese language is suffused with connotations
of differentiation.

Centuries of tradition have left the Japanese with a clearly
gerontocratic social order: The most widespread basis of differentiation is simply age. Rank, respect, and usually power and privilege
correlate closely with age in Japan. There is, furthermore, a sharp
differentiation of sex roles, with women accorded a lower status
even though their role as homemakers and caretakers is regarded
as critically important. Historically, Japanese society was also
sharply differentiated by class. With the abolition of class at the
end of the nineteenth century, education emerged as an important
basis for differentiation in addition to age. Although division by
race does not plague Japan to the same extent that it does the
United States, this may be not so much because Japan is less
racist but because the population is remarkably racially homogeneous. In fact, discrimination against even long-established groups
of Koreans in Japan and the historical distrust of all foreigners
suggest that the all too human tendency of associating differences

of race with differences of character is not alien to the Japanese culture.

In summary, the American vision of society rests on a premise of equality, but legitimizes merit as a basis for differentiation. This attempt to achieve a meritocratic social order is frustrated by difficulties with the measurement of merit. The Japanese vision of society begins with an acceptance of the necessity of differentiation, and legitimizes sex, age and education, all more objective than merit but only weakly linked to performance, as the criteria for differentiation. There are immense pressures in modern Japan that are operating to undermine this reality, but for the most part the traditional Japanese vision of society continues to dominate. Curiously, in spite of the American ideal of equality and the Japanese acceptance of differentiation, American society seems to contain a much greater variation in the distribution of power and privilege. For example, the difference between the highest and lowest salaries of a typical business organization in the United States can be ten or twenty times the difference in Japan. Similarly, some symbols of differentiation, such as private offices and reserved lunchrooms, are widespread in the United States but relatively rare in Japan.

The *equality versus differentiation* drama is played out even more sharply in organizations than in the larger society, because organizations everywhere are blatantly hierarchical. The pyramid is the most common image for representing organizations with good reason: organizational efficiency and effectiveness virtually demand a steep gradient in the distribution of organizational power. The American employee is in a curious and unenviable position: Raised in an environment saturated with the ideology of equality, educated in schools where he or she is often encouraged to address teachers by their first names, the employee suddenly faces a lifetime of having to follow orders from people who must be acknowledged as "superiors." One suspects that this discrepancy between the environment and the organization contributes substantially to the American experience of organizational life as oppressive. For many, this frustration and resentment, even if experienced only unconsciously, is made worse by the extent of the inequality, especially with regard to income. American organizations attempt as a matter of policy, and law, to pursue the ideal of a meritocracy, but run up against the same problem of objective assessment of merit that the larger society confronts. One consequence of this state of affairs is the vast distance between "labor" and "management" that prevails in the United States.

Organizational realities and environmentally engendered expectations are much more closely aligned in Japan, with the consequence of lower levels of frustration and resentment. Deep divisions between labor and management are rare, made even less probable by the policy of exclusively internal promotions utilized by most Japanese organizations. Age, sex, and education determine rank and income in the early stages of one's career; at higher levels of the organization, promotion is determined by the additional criterion of performance in eliciting harmonious cooperation from subordinates and colleagues. In the assessment of these leadership qualities, the Japanese likely confront the same problem as faced by American managers in their attempt to measure merit.

Change versus Continuity

If there is anything in life as certain as death and taxes, it is change. Societies must change in response to changes in their environments or be doomed to serious decline. Processes internal to the society, such as science and technology, produce imperatives for change as well. But change is stressful, and humans come equipped with a decidedly finite capacity for change. Furthermore, many aspects of life are considered worth keeping constant, including time-tested values and political institutions. The very identity of a society depends on continued adherence to what it considers to be basic to its character.

Cultures differ in terms of the encouragement and legitimacy that they provide for change. The "frontier" mentality, the quest for change that is at the core of the immigrant's motivation, and the freedom to exploit abundant natural resources have given Americans a predisposition to embrace and perhaps revere change. Traditions acquire staying power over time, and America's relatively brief history has left it far less burdened by the inertia of ancient beliefs than Japan. The American economic system, with its free competition ideology and its protection of intellectual property rights, is perhaps the most energetic engine of change the world has ever experienced. The endless stream of scientific discovery, technological miracles, and new products that have issued forth from the minds of Americans have transformed not only the United States but the whole world as well.

Changes in the material conditions of life have a profound impact on social consciousness. At least in the past few decades, American society has undergone tremendous change: Each new generation seems determined to find its own way of life. Of these, changes in the fundamental institutions of marriage and family promise to have the most far-reaching effects.

Japan, too, has experienced tremendous changes throughout its history. Japan's economic performance could never have been what it is today without these immense changes, especially of the past 125 years. But the essential character of these changes differs significantly from the internally driven dynamic of change in the United States. Great change in Japan has been episodic rather than evolutionary and almost always triggered by external pressure. The most effective of such external pressure has come—and continues to come—from the United States. While the West was boldly marching into the twentieth century, Japan had shut its doors to the world in the seventeenth and imposed on itself a social system based on the philosophy of a sage who lived 2,000 years earlier. Commodore Perry's black ships triggered the downfall of the 250 year old regime of the Tokugawa shogunate and ushered in a revolution in Japan's way of life. The next great transformation in Japanese life was also brought about by Americans, during the allied occupation at the end of World War II. Once again, the Japanese people were subjected to a revolution in their way of life primarily under the influence of external pressure. The current attempt by the United States to force Japan to eliminate trade barriers continues this process.

In terms of the *change versus continuity* theme, Japanese culture urges continuity almost as much as American culture encourages change. At the core of the explanation for this difference lies the Japanese understanding of *time* as cyclical, more allied to the ebb and flow of the seasons than to the inexorable and linear march of events. The present confluence of circumstances is only temporary and thus does not call for an aggressive response. In time the disturbance will fade and things will return to their original alignment. This view also supports the Japanese tendency to avoid confrontation in interpersonal contexts.

For the Japanese, the continuity of their family's good name is a constant requirement in all their dealings with the world. The more ancient the family name and the good work associated with it, the greater is the honor it brings to the current generation. Ancestors are a palpable living presence in Japan, not merely memories but a spirit or *kami* that watches over its descendants. The Japanese individual is thus reluctant to deviate radically from the path laid out by his or her ancestors. In the case of social and political arrangements, Japanese culture provided the strongest basis for the legitimacy of the status quo: divine sanction. Any attempt to deviate from the status quo led to severe penalty, even death, especially under the Tokugawa regime from 1600 to 1868. Buddhism also contributes to the Japanese preference for continuity, through the resignation to destiny that it promotes.

The American enthusiasm for change and the Japanese preference for the stability of the status quo extends into organizations in each society. Effervescence, vitality—and turnover—characterize American organizations, many of which pursue new ideas relentlessly, as a matter of basic policy. This image of the innovative, adventurous organization must be tempered, however, with a reminder that American organizations do not ignore the need for stability. Large segments of the organization continue unchanged from day to day, and resistance to change is not rare. Similarly, Japanese organizations must also change if they are to succeed, and in some ways they display even greater flexibility than many American organizations. Change in Japanese organizations is more incremental and deliberate, however, and embedded in a context of continuity of the essential character of the organization, usually articulated as the founder's values. "Lifetime" employment and the avoidance of mid-career recruitment further contribute to the sense of continuity and stability.

Material versus Spiritual

For most of us, life is an endless series of interactions with the material world, forced on us by the simple necessity of keeping food on the table and a roof over our heads. Most of our goals relate to the business of improving the material conditions of our lives. Our preoccupation with the material world is reflected in the domination of materialistic concerns in culture. Still, since the earliest days of civilization, humans have taken time out from the pursuit of the *means* of existence to respond to a deeply felt need to ponder the *meaning* of existence. Cultures differ not only in the mix of answers to spiritual questions that they make available to people but also in the emphasis they place on the spiritual quest. In American culture, the spiritual dimension coincides almost entirely with the religious, which in turn is dominated by Christianity. Religion, and thus the spiritual quest, is regarded as being quite distinct from the secular, material world. This institutional separation does not prevent many Americans from integrating their religious beliefs with the rest of their lives, but for many others, spiritual and material seem to have no relevance for each other. Thus, the mix of answers to spiritual yearnings available to Americans is quite narrow, and the culture does not give the spiritual dimension any significant salience.

In Japan, until only recently, the emperor was considered to be a direct descendent of the Sun goddess, the highest deity of the Shinto religion. Shinto was at one time the state religion; at other times, Buddhism was actively promoted by Japan's rulers. Government involvement in religion is prohibited today, but for many Japanese, the material and spiritual aspects of life are inseparable. Survey results suggest that about 95 percent of the Japanese people subscribe to both Shinto and Buddhism. Shinto's *kami* are everywhere, in the forests and hills, but also in modern machines: The Japanese have a festival for the *kami* of the machine and make offerings at shrines of these *kami* to express their gratitude for the blessing represented by the machine. A Shinto ceremony is conducted, to give another example, for the souls of animals sacrificed in animal experiments.

Buddhism urges its devotees to work relentlessly to achieve enlightenment: Here, too, the effort is to be exerted in daily life, not in some sanctuary away from the material world. Buddhism penetrated into the daily life of the Japanese people even more thoroughly than Shinto through its association with almost every cultural activity popular in Japan: calligraphy, painting, poetry, and so on. In all of these, perfection is achieved only by approaching the activity spiritually, as a context for self-development.

It therefore comes as no surprise that in Japan the spiritual dimension is integrated into organizational life as well. Many Japanese organizations commit considerable resources to the pursuit of spiritual development by their employees. But even more fundamentally, organizational philosophies of Japanese companies often rest on the premise that work should be performed with the correct "spirit" or attitude. Poor performance is most often seen as a spiritual failure, and in severe cases employees are sent to boot camp-like programs for spiritual rejuvenation.

Many of the specific patterns of behavior of the Japanese people, both in and out of the organization, are more readily intelligible when viewed through the framework presented here. The selections included in this book are divided into five sections. Section I, "The Cultural Environment of Japanese Business," deals with the institutional arrangements and cultural forces that create the context for the Japanese organization. Section II, "Communication and Interpersonal Relationships in Japan," consists of selections on the behavior of the Japanese people in a variety of situations. Section III, "Institutional and Legal Environment of Japanese Business," examines the impact of government, law, and education on business in Japan.

Section IV, "Management and Marketing in Japan," has selections about some of the practical consequences of the impact of culture on Japanese business. Finally, Section V, "Manufacturing: The Japanese Approach," reveals some essential but less familiar "secrets" of Japan's extraordinary success with manufacturing.

SECTION I

The Cultural Environment
of Japanese Business

The basic premise of this book is that further progress in the commercial relationship between Japan and the United States will increasingly require a deeper understanding of Japanese culture. In these brief introductions to each section of the book, we attempt to draw out the cultural significance of the selections by linking the authors' writing to the framework discussed in the Introduction. In Section I, we bring together four articles that begin to describe the cultural context within which Japanese business operates. The sections that follow maintain this cultural focus, but apply it to more specific aspects of Japanese business.

The first selection, "The Source of Japanese Management," is an excerpt from an insightful book by Kunio Odaka. The change versus continuity theme is immediately engaged, as Odaka tries to resolve a conflict between two opposing theories regarding the origins of the personnel practices of modern Japanese business. The "immutability" theory insists that these practices were established during the Edo period (1600–1868), whereas the "postwar evolution" theory suggests that these practices are actually the result of Japan's rapid industrialization after World War II. Odaka finds the truth to be somewhere in between these two camps, but points out that modern Japanese business cannot be understood without reference to seventeenth and eighteenth century Japanese society. His review of that period of Japanese history confirms our suggestion in the Introduction, that traditions influence Japanese culture much more strongly than they do American culture.

Odaka's description of Japanese society during the Edo period provides substantial evidence for the proposition that, when it comes to the choice between freedom and order *and between* individual and society, *Japanese culture has consistently leaned toward order and society. Terms like* close-knit communities *and* groupism, *often used today to describe Japanese organizations, are apt descriptions as well of Japanese society more that two centuries ago. Then, just as today, the destiny of individuals was viewed as being firmly tied to the destiny of the community to which they belonged. Odaka finds that the most prominent characteristics of Japanese human resources management, such as lifetime employment, seniority-based promotion and rank, and the ideology of selfless devotion to the company, are a natural extension of the social reality of the Edo period.*

The equality versus differentiation *theme is also addressed by Odaka as he examines life during this period. The strongly hierarchical, seniority-based society that existed during this period is a direct precursor of the rank structure of modern Japanese business and society. Within the communities of the Edo period, seniority was a inviolable basis for status, and the "elders" commanded absolute obedience from the community at large. This is quite akin to the "gerontocratic" social order that prevails to this day in Japanese organizations. This juxtaposition of egalitarianism with a pervasive rank structure based primarily on age is one of the most interesting features of modern Japanese society.*

Tobioka Ken, in his chapter, "Japan's Matrix of Nature, Culture, and Technology," suggests that the high level of Japanese technology is intimately related to the spirit of traditional arts like flower arranging, tea ceremony, and so on. He traces the development of group orientation and the institutionalization of seniority to the impact of land and climate: wet-paddy rice cultivation required close cooperation among members of a community and survival in the face of the frequently violent weather required the kindness of neighbors. Hierarchical patterns of relating arise naturally in groups of people who cooperate to achieve common goals. Ken's chapter contains a series of fascinating suggestions about the genesis of the Japanese character, including, for example, eating, sleeping, and bathing habits. It is relevant to note that the existence of "group orientation" (individual versus society) and "institutionalization of seniority" (equality versus differentiation) is so commonplace and self-evident in Japan that Ken finds it unnecessary to try to demonstrate their reality and seeks only to explain their cultural roots.

In the excerpt from "Confucianism and Japanese Modernization: A Study of Shibusawa Eiichi," Kuo-hui Tai presents an insightful analysis of the life and work of Shibusawa Eiichi, who has been called the father of Japanese capitalism. In premodern Japan, the merchant class was accorded the lowest status in society, lower than the samurai, the warrior class, and lower even than the farmers and artisans. The samurai followed a strict code of behavior, called bushido, *which consisted of principles drawn mostly from Confucianism and included among its precepts fierce loyalty and high standards of ethics. The true follower of* bushido *considered the material world to be base and not worthy of the slightest attention, and thus a life devoted to material gain was viewed in old Japan as lowly and demeaning.*

Although the samurai exemplified the utmost application of bushido, *the code of the samurai became the ideal to which the rest of the population also aspired. Thus,* bushido *became identified as the Japanese spirit or, as Inazo Nitobe characterized it in a widely read book by the same name, "The Soul of Japan."*

It was in this context that Japan was faced with the challenge of modernization at the start of the twentieth century. Shibusawa Eiichi recognized that the widely held perception of business activity as base and demeaning would have to change if Japan was to enter the modern era. In this excerpt, Tai documents the extraordinary life of Shibusawa and his attempt to demonstrate that business is compatible with Confucianism and bushido. *Shibusawa's writings are still very popular in Japan, and his influence on Japanese business is immeasurable.*

Shibusawa urged on Japanese businessmen a unique marriage between bushido *and commercial talent. It is interesting to note that, although the other great Confucian culture, China, found it necessary to break with Confucianism in order to modernize, Shibusawa insisted that Japanese business retain the Japanese spirit. This reflects the strong tendency within Japanese culture to prefer* continuity *to radical* change. *There could be no better statement of this tendency than Tai's conclusion from his review of the history of Japanese industrialization: "What deserves our attention is that the Japanese always insist on maintaining the Japanese spirit: They can revise, reinforce, or adapt it, but never are willing to abandon it completely in favor of total Westernization."*

The other theme from our framework for which we find considerable evidence in Tai's article is material versus spiritual. *Not simply the constant reference to "the Japanese spirit" but the entire tone of Shibusawa's work reflects the greater comfort and concern that Japanese culture has with the spiritual dimension of human existence. In fact, Shibusawa's life's work could be summarized as*

*an attempt to endow business activity with a spiritual patina, a
task he presumably found necessary because of the prevalence of the
spiritual quest within Japanese culture.*

*The last selection in Section I, "The Influence of Confucianism
and Zen on the Japanese Organization," utilizes concepts from
Western social science to reveal the processes by which Japanese
culture has influenced the form and functioning of the Japanese
organization. Subhash Durlabhji, one of the editors of this book,
distinguishes between utilitarian and affective relationships and
demonstrates that, under the influence of Confucianism, the Japanese people find it difficult to establish utilitarian, contractual relationships. An affective, trusting relationship is a prerequisite to
even limited business interactions in Japan, which is why the most
frequently heard advice about doing business with the Japanese is
to take the time and patience necessary to build a relationship
before expecting successful business dealings. From Zen, according
to Durlabhji, "the Japanese people get a set of attitudes, predominant among which is a distrust of rational and logical processes."
Zen teaches the Japanese to be more in tune with the intuitive side
of their minds and to avoid exclusive reliance on the direct, logical
approach, both in the context of work and in the context of interpersonal relationships. Japanese involvement with Zen practices, even
in business contexts as indicated in this selection and also in the
selection by Thomas P. Rohlen in Section III, reflects the perception
held in Japanese culture that the truly meaningful life cannot be
achieved without the correct spiritual understanding.*

1

The Source of Japanese Management*

Kunio Odaka

[**Editors' Note:** In an earlier part of the chapter from which this selection is excerpted, the author discussed two theories regarding the origin of Japanese management. The "immutability" theory traces modern Japanese management to the values of premodern Japan, whereas the "postwar evolution" theory suggests that modern Japanese management evolved only after World War II and has little to do with premodern Japan.]

Although it may seem strange for there to be two drastically conflicting theories about when a given set of personnel policies was established, such disagreement is by no means unusual. What we have here are two theories, each stubbornly affirming one side of the same set of facts while denying the other completely.

As so often happens in such cases, the truth is somewhere in between, that is, the original form of Japanese management was, as the theory of immutability argues, molded out of values underlying Japanese society during the Edo period. In this prototype form, including both positive and negative aspects, it endured over

---

*Excerpted from *Japanese Management: A Forward Looking Analysis* (Tokyo: Asian Productivity Organization, 1986). Reprinted by permission.

the years until the end of World War II. Yet as the postwar evolution theory contends, Japanese management was modified and strengthened over the long decades of Japanese industrialization in the late nineteenth and early twentieth centuries, and it did not emerge in its present form until after World War II.

Any discussions of Japanese management today must deal with Japanese personnel practices in their present form. However, even though this present form has undergone substantial evolution, it must be recognized that Japanese management still retains its original character and effectiveness. The forces that produced the Japanese management prototype, for all its strengths and weaknesses, are still with us today.

The Close-Knit Communities of the Edo Period

In attempting to discover how Japanese management originally arose, we must first look at the seventeenth and eighteenth century society and the various close-knit communities that sprang up throughout Japan during that period.

The shogunate that Tokugawa Ieyasu founded in Edo in 1603 divided Japan into a large number of fiefs created by consolidating the domains the *daimyo* lords had held since the late sixteenth century. Each fief included the villages that already existed within its realm and the families that had settled them.

The word *family* here does not mean the nuclear family consisting of a husband and wife and their children, but the patriarchal extended family banded together to pursue wet-paddy rice farming in the traditional manner. A village of such families was a natural unit, unlike the artificial administrative units of modern times. Like the village families, the village itself was engaged primarily in growing rice in irrigated paddies. Given the demands of this work, the village's families and individuals had to cooperate to perform this work as efficiently as possible, and their cooperation readily extended to their other daily activities that they undertook to ensure the entire village's continuity and prosperity.

To the people who lived in them, these families and villages were close-knit communities sharing a common fate: Each community of people bound by kinship, land, or other natural ties, living together permanently in one place as a self-sufficient group in the true spirit of harmony and cooperation. The reason for calling such a community close knit is that its members were completely immersed in it for their whole lives. A person who became a member of such a community, regardless of his or her role and accomplishments, was inseparable from the community and its destiny.

Although the family and the village units arose spontaneously, the fiefs were artificially established for military or political reasons. Yet because the society and social structures that they encompassed consisted of a number of family and village communities, so in time did the fiefs themselves come to take on many of the features of those close-knit communities. During the 265 years that the Tokugawa shogunate lasted, many such close-knit communities were formed and flourished throughout Japan. Several factors made this possible.

The first factor was that the main occupation of the members of these communities was, as we have seen, wet-paddy farming. It was neither commerce nor industry occupations that keep people constantly moving to different places, but agriculture—the tilling of paddies by generation after generation of people living permanently in the same place. Having this land-rooted occupation basic to their entire way of life facilitated the formation of close-knit communities.

Perhaps even more important, however, were the special political and societal conditions of the Edo period. The Tokugawa shogunate brought peace to the land after nearly 150 years of civil war. When Tokugawa Ieyasu united the country under a stable, orderly government, the resulting political situation naturally favored the formation and prosperity of all sorts of close-knit communities, large and small. This was further encouraged by the shogunate's policy of sealing out foreign influence as the Tokugawa shogunate protected these close-knit communities from being undermined by foreign culture and civilization. Christianity, for example, was an important factor in fostering individualism in the West but remained inconsequential in Japan during these centuries.

Interpersonal Management and the Close-Knit Community

The close-knit communities that developed under the Tokugawa shogunate operated on the basis of a number of personal management principles or, from the standpoint of the community members, behavioral norms:

1. Total, lifelong membership. Most of the members of the close-knit community were born and raised in it, worked in it, lived in it, and belonged within the community. If events forced them to go into the outside world, they carried their community status and duties with them and retained these permanently. Throughout their lives, their destinies as individuals were tied up with the destiny of their community.

2. The duty of selfless devotion to the community. The primary duty of a member of a close-knit community was to devote oneself selflessly to the continued well-being of the community as a whole. There must have been people in these communities who desired personal distinction and happiness, but such desires were suppressed as the sustained, patient effort to ensure the continuity, prosperity, peace, and happiness of the group took precedence. Not until these things had been achieved for the community as a whole could individual members benefit from them, in proportion to the effort each had put into their attainment.

3. Discipline and seniority-based rank. Whether born or adopted into a household that already belonged to the village community, the individual's status in the community was defined from the very beginning as that of his or her household. From a young age, formally recognized members of the community were taught discipline and correct behavior so that they could grow into capable community leaders. They were taught not only the rules of personal relationships but also rules of moderation in food and dress and the accepted uses of leisure time. They also received thorough training in the household occupation, so that they could contribute properly to it, and through it to the life of the community. Although the training varied slightly from community to community, it was usually fixed and uniform in each community, aimed at turning out well-integrated community members. Little attention was paid to developing the individual's personality, talents, or ambitions. In fact this type of education was avoided because it might produce heretics who would disrupt the community order.

   Young people brought up under this discipline were first set to easy tasks as apprentices or helpers. As they grew older and gained experience, they were given more difficult and important work. As their roles changed, so did their status and the treatment accorded them. Thus arose the system of seniority distinctions among community members, and the seniority-based hierarchy.

4. Harmony and concerted efforts. A single close-knit community often contained subcommunities within it, either present from the beginning or created subsequent to the community's formation. In every village there were, for example, the separate constituent families, groupings of clan and kinship, and age groupings. Within a family, the subgroupings might include the main family and several branch families, direct and collateral bloodlines, and the group of hired hands. Each grouping would have its own role and rank, but the different groups were always expected to cooperate with each other and to respect the hierarchy of their relative positions. For its own continuity and well-being, the community demanded that its subcommunities work together to create and preserve harmony for concerted community efforts.

It was also important to maintain and promote harmony within the subcommunities. Harmony within the subcommunity may even have been more important, because without it there could not be true cooperation among the different subcommunities. One of the basic beliefs of the community leaders was that harmony among the members of the subcommunities was a motivating factor for all community members. It was to promote harmony within the group that competition among the members of a subcommunity was suppressed, and attempts to gain advantage over other people were quashed, and equivalent rank and treatment were accorded to group members of the same age cohort.

Because of these practices of harmony and concerted effort, less capable members who were unable to perform their set tasks well and delinquent members who abandoned their duties were helped out by the rest of their subcommunity and were gradually socialized to fit in with the group. After a while, they came to have the pride and feeling of worth that accrued from contributing to the entire community.

5. Authoritarian management and participative management. The highest status among the members of a close-knit community belonged to the village headman, the heads of households and other elders, and the leading adults appointed as their assistants. Having the authority to speak on behalf of the entire community's interests and needs, these people demanded absolute obedience from the general community at large.

In running the community's affairs, however, these men of authority did not use the arbitrary, one-sided decision-making process of despot kings or autocratic company presidents. In principle, all important decisions concerning the ruling and running of the community were made in councils, with all members participating. The elders' duty was to pass final judgment on the results reached by the council.

Decision in the various subgroups generated within the close-knit community were made in basically the same way, with the participation of all members. The oft-cited *ringi* system is simply the institutionalization of this type of decision-making process. What Vogel called the Japanese *bottom-up* method of corporate management already existed in the close-knit communities of the Edo period.

This Japanese management was participative in the sense that all members of the group joined in deciding its directions and planning its activities. Participation was a major feature of these close-knit communities. The reverse side of participation's coin— that no member of the group was individually responsible or even had to feel responsible for whether the policies and plans everyone decided on succeeded or failed—was equally important. Responsibility for the group's decisions and their implementation was borne not by individual members but by the group as a whole.

6. Concern for the person's total welfare. The final important feature of these close-knit communities was the way they looked after their members, seeing that they had the necessities of life: food, shelter, and clothing; protection and safety; education and training; health and hygiene; and leisure and entertainment. The peace and happiness of the life of the group could not be achieved without satisfying its members' needs.

If the community had not shown such concern for the welfare of its members, they would probably not have been willing, no matter how closely their own fate was linked with the group's, to give it their continued devotion and service. But with the members belonging to the group with their whole beings for their whole lives, it was natural for the close-knit community to show a constant, warm concern for the total life of each member. At the same time, however, the close-knit community's all-embracing concern for its members' well-being sometimes had the undesired effect of spoiling them and making them overly dependent on the community.

The Source of Japanese Management

The principles of personal management in these close-knit communities furnished their members with behavioral norms and structured their shared existence. By following these behavioral norms in their continuing common life, they were able to make their close-knit community a place of happiness, comfort, and peace. Satisfied with their community life, they could take pride in the worth of their daily work and devote themselves to the preservation and prosperity of the group.

This was no mean achievement. In later years, when more modern organizations were created in Japan's urban centers, the founders and managers of those organizations had the wit to try to make them as much like the former close-knit communities as possible. It was no accident that they modeled their personnel practices on the principles of personal management generally found in the close-knit communities. The value set that guided this wisdom was the theory that we are calling *groupism*.

However, this theory was first applied to create imitations of the close-knit communities long before corporations, factories, trading companies, and the like began to appear in Japan's cities. The commercial application of the values of groupism—the embryo forms of the Japanese management pattern—actually took place around the middle of the Edo period. The artificial bodies to which groupism was applied were still too small to be called *modern organization;* they lacked modern facilities, and the management was not very "rationalized." They were the mercantile houses with shops in large cities.

In the beginning of the eighteenth century, for example, the Mitsui, Konoike, Sumitomo, and other large mercantile houses flourished in Osaka, Kyoto, and Edo. These mercantile houses were originally family businesses, but they also engaged in shipping, mining, pharmacy, money changing, money lending, and other activities. They were quite distinct from the original close-knit communities, which were located in the country and practiced agriculture as their main occupation, but this very distance was all the more reason for their founders and managers to consciously model their shops and other places of business on the former close-knit communities. The fact that their personnel practices were based on the principles of personal management originally found in the close-knit communities was one of the secrets of their success.

Proof that such modeling actually took place can be found in the family precepts of these mercantile houses. According to Professor Yotaro Sakudo, a management historian at Osaka University, the major practices of later-day Japanese management, including lifelong employment, the seniority-based hierarchy, the apprentice system, training and discipline, respect for harmony, group decision making, and humanistic management, were often emphasized in the family precepts of the mercantile houses of Osaka and vicinity as basic precepts for employee management. Systematic Japanese management practices based on the theory of groupism already existed in a primitive but visible form in the eighteenth century.[1]

The fact that this special set of practices was inscribed in the family precepts is indicative of how effective they were in the mercantile houses' management. Indeed, large mercantile houses practicing this early form of Japanese management were established not only in the three large cities of Osaka, Kyoto, and Edo but also in outlying castle towns as well. During the long period between its original formation and the end of World War II, however, Japanese management was frequently modified to satisfy evolving requirements. According to Professor Sakudo, these modifications had already begun in the Edo period. Further modifications were made in the late nineteenth and early twentieth centuries, when Japan's industrial modernization was beginning to "take off" and modern enterprises were springing up all over the country. The pace of changes was particularly evident at the larger enterprises as they rationalized their organizations to make better use of the new, power-driven facilities they were installing.

Modern Business's Groupistic Management

The groupistic management that was applied in Japan's new, urban firms and factories around the turn of the twentieth century had the same ultimate objectives as the groupistic theory applied by the Osaka mercantile families in the eighteenth century but was adopted for slightly different reasons. In eighteenth century feudal Japan, groupism was applied to organizations that had started as close-knit communities but had become so large that they were losing their original community character, and groupistic management was intended to revive this community character and group values.

In the firms and factories of the late nineteenth and early twentieth centuries, groupism was applied to organizations that had never been close-knit communities but were completely new creations, rationally and artificially constructed in imitation of the corporate organizations of the advanced industrial countries of the West. Thus groupism was instituted and institutionalized at these organizations to make them more like the close-knit communities of old and, by introducing groupistic management practices modeled on the communities' personal management, to instill them with a community spirit and vigor.

Japanese management is not a style of corporate management that developed spontaneously at any one point in time or any one firm. Rather, the system of Japanese management practices was created intentionally and systematically to make the new corporate organizations resemble the successful close-knit communities of the past despite their modernity, rationality, and artificiality. Not created at any one particular time by any one individual or individuals, it was molded over a long period, undergoing modification and development at the hands of many individuals. What remained constant throughout the process of its formation was the effort to make the modern, artificial corporation a vital entity by imbuing employees with the spirit of company loyalty, community identification, and pride in their work.

Is Company Loyalty a Japanese Instinct?

Although the modern Japanese company as it emerged in the late nineteenth century was an artificial creation patterned after Western models, it was not simply an organization created for a single purpose. It was also a *gesellschaft*[2]—a company of individuals gathered together for their mutual benefit. No matter how culturally homogeneous the Japanese people might be, no matter how infused they might be with the spirit of harmony and cooperation, the new organizations were ultimately composed of people, both labor and management, pursuing their own individual interests. The bigger the enterprises grew and the more the individual's role was compartmentalized, mechanized, and automated, the truer this became. If the employees of such a *gesellschaft* had been left to work simply for the corporate profit, without receiving any independence or autonomy, they would eventually have lost their will to work for and identification with the company. They would have become the type of employees who are quick to gripe where their own ambitions and desires are concerned but are completely indifferent to the company's needs and interests.

Only the uninformed outsider, or nationalist seeking something to extol in the Japanese character, could believe that all Japanese have some kind of innate loyalty that would prevent the disintegration of the company even if nothing were done to strengthen and consolidate personal relations. Even if it could be demonstrated that modern Japanese workers are more loyal to their companies than American or West German workers, this would probably have to be done with a survey conducted at a Japanese company that had been practicing groupistic management and fostering employee loyalty for some time. Loyalty to the company is by no means an innate or instinctive Japanese trait.

Today as in the past, Japanese who work for a company work for their own needs and interests. If they work willingly, it is because the work satisfies their own needs and does not involve any undue suffering or sacrifice. If forced to perform dull, repetitive, compartmentalized tasks in a mechanized or automated plant without any discretionary freedom, even the most diligent Japanese worker would eventually lose the will to work and fail to identify with the company.

In fact, this very trend was already evident among employees at large, impersonal companies in the earlier-industrializing countries. Starting in the late nineteenth century, the entrepreneurs and managers of modern Japanese firms realized that Japan would suffer the same problem of labor alienation, with all of its dangerous consequences for their companies' survival and growth, if they allowed their companies to remain mere associations in the *gesellschaft* sense.

One option open to them for preventing such alienation was to take advantage of the employee's own self-interest to tie him or her to the company with rationalized working conditions, efficiency, pay, and improved treatment. This policy left the *gesellschaft* character of the corporation unchanged. The other side of this policy was to sharply limit the employee's actions and to punish or fire lazy or disobedient workers. This was the usual policy in the industrialized Western countries, and it was adopted by many of Japan's early modern companies.

Yet as the disadvantages of this policy orientation became evident starting in the early years of the twentieth century, large Japanese corporations shifted their personnel practices to the second option of conceiving the modern company's artificial structure as analogous to the close-knit communities of an earlier time. In effect, this was an effort to introduce groupistic management practices modeled on the personal management principles of the close-knit communities and hence to suppress the *gesellschaft* aspects and highlight the communal *gemeinschaft* aspects. On the whole, this policy was successful. Companies that introduced groupistic management practices found they had heightened the spirit of harmony, cooperation, and employee loyalty, people took pride in their work and its social worth, and there tended to be less personnel turnover. Because of these positive results and despite the serious problems inherent within the system, these groupistic management practices were preserved through World War II to become institutionalized at large corporations as fodder for the Japanese management myth.

2

Japan's Matrix of Nature, Culture, and Technology*

Tobioka Ken

The level of Japanese technology today, in almost all areas except the military, is among the highest in the world. For some time, Japan has been producing highly competitive automobiles, household electrical appliances, and iron and steel—our leading industries—and now it has become a top producer in microelectronics and mechatronics. Japan's robots, semiconductors, computers, video and copy equipment more than hold their own in the technological marketplace.

Why Japanese technology in mechatronics and microelectronics is so successful is no mystery if one examines the process of its growth. After the Second World War, Japan was quick to move into precision instruments, including watches, cameras, and electronic microscopes. It made rapid strides and joined the most advanced nations in this area first. An important subsequent breakthrough was the perfection, ahead of other countries, of the LSI manufacturing process using electron beams instead of photo beams, and that led to the recent achievement of very large-scale

*Reprinted, by permission of publisher, from *Management Review*, May 1985 © 1985, American Management Association, New York. All rights reserved.

31

integrated circuits with resolution capacity of 0.5 microns. One factor contributing to this crucial innovation was the superior level of technology in electronic microscopes, one of Japan's most highly developed precision industries.

Given their ingenuity in systematization techniques, it may have been historically inevitable that the Japanese would perfect and combine the two types of technology—electronics and precision engineering—to bring about a new system of mechatronics. Yet ingenuity alone cannot explain Japan's strength in precision industries and systematization. Nor does it account for Japanese skill in assimilating foreign technology. But it is important to understand just what else was involved in preparing the Japanese to forge ahead so quickly and with so few false diversions on the road to technological eminence. That background has a lot to do with the process of Japan's modernization and with the ways Japan will tackle difficulties in the future. I would like to examine how technological advancement—a central pillar in the prosperity of the economy—is related to Japanese culture and the natural environment that helped shape the culture. Then I will briefly consider the kinds of technological innovations and economic values that can be expected from Japan's cultural base as the society becomes progressively more international.

Evolving Traditions

An interesting episode revealing the close relationship between Japan's cultural tradition and industrial technology occurred in 1980. On a trip to Japan, the president of a large American electrical appliances company visited one of the factories of a leading Japanese manufacturer. When he was shown the production line, he was utterly amazed at the workers' absorption in their simple tasks and the diligence and precision of the women workers. He was so impressed, and believed it so important to analyze their motivation, that the president extended his stay in Japan. Thinking it might explain the difference in labor productivity between Americans and Japanese, he tried hard to discover the key to their work attitudes. He observed the same women as they worked on the assembly line for several days, until he finally decided that

the way these women approach their work reflects something of Japan's traditional spirit. They appear to work in exactly the same spirit as they might perform the traditional arts, like flower arranging or tea ceremony. These girls are not just mindlessly moving their hands as they work; they seem to find some delicate diversity in apparently repetitive and simple functions. As a result, their skills improve dramatically.

American workers were no match for the Japanese, the American businessman lamented.

This president later visited Kyoto, as most foreign visitors do. The buildings, gardens, and other spots he saw in the old capital demonstrated the same qualities of care, precision, and excellence that he found in the workers. To most foreigners the rock garden at Ryoanji temple is just another garden with an arrangement of stones and sand that one might find anywhere. But the balance in the geometrical pattern produced from the combination of ordinary stones and combed sand projects an expanse of universe within the confines of a small enclosure. Here, the American company president could see the influence of nature on cultural patterns, and appreciate the skill necessary to create a macrocosm from a microcosm.

There is a deep-lying connection between the high level of Japanese technology and the traditional arts—flower arranging, tea ceremony, *Noh*, indigenous architecture, and many more. If we can identify that connection, it ought to be easier to understand why Japanese technology has advanced so far and so quickly.

Land, Climate, and Sensitivity

To begin with, the land, which is the base of our culture: Japan is a long and narrow chain of islands lying off the eastern rim of the Eurasian continent. On one side is the Sea of Japan and on the other, the Pacific Ocean—two very different bodies of water. The islands are covered with mountains and valleys, and the monsoon climate pours two-and-one-half times the world's average rainfall over them. The precipitous landscape and abundant rain combine to produce a fine network of rivers, some of them roaring currents, others meandering streams. The richness of the natural environment is manifest throughout the islands in all four seasons. Winter brings arctic cold and wind to the north, and summer transports most of the land into a state of humid, semitropical heat. The seasons are punctuated by floods, droughts, blizzards, and typhoons.

Nature in Japan is violent and mild, delicate and rough. In its ever-changing diversity, it has gathered within the islands most of the variation in climate to be found anywhere. The range of plant life is vast, providing food from plain, mountain, and sea; animal life, particularly marine, is also abundant. The complex patterns of nature have molded the ways of settlers, forcing them to adapt to its vicissitudes. Having learned the methods of survival and growth in their own peculiar circumstances, the Japanese people, over a long, long period, have developed a unique set of national characteristics that reflect the diversity of nature but are still coherent.

Human sensitivity to nature's fertility has given birth to literally dozens of expressions to describe rain, for example. *Samidare* is early summer rain, *raiu* means thundershowers, and *kirisame* denotes misty rain. Nature wrought in the Japanese mind the ability to perceive complex diversity in terms of their own microcosm, or mandala. Thus, nature was never an enemy. Rather, all existence was seen as organically related, and man was made to live in harmony with it.

There is an interesting distinction between the Japanese deities and God. While Japanese mythology identifies the mother of nature as the virgin goddess Amaterasu Omikami (the Sun Goddess), in the Bible, creation is the work of the indisputably male God. Although traditions the world over refer to "mother" earth, is there not some correspondence between the respective creation myths and cultural attitudes toward nature? It seems to me that Japanese regard nature in a more "feminine" way, emphasizing harmony with and adaptation to its known patterns, whereas Western cultures appear to see nature in a "masculine" way, setting it up as a challenge to be overcome, an enemy to be fought and tamed. Is it going too far to say that similar differences mark ways of thinking; that Japanese are more flexible, more "feminine," while Westerners are more straightforward and rigid, more "masculine"? It may be that while Japanese enveloped themselves in the microcosmic nature of their land, Westerners tried to expand and advance their civilization by remodeling and manipulating the nature surrounding them.

In the course of time, rice, an import from the Asian mainland, became Japan's staple crop. Eventually, rice was grown all over the country, and the cultivation techniques were adjusted to suit the land and climate of each region. Japan's rice is mostly the wet-paddy variety, which requires a highly concentrated input of manual labor rarely seen anywhere else in the world. Most other rice-growing countries raise dry-field rice, or if they cultivate wet fields, they more often irrigate by channeling flood waters during the rainy season. They do not invest the degree of human labor seen in Japan. The Japanese system of irrigation depends on a series of ditches that draw water from rivers and man-made reservoirs, which allows artificial regulation of the level of water retained in the paddies. This technique was developed to conserve water from the two peak periods of rainfall in June and September, and to prevent the fast-flowing rivers from carrying all the rainwater out to sea.

Japan's wet fields are indeed an artificial product of technology created in response to the need to adapt an imported grain to the land. Moreover, as they carefully built the ditches and dikes for their wet fields, and as they grew and harvested the rice plants, many of the traits unique to the Japanese emerged. In the first place, agricultural activities, including reservoir building and clearing the fields, required people to work together. Our ancestors settled in groups on river deltas and alluvial plains near their fields, leading communal lives that centered on the unit of village, or *mura*. All members of a *mura* contributed to a shared goal, which is why the corporate ability of the group has always been considered more important than individual abilities. It was only natural, as in any communality, that a system of seniority should arise and become institutionalized. Japan may be unusual in that the institutions of the communal group were not wiped out or replaced when the center of gravity of the economy shifted from agriculture.

The Five Senses

Agriculture was the way of life for most Japanese until modern times, but it was not an easy one. The setbacks of natural calamities and epidemics were compounded by exploiting rulers and landlords who frequently pressured farmers to squeeze even more out of their land and mercilessly raised land taxes and corvees. The peasant population, forced to use all their resources, became keenly attuned to nature. They made rope from rice straw, wove straw shoes and tatami mats, and made good fertilizer by mixing straw with human waste. They used fermented rice to make saké, steam-roasted wood to make charcoal, and made a huge variety of ceramics from the different kinds of clay in each region. A lifestyle so deeply connected with the earth refined each of the five senses so that people could detect and respond to the slightest movement or change in nature.

Agrarian Lifestyle

Our ancestors led an agrarian life in a fixed abode, which enabled them to steadily improve their techniques and develop the optimum and intermediate technologies necessary to maintain and expand their activities. These techniques are receiving more and more attention today as our world begins to realize the evil, dehumanizing misery of excessive industrialization. The high level of acoustic technology, for example, might never have been possible without an acute sense of hearing. But, like other Asian cultures, Japanese have long had a variety of musical instruments, such as the koto, whose effect depends on subtle nuances in tone, quality, and rhythm. Strings for the koto are manufactured from tens of thousands of silkworm cocoons, and they produce an extremely delicate tone quality in comparison with the harsher synthetic or metal strings. A Japanese well versed in stringed instruments can tell from the sound of the strings just how far the silkworm had matured and even the manner in which the mulberry leaves fed to the worm were grown. That kind of perception grows in a land of diversity and subtle change. Japanese have unconsciously cultivated that sensitivity, and it naturally finds expression in their daily lives. Its constant application in the immediate demands of living is what has produced the traditional Japanese skills.

Japan and the West—Inherent Differences

How Japan's land and climate have affected its people comes out more prominently if we consider some of the differences between the people of Japan and the West, how they live and how that has influenced even their physical features. The physiological characteristics inherited by Japanese were formed in large part in the environment of rice-paddy culture of the Southeast Asian monsoon region, while the Caucasian physiology owes the most to a hunting culture that developed in a temperate region of "prevailing westerlies."

The rice-based Japanese diet, with its heavy emphasis on vegetable foods, compared with the Western diet and its stress on meat, has naturally had an effect on physical characteristics, but eating styles have also developed differently. Japanese, blessed with a variety of foods from land and sea, traditionally prefer small portions of a large variety of foods served in individual dishes, while the Western meal, prepared from the products of a relatively simpler ecosystem, follows a pattern of larger portions of fewer varieties of food on one plate. The gourmet's delight in the West is one plentiful course after another, whereas the best Japanese cuisine aims at preserving the natural appearance of the ingredients and enhancing their beauty by using a variety of vessels, which are set forth all at once. The vessel and the arrangement of food are meant to create a harmonious microcosm, which is an integral element in the visual balance of the whole. Spices are used in Western cuisine to bring out the best in a small number of foods, while in Japanese cooking, the goal is to preserve the natural flavor of each of the many items composing the meal.

Physiological and climatic differences also account for divergent sleeping and bathing facilities. The generally humid climate in Japan makes it necessary to take long hot baths to clean the skin, and to use bedding and clothing that absorb perspiration. That is why tatami floors and quilted pads for sleeping have been so well-suited to Japanese life. When one considers that until not long ago most of the population worked in muddy, wet fields all day, it is not surprising that the Japanese bath became a cultural institution. It was not only a place to warm the body and steam out the dirt, but also a place to relax. On the other hand, in the drier, temperature zones where Western culture developed, perspiration evaporates more easily, and clothing and bedding are made for warmth more than absorbency, and the Western bath is designed for washing more than soaking.

Again, while I can offer little hard evidence, it seems plausible that Japanese, who adapt so well to the changes of four distinct seasons, also developed an openness to new alternatives or additions. This openness facilitated the adoption of outside cultural elements. When cultural imports first arrive in the countries of Europe or the United States, they come into conflict with the established culture until they are rejected, or adopted to replace something else. In our country, the old culture is put away in storage, it is not abandoned, and new things are tried without resistance. Hence, in the West, the newly accepted cultural element usually becomes a permanent fixture, while in Japan, all those old items in storage are frequently brought back into circulation again.

The Japanese Refinery

Japanese may have finely honed sensitivities in many areas, but they have originated the basic principles for practically none—if any—of the technologies in use today. In almost every case, Japanese import the principles, refine and improve them, and come up with better techniques and products than the originals. This tendency can be traced back in history to the early contacts with the Asian continent many centuries ago, and it has gained for the Japanese a reputation as imitators. Two factors seem to account best for this inclination. One is that Japanese civilization emerged later than others, and incorporating outside ideas, techniques, and objects was one way to try to catch up. The other involves the Japanese way of perceiving whatever it is they are going to adopt. Take metal mirrors, for example. The first samples were brought to Japan sometime in the middle Yayoi, between the third century B.C. and the third century A.D., from the Han dynasty. Japanese appreciated their value for both practical and ritual use, and began making their own, modeled exactly on the Chinese prototypes, even though they did not understand the original purposes of the patterns on the back of the mirrors. The patterns on the back continued to be the same Chinese legendary animals, characters, and abstract designs for a time, but gradually they were superseded by the trees, birds, and other motifs more familiar to Japanese. Also, the Japanese increasingly used mirrors for symbolic or ritual purposes, in addition to their practical function of reflecting an image.

Finally during the Heian period (794–1185 A.D.) there appeared a new type of mirror that was uniquely Japanese, its design reflecting the surrounding nature. By the time glass mirrors emerged in the Edo period (1603–1868), the peculiar Japanese mirror had undergone a succession of changes. The evolution of the Japanese mirror was strongly affected, first, by the gradual modification of the Chinese patterns on the back to patterns reflecting nature in Japan, partly because the meaning of the Chinese letters and legendary animals were obscure to Japanese. Second, the native skills of Japanese were developed enough that they could produce their own mirrors. Third, the use of the mirror in Japan, including its ritual functions, differentiated it from its Chinese prototype.

The mirror provides a good example of the way cultural imports into Japan could be accepted without conflict. The outer form, the surface, is brought in and integrated with the indigenous culture by adapting its content, meaning, or inner substance as necessary. Thus, while the mirror had not such significance in China, it was revered as one of the three sacred treasures of the Yamato Imperial Court (300–710). The same thing happened again and again when the steady influx of imports from the West started in the Meiji period (1868–1912). Beef, for example, was introduced in the late nineteenth century, but Japanese chose to prepare it their own way using soy sauce. That gave rise to sukiyaki. I think the talent for incorporating foreign cultural elements without creating internal conflicts was nurtured by the rich and varied natural environment of Japan. Not only their climate and geography, but also their physiology, has wide variations, giving Japanese an affinity for the cultures and techniques of other peoples. With almost no psychological barriers to imported ideas, techniques, or objects, it is easy to adapt something new, no matter how "foreign."

Sartre and Dogen

The diverse nature of our land may also help to explain why modern technology in Japan could quickly equal, and in some fields surpass, that of other countries. Of all the climates prevailing in most of the world, probably only the scorching heat and sand of the desert cannot be experienced in Japan. When a people must adapt their lives to constant change in weather, and to wide variations in climate and topography, they develop a degree of sensitivity and perception so fine as to prepare them to tackle almost anything with competence. It may be that the subtlety of the environment is passed on to the people who live in it.

The late Dr. Yukawa Hideki, physicist and Nobel Prize winner, relates in his autobiography an experience he had on a visit to Greece. Standing before the Parthenon, looking out over the Mediterranean, he suddenly understood, he said, why in Greece, men of the ancient civilization so ardently pursued the origin of matter and discussed the cosmos. Laid out before him, the sea and the islands made a vast, uniform panorama that must have taunted people to seek a single essence. The diverse scenery of Japan, in contrast, seems to lure one to focus on phenomena that are the expressions of existence rather than the essence. Here, said Dr. Yukawa, lay the conditions that gave rise to the difference between the two cultures.

Japan is generally considered to lag behind the West in seizing the essence and structure of a given phenomenon, especially in the area of technology. Japanese are not recognized for new inventions derived from their grasp of the basic principles, or essence. But producing relatively few original modern inventions does not mean they lack the ability to grasp the basic principles. Recently several studies have appeared comparing Heidegger, Sartre, or other twentieth century Western philosophers with Dogen, priest of thirteenth century Japan. Dogen's analysis of the concepts of time and space, matter and spirit, or phenomenon and essence often seem to be deeper and far more systematic than those of Sartre or Heidegger. When one considers that seven centuries separate Dogen in time from our modern-day thinkers, the magnitude of the priest's ideas is amazing.

In *Shobogenzo* (literally, Treasury of the Correct Dharma Eye), an essay on Buddhism, Dogen presents a grand, well-coordinated system of knowledge in which he reveals an order behind complex phenomena. This great work is not yet widely known in the world. Very rarely, in fact, has any profound system of knowledge born in the Oriental monsoon region been diffused to their civilizations, or its knowledge translated and applied in practical activities. But the spirit of Buddhism, which is that of the "mandala," or microcosm, has the potential for practical use. That potential would have been realized much more fully had temporal, utilitarian incentives been stronger. To see the totality of an object with maximum objectivity, personal bias removed, is deeply rooted in the Japanese way of thinking. Good, for example, is taught to be a spiritual awakening at a microcosmic level to the totality of the macrocosmos.

A study of Japanese Buddhist philosophy teaches one that Western concepts were not necessarily unique to the West; concepts originating in the Middle East and India spread both east and west. In the Western cultures, in which nature was seen as a force to be manipulated, these concepts were readily adapted to the needs of scientific inquiry, leading to the rapid development of science and technology. Even then, three important inventions of the Renaissance period, gunpowder, the compass, and the printing press, had been discovered long before in ancient China. In either case, the seed of technology cannot grow unless soil in which it can be nurtured is present.

Perhaps, therefore, the skill of Japanese in imitating, modifying, and improving on foreign imports lies in the relatively late maturation of its culture. Japan could find good teachers outside, and the peculiar character of the natural environment worked to ease any conflict or psychological barriers against new things from other lands. At the same time, the refined sensitivity and perception of the people, nurtured by the natural environment, and the particular attitudes and technical skills shaped by those qualities, gave Japanese the ability to transform, almost instinctively, foreign imports through the elaborate workmanship that one sees in everything, from poetry and crafts to precision instruments. Japan's twentieth century success story bears witness not to innately superior abilities as much as a talent for making the most of the strong points in their culture and traditions.

Towards Internationalization

Looking forward, it is important to try to project how the characteristics of our culture will develop as our society becomes more internationalized. Many aspects of the economy have already been restructured since 1945, and today Japan maintains one of the strongest growth rates among the advanced nations. Its level of technology in electronics and high-precision instruments, in life sciences, in developing non-oil energy sources, systematization techniques, and manufacturing processes, among others, is already high, and expected to keep on advancing. Habits, skills, and attitudes bred into the Japanese during long centuries as an agricultural society were brought into play to support the successful shift to modern industry and technology. Their sensitivity, their perception of work as a virtue, their perfectionism in technical skills, the potential of the language, traditional techniques (fermentation using pure water, for example) their delicate sense of nature—all these and more lie behind today's Japan. The same qualities will undoubtedly continue to serve economic and social progress in the future.

As a case in point, the Japanese language uses the digital characters of the *katakana* and *hiragana* phonetic alphabets as well as Chinese ideographs, and most of the population are able to use the Roman alphabet as well. That flexibility will be a valuable asset as computer logic and pattern cognition become part of daily life. Japanese seem to be linguistically well prepared for the age of analog and digital computers. In the life sciences, likewise, Japanese have a wealth of experience that could contribute a great deal to the world. Settled in areas where temperature and humidity are both high, many Japanese learned how to exploit and devise countermeasures against the harmful effects of bacteria and germs, as in the production of *natto* (fermented beans), *yokan* (bean cake), and saké. This kind of knowledge, combined with their technological dexterity, holds great potential for the future.

Tradition has been woven into the economic and social fabric of Japan in the international age, and the combination has sustained the vitality necessary for growth. A reputation has been made, and now Japan is expected to maintain superior standards of quality and efficient production. But if our cultural traits are not understood by others, and if we do not sufficiently appreciate foreign cultures, our system of production will be restrained by political, social, cultural, and, particularly, economic differences with other countries. Those differences will cause friction when they meet in an international context, and our economic growth will be held in check.

My comments on Japan should serve mainly as an example of the way a country can identify and use its assets. It is vital for developing nations to examine their natural environment, historical heritage, and cultural traditions, and to draw on them as a resource pool, selecting and building on those points with potential value for their nation of tomorrow. Japan's role would be to help in the investigation. In re-examining the modernization of Asia as a whole, it is very important to identify the experience and processes common to Asian and Western cultures, and to recognize the aspects of modernization in Western cultures that do not lend themselves to Asia. This is an ongoing task that no single nation, certainly not Japan, can direct itself; countries must share their experience and ideas, and each one must help in areas where it is better equipped than others.

3

Confucianism and Japanese Modernization: A Study of Shibusawa Eiichi*

Kuo-hui Tai

Introduction

As scholars in East Asia, Europe, and the United States are now reassessing the role of traditional Chinese culture and thought in the process of economic development, the issue of Confucianism and modernization has become once again an intriguing question to me. More than thirty years ago I first confronted the subject. In 1955, I was a graduate student at Tokyo University attending a class on Japanese economic history taught by Professor Tsuchiya Takao. An economist employing Marxist methodology in his studies, Tsuchiya was then discussing the life and career of a man who might be called the father of Japanese modern industries or the father of Japanese capitalism: Shibusawa Eiichi. As the editor of the collected works of Shibusawa, Tsuchiya introduced to his class

*Excerpted from "Confucianism and Japanese Modernization: A Study of Shibusawa Eiichi," by Kuo-hui Tai in *Confucianism and Economic Development: An Oriental Alternative?* edited by Hung-chao Tai. Reprinted with permission from the publisher, Washington Institute for Values in Public Policy, Washington, D.C., 1989.

a number of best sellers by the famed Japanese businessman, including *Seienhiyakuwa*. A compilation of Shibusawa's words and deeds, *Seienhiyakuwa* went to the eight printing in 1912, the very year it was published.

Tsuchiya then mentioned another, even more popular book by Shibusawa, *Rongo to Soroban*. First published in 1928, it is still widely read today, twice reprinted in 1985. Upon hearing the title of this book, which means *The Analects and Abacus*, I was astonished and puzzled. For *The Analects*, the most important book identified with Confucius, always was perceived by Confucianists as a body of moral norms diametrically opposed to the concept of profit-making, of which the abacus was seen in Far Eastern societies as both a symbol and an instrument. It was totally inconceivable to me how *The Analects and Abacus* could be linked together. That this book was highly recommended by a Marxist economic historian was all the more astonishing. Yet the book proved to be something refreshing and exciting, whetting my curiosity.

The Life of Shibusawa[1]

Shibusawa Eiichi was born in Saitama, Japan, in 1840. The Shibusawa family was then operating what may be called an estate-based business composed of three components: farming, commerce, and finance. In farming, the family raised rice, wheat, and silk; in commerce, it manufactured and sold fabric dyes; in finance, it managed small local banks. The operations of this sort of agricultural-industrial-banking conglomerate deeply affected Shibusawa's life and thinking.

It should be noted that in the era of Japan's modern transformation, Shibusawa was well educated in traditional Chinese studies. First receiving the Han learning from his father, he enrolled at the age of seven in a private school to study the teachings of Confucius and Mencius.

In the spring of 1866, Tokugawa Yoshinobu became the fifteenth *shogun*. This event placed Shibusawa in a dilemma. On the one hand, he was against the rule of *shogun* and was unwilling to be part of what he considered a soon-falling military government. On the other hand, he did not want to betray the friends who had recommended him to the Tokugawas. He tried in vain to persuade Yoshinobu not to become the *shogun*, but an event spared him of ensuing trouble. In 1867 he became an aide to Yoshinobu's brother, Akitake, who was then leading a mission to Paris to visit the World Fair. Shibusawa joined the mission and stepped into a capitalist Europe which, in his view, created "in less [than] one hundred years a new civilization exceeding all the human progress in the last several thousand years." This trip not only saved him from involvement in the political turmoil that precipitated the fall of the Tokugawa regime, but also opened for him a great new vista—modern capitalism.

At the end of 1868, he came back from Europe to participate in the new government under the Meiji Reform. In the Ministry of Finance, he first helped institute reforms of the finance, banking, and monetary system. He became the head of the ministry's taxation division in 1872. Two years later, in 1874, because of policy differences within the government, he and Finance Minister Inoue Kaoru resigned from the government. In the same year, he joined the business world and created the first modern banking institution in Japan—Daiichi Kokuritsu Bank.

Before he died in 1931, Shibusawa organized more than 500 business enterprises which dealt with banking, textiles, real estate, paper mills, shipbuilding, ocean freight, railroads, motor vehicles, beer, petrochemicals, hotels, and insurance. These covered practically every line of modern business. In addition, he participated in the establishment of Hitotsubashi University, an institution noted for turning out today's Japanese business elite.

Of his ninety-two-year life, he devoted more than seventy years to business. Spanning the reigns of Tokugawa, Meiji, Taisho, and Hirohito, his career was in a sense the life history of modern Japanese economy. No wonder he became known as the father of Japanese capitalism. An analysis of his life will enable us to unlock some of the secrets of the Japanese economic miracle. Moreover, we will be able to see how he used *The Analects* to achieve success in business. He gave Confucianism a new meaning, making it a catalyst for the social and economic transformation in Japan.

Shibusawa's Works and Thoughts

Before we proceed to introduce Shibusawa's works, it is appropriate to reiterate three factors influencing his thinking. First, his life coincided with a great transformation of Japan. He witnessed the emergence of an economic and social foundation that supported capitalism. He saw his country forced to open its doors to the West but not subjected to colonial rule, as had happened to Japan's neighbor, China. And he participated fully in the Meiji Reform to bring capitalism to his nation. Second, his formal education was limited to that of a private school whose curriculum was centered around Confucianism. He never went to a modern school, nor studied abroad.

Third, his on-site observation of Europe whetted his appetite for European capitalism. Under the influence of these three factors, Shibusawa skillfully dovetailed Confucianism with modern business and integrated the essence of Eastern and Western civilization in order to advance Japanese industrialization.

Shibusawa devoted his whole life to this endeavor, first expressing his ideas about Confucianism in *Ama yo gatari* (a memoir) and the previously mentioned *Seienhiyakuwa*. Both were memoirs. Both remain popular in the Japanese business community even to this day. In these works, he discussed from the perspective of a business leader during the Meiji Reform his views on life, society, the nation, religion, youth, and enterprise. But it was in *The Analects and Abacus* and *Rango Kogi* (The Essence of the Analects) that he focused more narrowly on the relationship between Confucianism and modern enterprise.[2]

Like his other works, *The Analects and Abacus* is not an academic treatise but a collection of personal thoughts and speeches derived directly from his business experiences. Today, as we open the volume half a century after its first publication, we do not see a stale book but a work of fresh, lively, eloquent ideas—and full of inspiration. The book contains ten chapters, under the following headings: 1. Mottoes of life; 2. Goal setting and studies; 3. Common sense and customs; 4. Righteousness and prosperity; 5. Idealism and superstition; 6. Character and cultivation; 7. Abacus and power; 8. Enterprise and *bushido*; 9. Education and empathy; and 10. Success and failure and fate.

As can be seen from these topics, the book is as much concerned with philosophy and ethics as with profit-making. The central theme of the book, however, is to reconcile righteousness with profit. Shibusawa writes in the very beginning of his book:

> The origin of today's moral norms can be traced to the book that embodied Confucius's words and deeds as recorded by his disciples—the well-known *The Analects*. [On the surface,] this book has nothing to do with [profit-making as symbolized by the instrument] abacus. But I am fully convinced that abacus is wholly compatible with *The Analects*, whose true value

can be realized through abacus. The relationship between *The Analects* and abacus is at once distant and close...I believe that without a strong profit motivation, no improvement of the popular welfare is possible. Similarly, people seeking abstract theory will not be able to find truth. Today, our task is not only to curb the arbitrary power of government and the military forces but also to expand business. Without business expansion we can never achieve national prosperity. On the other hand, national prosperity will not last long if it is not based on the moral principles of benevolence and righteousness. Our urgent task today is to unite *The Analects* with abacus.[3]

Shibusawa thus charted a mission for the Japanese: to reinterpret Confucianism to meet the needs of the day. This stands in stark contrast with China, which has seen the emergence of a movement resisting Confucianism. In the Tokugawa and early Meiji times, the Japanese—like the Chinese—accepted the orthodox view of Confucianism, which belittled the social status of business.[4] But as soon as the Meiji government commenced its modernization program, the Japanese did not condemn Confucianism—as some Chinese did during the May Fourth Movement—but set out to make Confucianism serviceable to their new way of thinking. For that purpose, Shibusawa coined the term "shikon shosai," literally a union of *bushido* and commercial talent. *Bushido*—the moral code of the samurais—was the embodiment of the Japanese concept of Confucian ethics; commercial talent referred to modern managerial skill. Shibusawa observed:

Sugawara Michizane has coined a very interesting term *Wakon kansai* [Japanese spirit, Chinese talent]. I am advocating *shikon shosai* [scholarly spirit, commercial talent]....
In order to gain social respect one must follow *bushido*, but if one goes into business by following *bushido* and possessing no commercial talent he will be certainly doomed to failure. To cultivate the scholarly spirit, one must not only read many books but also follow the moral precepts of *The Analects*. But then how does one develop the commercial talent? One can develop commercial talent by following *The Analects* too. For commercial undertaking without a moral basis borders on deceit, dilettantism; it is chicanery, sophistry, but not truly great commercial talent. A man who wishes to acquire true commercial talent must learn from *The Analects*.[5]

Looking at Shibusawa's career, one feels that Shibusawa himself exemplified *shikon shosai*. When he joined the Meiji government in the 1870s, the bureaucrats still adhered to a traditional interpretation of Confucianism, belittling business. With the Meiji Reform, the Japanese downgraded the samurais but did not elevate the status of business. Indeed, the reform initially brought about an uncertain future to Japan's emerging capitalism. Under the circumstances, Shibusawa thought it necessary to devote himself to the creation of a socially respected business class capable of rational management of large modern enterprises. It was at least partially for this reason he resigned from the government and began to pursue a business career. Thus, in *Shibusawa Eiichi den* (The Biography of Shibusawa Eiichi) Tsuchiya Takao observed:

> [In 1871, as the head of the Commerce Division at the Ministry of Finance,] Shibusawa was in frequent contact with many businessmen in Tokyo and Osaka. The subservient attitude of businessmen was still a social custom not yet eliminated. They bowed their heads deep when facing government officials; they had neither learning nor influence; they had never thought about the need for business reform and business regulations. Japanese businessmen and the French businessmen Shibusawa had met in Europe lived in two entirely different worlds.
>
> Under the circumstances, all that Shibusawa could do was to help the government formulate a new monetary law to stimulate business development. He considered Japanese businessmen of the day would never be able to make a contribution to industrialization. For this reason, he left the government and joined the business world so that he could devote himself to the cultivation and promotion of a new business class appropriate to industrial development.[6]

Thus, in promoting *The Analects* and abacus, Shibusawa hoped to reshape the Japanese businessman's personality. He wanted his new businessman to possess both a knowledge of economics and business ethics, so that he would feel equal to government officials. In the chapter on "Enterprise and *Bushido*" Shibusawa stated:

> As the highest social norms of Japan, *bushido* had long been followed in the gentlemen's circles but was not applicable to those in the business world. In the past, merchants and arti-

sans clearly misunderstood *bushido,* seeing righteousness, integrity, and magnanimity as incompatible with business transactions. They considered the *bushido* concept "*bushi wa kuwanedo takayoji*" [the samurai would rather starve than misbehave himself] as a bane to business. This may well be so under the circumstances of the time. However, just as the samurais could not live without *bushido,* businessmen could not survive without a moral code of their own....

The notion that *bushido* and profit-making were incompatible was erroneous in the feudal times just as it is today. People now have seen the reason why benevolence and prosperity are not contradictory. Confucius said: "Riches and honors are what men desire. If they are not obtained in the right way, they should not be held. Poverty and lowliness are what people dislike. If they are brought to the people in the right way, they should not be avoided" [*The Analects,* Book IV, "Li Jen"]. This saying is consistent with the essential precepts of *bushido*—i.e., righteousness, integrity, and magnanimity. The Confucian idea that poverty and lowliness should never deter one from following the right way is quite similar to the *bushido* notion that the samurai should never run away from his enemy. Moreover, the Confucian idea that one cannot truly enjoy riches and honors if they are not obtained in the right way is exactly the same as the *bushido* exhortation that one should never take a penny in the wrong way. Of course, even the sage desires riches and honors and dislikes poverty and lowliness. However, the sage regards morality as of primary importance and the issue of wealth and poverty as a secondary importance. In the past, many businessmen practiced otherwise. They were mistaken...*Bushido* and enterprise, I believe, must have and can have the same spirit.[7]

Shibusawa emphasized that the idea of uniting righteousness and profit was consistent with the original teaching of Confucius, but that many latter-day Confucian scholars mistakenly considered benevolence and wealth as contradictory.

In his preface to *The Works of Mencius,* the great Confucian scholar of Sung Dynasty, Chu Hsi, stated: "Obtaining business achievement through calculation is selfish; such an endeavor is a world apart from the way of the sages." This statement really belittles the idea of making profit through production.... Viewed in another way, this statement means

that righteousness and morality are the exclusive character-
istics of god-like sages, not at all applicable to businessmen.
This cannot be the essence of the teachings of Confucius and
Mencius.[8]

From Shibusawa's writings, one discovers that during the
late Tokugawa Period and the Meiji Reform there were two transformations in the Confucian ideology. The first was to reinterpret
the Confucianism-based *bushido* so as to make it a new national
ethos to sustain the emerging Japanese capitalist system. Both the
social and economic conditions within Japan and the international
environment surrounding the country made this transformation
possible.

Irobe Yoshiaki, former Chairman of Koyo Wa Bank and the
Japanese business leader best known in post-World War II Japan
for mastering Confucianism, has flatly stated:

> The moral code of traditional Japan—in both the Tokugawa
> and Meiji periods—did not come from Buddhism, nor from
> Christianity, but only from Confucianism. Japan's civic virtue
> as revealed in the *"Kyo iku chiyoku go"* ["Guides for Educa-
> tion"] clearly indicates the influence of Confucianism. The
> religious concept of divinity is non-existent in Confucianism,
> and since the Middle Ages, the Japanese sense of guilt had
> come about only as a reflection of Confucianism.... Confucian-
> ism became the foundation of Japanese social norms vitally
> affecting *bushido*. The schools in Edo and Osaka and all the
> famous *han* schools in *daimyo* promoted the study of *The
> Analects*. Among the disciples of Confucianism were the
> young members of the samurai families who naturally had a
> respect for ancient Chinese moral precepts.[9]

As to the second transformation of Confucianism in Japan,
one may discern it from Chio's writings:

> Shibusawa's theory is designed to unite what had tradition-
> ally been considered opposite ends—morality and economics.
> To do this it is necessary to negate to a certain extent both of
> them; it would then be possible for a new, mutually adaptable
> content to appear. Shibusawa's conception of *The Analects*
> seeks in the contemporary times a transformation of the for-
> malistic Confucianism as represented by the Chu Hsi School
> and a renaissance of the classical Confucianism. Shibusawa's

thoughts about economic enterprise negated the idea that business was a purely profit-seeking proposition. He regarded commerce and industry as vital components of modern business.... He was not worshipping a dead Confucius, but was looking for a living Confucianism marching in the real world. Thus, the spirit of Confucius would be a spirit for objective inquiry that can bring about knowledge through a thorough study of the physical world.[10]

The Impact of Confucianism on Modern Japanese History

Shibusawa advocated *The Analects* to emphasize righteousness; he advocated abacus to seek profit. Shibusawa's education was Confucianism-based Chinese learning; his career was immersed in Western-type business practices. Shibusawa's task, one can therefore suggest, involves a transformation of *Kankon* (Chinese spirit) into *Wakon* (Japanese spirit) and then a union of the latter with Western technology. Many Japanese who consider Shibusawa merely a representative of *Wakon Yousai* without noticing his contribution in the transformation of *Kankon* into *Wakon* miss a significant point.

Indeed, Sugaware Michizane (845–903) long ago proposed the concept of *Wakon Kansai* (Japanese spirit, Chinese talent). Only when Chinese learning lost its utility in modern times did the Japanese seek Western learning. This change occurred during the Meiji period, when *Wakon Yousai* substituted for *Wakon Kansai* as the slogan of the day.[11] What deserves our attention is that the Japanese always insist on maintaining the Japanese spirit; they can revise, reinforce, or adapt it, but never are willing to abandon it completely in favor of total Westernization.

Shibusawa's effort to transform or reinterpret Confucianism has several manifestations.

First, in modern China many people tend to hold two extreme views of Confucianism. Some would like to see a total liquidation of Confucianism; others consider it a moral code good for all times. In a sense, both look at Confucianism as an instrument of governance, a means to rationalize the family based bureaucratic system. What Shibusawa did was to step out of the sphere of politics, liberating Confucianism from its position as an instrument of governance and gave it a new, economic interpretation. He made *The Analects* the dialogue of the business class, the ethics of modern business.

Second, during Shibusawa's time, the mainstream Confucianism was dominated by the Chu Hsi School, which had rendered Confucianism into an ivory-tower learning for a small cluster of orthodox Confucian scholars. Shibusawa daringly challenged the orthodoxy, liberating *The Analects* from the constraints of the Chu Hsi School and giving it a new life. In other words, he removed Confucianism from its doctrinal, religious cast and returned it to its original form. The reinterpreted *Analects* became a practice-based learning; as such, it could apply to economics and become the guiding principle of modern business.

Third, Shibusawa used the Confucian notion of "deriving knowledge from studying the physical world" as a way of comprehending the meaning of life. Embracing the idea of "uniting knowledge with practice" as proposed by the great Confucian scholar Wang Yang-ming, Shibusawa launched *The Analects* on a path entirely different from the Neo-Confucianism of the Sung and Ming times, which Wang Yang-ming had challenged. In his *The Analects and Abacus*, Shibusawa attempted to use *The Analects* to interpret his personal experiences, his contacts with others, and his observations during his trip to the West. Relying on intuition as well as reasoning, he purged Confucianism of its conservative and formalistic features, creatively transforming it, improving it, and eventually reshaping it into the spirit of modern Japanese capitalism. In a sense, Shibusawa's writings can be considered his response to Max Weber's critique of Confucianism. Shibusawa used Wang Yang-ming's idea of "uniting knowledge with practice" to create *The Analects and Abacus*, and his reinterpreted Confucianism is different from the Confucianism as perceived by Weber. He has made a lively use of Confucianism with which he bridged tradition and modernity.

Finally, a close reading of *The Analects and Abacus* would reveal that Shibusawa praised Confucianism but did not worship it blindly. He found that in its original content *The Analects* was very much concerned about interpersonal relations but not much about individuals themselves. He noticed that Confucian teachings touched more on the process of governance than on the position of the governed. Such teachings, in Shibusawa's view, deprived the masses of their sense of personal independence, making them subservient to the ruling class and tolerant of political authoritarianism. To remedy this shortcoming, Shibusawa devoted one section of his book *Seienhiyakuwa* (Section 72) to a discussion of the concept of self-governance.

Similarly, modern businessmen must possess, he believed, a

self-reliant, self-sustaining spirit so that they can decisively, promptly, and effectively handle their business in a highly competitive environment. Here, Shibusawa raised a very important question—the autonomy of businessmen. When he resigned from the Ministry of Finance, he did so not only because of disputes within the Ministry but also because of his dissatisfaction with the subservient attitude of businessmen toward officials. He believed that if businessmen lacked a sense of independence, a will of their own, their business could not long endure and flourish. A nation could create economic institutions by imitation but could not develop a business spirit by import. The business spirit had to emanate from the nation's own cultural and social conditions. In Japan, the transformation of *Kankon* (Chinese spirit) into *Wakon* (Japanese spirit) and the acquisition of *Yousai* (Western learning) forged a powerful force pushing forward Japanese capitalism and modernization.

Conclusion

Having introduced Shibusawa's thinking and the fate of Confucianism in modern Japan, I would conclude with two points of interest.

The first relates to the issue of economic growth in the so-called "Confucian cultural area." The economic achievements of Japan, South Korea, Taiwan, Hong Kong, and Singapore in the last twenty years makes it necessary to revise Max Weber's theory. Many Western scholars have raised the question, as Mineo Nakajima has noted, whether "there is a [new] model of economic development in the Confucian cultural area."[12] Those who answer the question affirmatively, such as the new Confucianists, attempt to explain the economic performance of East Asia from structural and cultural perspectives.

Structurally, they believe that East Asia differs from the West in the area of political institutions. The governments in East Asia have established a rationalized bureaucracy dedicated to the promotion of industry and commerce. These governments have been engaged in a prudent administrative engineering. Culturally, the new Confucianists look on East Asian countries as having embarked on the path of "Confucian capitalism"—a third phase of Confucianism, following the Confucianism of the Han Dynasty and the Sung/Ming dynasties. As such, it is a creative response or challenge to Western culture.

These explanations of the economic success of East Asia seem to be a rather simplistic *post facto* rationalization. The internal and external conditions surrounding economic development have been and remain vastly different. The five countries can be divided into three categories: (1) Japan, (2) Taiwan and South Korea, and (3) Hong Kong and Singapore. Japan is the only completely modernized country in East Asia—far more industrialized than any of the rest. Taiwan and South Korea obtained the pre-conditions for capitalism during the Japanese rule prior to the end of the Second World War; both countries subsequently have been under the influence of the United States, separating themselves from mainland China and North Korea, respectively. Hong Kong and Singapore are city states without any substantive agriculture; they derive their income from commerce, industry, and tourism. Hong Kong cannot survive without the market of the Chinese mainland; nor can Singapore without the market of Malaysia and Indonesia.

With such diversity in the "Five Dragons," it is important to carefully delimit the role of Confucianism in economic development. What Confucianism needs is to adapt itself to changing historical circumstances. In addition, in the study of Confucianism, current research should not be confined to the area of philosophy and history but should relate Confucianism to business, thereby creating a business ethic that can truly merge Confucianism with modern management.

This relates to a second point of interest. Shibusawa's thought really represents a balance between righteousness and profit. Though devoting his whole life to capitalism, Shibusawa discovered certain problems in modern capitalism. These include rising materialism among the general populace and seeking profit by the capitalists at the expense of social responsibility. Facing these, Shibusawa thought it necessary to use Confucianism to reshape society. In advocating the idea of "moralized profit-making," he sought a union of business development and social responsibility. Successful businesses, he believed, must assume responsibility for improving social welfare, education, and the environment. A stable society, harmonious labor relations, healthy social environment, and widespread education—these are conditions leading to a healthier and more prosperous economic development. Many leftists in Japan might criticize Shibusawa for having served the interests of the bourgeoisie, being himself a conservative business tycoon. But for a man coming out of the feudalistic Tokugawa reign, Shibusawa's accomplishment is extraordinary.

At present, while many East Asian countries are under the

sway of commercialism and materialism, it is sobering to study Shibusawa's *The Analects and Abacus*. By embracing the moralism of Confucianism and the best of Western technology, these countries can achieve further successes without suffering from the social ills of Western capitalism.

4

The Influence of Confucianism and Zen on the Japanese Organization*

Subhash Durlabhji

It is a great mistake to adjust everything to the Procrustean bed of logic, and a greater mistake to make logic the supreme test in the evaluation of behavior.[1]

The success of Japanese work organizations as productive systems is certainly remarkable, but a large part of it is attributable to what the Japanese borrowed from Western culture. What is truly unique and original about Japanese work organization is its success as a social system, a goal that Western Organization Theory has pursued since the birth of the Human Relations School. It is the purpose of this chapter to suggest that the success of the Japanese work organization as a social system is attributable primarily to Eastern culture: to Confucianism's single-minded search for *Wa* (Harmony), and to Zen's more complex vision of human beings. Concepts of Eastern culture have remained somewhat inaccessible to the West; hence, the discussion in this paper is placed in the context of concepts developed in the West. Confucianism's influence on

*Reprinted, by permission of the publisher, from *Akron Business and Economic Review* 21, no. 2 (Summer 1990).

the Japanese work organization can be discussed in terms of *primary* and *secondary* relationships and the related concept of *gemeinschaft/gesellschaft* social systems. Zen's influence can be understood in terms of the concept of the *unconscious*.

Figure 4–1 contains an outline of the argument presented in the paper. Confucianism is described to demonstrate that it contributes to the *gemeinschaft* nature of Japanese society and Japanese organizations. The depth of penetration of Confucianism in Japanese life is revealed to indicate the extent of its influence on the Japanese organization. Zen's influence on the Japanese mind is similarly demonstrated. These forces combine with the policies of Japanese organizations to result in the engagement of the unconscious energies of Japanese employees in work-related behavior.

The discussion points to some new directions for debate and research in our continuing quest for work organizations that allow for high productivity in socially satisfying, if not exciting, contexts. The chapter concludes with a discussion of theoretical and practical implications of the ideas presented.

Confucianism

This part of the paper seeks to suggest that the Japanese work organization is a *gemeinschaft* social system, and that Confucianism is largely responsible for this fact. The first section reviews concepts that will be utilized to conduct the discussion. The *gemeinschaft* character of the Confucianist ideal of society is revealed next. The extent of the influence of Confucianism in Japan is then indicated. Finally, the *gemeinschaft* nature of Japanese organization and Japanese society is discussed. The relationship of the *gemeinschaft* character of Japanese work organization to the "success of Japanese work organization as a social system" will be made explicit in a later part of the chapter.

Primary and Secondary Relationships

Tonnies,[2] in a highly acclaimed book translated into English as *Fundamental Concepts of Sociology,* has distinguished between *gemeinschaft* societies and *gesellschaft* societies in terms of the form of relationship among people predominant in each type. Tonnies suggests that the key difference between relationships in the

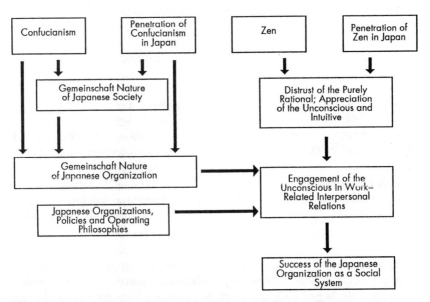

Figure 4.1 Influence of Confucianism and Zen on Japanese Organizations

gemeinschaft and *gesellschaft* societies is that relationships in the former are based on "natural will" and in the latter on "rational will." When a relationship is formed because those involved wish to attain a definite goal, then the basis for the relationship is rational will, in which means and ends have been sharply differentiated. When people associate because they think the relationship is valuable in and of itself, it is natural will that predominates. In other words, *gesellschaft* social systems are composed of mostly utilitarian relationships, whereas in *gemeinschaft* social systems relationships between individuals go well beyond being merely utilitarian. Tonnies identifies five main *gemeinschaft* ties: mother and child, father and child, sisters and brothers, friend and friend, and rulers and subjects.

Durlabhji[3] has suggested that this distinction can be viewed in terms of the concepts of *primary* and *secondary* relationships. Based on his review of Cooley,[4] who first introduced the term "primary group" to social science, and other authors[5] who have further developed and utilized the concept, Durlabhji has summarized the distinction between primary and secondary relationships in Table 4.1.

Gemeinschaft social systems consist of predominantly primary relationships. A fundamental difference between primary

Table 4.1 Main Distinctions Between Primary and Secondary Relations

PRIMARY	SECONDARY
Based on natural will	Based on rational will
Ends in themselves	Means to an end
Whole persons involved	Segments of persons involved
Face-to-face interaction	Mediated interaction
Long term	Often brief
Frequent contact	Intermittent contact
Spontaneous and informal	Structured and formal
Warm, intimate, personal	Indifferent and impersonal

and secondary relationships is their reason for existence. A secondary relationship is entirely utilitarian; conversely, a primary relationship is not goal-directed, but exists for its own sake. In the Freudian perspective, the energy in the conscious level of the mind is viewed as being bound and goal-directed, while the energy in the unconscious is free floating. If the characteristic of secondary relationships is that they are goal-directed, and the characteristic of the energy in the conscious level of mind is also that it is goal-directed, it may be reasonable to suggest that a secondary relationship between two individuals is predominantly a relationship between the conscious levels of their minds. In contrast, a primary relationship involves an engagement of unconscious energies.

The other dimensions along which primary and secondary relationships can be distinguished (see Table 4.1) are consistent with this interpretation. Secondary relationships involve only those conscious segments of the mind that are relevant to the accomplishment of the goal around which the relationship is constituted. Primary relationships require face-to-face interactions, in which communication is largely a matter of unconsciously transmitted cues picked up unconsciously by the persons involved. Adjustment of two individuals to each other at the limited, conscious levels can be achieved in short-term associations with intermittent contacts that are characteristic of secondary relationships. Adjustment at the deeper, unconscious levels would require a long-term relationship with frequent contacts, which alone provide the opportunity for the two people to interact with their defenses relaxed.

Gemeinschaft Nature of Confucianism

The Confucian ideal of society has a striking resemblance to Tonnies's *gemeinschaft* society. Confucius was, above all, a social reformer, convinced that, if the "Laws of Heaven" were adhered to by men, the same harmony that rules Heaven would come to reign on Earth. Perhaps the most succinct statement of the core of the Confucianist ideal of society comes from Chu Hsi (1130–1200 A.D.):

> The universe is governed by the laws of Heaven, so are human affairs. These laws require of each of us to observe what is proper to him. He has a "name," he performs a certain "part" as he occupies a definite position in society. This network of social relationships is not to be ignored if the peace and happiness of its components are to be preserved and enhanced.[6]

According to Confucius, if people do not observe propriety in all matters, especially in all social encounters, anarchy and disorder would surely follow "as night follows day." The most important requirement for social order and harmony is for each and every individual to be continuously aware of his or her position in society and to act in strict accordance with what society demands of the incumbent of this position. In other words, harmony (*wa*) is of paramount importance. Propriety in interpersonal relationships is the essential requirement for the achievement of harmony.

Among the rules of propriety, filial piety is by far the most sacrosanct. Honor and respect for parents is an imperative: Without it, social life is simply impossible. At the heart of Confucianism is the "way" of *jen* (not to be confused with "Zen"). *Jen* signifies compassion, and it is the way of *jen* that must be followed in all human affairs for harmony and social order to flourish. The root of compassion in the heart of every individual is filial piety. It is in the primal bond between parents and children that the seeds of compassion are sown. Filial piety thus becomes the cornerstone of the Confucian social ethic, and the parent-child relationship becomes the model for all other relationships, as well as the chief source of the development of compassion. The family is by far the most important institution for Confucius; the state is thought of as an enlarged family. It is of utmost importance for children to serve, support, and obey parents, and to honor ancestors, for filial piety is the starting point of all virtues.

Confucius lists five relationships in which the way of *jen* must reign for there to be harmony in society. These five are father-son, ruler-minister, husband-wife, brother-brother, and friend-friend. It is clear that the Confucianist ideal of society is identical to Tonnies's *gemeinschaft* society. The overriding concern in Confucian thought is social harmony, and the central path to such harmony is the creation and maintenance of primary social relations at every level of society.

Confucius in Japan

Students of Japan, both Japanese and non-Japanese, agree that one of the strongest influences on Japanese social relations has come from Confucianism. The ideas of Confucius (551–479 B.C.) have had, and continue to have, a fundamental influence on Japanese society. It is impossible to trace all of the avenues through which Confucianism entered Japan and influenced the Japanese people throughout their history. There is no reliable history of Japan in which Chinese influence is not present from the earliest days of Japan. The earliest writing in Japan is thoroughly suffused with Chinese thought.[7] Confucianism spread to Japan almost as soon as it gained popularity in China and affected Japanese society as deeply as it affected China. The author of Japan's first constitution, Prince Shotoku (573–621 A.D.), was a renowned Confucian scholar, and much of the constitution itself is Confucian in character. The first article of this seventeen article document, proclaimed in 604 A.D., is taken verbatim from the Analects of Confucius: "Harmony is to be valued, and an avoidance of wanton opposition to be honored."[8] The Shotoku constitution is significant not only for the effect it had at the time but also for the tone it set for Japanese society for many centuries to come. Through Shotoku, Confucianism was adopted by the early Japanese as the state creed and cult. "It was expounded in the imperial university, incorporated into the civil service examinations, and systemized by scholars working for the Throne who tried to arrive at a definite version of the Confucian classics."[9] Knowledge of the Confucian classics became the first requirement in the education of all government and court personnel.

Through the centuries, Confucianism, Neo-Confucianism, Han Confucianism, and various other schools or interpretations of Confucianism have flourished in Japan. While it is thus true that there has never been a time when Japan was free of Confucian influence, it was during the Tokugawa era (1600–1858 A.D.) that modern Japan became firmly Confucianist. Ieyasu Tokugawa's first task after becoming shogun in 1603 was to restore social order, stability, and peace to a country grown very weary after endless years of war and strife. Ieyasu Tokugawa adopted Confucianism as his official philosophy, and set about earnestly to set all of Japanese society into a Confucianist mold. Tokugawa's regime employed almost draconian measures to enforce the Confucian ideals. For example, "proper" behavior for all classes of Japanese was specified in great detail, and the power of the military was utilized to ensure strict observance of the rules. The whole country was organized into groups of five families each, in which every member was held responsible for the actions of all. Since these practices were in force for two centuries, they penetrated deeply into the Japanese psyche.

Japanese Organizations. While there is variation in the nature of Japanese work organizations, the general tendency is for them to be "familylike."[10] Some of the characteristics that organizations either already possess or aspire to possess are: lifetime employment, mostly seniority-based rank and promotion system, extensive employee welfare programs, frequent and intensive attempts to inculcate in employees a sense of community, and an almost total absorption of the individual into the "collective conscience."[11] A few brief quotations from a variety of sources will demonstrate that Japanese organizations seek to achieve, usually with success, *gemeinschaft* social systems:

> The Japanese employee is a member of the company in a way resembling that in which persons are members of families—in the U.S.[12]

> There is a tacit recognition by management that the relationship between the company and the worker is not simply a function of the economic convenience of the two parties.[13]

> The term *kaisha* (my company) symbolizes the expression of group consciousness. *Kaisha* does not mean that individuals are bound by contractual relationships into a corporate enterprise, while still thinking of themselves as separate entities; rather, *kaisha* is "my" or "our" company, the community to which one belongs primarily, and which is all important to one's life.[14]

Ouchi and Johnson explicitly equate the "Type Z" or Japanese Style Organization with *gemeinschaft*:

In the descriptions of the Type A and the Type Z organization we find forms of social organization which bear a striking similarity to earlier and, by now, classic descriptions of whole societies. Our description of Type A is very similar to the common description of the *gesellschaft* or contractual society. Similarly, the Type Z description sounds much like the *gemeinschaft*, village, or non-contractual, society.[15]

Japanese Society.   Examples are readily available of *gemeinschaft* work organizations operating in a mostly *gesellschaft* social environment, such as some of Peters and Waterman's[16] "excellent companies." But in Japan, the *gemeinschaft* tendency of Japanese organizations seems to have emerged from, and is in any case nurtured by, a strong *gemeinschaft* bias in the larger society. DeMente suggests that the Japanese do not feel comfortable or "right" in any person-to-person relationship that does not include "a feeling of complete trust and confidence, not only that the other party will not take advantage of them, but also that they—businessmen or private individuals—can presume on the indulgence of the other."[17] In other words, the Japanese do not feel comfortable in any interpersonal contexts not characterized by primary relationships: "—for a variety of reasons it is difficult for a Japanese to establish operational (i.e., functional) contractual personal relations—. Once a relationship is established, both parties tend to expect more from it than work itself, and so involve themselves emotionally."[18]

Japanese society is a collection not of individuals but of groups. The identity and self concept of the Japanese individual is almost completely defined by his or her membership in a group. In almost all transactions with the world outside the group, the Japanese is always a representative of the group, linked to it by strong bonds of loyalty and obligation. In all circumstances the Japanese is likely to ask not, "What should I do?," but, "What am I expected to do?" Furthermore, all these groups are overwhelmingly of the primary type. The most important of these groups is the family, but other groups acquire the status of the family, as suggested earlier, before they become fully operative. A group may have its origin in the utilitarian end for which it is formed, but it really does not exist, and certainly does not begin to function, until it has become a primary group through frequent and intense face-to-face interaction. Once groups are formed, they are expected to endure. Conversely, a secondary group would lose its reason for existence as soon as the goal for which it had been created is accomplished.

Zen: Theory and Practice

"Those who know do not speak; those who speak do not know." So goes a common, and typical, Zen saying. It is thus perhaps foolhardy to attempt to communicate in words a feel for the nature of Zen. Nonetheless, the attempt must be made, for nothing Japanese can be adequately understood without Zen. What makes Japanese society and Japanese work organizations so remarkably different from Western society and organizations is a profound difference in the concept of human nature that forms the core of each culture. For more than 2,000 years, Western civilization has held rationality to be the true human quality, that which distinguishes us from mere animals. Modern Western civilization, especially science and technology, is the triumph of this concept of the nature of humans. Western work organizations embody this same concept of human nature. During the same period, Japan, largely through the influence of Zen Buddhism, developed a civilization where human rationality came to be viewed as relatively insignificant, compared to the forces that lie below the level of consciousness. This view of human nature is so central to Japanese thought that reason and logic are widely mistrusted in today's Japan, for nothing as complex as the affairs of even a simple person can be captured in words and arguments.

In this part of the chapter, a brief historical review of Zen is followed by an attempt to describe Zen. Zen's insights about the dynamics of human behavior, especially as they are influenced by the unconscious, are revealed. Zen's deep influence on the Japanese people is then established. The consequences of the Zen view of human nature for the modern work organization in Japan are suggested, especially as they relate to its success as a social system. The final part of the paper then weaves the strands thus far developed to come to the conclusion stated to be the purpose of the chapter.

Zen Origins

The word "Zen" is the Japanese transliteration of the Chinese "Ch'an," which in turn is the Chinese version of the Sanskrit "Dhyana." Sanskrit is the classical language of India, the birthplace of the Buddha. Zen is, of course, a sect of Buddhism, and thus has its origins in India four centuries before the birth of Christ. "Dhyana" means meditation; thus, Zen emphasizes meditation as the path to the attainment of Buddhism's goal, which is always enlightenment. In India, enlightenment has been viewed for thousands of years as the highest spiritual state attainable by humans. Enlightenment is regarded "as a new insight or vision which breaks suddenly on the inner eye and is taken up in the consciousness."[19]

Buddhism was carried to China and was already widespread there by the fourth century A.D. Whereas Buddhism in general retained the Indian notion that enlightenment required many lifetimes to achieve, there developed in China a school of Buddhism that asserted the possibility of "instantaneous" enlightenment. "Because of his doctrine of instantaneous enlightenment, Taosheng (360–434 A.D.), one of the followers of the Indian monk Kumarjiva, has been called the founder of Zen."[20]

Buddhism was introduced to Japan from China, and gained tremendous popularity there. Prince Shotoku, mentioned earlier, was a devout Buddhist and did much to promote Buddhism in Japan. The origins of Zen in Japan can be traced to the seventh century. Interaction between Chinese and Japanese Zen monks continued thereafter, and Japanese Zen became a strong movement in its own right. There were, of course, ebbs and flows in the strength of the movement over the centuries, but Zen was firmly rooted and was never seriously under any danger of elimination. Zen's influence on the Japanese mind cannot be overemphasized: "Zen has entered internally into every phase of the cultural life of the Japanese people."[21]

Zen Theory and Practice

"Before your father and mother were born, what was your original face?"

If your mind was perplexed into silence on reading this *koan*, even if only for a brief moment, then you have already experienced a Zen moment. If this brief silence was quickly overtaken by an attempt to understand the "meaning" of this question, or if you dismissed the question as frivolous and meaningless, then you have also come face to face with the main obstacle in the path of the attainment of Zen's goal.

Zen, we are told again and again, is beyond words and beyond the grasp of the reasoning mind, and can ultimately only be transmitted from master to disciple. Zen subscribes to the development of the usually untapped powers of the mind as the path to the achievement of enlightenment. The primary mechanism for the development of the powers of the mind is meditation. Concentration, the state of mind in which all of one's attention is focussed on a single object or image, is the key to the practice of meditation: The development of the powers of the mind can be understood as the result of the struggle to maintain concentration in the face of the irrepressible tendency of the mind to wander. When this concentration or "one-pointedness" becomes effortless, a certain transformation is said to take place, through which the practitioner gains access to the allegedly incredible powers of the mind.

This brief description of Zen goals and practice already suggests that the "field" of operation of Zen is the unconscious mind. Zen is vehement in its claim that the logical, rational mind is not only incapable of penetrating the mysteries of Zen but also the main stumbling block to the achievement of enlightenment. For Zen, the habit of the conscious mind of constantly attempting to understand reality is the chief source of the doubts and hesitations that prevent us from tapping into the limitless power of the mind. "When the ultimate perfection is attained, the body and limbs perform by themselves what is assigned to them to do, without interference from the mind."[22]

The paradoxical quality of the Zen quest, that of seeking a state of "effortless effort," is utilized by Zen masters in their training at every turn. To bring the conceptualizing mind to an intellectual impasse, a deadlock from which it cannot escape with the resources at its command, is the central aim of all that Zen masters say and do to their disciples. The *koan*, or "spiritual problem," of which an example was given at the beginning of this section, is typical of this method. An intellectual response seeking clarification or explaining the physical impossibility of the act would be offered by only the most naive seeker. To earnestly seek meaning in these puzzles is to exhaust and frustrate the mind—which is precisely their purpose. There are, of course, no "rational" answers to these questions, yet the poor disciple, in his weekly interview with the master, is asked to meditate on the *koan* that is given to him and bring an answer. After weeks, months, and even years of such effort, the disciple learns to silence his reasoning mind, and let the "answer" flow from the depths of his unconscious, unmediated by his intellect. The answer itself may be as oblique as the *koan*, or it may consist of a shriek, or of breaking a bamboo staff in two—but it cannot be feigned, for the master knows when it is genuine and when it is only another example of the mind's cleverness.

Zen in Japanese Life

The claim that "nothing Japanese can be understood without Zen," made earlier in this chapter, is based not on Zen's unconventional approach but on the fact that it managed to penetrate deeply into almost every facet of Japanese life. From the time it was introduced to Japan from China in the sixth century, Buddhism has not limited itself to purely "religious" teaching. Buddhist temples were centers of learning for Chinese classics, literature and poetry, and all kinds of arts. Simplicity, elegance, unobtrusiveness—these are the values that have influenced all facets of Japanese culture from the early centuries of the Christian era, and there can be little doubt that these values are rooted in Buddhism. The Zen attitude of no-mind or egolessness, the Zen requirement of discipline and diligent practice and the Zen insistence on concentration and detachment are even now at the foundation of almost all Japanese arts including calligraphy, ceramics, poetry, the theater, and painting. The tremendously popular *haiku*, the famous seventeen-syllable Japanese poem, is testimony to Zen's widespread influence on the Japanese mind. For the *haiku* poet, the challenge consists of expressing in seventeen syllables not only the essence of some simple aspect of nature that he has observed but also the "cosmic significance" of the event. The *haiku* poet is a passive participant in the flow of life, and the poem is always an expression of a "Zen moment":

> A little frog
> Riding on a banana leaf
> Trembling

Even relatively mundane activities such as flower arrangement and tea-drinking have been converted, by Zen, into occasions for spiritual development. It is perhaps not an exaggeration to suggest, therefore, that Zen attitudes and sentiments have entered into the bloodstream of the Japanese. But the most powerful impact of Zen on the Japanese character has come through its intimate association with *bushido*, "the way of the *samurai*."

The *samurai* has been called the "flower of Japanese culture," and is, to this day, a source of immense pride for the Japanese. *Samurai* were formidable warriors, best known for their willingness to commit ritual suicide, called *seppuku*. *Seppuku* involves slitting open one's abdomen, with ceremony and dignity, and without a flicker of emotion of any kind. For the *samurai*, the only satisfactory meaning of life is to die with honor, in the service, or at the command, of his lord, the *daimyo* or warrior-chief to whom he has pledged complete and unwavering loyalty. In the hands of the *samurai* the sword—itself a miracle of Zen-inspired craftsmanship—became the most lethal weapon of hand-to-hand combat ever known to man. With the long, razor-sharp sword that the *samurai* always carried with him, he was capable of slitting men into two halves, head to toe, in one powerful yet effortless stroke. With the other shorter sword that he also always carried with him, the *samurai* was always ready to commit *seppuku*, either because he had failed to accomplish his mission, or because he found himself in a position from which he could not escape with dignity, or simply because his lord had ordered him to do so, even if for no apparent reason.

The significance of the *samurai* for the purposes of this paper is that, in death as in life, the *samurai* never lost control, never allowed any human frailties—fear, doubt, love, or even hate—to interfere with the performance of his duty. Even the least accomplished of *samurai* demonstrated an incredible power over his unconscious mind, and it was through the discipline of Zen that he achieved this power. Survival is perhaps life's deepest instinct, so that if the fear of death is conquered one has gained tremendous mastery over one's instincts—that is to say, over one's unconscious mind. Or, to state it in terms of Freudian concepts, when the fear of death is eliminated, a vast amount of energy that was cathected to this fear is freed up and becomes available for the development of other capabilities. This is precisely the path followed by the *samurai*:

> As long as the thought of death is in the consciousness, it will unconsciously but inevitably lead the swordsman in the direction he is most anxious to avoid. When one is resolved to die, that is, when the thought of death is wiped off the field of consciousness, there arises something in it the presence of which one has never been aware of. When this strange presence begins to direct one's activities in an instinctual manner, wonders are achieved.[23]

The *samurai* were the unchallenged heroes and rulers of Japan for centuries, and even today much popular culture— movies, plays, novels—glorify the *samurai* tradition. If Zen is today a household word in Japan, it is partly because one cannot think of the *samurai* without thinking about Zen—and one cannot avoid thinking about the *samurai* in Japan.

This is not to suggest that Japanese workers and managers are descendants of *samurai*, or that they actively practice Zen, though doubtless many are, and do. However, almost every Japanese individual does take up some "extra-curricular" activity that has procured the basic elements of its training from Zen. Such activities are considered an essential part of the development of character in Japan. Whether they are calligraphy or flower-arrangement, swordsmanship or the tea-ceremony, they all share the Zen goals of concentration and mastery of the principles of the activity through diligent, "egoless" practice. Accomplishment in these arts is not so much a matter of creativity or uniqueness of expression but of a freedom and power of movement which reflects "effortless effort," a flow of energy from the depths of the unconscious without mediation by the conscious mind.

This intense involvement with activities that are based in Zen cannot fail to transfer to the world of work. The president of a large American company, after careful observation of women workers at a large Japanese factory, came to the conclusion that "the way these women approach their work reflects something of Japan's traditional spirit. They appear to work in exactly the same spirit as they might perform the traditional arts, like flower arranging or tea ceremony."[24]

Furthermore, Zen-based *seishin kyoiku* or "spiritual education" is a large part of the substantial amount of training that most Japanese companies provide for their employees. Japanese companies place considerable emphasis on the "right" attitude toward work and company: "Enjoyment of work has less to do with the kind of work performed than with the attitude the person has toward it."[25] This viewpoint itself is borrowed from Zen, since the goal of enlightenment is, at its root, no more than a profound change in attitude. More significant, the exercises through which the "right" attitude is to be attained can be traced to Zen.[26]

Discussion

What the Japanese people get from Zen is a set of attitudes, predominant among which is a distrust of rational and logical processes which are dismissed as "cleverness": "The great majority of Japanese simply do not wish to speak in clear, concise, logical fashion. Japanese shun explicit, clearly reasoned statements in favor of indirect and ambiguous ones basically designed not to communicate ideas but to feel out the other person's moods and attitudes."[27]

It is not clever ideas but a sensitivity to the unexpressed feelings of others that is more highly valued in the Japanese work organization. The cardinal sin in Japan is to cause someone to "lose face," and the Japanese will go to great lengths to avoid causing embarrassment to others, even their rivals. What these concerns require is an awareness of the complexity of human motivation and a conviction that the "real" forces that determine behavior are usually invisible. This is what Ouchi[28] calls "subtlety," and what Pascale and Athos[29] refer to as tolerance for uncertainty and ambiguity. What it amounts to is that the Japanese learns to trust his gut feelings and intuition, that is, the promptings of his unconscious mind, rather than logical conclusions based on the "facts."

It is not difficult to conclude, then, that Japanese interpersonal behavior is informed at every point by a complex vision of human nature, one that fully incorporates unconscious processes. Consider, for example, Mushashi's advice concerning the "Real Art of Japanese Management": "Perceive that which cannot be seen by the eye...make profound observation of the essence of things primary and observation of the movements of surface phenomena, insignificant actions, what your opponent wants you to see secondary..."[30]

This view of human nature interacts with the *gemeinschaft* tendency of the Japanese work organization to result in a social system where sentiment is not only tolerated but honored, and harmony is the supreme value. The Zen-engendered predisposition of the Japanese people to engage their unconscious energies in inter-personal relations finds a conducive environment in the Confucian-inspired social structure of their work organizations. If the predominant inter-personal relationships in Japan are primary, then the current superior performance of Japanese organizations may be due, in part, to the greater involvement of the unconscious obtained from their employees. More significantly, the success of Japanese organizations as social systems, in the sense of their being satisfying contexts for humans beings in interactions with each other, can be attributed to the relatively unthreatening environment that exists in *gemeinschaft* social structures. Defenses are constructed by the conscious mind when it comes into contact with a "reality" that renders free expression of impulses originating in the unconscious dangerous to the survival or well-being of the individual. In other words, the free flow of energy from the unconscious to the pre-conscious and conscious levels is blocked by defenses and repressions when this free flow would lead to a situation in which the individual's life, livelihood or self-concept is threatened. If expressing what I really feel or acting according to the dictates of my instincts leads consistently to loss of "face" or some other punishment, I will soon cease to express my feelings or act according to the dictates of my instincts. This is perhaps what happens, all too often, in the typically *gesellschaft* Western organization. In contrast, "one of the charms of Asia is that you need have no fear of being insulted or having your dignity threatened in public. *You can lower your defenses and relax.* No one will insult you or cause you emotional pain."[31]

Along with the cultural tendencies that contribute to the success of Japanese organizations as social systems, policies and operational procedures of Japanese organizations further create the conditions by which unconscious energies of employees are engaged at work. If one were to design an organizational environment in which the unconscious has relatively free play, it would not be surprising if the characteristics considered necessary closely resembled Ouchi's[32] Type Z characteristics. (Table 4.2) High on the list would be job security of the kind provided by the lifetime employment system in Japan. There is probably no other circumstance as effective in putting employees "on guard" as the threat of loss of livelihood.

The second dimension on Ouchi's Type Z list, infrequent evaluation and promotion, would similarly serve to relax employees' defenses or, rather, prevent them from being created in the first place. It is not hard to imagine the differences between the states of mind of the typical American employee who is more or less constantly haunted by the prospect of an upcoming performance review, and his or her Japanese counterpart, who is relatively free from such concerns. The environment of the American employee is much more likely to be perceived as containing dangers that

Table 4.2   Ouchi's Type Z Characteristics

Long-term employment
Infrequent evaluation and promotion
Implicit, informal evaluation
Nonspecialized career paths
Collective decision making
Collective responsibility

threaten his or her livelihood and career goals. The differences in the criteria used for control, evaluation and promotion in the two systems point to the same conclusion, that the Japanese worker is relatively free to act intuitively, in harmony with his or her deeply felt nature. It is wisdom, experience, and subtlety that are valued in Japanese organizations, in contrast with the emphasis on quantifiable criteria in American organizations. The specialized career paths of employees in American organizations produce "a set of individuals of widely differing talents, skills, and objectives. Such people are in an important way strangers to one another."[33] It is in the company of strangers that one is most "on guard," most likely to deny expression to impulses originating in the unconscious.

Collective decision making and collective responsibility typical of Japanese organizations further reduce the burden on individual employees of having to base their contributions on arguments that are capable of rational and logical expression. By now, the importance Japanese organizations place on philosophy of management and company values is well known. Japanese organizations expend considerable effort in the indoctrination of employees to company philosophy and values. In many organizations all over Japan employees begin their work day by "reciting the code of values and singing [the company song] together."[34] In the Matsushita Electric Company, every employee is asked at least once every other month to give a ten-minute talk to his group on the firm's values and their relationships to society.[35] Through such mechanisms, the Japanese employee comes to identify deeply with the company philosophy and values. Stated differently, the company philosophy and values become deeply imbedded in the employee's unconscious. It is only in the context of this deep identification with company philosophy and values that the willingness of Japanese organizations to allow employees to act according to the dictates of their instincts can be understood.

It may be observed that rather than being free and uninhibited, Japanese employees are quite constrained in their interpersonal conduct by considerations of propriety. This does not, however, contradict the suggestion made in this paper, for the following reason: while unconscious energies may be engaged at work, the *contents* of the unconscious are a function of the conditioning that the Japanese are subjected to in their early socialization. In fact, this conditioning consists of a heavy dose of Confucianist rules of propriety. In other words, considerations of propriety are deeply imbedded in the unconscious of the typical Japanese individual and hence operate in the organizational environment. The constraints on interpersonal behavior that the Japanese culture imposes on the Japanese people serve the overriding goal of harmonious co-existence, a goal that requires awareness of the sensitivity to the unconscious processes that underlie human behavior. Confucianism and Zen thus reinforce each other.

Conclusion

"Japanese and American work organizations are 95 percent the same—and different in all the important respects."[36] This chapter has suggested that these crucial differences have emerged from cultural forces originating in Confucianism and Zen Buddhism, and are primarily responsible for the success of Japanese organizations as social systems. This chapter's principle contribution to theory consists of the links suggested between concepts developed in the West (*gemeinschaft/gesellschaft*, primary/secondary, and the unconscious) and in the East (Confucianism and Zen). On the practical side, at the least this paper contributes to an understanding of Japanese culture and its influence on Japanese organizations.

The ideas presented here could also lead thoughtful managers to a fundamental re-examination of their organizational philosophy and practice. Work organizations constructed around a rationalistic view of human nature, and hence *gesellschaft* in character, may not provide the context for satisfying and enriching social relationships. It is widely acknowledged that no more than a fraction of the potential of human beings is normally utilized, with much of the rest being bound up in anxieties, fears, and defenses. Work organizations designed to appeal only to the utilitarian instincts leave out the larger part of what humans are made of, that is, the unconscious energies, which, if a rightful place can be found for them in the work organization, can contribute a great deal to productivity. The persistent effort in the West to create work organizations governed by rationally determined rules of behavior *to the exclusion of emotion and sentiment* render these organizations cold and undesirable places for people to be in. The Japanese example suggests that work organizations can be contexts for personal, social, and even spiritual satisfaction.

What is being suggested here is not that rational design of organizational structures and processes be abandoned, but that our vision of work organizations be expanded to allow them to embrace a fuller vision of human beings. There are too many differences between the cultures of Japan and the United States to allow for any one-to-one duplication of Japanese organizational mechanisms. Perhaps the lessons for us from Japan have eluded us largely because of our tendency to look for specific ideas that can be rapidly implemented here. The true significance of the Japanese social structure for the West may be related to more basic issues, such as the concept of human nature that underlies social structures, rather than to techniques such as quality circles. The Japanese emphasis on harmony, in the context of the intricate interdependency in human affairs, seems more "rational" than the core Western value of freedom. Could it be that freedom—from crime, fear, and loneliness—is a by-product of harmony, rather than the other way around? If this chapter triggers such a questioning of our basic assumptions, it will have served its purpose.

What the Japanese example challenges Western managers to do is to begin their analysis of organizational design not with the question of "what our business is, and what should it be," but with the question: "Who are we as people, and what do we want to be?" If the answer is in terms only of task performance or material gain, then perhaps the typical Western organization design will be quite adequate. If the answer is in terms of more earthy sentiments such as friendship and good cheer, a sense of belonging and significance, then room will need to be made in the organization for tradition and ritual, for informal contact and frivolous banter. Questions regarding the relative role of merit and attitude, talent and character will have to be raised. The balance, in short, between success of the organization as a productive system and as a social system will have to be explicitly examined.

SECTION II

Communication and
Interpersonal Relationships in Japan

At the heart of all business interactions is communication. But patterns of communication are so thoroughly bound up with culture that communication across cultures cannot possibly succeed in the absence of cultural understanding. Learning the language is an important first step, but is by no means a substitute for an awareness of how the words and phrases relate to attitudes and beliefs, especially regarding interpersonal relationships. The selections included in this section provide the reader with a perspective from which to gain better insights into the cultural aspects of language.

The reality behind the stereotypes of Americans as frank, self-assertive, spontaneous, informal, and talkative compared to Japanese as formal, reserved, evasive, and silent is explored by Dean C. Barnlund in his chapter, "Public and Private Self in Communicating with Japan." Barnlund suggests that the Japanese "public self," that is, the aspects of the self made accessible to others, is much smaller than is the case in the United States. After reviewing the evidence for this suggestion, Barnlund points out that this difference is related to the fact that the group is central to the self-identity and security of the Japanese individual. The group's needs take priority over the individual's. "Too frequent or too strong an assertion of the self threatens group solidarity." Barnlund then goes on to a broader cultural analysis and finds, in a strong endorsement of the discussion in the Introduction, that Japan can be characterized by the words homogeneity, hierarchy, collectivity, and harmony, in contrast to heterogeneity, equality, individualism, and change for the United States.

"The Vocabulary of Human Relationships in Japan" is an

excerpt from a book by Edward Hall and Mildred Hall in which they seek to reveal some of the less obvious and often misunderstood aspects of Japanese culture and behavior. In this excerpt, the Halls discuss Japanese psychology and culture by explaining the significance and role of a number of key Japanese terms, most of which have no simple translations into English. The Halls distinguish between "High Context" words, which can be understood only with reference to the context in which they are used, and "Low Context" words, which have a fairly universal meaning. Their analysis of the Japanese language leads the Halls to the conclusion that it is a High Context language. The implication is that a full understanding of Japanese conversation cannot be achieved without a relatively detailed knowledge of the particular situation in which it is taking place. If only a written transcript of a conversation in Japanese were available to us, we would not be able to as fully discover the contents of the conversation as we would if the language in question were, say, English.

The Halls discuss a number of key terms of Japanese interpersonal relationship, but underlying each of them we can see the tendencies suggested in the Introduction. The Japanese people operate in an interpersonal environment that presses on their every action much more heavily than for most Americans. The emphasis on obligation and interpersonal propriety that was discussed in the Introduction is revealed in this selection when the authors declare that "a sense of indebtedness is ever present in Japanese society." In numerous ways, Japanese culture continually emphasizes the priority of society and social order *over the* individual and individual freedom.

Harumi Befu's chapter, "Gift-Giving in a Modernizing Japan," reviews the long tradition of exchange of gifts in Japan, a practice that is often perplexing to foreigners. Befu calls gift giving in Japan a "minor institution," with complex rules covering everything from when gifts are mandatory to how they should be packaged and presented. He traces the origins of gift giving to the custom of offering gifts of food to gods and reveals the various motivations behind gift giving in modern Japan. Perhaps the most important motivation is to manage the intricate web of social obligation and gratitude that is at the heart of Japanese interpersonal conduct. Gift giving within the context of business relations is just as prevalent, and proceeds from essentially the same motivation. It is also in the Japanese tradition, and one does not deviate from tradition lightly in Japan: "One is morally obligated to give a gift when custom demands it." Thus, in Befu's rich description of gift giving in Japan we find fur-

ther manifestations of Japan's preference for society over individual *and* continuity over change.

Note also that this "minor institution" of gift giving in Japan creates a lucrative market for American products, but one that will remain inaccessible without a detailed study of the rituals and customs associated with gift giving. Thus, Befu's article can contribute not only to the effort of American executives to establish relationships with their Japanese counterparts but also to American companies attempting to market their products in Japan.

The last selection in this section is also from Harumi Befu. In 'An Ethnography of Dinner Entertainment in Japan," Befu turns his perceptive eye toward another Japanese custom with which foreigners are bound to come into contact. Going to a bar for drinks and going to dinner together are essential features of the development of business relationships in Japan. But almost all public behavior in Japan is ritualized, and one risks damaging the delicate process of building trust and friendship if one does not know the rules of the game. Befu provides an accurate and informative portrait of an important Japanese ritual and an insightful analysis of the cultural foundations of this ritual.

5

Public and Private Self in Communicating with Japan*

Dean C. Barnlund

Nearing Autumn's close,
My neighbor—
How does he live, I wonder?

—Basho

When these words were written nearly 300 years ago, Basho's "neighbors" referred to people like himself—similar in dress, customs, manner, and language—who happened to live next door. Today few of us are surrounded by people who are carbon copies of ourselves. We may spend our lives in the company of those who speak in other tongues, move at a different pace, or interact in unexpected ways. And we may find that increasing proximity and social equality aggravate interpersonal frictions instead of dissipating them. Anyone who has ever struggled to understand someone else—even someone very much like himself—can appreciate the challenge of understanding someone with a different set of val-

*Reprinted from *Business Horizons* 32, no. 2, Copyright © 1989 by the Foundation for the School of Business at Indiana University. Used with permission.

ues or motives. Technical advances—satellites, jet aircraft, computer technology, and ballistic missiles—remind us that a global village is more a reality than a poetic metaphor. Can we master the cultural attitudes and new communicative skills required for collaborative management under these emerging conditions?

Because cultural parochialism has always flourished on cultural isolation, wider and more frequent contact is obviously essential in promoting understanding. But too often we have regarded increased contact across national borders as a necessary and sufficient means of improving international rapport. Research does not confirm this simplistic notion: contact between nations has, more often than not, actually exacerbated existing antagonisms. Armed hostilities are more common across the borders of neighboring cultures than between cultures separated by great distances. Familiarity, it is said, breeds contempt, especially when contact consists only of uncomprehending confrontation.

More than mere contact is required. People must become capable of projecting themselves into the unconscious premises of an alien culture. When we understand how people of another culture view the world and relate to one another, encounters with them are more likely to succeed. And our success can be even greater when we become capable of articulating our own views in the same communicative style they employ.

"One of the handicaps of the twentieth century," writes Ruth Benedict, "is that we still have the vaguest and most biased notions not only of what makes Japan a nation of Japanese but of what makes the United States a nation of Americans, France a nation of Frenchmen, and Russia a nation of Russians. Lacking this knowledge, each country misunderstands the other." This handicap promoted our effort to explore some of the differences in the communicative behavior of Japanese and Americans, differences that might reveal why some encounters fail and others succeed.[1]

One of the first questions to arise in any cross-cultural study is the extent to which the two cultures are alike and different. In creating profiles of Japanese and Americans our research found that the Japanese characterized themselves, and were characterized by non-Japanese who knew them well, as "formal," "reserved," "cautious," "evasive," and "silent." Americans described themselves, and were described by the Japanese, as "frank," "self-assertive," "spontaneous," "informal," and "talkative." Interestingly, the Japanese scored near zero on the attributes of Americans, and Americans scored near zero on the qualities assigned to the Japanese. To be useful, however, such broad assessments must be traced to concrete behaviors and to the cultural norms on which such behaviors rest.

Public and Private Self

It was hypothesized that the Japanese would prefer an interpersonal style in which aspects of the self made accessible to others (the public self) would be relatively small, while the proportion of the self not revealed (the private self) would be relatively large. If minimal exposure is a cultural value, this trait should be displayed in a number of ways. The Japanese might prefer to interact more selectively and with fewer persons, prefer formal rather than spontaneous encounters, disclose their thoughts and feelings less openly, be less demonstrative physically, and prefer more passive ways of responding to threatening situations. All of these strategies reduce the unpredictability and emotional intensity of personal encounters (see Figure 5.1).

The Americans, it was believed, would prefer a communicative style that stands in contrast to the Japanese, one in which the public self dominates the private self. If the fullest possible sharing and expression of the self is an important cultural value, it too should be manifest in a number of communicative strategies: Americans might seek to communicate less selectively and with a wider number of people; prefer informal to ritualized forms of communication; talk about a wider range of topics in more personal ways; be less inhibited physically in showing their feelings; and prefer to respond more aggressively in threatening situations (see Figure 5.2).

What is suggested here is a difference, not of kind but of degree, between the psychic structure and cultural norms of Japanese and Americans. This contrast in personality structure, reflecting the cultural assumptions and values of Japan and the United States, should dispose members of the two societies to communicate differently—about different topics, to different people, in different ways, with different consequences.

Relations with Strangers

To test speculations, conversational norms were explored through surveys in the two cultures. Although not tested directly, there was indirect support for the idea that Japanese and American hold

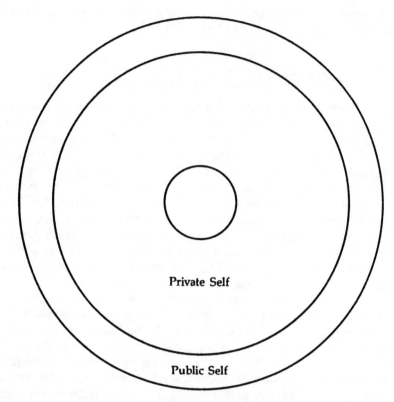

Figure 5.1 Japanese Public and Private Self

different attitudes about interacting with strangers, the Japanese preferring to interact less frequently and disclose less of themselves to unfamiliar people than do Americans. The barrier separating people one knows and feels comfortable with and those who are unknown is more formidable in Japan than in the United States. (This has been fully confirmed through recently published research.) The unpredictability of encounters with unfamiliar people, combined with the obligations such encounters might impose, appear to discourage Japanese from talking with strangers. Americans, in contrast, appear to welcome such occasions and to talk almost as freely and openly with people they do not know as with those they do. The foreigner working in Japan may sometimes find his special status exempts him from this rule, but not always, and it often makes spontaneous creation of temporary working teams composed of unacquainted colleagues difficult or impossible.

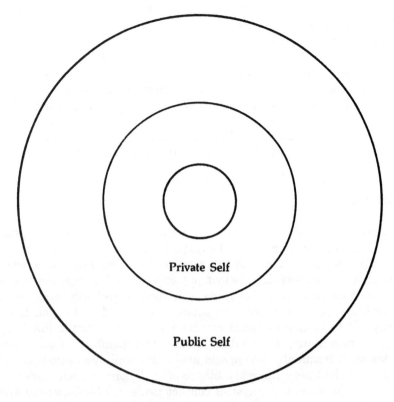

Figure 5.2 American Public and Private Self

Conversational Styles

With regard to preferred topics of conversation, however, we found considerable agreement between the two cultures. For example, Japanese and Americans both preferred to talk about such topics as their "interests," "attitudes toward work," and "public issues"; both preferred not to talk about their "financial situation," "personal strengths and weaknesses," or "physical condition." Japanese and Americans were most open and revealing with peers and parents, least open with strangers and people they did not trust. Japanese, however, differentiated between what they would reveal to same- or opposite-sex associates and to mothers and fathers; Americans tended to disclose equally both to parents and male and female friends.

The widest cultural contrast appeared, however, not in the

topics of conversation but in the depth of personal disclosure. Japanese rarely talked about their partners in more than the most general terms, disclosing little about their inner thoughts. Americans, in contrast, disclosed more on all topics to all people at deeper levels, expressing their own feelings more fully. This held true for the "most sensitive" as well as the "safest" topics. Indeed, Americans disclosed nearly as much to strangers as the Japanese did to their own fathers. The precise boundaries of the public and private self in the two countries is illustrated in Figure 5.3, Americans disclosing at a level about 50 percent higher than the Japanese.

Physical Style

Where the verbal channel for sharing ideas is more restricted, one might expect greater physical expressiveness as a form of communicative compensation. But this was not the case. Physical expressiveness duplicates the distinct patterns of verbal expressiveness in the two countries. Japanese and Americans both were more physically demonstrative with people they felt close to than those they felt to be more distant psychologically (a principle that may hold across many, if not all, cultures). And members of both societies most frequently touch, and avoid touching, the same areas of the body. But here the resemblance ends: There is a wide discrepancy in the extent of physical contact preferred by Japanese and Americans during conversation. Americans reported two to three times greater physical contact with friends than the Japanese. Americans tend to be more disclosing of their inner reactions both verbally and physically. The two cultures cultivate and enforce distinct communicative norms with respect to the public expression of private thoughts and feelings.

Defensive Styles

The impulse to communicate arises from the necessity of accommodating the meanings each of us assigns to our experience. If every object or event elicited an identical response from all who witnessed it, there would be little need for humans to communicate at all. But every event is construed in a different way by every observer, reflecting his or her past experience, current perspective, and emerging motives.

For most of the human race, differences are threatening. To

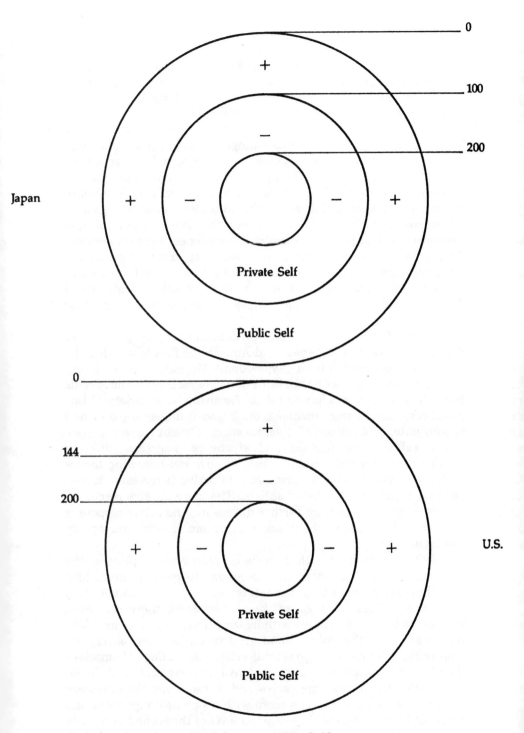

Figure 5.3 Precise Boundary of Public Self

be brought face-to-face with discrepant facts, opposing opinions, or alternative judgments arouses our defenses. The deeper the difference in meanings, the more it threatens us by throwing into question our ways of making the world intelligible.

Communication, since it is usually prompted consciously or unconsciously by the desire to change another person—in what they know, feel, or think—threatens most people. The deeper the implicit change, the more threatening the encounter may appear. In ordinary conversation, where much of the talk is formalized (even between people of diverse cultural backgrounds), things tend to run smoothly. It is in moving beyond the rituals of conversation and into areas of potential conflict that defenses may be aroused. And it is precisely under these conditions that cultural contrasts in communicative behavior are most likely to surface in cross-cultural negotiations. For this reason the defensive strategies of Japanese and Americans might throw the sharpest light on their cultural differences.

Three factors seem critical in determining the patterns of defense displayed by Japanese and Americans: first is whether the threat is of low or high intensity; second is the extent to which preferred defenses vary with the status of partners; third is the specific form that defensive behavior takes. Accordingly, a variety of targeted companions were included: older and younger; superior and subordinate; same or opposite sex; respected or not respected associates; relatives or friends; and strangers. Fourteen different options were included, ranging from passive (withdrawing tactics such as argument and denunciation) to active (aggressive tactics such as argument and denunciation). The more passive responses permit one to retreat from further disclosure; the active responses are difficult to use without becoming more deeply and openly involved.

When confronted with disturbing questions or opinions, the most popular choice among Japanese was to remain silent, hint that they do not want to discuss it, or actually say "I do not want to discuss it." As the level of threat increased, there was even greater reliance on passive-withdrawing forms of response. The Americans, on the other hand, relied almost exclusively on answering threatening ideas directly, defending themselves through explanation and argument. All of their preferred defensive tactics fell on the aggressive end of the scale; the Japanese varied their defensive tactics more with different companions and different levels of threat. Varying the level of threat had very little effect on the aggressive tactics favored by Americans. And each culture, particularly the American, scored very low on the strategies the other culture preferred. As Fosco Maraini once observed, "Americanism rises on the foundation of ultimate dissent; Japan on the foundations of ultimate assent."

In these contrasting patterns of defensive behavior there is a suggestion of cultural circularity. A society that favors less disclosure and maximizes agreement is unlikely to cultivate the skills of analysis and argument; a society that encourages the self-expressiveness that increases the incidence of disagreement must cultivate the skills of containing and resolving such conflicts through argument.

Psychological Implications

After identifying these two communicative styles, we can now examine their significance for the individual and for interpersonal and intercultural encounters. How do they diminish or enrich human relationships? Does discouraging expression of inner thoughts and feelings reduce opportunities for self-realization? Or, conversely, does wider and fuller self-expression contribute to growth?

The ability to expose one's self, to be known to at least one other person, argues Jourard, is a prerequisite for a mature and productive personality. To many, like Picasso, the inducement to express one's self arises out of contact with others: "To fall back, to live on oneself, to withdraw is sterility." The encouragement to express an opinion is often the stimulus for having an opinion.

Eastern culture takes some exception to the charge that restricting self-expression limits growth. Is not silence as essential as speech in the cultivation of personality? The self, it is argued, grows not only through noisy argument, but also through quiet contemplation. All conversations need not take place out loud; internal conversation can be as stimulating as external conversation. Meditation and silence are respected not because they imprison the mind but because they free it. If inhibition sometimes contributes to psychic impoverishment, cannot excessive verbalization also cripple? "Speech," writes Kyoshi Ikeda, "draws everything out of a man, and when words have been spoken there is nothing left in him." The compulsion to express oneself may be as great an impediment to selfhood as cultural norms that inhibit such disclosures.

This difference in self-disclosure results from differences in child-rearing practices in the two countries. An American infant is surrounded from birth by an appreciative audience constantly provoking some sort of communication. To hold the attention of this audience and secure its approval, children learn to speak constantly, loudly, and dramatically. In adulthood it is not surprising if this preoccupation with verbalizing one's thoughts should continue as a means of securing recognition and love. Japanese children are loved no less, but they are rarely subjected to such stimulation from parents. Words are less important; silent rapport is quite enough. Among Americans greater disclosure may result from a continual craving for attention and affection or simply an emphasis on self-realization. Among Japanese a reduced need for self-expression may suggest a repressing of natural impulses or simply lack of a need for such constant reassurance of one's status.

In one culture communication turns principally outward, an opportunity for self-actualization and achievement. It is a way of influencing and affecting the outer world. In the other the communication process turns more inward, less a means of gaining attention or influencing events than a way of finding inner serenity and preserving harmonious relations with society. Such a contrast in communicative thrust understandably affects the character of conversation in the two countries.

Even the concept of the self differs. Every society creates some unit that serves as the psychological core for its members, the ultimate source of meaning and the base for the interpretation of events. In some it is the individual; in others it is the group. In the United State and most Western cultures, this psychological unit is the solitary human being. The individual is the measure of all things. To preserve a sense of personal uniqueness the individual must stand apart, or even against, other members of his or her family, office, or nation.

In Japan the group is the measure of all things; at first the family and later one's work associates. A sense of identity and security against the hazards of life comes from group strength, not from the strength of the individual. To protect this identity the needs of the group must prevail over the needs of any solitary person. Too frequent or too strong an assertion of the self threatens the group's solidarity.

Perhaps these two cultural perspectives define the pathological extremes on a continuum of self-disclosure. Both the person who rarely discloses himself and the person who is preoccupied with disclosure may appear maladjusted and unable to maintain close working relationships. In a communicative mature person, private reflection and public expression may merge. Here there is a capacity for private, silent contemplation, that is neither a product of repression nor a defensive retreat, and a capacity for self-expression that is neither an aggressive exploitation nor a compulsive need for attention.

Communicative Implications

Specialists in communication are understandably fond of repeating that, in human affairs, "misunderstanding is the rule and understanding the happy accident." There is reason to respect this assessment, for understanding is often difficult to achieve—even between members of a single culture. The issue is to what extent the communicative norms of Japan and United States aggravate or diminish the inherent difficulties in this process. Japan, with its emphasis on formal relationships, appears to reduce the scope of verbal disclosure, limit physical expressiveness, and encourage withdrawal from threatening confrontations. The United States encourages greater informality, values verbal candor and physical spontaneity, and favors more aggressive approaches to conflictful situations.

Yet the depth of conversations suggests that human contact is somewhat superficial in both countries. Even among intimate acquaintances, large areas of thought and feelings remain unexposed and unshared. As Edward Albee once put it, "We are all lonely at times, fearful of others, and pained most of the time. Why we do not make use of such kinship rather than ignore it, is a question worth answering." If cultures could be placed along a "disclosure gradient," neither Japan nor the United States would occupy the extreme ends. But there would be a wide gap separating them.

In infancy there is no private or public self, only a single undivided self. It is the uncensored expression of every feeling that makes children so appealing. Yet societies oppose this "childish" impulse to say whatever one thinks or feels, and by adulthood the inner self is split and compartmentalized. This split, necessary or not, is bought at a price; it takes immense energy continuously to monitor inner reactions, to segregate what can be expressed and what must be concealed. The result may not only alienate people from one another, but from themselves as well. It would be surprising if such concealment, practiced over a lifetime, would not limit the capacity for intimate relationships.

Still more serious is the way such interior manipulation of the self corrupts communication between people. Even when people earnestly want to understand each other, there are difficulties that make such agreements doubtful. No two people perceive alike, or believe alike. Each brings to every conversation a different personal history, different assumptions, motives, and expectations. And the words and gestures we use to cross this experiential divide are themselves ambiguous, provoking discrepant meanings in those who hear and see them. Such normal difficulties are compounded when conversational partners do not allow themselves to be known as they really are. Messages that ordinarily might be regarded as clues to inner meanings are now deliberately manipulated to camouflage. If communication is difficult when people express themselves honestly, imagine the complications when each presents a person who is not really there. Concealment does not merely complicate understanding, it encourages misunderstanding. As Figures 5.4 and 5.5 suggest, not only are there the normal areas of agreement and disagreement to be expected in any discussion (shown by the + and - signs in the lightly shaded areas), but these are now compounded and aggravated by differences in the communicative norms of each culture (the - signs in the darker areas). Each participant, Japanese and American, tries to tailor the conversation according to his own rhetorical tradition; each strives to impose a different set of norms, a different degree of personal involvement, a different form and pace for conversation.

In the first instance the American conversational norms prevail, either because of their forceful assertion by the American or the reluctance of the Japanese to resist them. In the second instance, the Japanese norms prevail, again because of the unwillingness of the American to oppose them. In most cases some tenuous compromise or vacillation between the two sets of norms will result. But neither will eliminate feelings of awkwardness or frustration.

Each, blindly conforming to his own cultural script, asserts his own approach to problems, level of frankness, and evaluations of the negotiations, and each finds he lacks a frame for comprehending the other. The Japanese may be frightened at the prospect of being communicatively invaded (because of the unexpected spontaneity and bluntness of the American); the American is annoyed at the prospect of endless formalities and tangential replies. The cues that are impeccable guides to interpretation within each culture have become obstacles to rapport and comprehension of messages from the other culture.

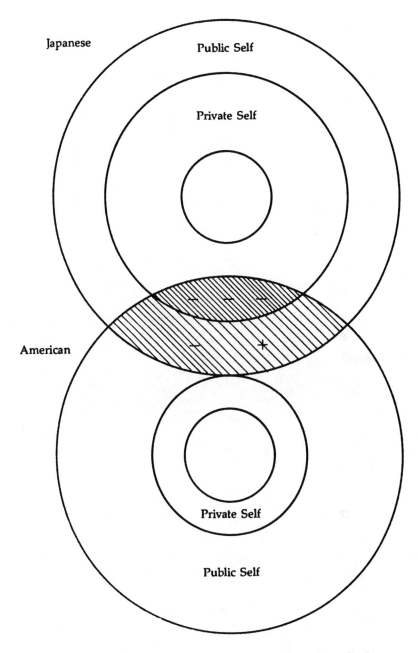

Figure 5.4 Intercultural Communication: American Style

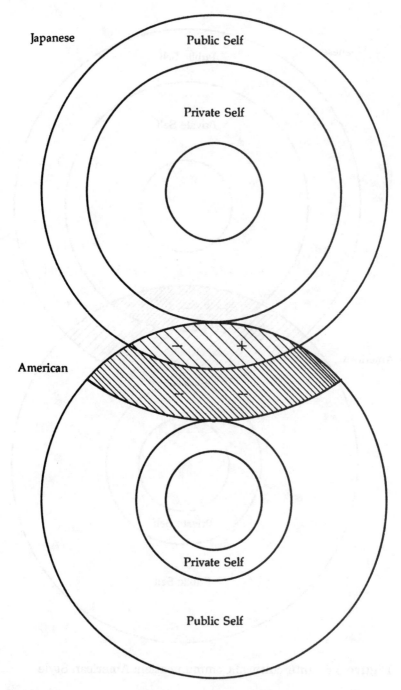

Figure 5.5 Intercultural Communication: Japanese Style

The Japanese may be frustrated by flippant attitudes toward formalities, "insensitivity" to status differences, "blunt criticism," "prying questions," and a predilection for "premature" decisions. In the Japanese culture these are the meanings that would be attached to "American" behavior. The American talking to Japanese associates, is equally baffled by conversations that seem "pointless," silences that "waste time," delays that are "inexcusable," the "distant and cold" demeanor of his counterparts, and their "evasive and ambiguous" remarks. This is how he might interpret the same acts displayed by a fellow American. What seems clear to one is unclear to the other. And what seems clear may actually be misunderstood.

There is still another way in which cultures affect the course and quality of communication. To interact requires not only the encoding or symbolizing of inner thoughts, but decoding and interpreting the symbols used. American emphasis on self-assertion and talkativeness cultivates a communicator who is highly self-oriented and expressive; the Japanese emphasis on "reserve" and "sensitivity" cultivates a communicator who is other-oriented and receptive. As one Japanese reminded a talkative American who criticized his quietness, "I want to understand this other person and the only way I can put myself in his shoes is to empathize with him. And that is impossible if I am always shouting at him." Each culture thus may foster a sort of communicative specialization (and communicative negligence). Yet both the ability to express oneself and to sensitively hear what others are saying are essential in the search for mutual understanding and agreement.

Cultural Implications

If one were forced to choose only a few words to capture the ethos of these two societies, the words might be these: homogeneity, hierarchy, collectivity, and harmony for Japan; heterogeneity, equality, individualism, and change for the United States.

Is there any large country that can match Japan in the homogeneity of its people? As a nation it has deliberately cultivated "Japanese-ness" for hundreds of years, isolating itself from foreign influences and promoting the greatest possible consistency in language, values, architecture, clothing, and life-style. The more any two people communicate, the larger their store of common meanings, and the more they share a common outlook. And the more two people resemble each other, the easier it is to convey complex meanings by the most rudimentary messages. If true, then the ambiguous character of Japanese communication so often noted by observers may be simply a reflection on a national scale of the same phenomenon found within any family. The greater the cultural homogeneity, the more that can be conveyed in a single word, the more that can be implied without being stated explicitly.

Nearly all communication in Japan takes place within an elaborate and vertically organized social structure. Everyone has a distinct place within this framework. Rarely do people converse without knowing, or determining, who is above and who is below them. Associates are always older or younger, male or female, subordinate or superior. And these distinctions all carry implications for the form of address, choice of words, physical distance, and demeanor. As a result, conversation tends to reflect this formal hierarchy. It has, however, two further effects: it moderates the advocacy of differing points of view and, at the same time, increases preoccupation with losing or saving face.

As noted earlier, group identification is paramount in Japan. The boundaries of the ego appear weaker and more permeable than those that surround the collective unit. The Japanese tends to be more other-directed than self-directed, more interdependent than independent, more conscious of responsibility to others than to self. It is the group that should grow, prosper, and survive; it is the group from which the individual obtains support, identity, and pride. Much of Japanese communicative behavior is focused not on securing attention or advantage for oneself, but on securing advantage and prestige for the group.

To preserve harmonious relations becomes the overriding concern in most interpersonal encounters. Each person must be sensitive to the status of others and to the possibility that some thoughtless remark may weaken or dissolve the group. Great social sensitivity and elaborate social rules protect against the destructive potential of unanticipated and uncongenial remarks. A concern for others, and loyalty to the group, are valued above a concern for self; courtesy and tact are valued above honesty and sincerity.

Standing in sharp contrast to the homogeneity of Japanese culture is the heterogeneity of the United States. Immigrants continue to arrive in increasing numbers. The result is a society that is a mosaic of cultures. While the process of assimilation continues, understanding cannot be taken for granted.

In spite of such heterogeneity, or perhaps because of it, equality has always been a dominant cultural theme. The merest suggestion of privilege or unequal advantage is automatically condemned. It has been suggested that deference to others is among the most painful emotions for American to express. As Eric Larrabee once argued, "Compared to any country in Europe" (and Japan would represent an even more extreme case), "the United States is so lacking in traces of status as to have virtually no social system whatsoever." Lack of complicating status considerations may ease communication and may invite, or even require, greater expressiveness.

This same equality, it is thought, contributes to the extreme individualism that is the most marked feature of the social landscape. Equality, as de Tocqueville emphasized, places people side by side, not above one another, forcing each to find and articulate his own views. If group affiliation is the incentive to communicate in Japan, it is self-realization that is the compelling motive in the United States. America is, as one foreign student put it, "the land of the Big I." The urge to express personal opinions is so compelling that automobile bumpers carry arguments, proclamations cover the walls of buildings, political posters hang from house windows, announcements overflow bulletin boards, graffiti fill the walls of public toilets—even lapel buttons make a statement. Strength lies not in the capacity to surrender to the group, but in the capacity to stand alone, or even against the group. Personal disclosure, even if it involves more provoking conversations, is the course for fulfilling this aim.

The American cultural scene is also distinguished by its commitment to change. The nation was born of dissatisfaction with traditional institutions, and the geography of the frontier further encouraged a pragmatic attitude. As a result, not only the land but social institutions and even personalities came to be seen as resources to be cultivated and improved. In this sense the United States resembles a nation of missionaries. Everything is, and should be, made over. The validity of change, cultural or personal, is tested through dialogue. Discussion and debate, the most characteristic communicative forms of Western cultures, involve proposals and counterproposals, assertions and refutations, leading to agreement.

One suspects that the two cultural styles differ not merely in this or that technical feature, but that they spring out of differing conceptions of the role of communication in human society. In one there is continual reference to the search for harmony, a stress on form, the cultivation of empathy, the sharing of a mood, the search for consensus. The view and vocabulary are essentially esthetic. In the other there is a search for truth, cultivation of independence, exploration of differences, desirability of confrontation, respect for facts and arguments, and achievement of compromise. The view and vocabulary are essentially pragmatic. In Japan communication seems better suited to preserve the peace; in the United States is seems better suited to disturb the peace.

Extremes, of course, exist in both cultures. There are Japanese who are open, impulsive, direct, talkative. And there are Americans who are quiet, reserved, introspective. Contact at this border demonstrates the possibilities of intercultural rapport. But there is another border—when a formal and inarticulate Japanese meets face-to-face with a voluble and aggressive American. Here one glimpses the immense challenge of intercultural negotiations.

If one society seems threatened by a fanatic individualism, the other may be vulnerable to a fanatic collectivism. Where rights are emphasized in one, obligations dominate in the other. To Americans, the Japanese might well say, "You Americans so inflate the importance of your private selves that you run the risk of destroying the bonds that hold a society together." To this an American might reply, "In your concern with harmony you run the risk of discouraging individual initiative, which is the ultimate strength of any social system." Obviously both countries have much to say to each other. Person and group are inalienable: no human being ever matured without the stimulation and incentive of a surrounding community; no society can survive or grow without continual fertilization from creative individuals.

Finally, tempting as it is to view Japanese communicative style as a prototype of all Asian or Oriental cultures, it is a stereotype that must be resisted. There are as wide differences in communication styles among the cultures of the Far East—Philippine, Cambodian, Chinese, Indian—as between Japan and United States. A recent comparative study of Japanese, Korean, and American communicative behavior using the same methodology reported here found Koreans resembled the Japanese in several respects but were nearly the opposite in others; close to the American style in some respects but highly contrasting in others. This tendency toward oversimplification of the cultural variety that exists in the world is another hurdle to overcome in selecting, training, and assigning executives to work in foreign countries.

No one obtains much nourishment from his image in a mirror, or from someone who is only a reflection of himself. There is a communicative paradox here: The more one human being resembles another, the more effortless their relationship and the greater the likelihood of understanding one another, but the less they can learn from each other. The more another person differs, the more puzzling and challenging is the relationship, but the more each can gain.

The boundaries of our countries can no longer be the borders of our minds. In an increasingly interdependent world, it is essential—perhaps even a matter of survival—for us to learn to see and appreciate the world from the perspective of cultures other than our own. As well, it becomes a way of expanding and deepening our knowledge of ourselves and our culture.

6

The Vocabulary of
Human Relationships in Japan

Edward T. Hall and Mildred R. Hall

Knowledge of the meaning of a number of key Japanese terms makes it possible to understand some of the heretofore hidden features of Japanese psychology and culture. One of the strengths of modern science is a shared agreement as to the meaning of scientific words and symbols; if there were no agreement, unified science would be impossible. To understand the Japanese, Americans must learn some new terms, words whose equivalents do not exist in English; these words have immediate and profound meanings to the Japanese, but would require volumes to be explained fully to Americans. These terms are very high on the context scale and constitute vital elements in the vocabulary of human relationships in Japan; they are well worth the effort required to appreciate their meaning.

Amae

We begin with the term *amae*, a word with many meanings and varied connotations depending on the context. The closest English

*From *Hidden Differences: Doing Business with the Japanese,* by Edward T. Hall and Mildred Reed Hall. Copyright © 1987 by Edward T. Hall and Mildred Reed Hall. Used by permission of Doubleday, a division of Bantam Doubleday Dell Publishing Group, Inc.

word is "dependency," but dependency in the United States has a negative connotation that it does not have in Japan. *Amae* is the glue that holds Japanese society together.

Amae means feelings of closeness and dependency, the emotions an infant feels for its mother. These emotions and the needs they engender continue to operate throughout the Japanese lifespan. The loyalty that is felt between members of a work force is strengthened by *amae* among the group. A Japanese male, when embarking on a career, will knowingly enter into a dependency relationship with men of power, status, and influence. This binds him to them in a reciprocal relationship (the reciprocal term, *amaeru*, means "to depend on the affection of another"), and while he benefits from the favors (which must be repaid, of course) it is the emotional tie that is important to him.

Americans will find it difficult to understand how a man could actively seek dependence on another man. Our cultural currents (for males) run in the opposite direction—toward *independence*. Yet the *amae* syndrome is entirely consistent with other dominant themes in Japanese life. The Japanese find it easier to communicate with another human being if they are in a dependency relationship with that person.

The larger Japanese companies reflect *amae* in their relationship to employees by providing health and life insurance, housing for some employees and housing allowances for others, low-interest mortgage rates, vacation facilities, weekend retreats, athletic facilities and team equipment, and education and training both in-house and at technical schools and universities. In return, employees identify closely with the company, which gradually becomes at least as important as their family. Employees depend on the company just as the company depends on its employees.

The crucial point about *amae* is that one's personal identity is rooted in the soil of one's dependent and interdependent relations to others as a *member of a group*. In contrast, the American and the European seeks his identity not as a cog in a larger machines but as an individual. Not only must he free himself from his parents but also he must maintain some distance from all groups, even if he is a member of the group. For Westerners, being too closely identified with a group is tantamount to *giving up one's identity*. Herein lies the greatest distinction between Japanese and Americans. (For further information about *amae*, we refer the reader to Dr. Takeo Doi's insightful book, *The Anatomy of Dependence*.)

Strong drives to conform characterize the Japanese. The Japanese child is encouraged to conform at home as well as in school, where he is rigidly programmed; a child who tries to deviate from the prescribed lesson will be quickly brought back into line. As in calligraphy, there is one right way to do everything; nothing else is allowed.

In adult life, Japanese conformity focuses on the "reference group," the group with which one works in a company. Loyalty to the group is felt to be one of life's highest values and is the principal means by which an employee's worth is measured. Conformity is a strong and dependable indicator of the individual's loyalty.

Two important differences spring from the soil of Japanese group identity: Privacy for the individual is not important, and since the "public" is outside one's group, the Japanese have little of what Americans call "public spirit." To the Japanese the concept of individual freedom does not have the same value it has in the United States. To understand and appreciate such apparent contradictions, one must be able to "jump over one's shadow," as one of our respondents phrased it.

Giri and On

Closely related to *amae* is *giri*, which means one's indebtedness to others, past and present. A sense of indebtedness is ever present in Japanese society, and the concept of *giri* includes one's ancestors and all those who have gone before as well as one's contemporaries. In every relationship one feels the strong need for fulfill responsibilities.

On is the term for obligations, from minor matters to major concerns. It involves giving and granting favors, again with a burden of indebtedness. A Japanese feels special lifelong obligations to his teachers and his bosses, past and present. The passage of time never weakens this obligation. If anything, it results in even greater feelings of indebtedness.

Giri and *on* begin in infancy and are carried within the individual throughout his lifetime. How well one discharges one's responsibility is part of one's *kao* (face). English has no term comparable to *kao*. *Kao* encompasses pride, self-esteem, and reputation. It is vital to the Japanese. A foreigner should avoid criticizing a Japanese or demeaning him in any way, nor should one disparage his work. All of these actions are considered anathema.

A strong desire to maintain harmony characterizes the Japanese. They are very concerned about other people's feelings.

They hate to say "No." Instead, they say, "I will consider your request very carefully." Americans often complain that Japanese lead them to believe they agree to something which, it later turns out, they reject. Remember, when you ask for something, the Japanese avoid saying no, even though that's what they mean. You must therefore learn to read the subtle signs of a negative reaction. (We refer the reader to Masaaki Imai's book, *16 Ways to Avoid Saying No*.)

Since saving face is very important to the Japanese, they do not criticize and they hate to make a mistake. You don't hear Japanese saying, "I told you that wouldn't work." The Japanese do not understand people who criticize their own country or their company. They consider this extremely disloyal. Be warned—if you do this, you will lose face.

Ningen Kankei

If Japanese society is seen as a network of interlocking relationships, hierarchically arranged, the strands of that net are formed by *ningen kankei*.

Mark Zimmerman,
How to Do Business with the Japanese

Ningen kankei involves closeness and cooperation between people in mutually beneficial relationships which spring from a variety of sources. In addition to former classmates it includes people who come from the same town or who are working for the same company. All of these shared experiences create special bonds between people that are part of *ningen kankei*. These relationships are carefully tended over long periods of time. *Ningen kankei* furthers the goals of those involved and is reinforced by feelings of duty and obligation and sometimes genuine friendship.

Employees of the same organization tend to form *ningen kankei* with people of their same level but in different parts of the company (those in the same department might be in competition). *Ningen kankei* is greatly strengthened by afterhours socializing in bars or on the golf course over the weekend.

As a foreigner develops contacts among the Japanese he would be well advised to keep his contacts informed on all matters of interest to them. In all likelihood the Japanese will reciprocate

and the foreigner can start building his own all-important information networks. One never knows when a new acquaintance will
prove useful. Our advice is try to build as many relationships as
possible and remember that acts of thoughtfulness and kindness
will be repaid many times over. Cultivating relationships requires
time; one starts slowly and spends a great deal of time learning
about the background of people who might be helpful in order to be
contexted to their interests and needs.

Most important, remember that these relationships are based
on genuine good feeling, not exploitation. One gives and one
receives from the heart.

But do not expect that, once you know them, your Japanese
friends will then behave like Americans. The Japanese hide their
emotions, and are very restrained in showing feelings. As one
Japanese observed, "We share our sorrows and we hide delight."
When Japanese are complimented or congratulated, they look
abashed or embarrassed, which is confusing to Americans, who
expect them to smile and look happy.

As a corollary to *ningen kankei*, the Japanese distrust verbal
facility because they believe it denotes superficiality. They communicate their true inner feelings by innuendo and nonverbal means.
Chie Nakane, the distinguished Japanese anthropologist and
author of the classic *Japanese Society*, gives a perfect example of a
high-context interaction in her description of a Japanese dealing
with his own group:

> members of the group know each other exceedingly well.
> One's family life, love affairs, even the limits of one's capacity
> for cocktails are intimately known to others. Among fellow
> members a single word would suffice for the whole sentence.
> The mutually sensitive response goes so far that each easily
> recognizes the other's slightest change in behavior and mood
> and is ready to react accordingly.

Other High-Context Terms

There are many other important terms in the Japanese vocabulary
of human relationships. The list that follows suggest several
things: First, a lesson that Americans seem to need to learn again
and again—namely, that High Context systems, by virtue of the
fact that context is widely shared, are systems of great and deep

involvement of the participants with each other. The closest ana-log most people know is that of twins who have grown up together or people who have been through a great deal together over a long period of time. In this sense, it is sometimes convenient to think of Japan as a very large family with the emperor as the head of that family. Second, shared information means not only high involve-ment but also many ways of talking about the subtlety of that involvement. The shared behavior patterns inherent in these con-cepts make the Japanese sensitive to even the subtlest of changes in emotional tone. They are sensitive to feedback from friends and colleagues, and their awareness of nuances of response in the mar-ketplace make American marketing analyses seem crude. Third, as there are insiders, there are also outsiders and specified emo-tions and commitments (or lack thereof) for dealing with them. Japanese can be ruthless with outsiders. Therefore, it is not sur-prising that the Japanese are considered ethnocentric. We heard many accounts of discrimination against foreigners, Asians as well as Westerners of all nationalities. The use of the term *tanin* is sig-nificant: "other persons" roughly translate to "nonpersons." Unless the visiting businessperson is a tourist with nothing at stake, it is dangerous to maintain the status of *tanin*. In Japan, connections and friends are imperative.

Some important additional high-context Japanese terms:

haragei	belly language; nonverbal communication to con-vey true intentions
jibun	one's self; awareness of self
enryo	special consideration for another, taking into account the fact that by holding back part of one-self one may not satisfy needs for *amae* (dealing with Americans requires *enryo* for most Japanese)
kao	face; personal honor
kimochi	feelings (very important, even in business)
nemawashi	preparing the groundwork
ninjo	ability to read and experience feelings of others
omote	front; the face or image one presents to others (one is "on guard")
ura	back; real feelings (one is "off guard"); related to *tatemae* and *honne*; see below

tatemae	front face; what is presented
honne	true feelings privately held (*tatemae* and *honne* are interdependent)
uchi	inside; insider; member of group
soto	outside; outsider; not one of the group
wa	harmony (vital)

7

Gift-Giving in a Modernizing Japan*

Harumi Befu

Introduction

The prevalence of gift-giving in Japan is well known. Even the casual visitor sojourning in Japan for a few weeks will find himself presented with a gift from his Japanese friends or business associates. The full-page ads of midyear-gift (*chugen*) sales by major department stores, the rows of gift shops in any resort town, the displays of gift-wrapped presents in stores at railroad stations, these are among the innumerable indications of the extent to which the Japanese are involved in gift exchange. Although no one knows for sure how much the Japanese spend on gifts every year, since no adequate statistics are available, the figure is undoubtedly high.[1]

Indeed, gift-giving is a minor institution in Japan, with complex rules defining who should give to whom, on what occasions he should give, what sort of gift is appropriate on a given occasion, and how the gifts should be presented. To take an example, a properly wrapped gift for a happy occasion should bear an intricately folded decoration known as *noshi* (nowadays, however, it is enough to

*Reprinted, by permission of the publisher, from *Monumenta Nipponica* 23 (1968).

have its picture printed on the wrapping); but a gift on an inauspicious occasion would not have the decoration on the wrapping. This practice goes back to the days when *noshi* was a strip of abalone, which, when attached to a gift, indicated that the occasion did not call for abstention from meat owing to death or other misfortune in the family. It is for this reason that a dried fishtail or fin is used in some rural areas as a substitute. For the same reason, a gift of fish does not require a *noshi*, since the nature of the gift itself indicates that abstention is not necessary and that the occasion is a felicitous one.[2] Most Japanese, particularly young urbanites, are no longer aware of this origin of *noshi*, which indicates the extent to which gift-giving customs have changed. In this chapter I wish to explore the origin of gift-giving in Japan and consider recent changes in it. I hope that this little exercise will help clarify the process and the present status of Japan's modernization.

Methodological Remarks

Reconstructing the past is not easy—even for a culture like Japan's which has a long written history—when the task is to outline the origin and development of a commonplace custom like gift-giving, which few literati and historians have thought worthy of documentation or study. Rather than to the historians and historical documents, then, we must turn to the folklorists and folk customs. As in so many instances, it has been the Yanagita school of folklore study that has contributed most in unraveling the past of the custom of gift-giving. To accomplish this, Yanagita and his students have had to analyze varied but similar and related gift-giving practices in many different regions of rural Japan, often in isolated communities and on offshore islands, to compare these variant practices, to dip into the etymologies of terms related to gifts and gift-giving, and to juxtapose past customs remembered by old-timers with present practices.

One major methodological problem that confronts us in using folklorists' data and interpretations concerns the temporal referent and sequence, a blind spot in folklore study which the anthropologist Eiichiro Ishida[3] has noted in his sympathetic assessment of Yanagita's scholarly contributions. Folklorists, working almost exclusively with oral tradition and unrecorded folk practices, have generally been reluctant to specify the definite point in time for any event. They discuss events of the past in terms simply of the "past," without indicating the absolute time referent. Consequently, it is extremely difficult to work out a sequence of stages or of events leading up to the present.

What follows is a composite picture of how, in general, gift-giving practices have originated and developed in Japan over an undefined period of time, based in good part on the findings of folklorists and also on a comparison of rural and urban practices. Urban data were mostly obtained through the writer's own investigation.[4]

The Supernatural Past

The custom of offering foods to gods and other supernatural beings—still a common practice in Japan—may seem unrelated to our concern, but in fact is an appropriate starting point.[5] Examples are numberless. In many households today, rice is offered to family ancestors at the household altar every morning. Village Shinto shrines and roadside *jizo* shrines are offered glutinous rice cake and other foods from time to time. The New Year is the time to offer rice cake to the New Year's god. And so on. Folklorists have shown that such food offerings are historically related to *naorai*, the custom according to which gods and mortals shared foods together.[6] *Naorai* is now commonly understood to refer to the feast held after a religious ritual proper, but this is evidently a later modification. In the original form of *naorai*, offerings to gods were gifts to gods, and these gifts were returned by gods as their gifts for mortals to share with them, so that the mortals might partake of the divine power of the gods to whom gifts were originally offered.[7] The symbolic significance of communal eating has been well argued by De Vos in his recent study of outcasteism.[8] He argues that the abhorrence of commensalism with members of an outcaste group is an essential psychodynamic ingredient of outcasteism. For us, this abhorrence is simply the other side of the "deeply social act [of eating together] symbolizing a form of communion, whether it exists as part of a ritual or as part of the daily habits of life."[9]

The ritual importance of saké is also apparent, as the practice of offering it to gods is still very much alive. Originally, the saké was first offered to gods, and then shared by mortals in *naorai*.[10] This custom is still very much alive in Shirakawa, Gifu Prefecture, where once a year *doburoku* (a type of raw saké) is prepared in a large tub, offered to the tutelary god of the village, and consumed communally by all villagers and also by visitors who wish to receive supernatural power from the local god.

The pervasive custom in Japan of giving the first crop of the field to neighbors and relatives is also derived from the past practice of offering the first fruits to gods, and thereafter sharing them among the community.[11] The word *otoshidama*, which nowadays refers to the New Year's present to children (usually money), also originally denoted offerings to the god of the New Year, which were later eaten by men as the god's gift.[12]

It is because communion with supernatural beings was achieved primarily through commensality that offerings to gods were, and still are, largely foodstuff, and also that even now food is considered the traditional type of gift in Japan and that in fact it is the most popular type of gift.[13]

In the past, commensality was not only a device for transferring supernatural power to man, but also a means by which members of the community could partake in one another's power and be brought into a mystical union. After all, the gulf between mortals and gods was not felt to be great; what gods were capable of, men were capable of, too, to a lesser extent. Otherwise, how could men hold communion with gods in *naorai*? Indeed, because of the belief that men are simply less powerful gods, but still susceptible to magical contagion through commensality, it happened that when *naorai* came to be separated in time and place from the ritual proper, the feasting retained its supernatural efficacy. The belief in magical contagion accounts for the banquet held for a person of an unlucky or "calamitous" year (*yakudoshi*), in which the combined power of all the guests was believed to dispel the danger of misfortune.[14] In addition to the magical function, such communal feasting of course served to reinforce the social solidarity of the group.[15]

If magical power could be shared by mortals through a communal meal, as Yanagita has argued, it could also be shared by the giving and the receiving of a gift of food. For example, folk medicine practiced in many rural areas of Japan until recent years prescribes that a person suffering from an eye disease should go to houses in the neighborhood and beg for food.[16] By consuming food from families in which no one was suffering from the disease, one could absorb magical power from these families to help cure the disease. In fact, giving a food gift to a sick person—something frowned on in the U.S. for medical reasons—was generally thought to be a way of giving the power of health inherent in the giver, so that the sick might recover from illness through the power of the healthy. Another custom related to gift-giving to a sick person is also based on the magical power of a food gift. Ordinarily, when a gift is given in Japan, the receiver returns a token gift, such as a box of matches or a bundle of paper, at the time the gift is made.[17] When the gift is to a sick person, however, the custom is not observed owing to the belief that such a return gift has the power of making the healthy person sick. The same belief in ritual pollution through commensality with a ritually impure person explains the customs of avoiding gifts from a person of an unlucky or calamitous year.[18] The customs of giving food gifts to a newborn baby and of having a seven-year-old child solicit food from seven neighbors, which have been seen in many rural areas of Japan until recently, are also believed to be means of building up strength by "borrowing" power from others.[19]

The Traditional Social Framework[20]

The folklorists' work on the supernatural origin of gift-giving has tended to give the impression that the origin of gift-giving in Japan was entirely magical and religious. To claim that gift-giving in Japan used to be entirely supernatural in its significance is to claim an unproven and probably false proposition. We have discussed the supernatural aspects of some gift-giving customs only because most of us know Japanese gift-giving in its secular forms. It is important to note that in rural Japan these gift-giving practices, whether supernatural or secular, were, and still are, imbedded in the traditional social structure, in which we find the household as a basic social unit, the values of *giri* and *on*, and the principle of social reciprocity. Let us examine the ways in which gift-giving is related to these elements of the traditional Japanese social organization. (I do not suggest that this social framework operates only in rural Japan. It is very much alive in urban Japan, too; but there one finds new social elements manifested in gift-giving practices, as we shall see later.)

The importance of the household as a basic social institution in Japan has been reiterated by generations of anthropologists, both Japanese and Western and scarcely needs emphasis here. Suffice it to add that even when a gift is seemingly intended for one individual—e.g., a sick member of a household—and is sent from a certain individual—e.g., the sick person's uncle—the gift is still regarded as a gift from the uncle's household as a corporate unit to the sick person's household as another unit. Magically, as we saw above, such a gift may be intended for a given individual; but in terms of the working of the society, it is a gift to a group, of which the individual is merely a member. The significance of this fact will be seen when we consider how the principle of reciprocity operates.

In rural Japan, probably the most important motivating force behind gift-giving is the concept of *giri*. *Giri* is a moral imperative to perform one's duties toward other members of one's group. Gift giving falls squarely in the sphere of *giri*; one is morally obligated to give a gift when custom demands it. *Giri* is bound up with the institution of gift-giving in another way, namely, reciprocation. To the extent that one man's relation to another in Japanese rural society is defined in reciprocal terms, in which the give-and-take of social relations should be fairly rigidly balanced, the concept of *giri* evokes in the tradition-minded rural Japanese the obligation to reciprocate. Since gift-giving is an act of *giri*, and since *giri* requires reciprocation, a gift naturally calls for a return gift. The moral obligation to give, to receive, and to return gifts is as much a part of traditional Japan as it is of the archaic societies with which Marcel Mauss[21] concerned himself in his famous essay on the gift.

So important is the concept of *giri* in gift-giving that many rural Japanese interpret *giri* to mean strict observance of the etiquette of gift-giving.[22] Dore's account of Shitayamacho in Tokyo shows how important the concept is in the operation of gift exchange even in cities.[23]

We have seen that the institution of gift-giving requires that giving be balanced by returning. The operation of this principle of reciprocity in its most elementary form is readily seen in the customary donation of "incense money" (*koden*) at funerals. The family of the deceased keeps a careful record of each donation, and when death occurs in a family which has given incense money, an identical amount of money is returned.[24] Similarly, when the roof of a farmhouse is to be rethatched, neighbors and relatives donate labor and materials, such as bundles of grass and rope. When the time to rethatch the house of one of the helpers comes around, exactly the same amount of labor and material is returned.

Reciprocation, however, need not be in kind. A gift may be given for a favor done, or vice versa. When the relationship between households is a vertical, hierarchical one, this type of "heterogeneous" exchange is likely to take place. A man brings gifts to his *oyakata* in the New Year, or to his landlord at *o-bon* in thanks for the *on*—the past favor granted and assistance received.

Or again, a recovered patient may bring a gift—in proportion to the seriousness of his illness—to this doctor to thank him for the medical attention given. On such a gift-giving occasion, the social superior does not reciprocate with a gift of the same type or value. For the gift is already a return for the past favor, and to return in kind and in value would reduce the status of the superior to that of the giver.

In short, in rural Japan, whether and how well a person observes the rules and etiquette governing the who, the what, the when, and the how of gift-giving are important ways of judging his social character. One who observes them meticulously is a responsible, trustworthy individual; he is *giri-gatai.* If, on the other hand, a person sent a gift disproportionately cheaper than the social equation of gift-giving calls for, people would gossip about the cheapness not only of the gift but also of the giver's character.

Modern Changes and Innovations

In modern urban Japan, the religious origin and significance of gift-giving discussed above has been forgotten by most people. By contrast, the social context in which gift-giving is practiced in rural areas is still of critical importance for the city dwellers. They are quite conscious of the concept of the household as a unit in gift-giving, and the continuation of their household-based customary gift exchange is very much motivated by the concept of *giri.*

This is not to say that city people uniformly approve of the traditional etiquette of gift-giving. The more educated urbanites feel very much constrained by the social obligation of *giri,* which they contemptuously label "feudalistic." It is because *giri*-based gift-giving is looked on as a nuisance and with disfavor that the Japanese often scarcely consider the appropriateness of the content of a gift. Instead, gift-giving is treated as an empty formality. One simply buys a piece of merchandise of proper monetary value. Or, as it so often happens in returning from an extended trip, one simply buys so many dozens of the same kind of gift to be distributed among those to who one by *giri* owes a gift, irrespective to the individual tastes of the receivers. It is in this context that we can understand the practice of *taraimawashi,* in which a gift that a person receives, for which she (and anyone else, for that matter) would have no conceivable use, is simply passed on to another to meet the obligation of giving and returning. One reason why *giri-*

based behavior, including gift-giving, persists in cities, in spite of the negative attitudes toward it, is that such behavior is social insurance, as Dore puts it.[25] In case of an emergency, a person just might have to depend on neighbors and friends. If he had been recalcitrant and ignored *giri*-based etiquette, he might not be able to expect a helping hand at critical moments.

The strain of tradition thus presses heavily on urbanites. And city life, which does not depend very much any more on the kind of solidarity maintained by the traditional human relations and values of rural society, has to some extent permitted the discontinuation of the gift-giving that symbolized such solidarity. For example, in rural areas, at *o-bon* a social inferior traditionally makes a gift to his superior, such as a branch family to its main family or tenants to the landlord. In cities, the counterpart would be for employees to present gifts to their superior at work. While this custom does prevail widely, there are also a large number of city people who no longer practice it. In some business firms it has become an established practice not to give gifts to superiors at *o-bon*; in others certain superiors have explicitly prohibited the practice.

City dwellers, however, have not merely let old customs fall into disuse. They have added new practices or at least elaborated on existing customs and made them popular. One such practice is gift-giving between individuals *qua* individuals, without encumbering their households. This is not likely to occur in one's neighborhood, between relatives, etc., where households are already the interacting units. It is more likely to occur at work or at school, where individuals have opportunities to interact as individuals. School friends and work mates give gifts on birthdays, at weddings, and on other occasions. In marked contrast to the traditional type of gift-giving, in which social obligations (*giri*) is the prime mover of gifts, the motivating force in individual-to-individual gift-giving tends to be one's personal affection for the receiver. It is *ninjo*, if you like, rather than *giri* which is the basis (although few modern urbanites would want their personal motivation identified with such a traditional, and therefore feudalistic, concept as *ninjo*).

In this personal type of gift-giving, in contrast to the *giri*-based type, the giver cares a great deal about what he gives because he is not simply meeting an unpleasant obligation. Much thought goes into the choice of the gift; he does not simply buy something of proper monetary value or resort to *tataimawashi*, as mentioned above. Moreover, the concept of balanced reciprocity, so important in *giri*-based gift-giving, here breaks down. In *giri*-based gift-giving, it is extremely important to consider the value of the gift in relation to what it is a return for, if it is a return gift, or in relation to the relative social status of giver and receiver and the specific occasion for which the gift is intended. In the personal gift, one may choose to give very little, or something of great value. Since mutual trust is already established between the giver and the receiver, it is not necessary to regard gift-giving as an indication of the giver's social character, whereas in *giri*-based gift-giving, it may be recalled, one's character was judged to a considerable degree by the extent to which one observed gift-giving etiquette. Thus the personal type of gift-giving is associated with a whole complex of different attitudes. These attitudes have come into being as a result of the process of individuation that modern city life encourages.[26]

Another innovation associated more with urban than rural Japan is what I might call "collective" gift-giving. It occurs most often in situations in which personal gift-giving described above is likely to occur (such as school or work), but it may also be seen in the neighborhood, since the basic unit of "collective" giving may be either the individual or the household. Whichever the unit may be, givers in this type are either already organized into a group—such as clubs at school or neighborhood associations—or organize themselves into a group on an *ad hoc* basis. Each member of the group contributes an equal amount of money, and the total collection is then given as a cash present to the recipient, or a gift is purchased with the collected money and given him. This type of gift-giving is suitable when the giver does not feel very close to the receiver and does not wish to spend much money or time in buying a gift, but he nonetheless feels the obligation to give. In short, "collective" giving occurs as a response to the dilemma in which urbanites are often caught between the lack of personal motivation to give and the persistent social obligation—*giri*—to give.

A third type of gift-giving practice more characteristic of the harsh competitive world of cities than of the corporate community of rural Japan is one based on ulterior motives.[27] Since a gift traditionally comes wrapped, since the giver, according to etiquette, belittles the content of the gift, and since a gift should not be opened in front of the giver, it is impossible to foresee the value of the gift, which may far exceed the amount deemed proper by the normal measure of balanced reciprocity. In addition, the obligation to accept, once a gift is presented, is as binding as the obligation to give and to return. These norms governing the ritual of gift-giving provide the giver with a vast advantage—unfair though it is—in furthering his objectives. The social obligation thus created by an expensive gift requires in return a special favor for the giver which the receiver would not perform under normal circumstances. It is possible to cancel the debt incurred by the expensive gift by returning an equally expensive gift. But ordinarily, the circumstances make it evident that the giver wants a special favor in return. For example, a teacher who receives a very expensive gift from his student's father is fully aware that the father wants to have his son's grade improved.

We regard this type of gift-giving as bribery in America. But because gift-giving is so pervasive in Japan, and the obligations to give, to receive, and to reciprocate are so strongly entrenched in the traditional social system, it is extremely difficult, if not impossible, to discern whether a gift is legitimate or illegitimate. As Dore notes, "only a hairline separates the mere token of gratitude from the bribe."[28] Because the term "bribery" has a narrow legalistic tinge and because it is difficult to tell when gift-giving is bribery, we shall use the term "ulteriorly motivated" gift-giving. This type of gift-giving is an expression of urban conditions where anomie prevails; that is, emphasis on goals has take precedence over the culturally approved means of achieving the goal.[29]

One final type of gift-giving should be mentioned briefly. I refer to altruistic donation. Donation as such is nothing new in Japan. It is collected in the village association, in the neighborhood association, in the PTA, etc., for constructing a community hall, a school gymnasium, or recreation facilities for children. Such a donation, however, is not usually based on true altruism. Instead, it is a way of expressing one's loyalty to the group, of demonstrating one's economic affluence, or of impressing other members of the group with the important contribution one is making for the group. In short, most Japanese make donations in order to fulfill their social obligations or social ambition. This type of giving is not an expression of altruism, since the motivation is based on considerations of the psychological reward one receives from others through their approval, esteem, or even envy.

True altruism, on the other hand, is based strictly on the satisfaction derived from the simple act of giving. No one has to know one has given, or how much one has given. True, such altruistic giving is not unknown in Japan. Even before the war, for example, commuters saw students standing in front of train stations asking for donations to help starving farmers of Tohoku, where severe cold had destroyed crops. In the postwar years, we see other kinds of street-corner donation drives, such as the "red feather" or "green feather" donations, copied after the American Community Chest. Although no one knows how much such strictly altruistic donation amounts to in Japan every year, the amount probably is not very large. For such donation is based on a universalistic orientation, in which one does not seek through the donation the approval of "meaningful others," such as kinsmen, friends, and neighbors who "count" in one's social life. To the extent that Japanese are highly interdependent in their emotional patterning,[30] they find meaningful social life in particularistic relationships with others. Altruistic donation is not likely to be very successful in this sort of social context.

Conclusion

Let us now enumerate the significant cultural features of traditional Japan that are discernible in gift-giving practices:

1. The supernatural significance of magical contagion through communion and commensality as well as through gifts of food.

2. The household as a basic social institution.

3. *Giri* as a central motivational value in maintaining the custom.

4. Reciprocity as a principle of interaction.

While all these features except the first are still prevalent in modern Japan, there are new trends and changes that are discernible, particularly in urban areas. Let us list these:

1. Secularization, or a gradual loss of religious and magical meanings in gift-giving.

2. Individuation—the opportunity of individuals to interact as individuals and to express personal affect.

3. Instrumentalism, or ulterior-motivated behavior.

4. Weakly developed altruism.

These old and new elements of Japanese culture revealed in gift-giving practices indicate something of the general trend in the modernization of Japan. First, secularization—the decreasing reliance on religion and magic for solving worldly problems—is a natural evolutionary process.[31] Along with the secularization of the society in general, it is to be expected that gift-giving would have

less and less religious and magical significance. Second, as Dore
has observed, the complex city life of industrialized society encourages individuation; as social interaction is conducted on an individual basis rather than on the traditional household basis, it is
natural for gift-giving to express this changing social pattern.

Third, I have alluded to the concept of *ninjo*—a concept as old
as *kabuki*—in reference to the increasing tendency for expression
of individual affect in modern Japan. But there is a basic difference between *ninjo* and the modern expression of personal affect—
not so much in their contents as in their social contexts. In traditional Japan *ninjo* was placed in opposition to *giri*, as Benedict
elucidated years ago.[32] The concept of *giri* defined proper conduct,
whereas *ninjo* implied human failure to carry out *giri*. Society thus
had no legitimate place for *ninjo*. Expression of personal affect, on
the other hand, is now beginning to win a legitimate status in the
modern social order side by side with *giri*.

Fourth, while the society is changing in a secular and individ-
uated direction, it has also retained certain traditional features,
such as the concepts of household and *giri*. What is important to
note here is that these features are not simply anachronisms, the
cuff buttons of modern Japan. Instead, they have played a crucial
role in effectuating the process of modernization in Japan.

Lastly, the weak development of altruism also points to the
strength of such traditional values as *giri*, which emphasize one's
obligation in a particularistic setting. Since the roles of individuals
are by and large defined in particularistic terms even in modern
Japan, the most effective way to get things done is to take advantage of traditional motivational values. Basing social roles on universalistic criteria, on which altruism is ultimately dependent, is
correspondingly rare in Japan. Altruistic gift-giving therefore will
probably remain insignificant in Japan as long as the basic value
orientation of the people does not change from particularism to
universalism.

These observations lead us to consider Japan's modernization
from the theoretical standpoint. There are two possible positions
one might take. On the one hand, one may argue that in spite of
an outstanding performance in the economic sphere, Japan lags
behind in its social and cultural modernization, since it retains
many traditional elements. On the other hand, one may argue
(and many scholars have) that Japan's spectacular economic
achievement has been accomplished by exploiting its traditional
social and cultural patterns. The former position is based on the
assumption that modernization as an end-state ultimately implies

a uniform cultural manifestation, disregarding the heterogeneity cultures may display in the process of arriving at the end-state. The second position, which has been advocated by, among others, Ichiro Nakayama,[33] argues for a parallel development, namely, that although modernization may denote technological efficiency, for which all modernizing nations strive, there are different avenues by which to arrive at it, and moreover that in its social and cultural spheres a modernized nation can retain its traditional patterns.

Although the future is anyone's guess, the "uniform end-state" theory takes a position which has not been empirically demonstrated. The parallel development theory, on the other hand, is based on the widely substantiated position that each modernizing culture, while striving toward a common goal of more efficient integration and organization of its cultural legacy, attempts to achieve this goal through its unique set of cultural "equipment." In conclusion, then, those cultural patterns of Japan that are adaptable to and facilitate modernization will probably remain, and gift-giving as a medium for expressing these patterns will similarly be found in Japan for years to come.

8

An Ethnography of
Dinner Entertainment in Japan*

Harumi Befu

Entertainment in Japan is a highly ritualized activity, full of set procedures and etiquette. Limiting the analysis to entertainment in *ryootei*, or the Japanese-style restaurant, essentials of these procedures and etiquette are outlined. Aside from the sheer behavioral side of the entertainment ritual, symbolic meaning given to such behavior is complex and often too subtle to be perceived by untrained eyes. This chapter discusses how symbolism is used in entertainment interaction.

Superficial understanding of a culture is often said to be worse than no understanding at all. The reason is, of course, that a little bit of knowledge is a dangerous thing: It gives one a false conviction that he knows it all. Foreigners who have been living in Japan for a while and begin to manage their daily routines often lodge the allegation that Japanese say or do things that they do not mean, implying the insincerity of Japanese. True, a Japanese would offer a gift of a bottle of Johnnie Walker Black Label scotch, saying, "Please accept this worthless gift..." Or, when you are invited to a Japanese home, the hostess is likely to say in an

*Reprinted, by permission of the publisher, from *Arctic Anthropology*, Vol. 11, Suppl., 1974.

embarrassed voice, "Our house is in a cluttered mess, but please come in," but you will find the house immaculately clean. It is only the foreign novitiates to Japanese culture who are surprised by the contradiction. A Japanese guest would expect the house to be clean. If the house is in fact the cluttered mess the hostess says it is, the guest is entitled to surmise that he is not as honored a guest as he thought he was.

I recall the time I was invited to a Sunday lunch by a Japanese friend when I was collecting data on gift-giving in Kyoto. I was temporarily alone in Kyoto, my family having gone to visit a relative in western Japan. The friend, in the course of conversation about various and sundry things, found out I was alone and asked if I would come next Sunday. First, I had to judge whether my friend indeed meant to invite me or whether the invitation was a meaningless *pro forma*, uttered simply to fill time and to convey friendship and no more, much as Americans say, "Hi, how are you.... Oh, I'm fine," not as a way of conveying a message about one's state of affairs but merely to indicate one's readiness to enter into further interaction. Invitations are often extended in Japan without meaning to invite anyone when (and because) the context of the invitation makes it obvious that an invitation is not really intended and the invited person is expected to politely decline. Had I sensed that the invitation was of this variety, of course I should not have accepted it. Interpretation of the invitation was tricky in this instance, complicated by local custom. On one hand, Kyoto people are known for extending "false invitations" more sincerely than other Japanese and are fond of ridiculing others in private for misinterpreting them and, on the other hand, this hostess was unusually insistent on inviting me, even for a native-born Kyoto woman. Did she mean it or didn't she? Since etiquette requires me to decline any invitation initially anyway, I took advantage of the time required in the repeated give-and-take of declining and inviting several times to weigh all evidence to see if she really meant it. I finally decided that she really meant to invite me and I accepted the invitation. To this day, however, I do not know, and I probably never will, if my interpretation was in fact correct.

Be that as it may, when I accepted the invitation, the hostess asked me what I would like to have for lunch. I was, of course, quite well aware of the Japanese etiquette of not making demands on others. So I told her that anything would do. But she insisted that I specify what I wanted. I kept insisting I had no preference, knowing full well I would soon have to tell her what I wanted. However,

I knew that protocol required that I wait until the hostess had made several urgings, after which to state one's wishes would not seem too forward. Following what I judged to be an appropriate number of urgings, I said to the hostess that *ochazuke* would be just fine. *Ochazuke,* a bowl of rice with hot tea poured over it and served with one or two pickled dishes to increase the appetite, is one of the simplest meals in the whole Japanese culinary repertory. The hostess said fine, that she would serve me *ochazuke* as I requested. The following Sunday she did indeed serve me *ochazuke.* It turned out, however, to be the last, small appendage to a sumptuous luncheon served with elegant heirloom utensils starting with a bowl of fine soup and vinegared vegetables. *Saké* was served with fish of the season and a half dozen varieties of *tsukundani* (vegetable and sea food preserves—which are specialties of Kyoto) were brought out as hors d'oeuvres. At last, almost as an anticlimax, *tsukemono* (pickled food) and *kamaboko* (fish preserve). Was I surprised? Yes and no. Indeed, I asked for the simplest dish imaginable and got a feast instead. I should be surprised. On the other hand, knowing my relationship to the hosts, something more than a bowl of rice with tea poured over it was definitely in order, although the meal might have been a trifle more elaborate than I had expected. I would have been indeed surprised had the hostess simply served a bowl of rice with tea over it. It would not have been far from the mark in interpreting the event to mean either that the friend's luncheon invitation was actually *pro forma* and I shouldn't have accepted it, or that the invitation was meant but I wasn't highly thought of. Knowing my relationship with the hosts, I felt they meant to invite me and I was reasonably sure they respected me. Knowing this then, the feast I was offered was no surprise. But the rub is in the fact, or in the cultural rule, that the guest in this situation ought to act as if he was surprised. Like a good Japanese, I expressed much surprise with such a treat, while saying to myself, "this is about what I expected."

Now, did my hosts tell me a lie? Were they insincere? Or did they try to mislead me when they had agreed to treat me to *ochazuke?* If you assume that people always have to say what they mean literally, then the answer is yes. But an intriguing part of the cultural assumption operating in this context is that both hosts and guests are supposed to say what they do not mean, that they are supposed to know that they each know what the others really meant to say but did not say without being told. Hosts and guests are thus in collusion, acting out their parts in the everyday drama of Japanese social life.

Japanese do not have monopoly over such contrived behavior. Variance between intention and declaration is something we see everyday among Americans, who take pride in their being straightforward, in saying what they mean, and chastise people who are roundabout and cannot come right out and say what they have on their minds. As Sunday dinner guests leave, an American host is likely to say, with a big happy smile, "Good-bye, now. Come back any time." But he would be most surprised if any of them returned the next morning unannounced. He can tell such a blatant lie because he knows his guests know that he does not mean it. To take another example, "if there is anything you need, just let me know" may be a way for your newly acquired friend to say, "I like you, let's be friends." But the court would not honor your claim for a breach of contract if he refused to give his $50,000 home for the asking. Here again is a collusion. Both parties know what is claimed is not to be interpreted on its face value. That is in fact why a lie can be told with such sincerity.

A representative of a business firm in Japan, when negotiating a contract with another firm, is often invited by his counterparts in the other firm to play mah-jongg. The counterparts, who are normally very good players, then begin to lose one game after another, while placing heavy bets. The representative, knowing all the different ways in which Japanese firms try to entice contractors, would suspect, and correctly so, that he is being allowed to win, that this is a form of semi-sophisticated bribery, the money having been probably supplied through the company's expense account. Upon detecting this, the representative must not only continue to play games of mah-jongg, but also play the game of pretending to play a serious game of mah-jongg. There should not be even a hint that they are intentionally losing the game and that the money the representative won is meant to be a bribe. But after the game is over, without anyone telling him, he would try his best to get a contract with that company.

In sum, then, face-to-face interaction is like a drama, in which each actor knows what the others are supposed to say. Part of what this means is that multiple meanings of expressions are correctly sorted out by participants and behavior appropriate for each meaning is acted out in appropriate contexts.

Dinner entertainment in Japan illustrates workings of numerous cultural assumptions such as the above, many of which remain implicit and unstated. Spelling out these assumptions will hopefully help understand the general nature and quality of

Japanese human relations in a way in which they are not ordinarily discussed.

Japanese prefer to entertain their business associates at a restaurant rather than at home. Japanese say that their homes are too small, that their kitchen is inadequate for preparing foods for guests, or that the wife lacks appropriate culinary skills. Such factors are not to be denied, of course, but business executives with large homes and adequate kitchen facilities still entertain their guests by and large in restaurants, which suggests that there may well be other factors.

There is indeed a very important social reason for not entertaining business associates at home. Home for Japanese is very private. Besides their own families, it is generally open only to relatives, long-time friends, children's friends and, occasionally, a man's subordinates at work. These are mostly people with whom one shares a great deal of affect and intimacy. They are, in other words, people with whom one need not be businesslike. Even subordinates at work, when visiting, tend to discuss personal matters or family problems about which they seek psychological support as much as, or more than, practical solutions.

Penetrability of American homes is seen by the eagerness with which the hostess will show her guests around the house, all the way to bedrooms and even bathrooms, as if they deserve the special admiration of the not-so-interested guests. This is a symbolic gesture which parallels the expression, "my home is yours; please feel at home." Of course such an expression is another of those agreed-on lies, but it nonetheless does indicate the relative openness of American homes. Not so in Japan. There is no Japanese expression comparable to "my home is yours." Guests are expected to act like guests. They are never shown around the house. They are taken to a room specifically designed for outsiders known as *kyakuma* (guest room) or *oosetsuma* (reception room), where guests stay put.

Japanese have invented the neologism "my-home-*shugi*" or "my homism" to express the idea that the home is a fortress of privacy closed to people with whom affect is not shared to a great extent. Neighbors, shopkeepers who come around to take orders and others who are excluded from the circle of intimacy must stand at the entrance (*genkan*) or the service entrance (*katteguchi*) and carry on their business, even though the business may take half an hour or a whole hour. The mistress of the house, being a paragon of propriety, will bring out a cushion (*zabuton*) for such people to offer a comfortable seat, but implicitly to convey the message that the visitor belongs at the entrance and no further inside the house. This parallels an American housewife who stands at the front door, fully open but otherwise blocked by her bodily presence, to indicate to a Fuller brushman that she intends to cut him short and not to let him into the house where he can spread out his merchandise. I have seen a handful of neighborhood housewives with shopping baskets in their arms huddled together at street corners in Kyoto, where I lived in 1969–1970, talking for hours on end. Since they all do not want their neighbors to enter their homes just to sip tea and gossip, a street becomes a convenient open parlor for housewives to come and go and join and leave as time allows.

If neighbors are generally excluded from visiting, so are business associates whose visits home, in a sense, are tantamount to invasion of privacy. Excluded from the home, the only alternative is to entertain at a restaurant. While there are both Western-style restaurants serving Western dishes and Japanese-style restaurants serving Japanese dishes, practically all dinner entertainment of business associates, if done in style and if they can be called entertainment at all rather than just dinner, is done in a Japanese-style restaurant generally called *ryootei* or *ryooriya* rather than a Western-style restaurant. For the sake of brevity, we will refer to *ryootei* for Japanese-style restaurants. "Restaurant" would mean Western-style restaurants.

There are several reasons why *ryootei* are preferred to restaurants for entertainment. First of all, sitting in chairs is not the most relaxing posture for Japanese. At work, in school, and at other places like trains and buses, Japanese do, of course, sit Western style. But when they want total relaxation, they like to move their center of gravity close to the floor. No restaurant in Japan offers this comfort. Secondly, in restaurants, except for a large group, one has no privacy since the dining room has to be shared with numerous strangers, whereas in a *ryootei* each group of diners has a private room.

Thirdly, the role of service employees is different in the two situations. In a restaurant, waiters and waitresses are what Erving Goffman has called "non-persons." They interact with guests only to take orders and serve food; for the purposes of the dinner guests, they do not exist. Dinner guest ignore their comings and goings and recognize their presence only in connection with serving food. In a *ryootei*, the people serving dinner guests, who are always women, are not even called by the same name as their counterparts in restaurants. In a restaurant, they are called *kyu-*

uji or *jokyuu*, unless English terms such as "boy," "waiter," or "waitress" are directly used. In a *ryootei*, they are *nakai, neesan, okamisan, geisha, geiko*, etc. Far from being a non-person, a *ryootei* service worker is an integral part of the dinner entertainment. She is expected to participate in conversation, although unless she is a *geisha*, her role is by and large passive, speaking up when spoken to and not taking initiative in directing the trend in conversation. The extent to which she participates, however, is a function of the degree to which dinner guests are affected by alcohol, the size of the group, and other factors. When dinner guests are drunk and jovial, she too must join in to help maintain the joviality by being, for example, a little more risqué in her remarks, a little louder in speaking, etc. Her initial, reserved giggles should give way to uninhibited laughter. These changes must be executed even if she is not affected by alcohol herself. She is likely to receive offers of *saké* from time to time which she is expected to accept, but only in moderation so that she would not become truly intoxicated and fail to perform her duty in play-acting her intoxicated role.

In a *ryootei*, service workers serving in one private room are serving only one group of guests. At least during the time she is in the room, her services are monopolized. Even if they have other rooms to serve, they do not give a hint of it, so as to maintain an appearance, at least, of monopolized service which is not possible in a restaurant.

In *ryootei* entertainment, ordering of food is done by the host alone. Often this is done beforehand by telephone. And after the dinner is over, the host excuses himself from the dining room momentarily and pays the bill in the guests' total absence; the bill may alternatively be sent to the host's home or to his company if the entertainment is on the company expense account, as it often is. Thus guests do not see the menu with prices of each item printed or the total cost of the dinner on the check. All this helps to remove pecuniary aspects of dinner entertainment and helps to create a homelike atmosphere. This is a fourth reason why *ryootei* are preferred to restaurants for entertaining guests.

Fifthly, *ryootei* entertainment lends itself to creating a social environment conducive to group cohesion, at least for Japanese, because everyone—hosts and guest—have the same set of dishes. In a restaurant, each individual carefully studies the menu and orders his own unique combination of hors d'oeuvres, soup, salad (and salad dressing), main dish (not forgetting how the meat is to be cooked), side orders, and dessert as a symbolic way of asserting each individual's unique existence. In contrast, in the *ryootei*, by everyone having the same dishes, emphasis is placed on common sharing of experience. *Ryootei* entertainment thus strives toward negation of individuality and denial of uniqueness of each participant. Instead, it strives to create an atmosphere conducive to communion through commonality by emphasizing the sameness of everyone, by everyone having an identical set of dishes in front of him as it is in home dinner entertainment.

I have not exhausted all the factors of preference for *ryootei* over restaurant for entertainment. In fact, I have reserved probably the single most important reason, namely, that *saké* is served in *ryootei* while it is not served with Western dishes and therefore not in restaurants. The whole ritual surrounding *saké* drinking is unique, and is not replicated in drinking Western alcoholic beverages. For one thing, Western beverages, except for wine and beer, are generally not drunk with meals; they are more apt to be before-dinner aperitif or after-dinner "dessert." Drinking of grape wine has not caught on any wide scale in Japan yet, and its significance in Japanese dinner entertainment is still negligible. Beer alone has come to acquire some of the features of the *saké*-drinking ritual and is often used as a substitute.

Japanese folklorists tell us that *saké* was originally a sacred beverage produced as an offering to the gods. Mortals drank *saké* in a ceremony called *naorai*, which was held in front of the gods' altar, and drank it in communion with the gods. Mortals would assemble in front of the altar and share the spiritual essence of immortals by sharing the *saké* and other foods once offered to the gods and now given back as the gods' gifts. *Naorai*, while an occasion for communion with the gods, was at the same time an occasion for conviviality and re-affirmation of communal mutuality. Now, drinking *saké* is a completely secularized affair; its sacredness is gone. But still, its "communal" functions are deeply imbedded in ordinary dinner entertainment because the etiquette and numerous rules of *saké* drinking insures conviviality and communion.

One of the elementary rules of the *saké* party is that one does not pour for himself. Pouring is done for and by each other. It is a symbolic gesture of indicating that each is at the other's service. Since *saké* cups, except those used for solitary drinking called *guinomi*, are so small and allow only a few sips out of each cupful, this gesture requires constant surveillance of cups in front of others around you and an offer to pour as soon as a cup is empty or near-empty. At the same time, one should engage in absorbing conversation, an art which requires considerable training. An experienced host would, in fact, not wait until a cup is near-empty;

he would hold a bottle of *saké* in front of a guest, slightly tilted (nonverbally communicating his readiness to pour), and urge him to empty or "dry" his cup so he can pour more.

When *saké* is being poured, the "owner" of the cup is expected to hold the cup in his hand rather than leaving it on the table. Leaving it on the table while *saké* is being poured makes it possible for one to ignore the service another is rendering. One would thus be inadvertently impolite not to show proper appreciation for the service. Holding the cup in hand, on the other hand, requires one to attend to the pouring and obligates the expression of appreciation.

Pouring *saké* without spilling requires coordination between the pourer and the one holding a cup to be poured. A *saké* cup is small and at the same time, the bottle has a relatively large opening. Since the bottle is opaque, it is hard to know how much liquid is still in the bottle and how much the bottle should be tilted. There are three general ways of guessing how much liquor is left in the bottle, none of which is foolproof. One is to judge from the total weight. Since the weight of the bottle itself varies a great deal, past experience is not of great help. A second method is to remember how much one had to tilt the bottle the last time he poured. Since the same bottle is usually passed around from one end of the table to another, one does not always know how much to tilt the bottle he happens to be holding at a particular moment. The third means is to shake the bottle near one's ear if it seems light, and judge from the splattering sound of the liquid inside how much liquor remains.

After a considerable amount of alcohol is consumed, the man holding his cup and the man holding the bottle may not have perfect control of their arm and hand muscles, let alone of their swaying torsos. Yet both parties are sober enough to know spilling is bad manners. There is momentary concentration by the two individuals on the act of pouring and coordinating of hands to avoid spilling.

If a guest has had enough *saké* and wants to accept—only out of politeness—just a little more but not a full cup, then before the cup is full, he must move the cup higher and higher to prevent pouring of more *saké* while mumbling something to the effect that it is enough. A good Japanese host is not one who necessarily respects the other's wishes. He is more concerned with forcing his hospitality on the guest. He is thus prepared for the contingency of the guest attempting to refuse by raising the cup. The moment he senses this defense strategy of the guest, he counteracts by holding the bottle higher and higher, raising the bottle at precisely the same speed as the guest raises the cup, so that he can keep pouring *saké*. To do this, and do it without spilling a drop, especially after both parties are intoxicated, is no easy feat. I might add parenthetically that Japanese do not spend a great deal of time practicing pouring *saké*.

Numerous activities requiring various eye-hand coordination engaged in from childhood—goldfish scooping, using chopsticks, making paper-folding figures, playing with beanbags, etc.—all prepare Japanese for their adult life, an adult life which includes pouring of *saké* as an essential skill.

After the pouring is over, there have to be some gestural or verbal cues on the part of the receiver to indicate his thanks. He may bow ever so slightly or mumble something like, "aaa...." or "*doomo...*" or combine the two.

Etiquette requires that the host first pour *saké* for the guest, the host symbolically being the servant of the guest, and that the guest then reciprocate. It also requires that if a person of lower status wishes to exchange drinking with a person of higher status, the former first pours for the latter, and then the latter reciprocates. Also, if their seats are far apart, as they may be in a large party, the junior person is required to come to the senior person and ask him for the privilege of pouring *saké* for him.

This, incidentally, is a convenient ploy for a very junior person to approach a very high status person as a means of establishing an acquaintance, otherwise known as "buttering up." Offering to pour *saké* is a way of showing one's respect and paying homage to a high status person. It is thus socially correct, and offers a legitimate way for a lowly person to sit next to or in front of a high status person, a position he cannot otherwise occupy without seeming to be excessively forward. Thus he plays the game at two different levels at the same time. At one, he is showing respect to his superior and being formally correct; at another, he is furthering his personal gain by impressing the superior with his presence.

A practice unique to *saké* drinking is the offering of one's own cup to another person after drinking the contents. While pouring starts from a lower status person to a higher status person, or from the host to the guest, in offering a cup, the higher status person has the privilege of offering it first to a lower status person, or the guest to the host. This is followed by the same cup or the cup of the other person being offered to the superior or to the guest. Each such exchange is a symbolic handshake or embrace and is a reaffirmation of the social pact uniting those exchanging the cup.

When a cup is offered to someone, he is not required to return in immediately. Since normally a person drains a cup in several sips, putting it on the table at intervals of a few minutes, often someone else comes along to offer another cup before he finishes the first. When one finishes the first cup offered, he might offer it to the second person if he happens to be engaged in conversation with him. The upshot of this is that the route a cup travels forms a complex pattern indicating social statuses, cliques, ulterior motives, etc. Also, after a while cups are unevenly distributed, some people having several in front of them—typically high status persons to whom others have paid homage—leaving none in front of some of the lower ranking individuals. Since it is improper to leave people without cups to drink from, the *ryootei* management, concerned about customer's consumption (for which they can present a fat bill) as much as social propriety, will bring extra cups and leave them in the center of the table for this type of contingency. Thus, those without a cup may help themselves from the center of the table. High status persons should not hoard cups, however. They should try to drink up and redistribute them as fast as they can. Herein lies the reason why Japanese business executives are mostly heavy drinkers and why ability to absorb great quantities of alcohol is almost a *sine qua non* for upward mobility in Japan.

What makes excessive drinking inevitable in this sort of dinner entertainment is that there are no socially acceptable ways of refusing an offer of *saké* and at the same time making the occasion a success. Turning one's cup upside down and placing it on the table thus is a socially recognized way of saying, "No thanks, I cannot drink any more." But this is admittedly a socially poor thing to do, and if one must do this, he profusely apologizes for his ineptitude. If only one out of ten or twelve people is a teetotaller and if he is not a principal guest, then the atmosphere would not be affected appreciably since he may be ignored entirely and the entertainment can proceed without his social presence. But if there are more than one such persons in a small group and if they cannot be ignored because of their number or because of their position in the group, then the party cannot help being a failure.

On the other hand, succumbing to the insistence of the host and forcing oneself to drink when one does not wish to may not be pleasant at all. At least, however, it has the virtue of complying with the group norm and manifesting the willingness to sacrifice personal welfare for the good of the group. In the end, the participant may be dead drunk. He may say or do things he would not remember or prefer not to remember. But others observing him tend to be quite lenient in their judgment of his behavior. They are likely to show sympathy and some may wish he had a little more self-control. But one would not morally chastise him since such misbehavior is not a mortal misdeed, it is simply social misconduct. By the same token, even if drunkenness and possibly getting sick and throwing up at the end may be due to unswerving insistence of the hosts, who often equate the amount of hospitality forced on guests with the degree of success of the entertainment, it is quite improper for a guest to be angry with the hosts. The opinion of the community is on the side of the host, on the side of those who help lubricate social relations.

While a good deal of alcohol may be consumed in the course of a dinner, how drunk participants get is not absolutely a function of alcoholic intake. Socially defined rules of drunken behavior, varying from situation to situation, dictate how drunk one should appear. The help which alcohol provides in acting drunk is not to be minimized, of course. But we all know that the same amount of alcohol consumed in a party of congenial friends produces radically different results from that taken at home all alone. In a party, it takes very little alcohol to induce loud talking, shouting, loud laughter, singing and clapping of hands in unison with a wild, off-tune chorus of school songs. When the fun of the party is all over and it is time to go home, everyone except the few who lost control and are sound asleep by this time, regains his sobriety almost instantly and acts almost like a different person, like a group of actors leaving the stage after the curtain comes down. It is thus not strange that one almost never hears in Japan of a drunk, walking the narrow downtown street without sidewalks and teeming with cars day and night, being run over by a car or hit by a bus. Of course, he is almost invariably helped home by his more sober companions.

One important rule to be followed in dinner entertainment of a small party of five or six persons is to center the conversation of the entire group on one topic. Breaking up into groups of twos and threes rather than keeping the whole group united in a dinner situation is a sign of conspiracy, a gesture indicating lack of interest in the major theme of the play being enacted, and therefor an outright expression of a lack of respect and discourtesy to the honored guests of the party.

Those of higher status in the party should be allowed to dominate the conversation most of the time. Others are the supporting cast in this production. They should pitch in from time to time to punctuate the conversation and make it more interesting, throwing in little jokes and light remarks now and then, but they should make sure to leave any punch lines to the honored members of the party so that the dominant role of the principal actors of this drama is unmistakable to anyone. Supporting cast roles in this play are, of course, to enhance the dominant roles played by principal actors. The latter should be allowed to speak longer, introduce new topics more often, and make somewhat belittling remarks about comments of the supporting cast. They are privileged to cut into sentences of others, but the others must politely listen until they finish their remarks. The supporting cast might play its role by asking questions an honored member can answer with authority, so that in answering them he can reassert his dominant role, for example, by giving a glowing report of his recent trip to a place no one else in the company has been to, or by divulging some secret information he happens to be privy to. Supporting casts are supposed to express exaggerated interest, surprise, and other appropriate effects.

The drama cannot be enacted only with the effort of the supporting cast, obviously. Principal actors must know their roles well and read their script without making errors. When hosts expect the guests to dominate the scene, they must dominate. In order to dominate, they must know how to dominate. They must know interesting topics of conversation and know how to make conversation interesting. At the same time, even if the guest's talk is not too interesting, a good host would put on the appearance of being interested and attentive. In short, both sides—hosts and guests— must cooperate, saying what is appropriate at the right moment, giving cues to one another so that each knows when to offer a cup, pour *saké*, laugh, shake hands, etc. Seeing the appropriate and expected responses, others take this as a cue to proceed to the next scene of the play.

Flawless enactment of the entire drama and a smooth flow of each episode thus requires hosts and guests all to be familiar with the rules. This insures that the scenario is read flawlessly by all actors. This is more difficult than enacting a real play since, unlike real plays, the script is not written beforehand, but is being written from moment to moment as scenes unfold. Without rehearsal, each participant must play his part. As for the script, each participant must improvise his lines without delay as the drama develops.

Rehearsal of the play and the practice of improvising the script are actually found in each participant's daily living from time of birth. Learning to speak Japanese and learning all the hidden meanings and reversals of meaning, the meanings of hand and body gestures and the social system of hierarchy are all preparations for enacting the next drama of life.

When an American is invited to a dinner party in a *ryootei*, he naturally goes in without rehearsal and without the practice of improvising lines in the way appropriate to a Japanese social scene. He lacks the social accouterment necessary to act with grace and without flaw. The result is somewhat like an American wrestler having to play a match of *sumoo* with a *sumoo* athlete using *sumoo* rules. The result is a most awkward match. Since Japanese are too polite to tell their guest they are clumsy people, guests leave the scene believing they played their part according to the script. But actually, as in a real play, when one actor cannot play his part well other actors must strain themselves to make up for the deficiency, making their cues excessively obvious and covering up the mistakes made by the clumsy actor. Having an honored guest who does not know his part well in a dinner party requires that others help him to play his role so that they themselves can continue to play the hosts' role. If a clumsy actor is one who plays a minor role in the play, he can be almost ignored without causing much damage to the play. When the principal actor, which an American guest usually is, does not know the part or the script, the amount of effort required by the supporting cast is heartrending. It is almost like Fred Astaire trying to dance gracefully with a 200 pound woman who never danced before. After entertaining Americans, one often hears Japanese say they are all worn out. This is precisely because they try so hard to help Americans play the principal role without *faux pas* or try so hard not to make *faux pas* look like *faux pas* and even try to make them look as though they are charming improvisations of the correct script. In short, they try so hard to make American guests believe they play their role like Fredric March that in reality the Japanese are the Fredric Marches heroically helping clumsy and inexperienced American actors.

SECTION III

The Institutional and Legal Environment of Japanese Business

Japanese business operates in a unique social and political environment. While Japan shares with the United States the ideology of a free-enterprise, open market economy, in practice there are a great many differences. The selections in this section describe these differences. In "The Institutional Foundations of Japanese Industrial Policy," Chalmers Johnson makes the point that even terms like competition *and* private industry *cannot be applied to the Japanese economy in the same sense that they apply to the American economy. In fact, the existence of an "industrial policy" is itself a pivotal difference between Japan and the United States. The relationships between the state bureaucracy, the political system, and business create an environment for Japanese business characterized by a remarkable consensus regarding goals and national priorities among these centers of power. Johnson declares that there is no such thing as a government's not having an industrial policy, as government actions have profound effects on the markets within that economy. "The issue is whether a government's industrial policy will be ad hoc, incoherent, and run by and for insiders [as in the United States] or whether it will be consistent, long-term, and run for the sake of future generations [as in Japan]."*

This debate is closely related to the individual versus society *and* freedom versus order *themes of our framework. The idea of any kind of centralized economic planning by government is abhorrent to the American understanding of the proper role of government. In the American view, individuals and businesses left free to pursue their self-interest will automatically, through the operation of Adam Smith's "invisible hand," maximize the national interest.*

As Johnson describes it, the Japanese people are far less willing to trust the invisible hand, preferring instead to entrust the guardianship of the national interest to government, even at the cost of constraints on their own behavior.

American executives who are looking at Japan as a potential location for operations requiring the employment of Japanese individuals must be familiar with the legal aspects of the organization-employee relationship. Even for those only seeking to do business with Japanese companies, Toshiaka Ohta's "Works Rules in Japan" provides a look at Japanese perceptions of what constitutes minimum standards of working conditions. Ohta reviews the genesis of legislation concerning works rules and comments on their legal status. As can be expected, works rules cover minimum standards, and hence are more aligned with international standards than culturally specific practices. One culturally specific aspect of works rules requirements in Japan is the distinction made between male and female workers.

In modern societies, education is an important, perhaps the most important, vehicle by which cultural preferences are imparted to new generations. In "Learning and Working in Japan," Merry I. White surveys Japan's much admired education system and its relationship to the world of work and finds many contrasts with the American system. Even the care of infants at home is motivated by a different set of cultural assumptions: The American mother sees her newborn as a dependent being needing to be trained to be independent, while the Japanese mother thinks of the infant as self-oriented, needing to be made aware of its dependency on others. The individual versus society and freedom versus order themes are engaged almost as soon as the child is born, and continue to play a role throughout the early years. In the United States, children are impatient to grow up and be free of parental constraints; in Japan, the child savors the freedom of his young years, for he will soon grow up to lose much of this freedom.

School education in Japan is most remarkable for the socialization into group activity that it provides for all students. White describes how children are assigned to small groups that engage in almost every activity at school as a group. School experience in Japan lays the foundation for all the qualities of group interaction that will be important for the individual to "fit into" life in productive organizations. White also describes the pressures for conformity that exist in Japanese schools.

One feature of Japanese human resources management that is radically different from practices in the West relates to the inclusion *of the spiritual dimension in training and in day to day management. As suggested in the Introduction, Japanese culture predisposes the Japanese to pursue spiritual goals seriously. Buddhism teaches that the actions of the body are products of the spirit; therefore, first the spirit must be improved. Spiritual development most often refers to the development of self-discipline and an attitude of acceptance of destiny. Japanese culture is suffused with injunctions urging the Japanese to "improve the spirit," and even routine activities of daily life are viewed as occasions for spiritual development.*

It is not surprising, therefore, to discover that Japanese organizations incorporate the spiritual dimension in their Human Resources policies. Some aspects of this were discussed in the selection by Durlabhji included in Section I. In "'Spiritual Education' in a Japanese Bank," Thomas P. Rohlen takes a detailed look at how the organization actively promotes the spiritual development of its employees, and how it seeks to incorporate this dimension into organizational activities. Although this chapter discusses the internal practices of a Japanese organization, and thus may be more appropriately included in Section IV, it is included here to emphasize the fact that concern with "spiritual education" is a feature of the Japanese social and educational environment. Only a few decades ago, this kind of education was considered to be the responsibility of the formal education system, which has been taken up by organizations only because the schools no longer provide it.

Japanese culture emphasizes that one's experience of life as meaningful and fulfilling depends not on material conditions but on the attitude with which one approaches all tasks. Thus, Japanese organizations devote considerable attention to promoting the "correct" attitude, through frequent reminders of organizational philosophy and values, and through training programs designed to provide spiritual education.

New recruits in a bank in Japan received a three-month training prior to their first work assignment. Rohlen describes in detail the many activities designed to force trainees to confront the strengths and weaknesses of their own character. These included visits to Zen temples and instruction in the methods and practice of Zen meditation, visits to military bases, weekend "retreats," and a number of specially designed exercises with potential for intense, even traumatic, experience. Evidence for the bank's position on almost all the themes of the framework presented in the Introduction can be found in this article. Rohlen's report is a fascinating account of a peculiarly Japanese practice, and is essential reading for an adequate understanding of Japanese organizations.

9

The Institutional Foundations of Japanese Industrial Policy*

Chalmers Johnson

In talking about the Japanese government-business relationship, the first warning to be issued is to beware of the normal connotations of English language terms and to be prepared to use familiar concepts, such as parliament or bureaucracy, in a new way. The United States' leading legal authority on Japan, Dan Henderson of the University of Washington's Law School, puts it this way:

> Terms such as "competition," "private industry," or "free enterprise," commonly used in discussions of Japanese business, conjure up in the minds of readers in English quite different images from existing realities of Japanese business. "Collusive rivalry," "semiprivate industry," "quasi-public enterprise,' respectively, might be more apt expressions, precisely because their Western referents are unclear.[1]

The Japanese institutions of government and business are themselves quite different, and have quite different histories and functions, from those of the Anglo-American world, and these differences directly influence the kind of government-business relationship that exists in Japan.

- First, the Japanese state bureaucracy, particularly the economic bureaucracy concentrated in the ministries of Finance, International Trade and Industry, Agriculture, Transportation, Construction, Posts and Telecommunications, and the Economic Planning Agency, is an intrinsic meritocracy. Service in any one of these ministries is the most prestigious occupation in the country, and the senior public service is drawn primarily from the top 20 percent of the best law school in the country, that of Tokyo University. These men originate virtually all national policies, control the three unconsolidated national budgets, retire early and move on to top positions in business and politics (a process that is called *amakudari*, or descent from heaven, and that is directly opposite to the movement of talent in the United States from the boardrooms of private corporations to the government). These men also maintain legendary old-boy connections with each other during and after their period of public service. The state bureaucracy, particularly the economic bureaucracy, has supplied many of the most important prime ministers of postwar Japan, a source of political recruitment that is unknown and close to unimaginable in the United States.[2]

- Second, the parliament of Japan—the assembly of elected representatives of the people (known as the Diet)—is constitutionally the "highest organ of state power" (Article 41 of the Constitution of 1947), but in practice it is one of the weakest parliaments among all the advanced industrial democracies—and certainly weaker than the U.S. Congress, which is the strongest such institution in the world. In postwar Japan, an informal relationship between the Diet and the economic bureaucracy has developed in which the Diet reigns but the bureaucracy actually *rules*—or, to put it another way, the bureaucracy makes policy and the Diet merely rubber-stamps it. It should immediately be added that this is an unstable relationship and a moving target. At the present time, we are in a phase of relative Diet ascendancy; for example, tax policy, which was under firm bureaucratic control and not subject to political influence during most of the postwar period, is today more in the hands of the ruling conservative political party than in the past. But the relationship between the Diet and the economic bureaucracy is a cyclical one, with the bureaucracy always regaining influence in times of economic crisis, such as during postwar reconstruction or after the oil shock of 1973. To cite one example of Diet weakness, the bureaucracy's budget has been modified by the Diet only three or four times since the creation of the Liberal Democratic Party (LDP) in 1955, and these modifications always involved relatively minor changes in defense appropriations.[3]

· Third, big business in Japan maintains a skewed triangular relationship with the other two main power centers, the bureaucracy and the Diet. Big business keeps the Liberal Democratic Party in power by supplying enormous funds to the leaders of conservative factions (whose actual electoral constituencies are normally rural). This is important because since 1948 uninterrupted single-party dominance in Japan has been prerequisite to bureaucratic initiative and leadership.

Japan's single-party reign has not had the stultifying consequences of single-party rule in places such as the Philippines largely because Japan's LDP learned how to replace the head of the party, something it does with great frequency, through internal factional struggle. The party keeps itself in power through quite open subsidies to Japan's farmers, who are wildly overrepresented in the nation's system of electoral constituencies. At the same time, such payoffs to farmers have had powerful income redistribution and equalization effects and have eliminated rural poverty, which was the major source of instability in prewar Japan.[4] One consequence of the LDP's long reign—which shows no sign of ending soon unless the Americans destroy Japanese agriculture in the name of market-opening—is fairly frequent corruption scandals by politicians who have abused their access to the LDP-bureaucratic-big business nexus. The main advantage that Japan gets from its single-party system is simply that it allows for "solving problems with an eye to the economic system, rather than to a particular category of citizens."[5]

As we indicated earlier, the Diet tries, on occasion, to direct the bureaucracy, but this effort is weakened by the presence of large numbers of former elite bureaucrats within the ranks of conservative politicians. (Currently, about 20 percent of the Diet members are ex-bureaucrats.) The bureaucracy, in turn, supports the interests of big business, but it is not subservient to business because business financial support flows to the party. The bureaucracy supports big business primarily because it is interested in securing the economic welfare and economic defense of Japan as a whole.

· Fourth, the Japanese legal system derives from the Continental European tradition rather than from the Anglo-American common law tradition. This means that economic law, lawyers, detailed contracts, and adversarial relationships are relied on much less in Japan than in other open economic systems. Perhaps most important, and differing from both the Continental and Anglo-American traditions, administrative law is markedly underdeveloped in Japan. If a Japanese thinks that the executive branch has exceeded its mandate or is interpreting a law in an undesirable manner, he will not easily obtain relief by turning to the courts, which are also notoriously slow. The trend is toward an increased reliance on administrative law, as seen in the pollution suits of the 1970s, but this is not yet sufficiently advanced to make much of an impact. [6] Instead, bureaucratic power in Japan is checked by intense competition among the various ministries, by the use of Diet members to obtain advantages for particular groups (rather than to establish general policy), and through the practice of *administrative guidance*—meaning ad hoc, not legally binding agreements and arrangements between the bureaucracy and its clients in order to achieve common goals.

The Japanese government is extremely intrusive into the privately owned and managed economy, but it does this through market-conforming methods and in cooperation rather than confrontation with the private sector. Japan's economic bureaucracy is probably the most powerful of that in any contemporary capitalist democracy, but it is also the smallest, cheapest, and imposes the lightest tax burden of any capitalist democracy. With the exception of certain political sacred cows, such as the publicly owned railroads and rice-price supports for Japan's farmers, the economic bureaucracy tries to avoid subsidies, preferring instead the use of loans, seed money, tax breaks, and ad hoc benefits to promote its policies.

In talking about any government-business relationship, the issue is never government intervention in the private sector. *All* governments intervene in their economies for a variety of reasons, such as consumer protection, social welfare, national defense, and so forth. The key consideration is the functional priorities of a government in intervening. The first priority of the Japanese government in the private sector is not protectionism or neo-mercantilism (as in France), or regulation (as in the United States, with the exceptions of the defense and agricultural sectors), or welfare (as in Sweden or the Netherlands). Japan's first priority is, above all, *developmental*—meaning the effort by the government to secure Japan's economic livelihood through public policies based on such criteria as long-term dynamic comparative advantage and international competitive ability. The Japanese government's most important contributions to the economy are think-tank functions and supervision and coordination of the structural changes necessary to keep Japan competitive in world markets.

There are many other things one needs to know about the Japanese government and business community in order to understand and adapt to the relationship between them. Some of these things are:

- the similarities in outlook between public and private managers because of similar educational experience; lack of pronounced class, ethnic, or religious divisions in Japan; and widespread popular awareness of Japan's vulnerabilities and of the need to trade because it is an overpopulated, highly industrialized set of islands situated close to both China and the Soviet Union and with almost no natural resources;

- the oligopolistic organization of Japanese big business into bank- and trading company-based conglomerates or industrial groups (*keiretsu* in Japanese, descendants of the prewar *zaibatsu*), which means that profit considerations often take a lower priority to such criteria as market share, capital formation, research and development, and long-term market penetration;

- the fact that Japan's enterprises still obtain most of their capital via bank lending rather than the sale of equity shares, which means that Japanese managers are much less influenced by shareholders or securities analysts than in other systems, that they are much more influenced by the monetary policies of the central bank than in other systems, and that bailouts or reconstructions of the Lockheed or Chrysler types are common and not particularly controversial in Japan because banks and the government cooperate to protect their investments; and

- the history and norms of Japanese labor relations, which result in intense enterprise loyalties, an almost total absence of interfirm transfers but very extensive intrafirm transfers, enterprise unionism, and norms of consensus formation rather than majoritarianism in both governmental and enterprise decision making.

Many of these aspects of Japanese business are already familiar to Americans, and most of them have been extensively described in the numerous recent books in English on the Japanese political economy.[7]

The different priorities and political principles found in Japanese government, as contrasted with those of the United States, seem to me to be key to the highly controversial and even emotional debate in the English-speaking world about the Japanese economic challenge to the market economies of North America and Western Europe. There is no dispute about the *record* of Japan's high-speed economic growth, which lasted for about two decades during the postwar era and was then followed by a decade of slower but still impressive expansion of both production and productivity. Equally important is Japan's record of orderly shifts of industrial structure, first from labor-intensive light industry to capitalintensive heavy industry and currently to knowledge-intensive high-technology industry. Everyone knows that Japan is the world's largest manufacturer of automobiles, that it controls well over half of the world's market share for some important types of microelectronic components, and that other very rapidly growing capitalist economies of East Asia are explicitly modeling themselves on the Japanese economy. The dispute is about precisely what these facts mean. Above all, what are the political and intellectual implications for Japan's competitors of Japan's achievements?

Virtually the entire Western community of professional economists is united on one point: Whatever the data from Japan may be, they must not be allowed to challenge the prevailing theoretical paradigm of how market economies work. Professional economists are fundamentally hostile to "comparative economics." They conceive of their field as a theoretically and mathematically based science, one that seeks and allegedly has discovered a few universal laws, and in which comparative studies would be as irrelevant as they would be in, say, physics. Economists are uninterested in the thought that the *Wealth of Nations* actually concerned only one nation.

In recent times, comparative economics has had a brief flurry of interest as an adjunct to the study of Soviet-type socialism, but as

the Soviet economy began to falter, so too did comparative economics.[8] One would have supposed that the arrival on the scene of the
Japanese-type economies would have reinvigorated comparative
economics, but this has not happened (yet). Instead, most professional analysis of the Japanese economy "sees the basic source of
Japan's economic growth as lying in a vigorous private sector, ener-
getically, imaginatively, and diligently engaged in business, productive investment, and commercially oriented research and development and in the saving to finance those activities."[9] The discrepancy
between the performance of Japan and of other, no less diligent and
energetic market economies during various parts of the postwar
period is explained by a vast range of temporary or contingent factors: the especially propitious environment in which Japan found
itself (i.e., the same postwar environment as all other American
allies), mistakes by Japan's competitors in the management of their
enterprises, Japanese "free rides" of various kinds on the backs of
American scientists or taxpayers, secrets of Japanese management
(viz. the search for such secrets at the Harvard Business School in
Musashi Miyamoto's *Book of Five Rings*, a 1643 treatise on swordsmanship), Japanese workaholism, "creative Confucianism" in East
Asia, and so forth. However, economic punditry steadfastly avoids
analysis of the Japanese government-business relationship for the
simple reason that the comparison with the United States would
likely be damaging to both local theory and local practice.

As the American trade balance in manufactured goods with
Japan inexorably worsens each year, and as one quick fix after
another (e.g., elimination of non-tariff barriers, pressures against
the "undervalued yen") is attempted with no change, the professional economics approach has started to lose credibility. It simply
does not and perhaps cannot account for the numerous discrepan-
cies between theory and practice that are now commonplaces of
daily life in either Japan or the United States (the differences in
the cost of capital in the two countries, Japanese savings behavior
during periods of high inflation, etc.). This weakness of pure economics has produced a resurgent interest in the West in "political
economy," particularly in professional schools of business and in
departments of political science. By political economy I mean an
analysis of economic phenomena based on the explicit recognition
of the indivisibility of economics and politics—a view that has as
its corollary the understanding that "economic theory" is a totally
utopian subject unless and until it is translated into the real world
through institutions.[10] (As a practical matter this also means that
any discussion by political or business leaders in either Washing-

ton or Tokyo of the "glories of the free market" or of the "need to restore macroeconomic fundamentals" is purely ideological and probably designed to camouflage their real intentions.)

Even when they bear the same names—"labor union," "public corporation," or "stockholders"—the institutions of modern capitalism vary greatly among systems. There is no theoretical way to show what the "institutions of capitalism" ought to be. One can only show through comparative analysis the consequences, both intended and unintended, of particular institutional configurations. Equally important, the hypotheses of economic theory are not simply manifested in institutions; such institutions also have *political* foundations and political consequences that have their own theoretical rationales. The institutions that actually exist in a modern capitalist system owe as much to a nation's history as they do to either economic or political theory, which is not to say that such institutions are in any sense sacrosanct but only to indicate one of the kinds of knowledge that is needed if a nation wants to reform its institutions.

As should by now be obvious, I place myself in the school of political economists. I do not contend that Japan has repealed the "laws of economics," nor do I hold that the Japanese government in general or any individual agency of it in particular was the exclusive author of the postwar economic miracle. I do contend that the Japanese have put together the political and economic institutions of capitalism in ways that differ from the Anglo-American model and that this Japanese configuration has many different tradeoffs, not all of which have as yet become fully manifest to either the Japanese or Japan's competitors. The most obvious tradeoff is that in return for lesser levels of political participation than those prevailing in the United States, Japan has obtained a comparatively more effective and more efficient public economic policy.[11]

Embedded in Japan's institutional structure is something called "industrial policy." It is not possible to adopt a Japanese-type industrial policy without also adopting Japanese-type institutions, which suggests at the outset that Japan cannot be a model for the United States. The responsibilities, endowments, and political traditions of the U.S. differ too much for that. But it does not follow that a competitor of Japan could not match Japan's industrial policy within a very different institutional setting. Certainly during World War II and again today the United States has succeeded in matching and excelling its military enemies without copying their institutions. This is what, on the economic front, industrial policy is all about.

Industrial policy means the initiation and coordination of governmental activities to leverage upward the productivity and competitiveness of a whole economy and of particular industries in it. As a set of policies, industrial policy is the complement, the third side of the economic triangle, to a government's monetary and fiscal policies. Industrial policy is first of all an attitude and only then a matter of technique. Above all it means the infusion of goal-oriented, strategic thinking into public economic policy. There is no such thing as a government's not having an industrial policy—in the sense that any agency controlling 20 to 30 percent of the gross assets of an economy will have profound effects on the markets within that economy. The issue is whether a government's industrial policy will be ad hoc, incoherent, and run by and for insiders or whether it will be consistent, long-term, and run for the sake of future generations.

Industrial policy has its own macro and micro aspects. At the macro level it provides governmental incentives for private saving, investment, research and development, cost-cutting, quality control, improvements in labor-management relations, and in the appropriate education and reeducation of the labor force. At the micro level it seeks on the one hand to identify those technologies that will be needed by industry in ten to twenty years and to facilitate their development, and on the other hand to anticipate those technologies that will decline in importance and to assist in their orderly retreat or to support them on extraeconomic grounds (e.g., domestic food supply, weapons for defense, etc.). Micro industrial policy is also popularly known as "industrial targeting."[12]

In Japan, macro industrial policy has been of much greater, if unheralded, importance than industrial targeting. Japan's genuine successes with targeting have depended as much on the macro environment created by industrial policy as on the concrete policy measures intended to promote or support particular industries. Macro industrial policy a la Japan is not a matter of some new or esoteric technique of government; it is rather an emphasis on economic fundamentals in public policy making and the use of the criterion of international competitive ability in evaluating *all* governmental programs. The formulation and implementation of industrial policy in Japan depend as much on its depoliticization to the greatest degree compatible with democracy as on any economic mode of thought. Japan has been able comparatively to depoliticize its industrial policy because of widespread public awareness of Japan's dependency on imports for most of its fuel, food, and raw materials.

Japan's MITI has the primary although not the exclusive responsibility for formulating and executing national industrial policy. Concretely, what has MITI done in the past and what does it continue to do today? In the broadest sense MITI does four things:

- First, it makes medium-term econometric forecasts concerning the development of any needed changes in the Japanese industrial structure. Within this framework, it sets up goals which it believes the private sector must achieve if Japan is to remain competitive. These indicative plans—or "visions," as the Japanese call them—involve specific comparisons between Japan and its various foreign competitors of cost structures for different scales of production for each important industry. The major criterion (among many employed) in making industrial policy judgments is still income elasticity of demand, as it has been since the early 1950s.

- Second, MITI arranges for the preferential allocation of capital to selected strategic industries. It does this through the governmental and semi-governmental banks; and the Ministry of Finance guides the commercial banks to coordinate their lending policies with MITI's industrial policies. Financial support of an industry also implies guidance (not control) by MITI. This is usually quite indirect and subtle. For example, during 1984, the ministry exercised its influence over the biotechnology industry through preferential financing and ideas it disseminated to the unions of laboratory researchers at the various pharmaceutical companies.[13] Among MITI's most recent financial beneficiaries are so-called venture capital enterprises, which the ministry supports through the Small and Medium Enterprise Agency (an organ of MITI), the Japan Development Bank, and the 1983 law it sponsored to create "technopolises" in Japan—that is, new research cities modeled on California's Silicon Valley and aimed at stimulating synergistic influences among adjacently located high-tech businesses.[14]

- Third, MITI targets those industries it believes Japan must develop in the future and creates a package of policy measures to promote such development. In the past, MITI's prime promotional measure was protection against foreign competition in the Japanese home market. This was achieved through foreign exchange control (until 1964), protective customs duties (until the late 1970s), control of foreign capital investment (until about 1976), and control of imports of foreign technology (until 1980). As Andrea Boltho, formerly with the OECD in Paris, puts it, "Relative to other industrialized countries, Japan's effective tariff rates were higher, her quota system more comprehensive, and the ingenuity of her hidden trade barriers on manufactured imports and subsidies to manufactured exports almost certainly greater."[15]

Since the early 1980s, MITI has abandoned protectionism (although the culture and habits of protectionism continue with only slightly declining force in the general trading companies, regardless of official policy). Contemporary promotional measures stress financial assistance, tax breaks, incentives given through administrative guidance, and antitrust relief. Concerning the latter, Nobuyoshi Namiki, a former MITI official and one of its best-known theorists, defends research cartels in the targeted industries as Japan's only way to compete with the United States' much larger and richer research and development establishment. Targeting concentrates scarce resources and improves Japan's competitiveness vis-à-vis the U.S. in integrating basic science, applied science, production technology, and product development in the overall R&D process. "Establishing a well-defined and valid target," writes Namiki, "means that the goal has been obtained in large part."[16]

- Fourth, in addition to targeting and promoting industries for the future, MITI is also actively involved with formulating industrial policies for what the Japanese call "structurally recessed industries." Some of these industries became depressed because of the global recession that followed the first oil shock (e.g., ship building), or because of competition from the newly industrialized countries (textiles), or because of uncompetitive energy needs after the second oil shock (aluminum and petrochemicals). To create a general framework and a legal basis for governmental assistance to such industries, MITI wrote and sponsored passage by the Diet of the Special Measures Law for the Stabilization of Designated Recessed Industries of 1978, which it modified and renewed in 1983.[17]

Designation of an industry as "recessed" under the law causes the ministry responsible for the sector of the economy in which it is located (usually MITI but, for example, Agriculture in the case of some chemical fertilizers) to formulate a stabilization plan for the industry. This means that the ministry must forecast supply and demand (including exports and imports) for the industry on a periodic basis in order to measure excess domestic productive capacity and to allocate shares among enterprises for scrapping or mothballing such capacity. In drawing up these plans, the ministry must consult with an industrial advisory commission located in the Industrial Structure Council.[18] Costs of scrapping production facilities are divided between the private sector and government, with government normally raising its share through specific import duties. The Fair Trade Commission may reject or modify ministerial plans if it considers them excessively anticompetitive; but once the commission gives its approval, the activities of enterprises in the designated industry are exempt from the provisions of the Antimonopoly Law.

The essence of Japanese industrial policy is the attempt by the Japanese government to engineer comparative advantage in international trade for selected Japanese industries. It does this primarily through a broad range of macro industrial policies, but it also relies on industrial targeting to assist in shifts of industrial structure in a timely manner. On the record, as a matter of batting averages rather than individual successes or failures, Japanese industrial policy is the best in the world. For nations trying to compete with Japan on this dimension, the response seems obvious:

- learn from Japan the logic of what it is doing without attempting to copy Japanese institutions;

- bring under control the macro industrial policies of one's own nation and orient them to economic fundamentals;

- avoid protectionism at all costs; and

- inhibit political influence on economic policy making—if necessary through such drastic measures as constitutional amendments stipulating a balanced budget in peacetime, ultimate tax limits, and a line-item veto for the chief executive.

10

Works Rules in Japan*

Toshiaki Ohta

The role of works rules in different countries is closely related to the industrial relations system in force. In general, it tends to be minor in countries where collective bargaining is well developed, while in those where the collective bargaining system is still in its infancy it can be very significant indeed. This chapter takes a look at Japanese law on works rules and discusses the principal theories on their legal force and validity before examining their main contents, illustrated by specific examples drawn from a study published by the Japan Institute of Labor.[1] The concluding section analyzes the place occupied by works rules in Japanese labor-management relations.

The new Japanese Constitution adopted in 1947 shortly after the end of the Second World War guarantees the right of workers to organize, bargain and act collectively, and stipulates that standards on wages, hours, rest and other working conditions are to be fixed by law. In pursuance of these provisions, new labor laws such

---

*Reprinted, by permission of the publisher, from *International Labor Review* 127, no. 5 (1988).

as the Labor Standards Act of 1947, the Trade Union Act of 1949 and the Labor Relations Adjustment Act of 1949, were placed on the statute book. The Labor Standards Act, which was quite advanced in relation to the international labor standards of the time, contains detailed provisions governing the employer's responsibility for drawing up works rules and the procedures for doing so, their scope, and the relationship between works rules and laws, collective agreements and contracts of employment. It can be said that this act has done much to transform works rules from a social norm established by the employer for ensuring the smooth running of the enterprise into a legal norm for protecting workers' conditions of work and employment, and especially the large majority who are not covered by collective agreements. Let us begin by looking at the Act's main provisions on the subject of works rules.

Works Rules and the Labor Standards Act, 1947

Drawing up Works Rules

Section 89 requires employers who employ ten workers or more continuously to draw up works rules based on the provisions of the act, submit them to the Labor Inspection Office and bring them to the attention of their employees.

The Labor Inspection Office may order changes in the contents of the works rules submitted by the employer if they are not in accordance with the law or existing collective agreements. In 1981, 129,900 sets of works rules were submitted to the Labor Inspection Offices, of which some 7 percent were returned to the employers because they did not conform with the provisions of the Labor Standards Act.[2] The number of works rules submitted in 1987 was 135,477.

Section 90 of the act specifies that, in drawing up works rules, the employer must seek the opinion of the trade union representing the majority of the workers if there is one at the workplace or, if there is not, a representative of the majority of workers. When submitting the works rules to the Labor Inspection Office, the employer must attach a record of the opinions expressed by the trade union or workers' representative on their contents. This provision was included to prevent employers from acting arbitrarily. Although the employer must consult the union or the workers' representative, he does not have to obtain their consent; in theory he must take their views into account, but the final decision on the contents rests with him.

Section 106 specifies that the employer must bring the works rules to the attention of employees by displaying or posting them in conspicuous places throughout the workplace and by other means. This provision is pursuant to the principle of supplying information about conditions of work and employment laid down in section 15 which provides that in making a contract of employment the employer must inform the worker of his wages, working hours and other working conditions. To enable employees to determine whether the employer is providing proper conditions of work and employment, the Ministry of Labor has drawn up a model set of works rules which it takes great pains to disseminate in the enterprises.

The Scope of Works Rules

The Labor Standards Act lists a wide range of matters that must or can be covered by works rules. They can be divided into three categories: matters that employers must include in the works rules; matters that can be regulated only under the works rules; and matters that may be included voluntarily.

The following matters must be included in the works rules: (i) starting and finishing times of the working day or shift, breaks, rest days and holidays; (ii) the method of determination, calculation and payment of wages, the date on which they are to be paid, and provisions concerning pay scales and wage increases; and (iii) questions concerning termination of the employment relationship.

There are some matters on which employers are not obliged to make rules but which, if they do, must be included in the works rules with a view to spelling out the conditions of work and employment. In other words, employers are not allowed to make rules on these matters separately from works rules. They include: (i) severance pay, other allowances, bonuses and minimum wages; (ii) expenses incurred by workers, e.g. on food consumed at the workplace or working equipment; (iii) safety and health; (iv) vocational training; (v) accident compensation and assistance in the event of injury and disease not resulting from employment; (vi) rewards and penalties; and (vii) any other questions that concern all the workers in the enterprise.

Employers can make rules on other matters which are covered by the Labor Standards Act and include them in the works rules. Examples are disciplinary provisions, provisions concerning the interpretation of the works rules, and provisions concerning labor-management consultation over amendment of the works rules. Although their inclusion in the works rules is left to the discretion of the employer, once they are so incorporated they are binding on both the employees and the employer.

An employer having ten or more persons in his employ who fails to draw up works rules on obligatory matters or to submit them to the Labor Inspection Office is liable to a fine (section 120 of the Act).

How Works Rules Relate to Laws, Collective Agreements, and Contracts of Employment

Section 92 of the Labor Standards Act provides that works rules must not infringe any laws or collective agreements applicable to the workplace and that the Labor Inspection Office may order changes in the works rules if they are not in accordance with the law or collective agreements. It is quite natural that laws take precedence over works rules since these are considered to be private norms drawn up unilaterally by the employer.

As far as the relationship between works rules and collective agreements is concerned, the act gives precedence to collective agreements since these are concluded jointly between trade unions and employers. As works rules and collective agreements both cover a wide field, there is bound to be frequent overlapping. When collective agreements are comprehensive and detailed, trade unions naturally regard them as carrying more weight than unilateral rules.

Finally, section 93 of the act provides that any conditions laid down in contracts of employment that are inferior to those stipulated in the works rules are invalid and must be replaced by the latter. The act thus gives precedence to the works rules as an important means of ensuring uniform conditions of work and employment at the same workplace and of guaranteeing minimum labor standards.

The Binding Force and Validity of Works Rules

The source from which works rules derive their authority has been the subject of debate for some time. In Japan there are two main theories on the subject: the "contractual" and the "legal."

According to the contractual theory, works rules are a "model" of the contract of employment between the worker and the employer and their binding force stems from their contractual character. A worker is bound by the works rules because, when he enters into the employment of a firm, he is deemed to have accepted its works rules, explicitly or implicitly, as part of his conditions of work and employment.

The legal theory regards works rules not as part of the contract of employment but as part of the law of the enterprise which each employee accepts when he joins it. Like society, every organization, if it is not to become anarchic, must have its own laws, and it will generate them spontaneously. An employee submits to these laws voluntarily by the fact of taking up work in an enterprise, and must adhere to them. But this act of submission is not a contractual act. The validity of the contractual theory has been contested inasmuch as it regards works rules as a type of contract whether there is a formal agreement between the worker and the employer or not. It is the legal theory that has proved the more influential among Japanese labor specialists in recent years.

The most controversial issue concerning works rules is whether they remain valid when the employer alters their provisions to the detriment of the employees' conditions of work and employment. Theories on the validity of works rules are divided in much the same way as those on their binding force. The majority of theorists claim that changes detrimental to the employees' conditions of work and employment cannot be made in works rules unless the employees agree to them. But others claim that, at least from a practical point of view, the employer should be free to alter the rules even in a manner that adversely affects his employees, or some of them at any rate, because of the constantly evolving nature of labor-management relations and because changes in works rules may result in regulating conditions of work and employment more uniformly.

In the past judicial decisions also tended to be divided between these two schools of thought, but the Supreme Court finally came down on the side of the legal theory in the Shuhoku Bus Case of 25 December 1968. A number of employees who had been dismissed on reaching 55 years of age claimed that the dismissal was null and void because the new retirement age had been fixed by a unilateral change in the provisions of the works rules. The Supreme Court rejected their claim. In principle, it said, employees may not be deprived of their acquired rights nor may employers unilaterally impose worse conditions of work and employment on their employees by changing the works rules or drawing up new ones. However, if the contents of the works rules

are reasonable a worker cannot reject their application simply
because he disagrees with them. Works rules are intended to deal
with employees' conditions of work and employment collectively; in
particular, they serve to establish uniform conditions.

Although this ruling was severely criticized because the standard of reasonableness established by the Court was vague and the
decision had excessively harsh consequences for employees, the
Supreme Court reaffirmed its ruling on the validity of newly formulated or revised works rules in the Takeda System Company Case of
25 November 1983. Prior to 1982 this company had granted its
female employees special leave of up to 24 days a year without loss
of pay. However, it then decided that it would pay a maximum of 68
percent of the basic daily rate to female employees who took such
special leave. The eight appellants claimed that this was a unilateral change in the works rules and was therefore null and void. The
Supreme Court invoked the precedent in the Shuhoku Bus Case
that a company might change its works rules in a way that affected
its employees adversely provided the change was reasonable, and
referred the case back to the Tokyo High Court, instructing it to
review its earlier ruling that it was unreasonable for the company to
alter the works rules without prior union consent and to decide
whether the company's change of works rules was reasonable or not.

The Supreme Court also passed judgment on the validity of
rules governing severance pay in the Mikuni Taxi Company Case
of 15 July 1983 where a unilateral change in the rules was challenged by employees. The Supreme Court found no special circumstances to justify the change and, since the employer had failed to
offer compensatory conditions of work and employment to its
employees although the change affected them adversely, ruled that
it was unreasonable and hence invalid.

The Main Contents of Works Rules

Japanese works rules cover a very wide field. In this section the
main contents of works rules are examined in the light of specific
examples.

Personnel Matters

Recruitment. Although the inclusion of rules relating to
recruitment is not compulsory, almost all the examples examined
had provisions on this subject. For the most part these cover quali-

fications, selection methods, documents that must accompany the application, and the length of any trial period.

Transfer. Transfers are conducted frequently in Japanese enterprises since the efficient allocation of manpower is a necessary response to economic and social change and, besides, workers are not as a rule hired to work solely in a particular department of an enterprise. Transfers are also used to promote the career development of employees. In addition, there are many instances where workers wish to be transferred because of changes in their current job, work relations, state of health, change of residence, etc.

Almost all the examples contain provisions governing transfers. These usually state that employees may be required to accept transfers, may not refuse them without good reason and, in the event of refusal, may render themselves liable to penalties such as reprimand, reduction of pay, suspension or dismissal.

The company often consults and negotiates with the trade union on such matters as the reasons for the transfer, the employees to be transferred and the conditions relating to the transfer. Although there were few examples that laid down a procedure for consulting trade unions, a survey of job transfers made by the Japan Institute of Labor[3] found that 14.7 percent required union consent, 23.8 percent required prior union-management consultation, 29.6 percent required prior notice, and in 12.3 percent of the cases the union had to be informed *ex post*. It should be noted that more than 80 percent of the companies examined considered trade union involvement important.

Dismissal. Although the Labor Standards Act distinguishes between ordinary and summary dismissal, very few of the works rules examined make that distinction. Typical reasons for ordinary dismissal given in the examples are: (i) impossibility to continue working owing to physical or mental disability; (ii) a bad record of service; (iii) continued absence after the expiry of a period of suspension of the contract; and (iv) collective layoff because of the company's economic position.

While the inclusion in works rules of restrictions on the employer's right to dismiss an employee is not obligatory under the act, the latter does impose certain limits on the power of dismissal. Section 3 prohibits dismissal on the basis of nationality, creed or marital status; Section 19 prohibits the dismissal of a worker who is injured or falls ill while on duty, during the period of medical treatment and for 30 days thereafter, and also prohibits the termination of the contract of a pregnant woman or one who has given birth, during her leave entitlement and for 30 days thereafter. Section 20 requires an employer to give at least 30 days' notice or pay the equivalent of 30 days' average wages in the event of dismissal. However, this provision does not apply when the enterprise has to be wound up by reason of a natural disaster or another case of *force majeure,* or when the worker is dismissed for serious misconduct. Section 104 stipulates that a worker who complains that his conditions are inferior to those laid down under the act shall not be dismissed because of his complaint.

Suspension of the Employment Contract. This occurs when an employee is prohibited from or exempted from work for a certain period of time because of continuous absence due to a non-occupational injury or sickness; because he is seconded on outside business; because he becomes a full-time union official; because there is no suitable assignment for him; because criminal charges are brought against him; and so on. The main questions dealt with in the examples are: (i) reasons for suspension of the contract; (ii) duration of the suspension; (iii) treatment during this period; (iv) treatment after expiry of the period; and (v) treatment when the reasons for the suspension cease to exist.

Termination of the Employment Relationship. The Labor Standards Act makes it compulsory for works rules to contain provisions on termination of the employment relationship. In one example termination occurs in the following circumstances: (1) at the employee's own request; (2) on death; (3) on reaching the age limit; (4) on continued absence after the expiry of a period of suspension of the contract for non-occupational reasons; (5) on the expiry of a fixed-term labor contract.

Discipline

Although the inclusion in works rules of provisions on discipline and disciplinary penalties is not compulsory under the Labor Standards Act, any rules that are made on these matters must be so included; and most works rules do in fact contain such provisions with a view to maintaining order within the enterprise. This also helps to prevent arbitrary sanctions inasmuch as an employee may not be subjected to a penalty for a reason—or of a kind—other than those stipulated in the works rules.

The grounds for penalties can be roughly classified in three types. The first relates to conduct on the part of an employee that hinders the normal operation of work, such as absence without notification or just cause, late arrival or early departure, negligence, disobeying supervisors' orders, interfering with other employees' duties, causing disturbances in the workshop, etc. The second type relates to behavior by an employee that undermines mutual trust between labor and management, such as disclosing business secrets, defaming the company or otherwise bringing it into discredit, accepting money or gifts unconnected with his duties, and breaking the law. The third type relates to behavior that results in damage to company premises or equipment, such as causing accidents through negligence, causing wilful damage to company property, and affixing a poster without permission.

Works rules usually specify four types of penalties: reprimand, deductions from pay, suspension and summary dismissal. A *reprimand* is the lightest penalty: The employee is required to present a written apology and receives a warning for the future. He suffers no material loss but repeated reprimands usually lead to severer penalties.

With regard to *deductions from pay*, Section 91 of the Labor Standards Act stipulates that when this penalty is provided for in the works rules, the amount of the deduction must not exceed half of one day's average wage for a single violation or 10 percent of the total wage for all violations during a payment period. Almost all the examples examined contain provisions drafted in conformity with this stipulation.

Suspension means that the employee is suspended from his duties without pay for a certain period of time. For this penalty to be lawful, the period of suspension must be commensurate with the employee's misdemeanor and must not be unduly long.

Summary dismissal is the severest penalty: The employee is discharged without advance notice and, usually, without severance pay. Since a worker who has been summarily dismissed is likely to have difficulty finding another job, courts hearing cases contesting such dismissals carefully examine the appropriateness of the penalty. They have usually taken the view that mere formal compliance with the requirements for summary dismissal in the works rules is not enough, and that the employee's misconduct must objectively be serious enough to warrant such a severe sanction. The principles established by the courts have placed heavy legal restraints on this penalty and in practice it is very difficult for employers to make summary dismissals.

Working Conditions

Working Hours, Overtime, and Work on Rest Days. Section 32 of the Labor Standards Act provides for a maximum working day of eight hours (not including breaks) and a maximum week of 40 hours—although the present effective limit, established by decree, stands at 46 hours. However, Section 36 provides that employers may increase those maxima in agreement with the trade union representing the majority of workers at the workplace or, if there is none, their representative. The agreement must be submitted to the Labor Inspection Office in writing.

Women's working hours are covered by Section 64(2) of the act, which provides that women are not to work more than 2 hours of overtime a day, 6 hours a week or 150 hours a year, and are not to work on rest days whether or not the employer has reached an agreement under Section 36. However, this section does not apply to women who hold managerial posts or perform work requiring specialized or technical knowledge, and eases restrictions on the working hours of women in "non-industrial undertakings."

In addition to the provisions mentioned above, the act deals with exceptions to the prescribed working hours in the event of accident or cases of *force majeure* such as natural disaster; increased wage rates for overtime and work performed on rest days; working hours and rest days for minors; night work; etc. In these matters the works rules usually follow the provisions of the act, and most specify the number of weekly working hours.

Breaks. Section 34 of the act provides for a daily break of at least 45 minutes for employees working more than six hours and of at least one hour for those working more than eight hours, to be used by them as they please. In workplaces where work schedules and rest periods differ from the norm because of the type of production or work in which they are engaged, the breaks granted to the workers must be specified in the works rules.

Rest Days and Holidays. Section 35 of the act provides that the employer must grant workers at least one rest day per week or four rest days during a period of four weeks. In addition to weekly rest days, days off at the end of the year and New Year as well as on public holidays are provided for in almost all the works rules examined.

Leave. The Labor Standards Act contains provisions on annual leave with pay (Section 39), maternity leave (Section 65) and menstruation leave (Section 67). The law does not require the employer to pay wages during maternity leave or menstruation leave, but in many of the examples of works rules wages are paid to some extent. Almost all works rules provide as well for types of leave not mentioned in the act, such as "mourning leave" and "marriage leave"; in most of these cases, too, wages continue to be paid.

Wages

Although it is compulsory to include provisions on wages in the works rules, employers often have difficulty in spelling them out in detail. The manner of dealing with the problem varies from enterprise to enterprise but usually detailed rules governing wages are drawn up separately from the works rules.

Provisions governing the principles of wage determination are contained in almost all the works rules examined. One example states that wages are to be based on job content, individual ability and performance, and the employees' marital status. The manner of calculating wages—i.e. on a daily, monthly, or mixed daily and monthly basis—is usually specified in the works rules and varies according to the type of industry or work.

As for the method of payment, almost all the examples of works rules contain provisions reflecting the principle laid down in section 24 of the Labor Standards Act that wages must be paid in cash and in full directly to the workers, at least once a month on a specified date.

The wage structure generally depends on the specific circumstances of the enterprise and therefore varies considerably from one to another. While the wage structure is clearly set out in the works rules of the big enterprises examined, it is dealt with in only a very sketchy fashion in those of nearly all the small enterprises. As regards bonuses and allowances, however, even the works rules of small enterprises contain detailed provisions on, for example, post allowances, family allowances, commuting allowances, housing allowances and attendance bonuses (to combat absenteeism).

Since wage increases are among the matters which it is compulsory to include in the works rules, the criteria on which they are based and their amount and frequency have to be regulated. However, almost all the examples contain only very general provisions on the subject. One provides that, subject to the company's economic position, wage increases are normally granted once a year under the merit rating system and take into account such factors as job performance, ability, age, academic record and length of service; the amount is decided by the company.

Training

Japanese enterprises are paying increasing attention to in-house training in order to improve their employees' skills. The content of training programs has been radically altered, in particular, by the rapid changes in recent years in technology and work organization, which in turn have been brought about mainly by the application of microelectronics in factories and the introduction of computers in offices. While employers have to retrain workers who will be assigned to computer-related jobs or those made redundant by the introduction of new technologies, workers too need to adapt to change. Thus a comprehensive education or training program is essential for both companies and workers if the adjustment to new technologies is to proceed smoothly and rapidly. Nevertheless, provisions concerning training do not figure prominently in works rules. A typical example provides that an employee who is required to undergo training in order to improve his knowledge and skills cannot refuse to do so without a valid reason, and that he will continue to receive his pay throughout the training period.

Welfare

In recent years Japanese employers have been attaching increasing importance to enterprise welfare schemes in order to attract and retain a good work force. Accordingly, each enterprise devotes considerable thought and money to improving its welfare system. Nevertheless, few examples of works rules make any mention of welfare. In practice most enterprises provide for welfare facilities in detailed regulations distinct from the works rules.

Occupational Safety and Health

The legal framework for occupational safety and health was reinforced by the passing of the 1972 Industrial Safety and Health Act. There are few detailed provisions on the subject in the works rules examined, most of which lay down only general standards of industrial safety and health in accordance with the basic requirements of the act. Provisions commonly included are those on safety rules workers must observe; the organization of safety and health management; training in safety and health; limitations and prohibitions on recruitment for particular posts; and medical examinations required. Concerning more specific safety and health matters, almost all enterprises issue special rules, distinct from the works rules.

Accident Compensation

Accident compensation is regulated in detail by the Workmen's Compensation Insurance Act of 1947. Benefits payable in respect of employment injury under this Act are those covering medical treatment, temporary disability and physical handicaps, survivors' insurance, funeral expenses and permanent disability. Most of the examples of works rules merely reproduce the basic provisions of the act, but some stipulate the payment of additional benefits over and above those provided for in it.

Conclusions

In the mid-1980s there were 3,719,000 establishments covered by the Labor Standards Act. Of these the overwhelming majority— 2,913,000, or 78.3 percent of the total—employed fewer than ten workers. Those employing ten or more numbered approximately 806,000, or 21.7 percent of the total. However, the total number of workers in establishments employing between one and nine workers amounted to only 11,040,000, or 25.2 percent of the work force covered, whereas the total in establishments employing ten workers or more came to 32,807,000, or 74.8 percent of the work force.[4] Hence the provisions governing works rules apply to three-quarters of the total work force covered by the act.

Some circles maintain that, in the interest of protecting the workers, the scope of the Labor Standards Act should be extended so that every employer will be required to draw up works rules. Though this may be desirable in principle, in practice small employers would encounter difficulties in formulating the rules properly, and the Labor Inspection Offices are already too taxed to examine works rules with the necessary care. Thus it hardly seems practicable to extend the scope of the law to small enterprises at present. However, there is nothing to prevent employers with fewer than ten workers from drawing up works rules if they wish, in which case the provisions of the act are equally applicable to them. The Labor Inspection Offices in fact sometimes advise small employers to do so in order to spell out more clearly the conditions of work and employment in their establishments.

In some countries, such as the Federal Republic of Germany and Belgium, workers' representatives either determine or play a major part in determining the provisions of works rules. In Japan, on the other hand, workers' representatives have fewer rights in this matter. In adopting the present system of unilateral employer determination of works rules subject to certain limits, the Labor Standards Act implicitly designated the bargaining table as the place where workers can press for better conditions of work and employment. Japanese labor-management relations are based on the dialogue between enterprise unions and their respective enterprises. Collective bargaining is conducted almost entirely between the unions and the management of individual enterprises. The range of issues dealt with by collective bargaining is very wide and includes allowances, bonuses, lump-sum payments, severance pay, hours of work, days off, holidays, grounds for dismissal, disciplinary action, transfers, employment adjustment measures, welfare, safety and health, etc.[5] Hence there is no great functional difference between collective agreements and works rules. Both can regulate conditions of work and employment in the enterprise, even though, as noted earlier, precedence is given to collective bargaining.

Furthermore, the labor-management consultation system has developed considerably in recent years, particularly in large enterprises: conditions of work at the shop-floor level are frequently decided through some form of joint consultation machinery like the production committee. According to a recent survey conducted by the Ministry of Labor, 77 percent of establishments with 100 employees or more have established a permanent system of consultation.[6] The production committee provides labor and management with an opportunity to consult on monthly production and work schedules at factory and company level. The same union official and management representatives often attend both the collective bargaining session and the joint consultation meeting.[7] It is no exaggeration to say that day-to-day working conditions are increasingly decided through this system, and that it has come to have a greater influence even than collective bargaining on decisions regarding conditions of work and employment. In view of the spread of the labor-management consultation system along with the development of collective bargaining, the significance and role of works rules in large enterprises might well decline.

However, in small and medium-sized enterprises the situation is very different. Between 1977 and 1987 the unionization rate in Japan dropped from 33.2 to 27.6 percent, which means that at present over two-thirds of Japanese workers, mainly employed in small and medium-sized enterprises, are unorganized and are not covered by collective agreements (about 25.5 percent of the labor force were so covered in 1986[8]). Moreover, the labor-management consultation system is regulated exclusively by the works rules; and hence the role which works rules play for these categories of employees and establishments is very important—an importance that is heightened by the fact that employment contracts in small and medium-sized enterprises are generally not concluded in writing.

In particular, the number of precarious workers, such as temporary or part-time workers, has been growing recently and there has also been an increase in the proportion of women workers. These increases are due mainly to the reduced overall level of economic activity since the oil crisis. Although the unionization rate of these workers is remarkably low, the Japanese trade union movement has traditionally attached little importance to organizing them. As a rule, an enterprise union is made up exclusively of regular employees of the company, and temporary workers are very often excluded. According to the basic survey of trade unions carried out in 1983, only 4.8 percent of trade unions admitted temporary workers as union members, and 86.2 percent made no effort to organize them. In recent years national trade union organizations have become aware of the problem and have turned their attention to the organization of precarious workers in particular. But so far little progress has been made in this area.

As mentioned earlier, the government has issued model works rules in an effort to promote their wider introduction. In particular, it has begun to emphasize the need for drawing up works rules for part-time workers in order to secure better working conditions for them. In view of the significance and role of works rules both for precarious workers and for employees of small and medium-sized enterprises, greater promotional and information efforts are needed. At the same time trade unions also need to direct more of their energy to organizing these workers, while taking a closer look at the contents of works rules and seeing that more information on them is disseminated at the workplace.

11

Learning and Working in Japan*

Merry I. White

Japan is by many measures the most modern country in the world.
And yet, after the glitter of Tokyo's Ginza has faded in the experiences of everyday culture shock, one cannot help noticing that
modern doesn't have to mean Western. Learning from Japan is not
like technology transfer.

But many of us are indeed dazzled by the results of Japanese
educational mobilization. It has been said that the Japanese high
school graduate is as well educated as an American college graduate. College entrance examinations in Japan in science and math
test high school seniors at a level about equivalent to the third
year of specialized courses in an American university. There is the
expectation on the factory floor that any worker can understand
statistical material, work from complex graphs and charts, and
perform sophisticated mathematical operations. The consensus
that education is important, however simple it may sound, is the
single most important contributor to the success of Japanese
schools. Across the population, among parents, at all institutional
and bureaucratic levels, and highest on the list of national priori-

---

*Reprinted from *Business Horizons* (March–April 1989). Copyright 1989
by the Foundation for the School of Business at Indiana University. Used
with permission.

ties, is the stress on excellence in education—and this isn't just rhetoric.

These results make many Americans uneasy, especially those affected by trade politics, the declining American economy, and resultant protectionism. Volatile and ambivalent attitudes toward Japanese successes make some Americans blame Japan for their own problems. Before these people say that the Japanese child isn't fair—just as they say that the Japanese automobile industry isn't fair—we need to see a more complicated perspective on the challenge Japan offers, to emphasize cultural factors.

Chief among these, and at the base of Japanese educational strengths, are two factors:

- The relationship between culturally determined ideas about learning and the socialization and training in home and school; and

- The ideas themselves—the folk psychology of childhood—that parents and teachers use in home and school. Without attention to these factors, Americans looking for quick-fix solutions to our own problems—raising our 180-day school year to the Japanese 240-day level, for example—will be frustrated.

Japan's Educational System: The Background

Before going into more detail concerning the methods and outcomes of teaching in Japan, we need to study a few facts about schooling in Japan.

- Education is compulsory for ages 6–15 or through lower secondary school. Age is almost inevitably correlated with grade level, because a child is only rarely "kept back" and almost never "put ahead." Non-compulsory high school attendance, both public and private, is nearly universal—94 percent.

- There is extensive non-official education. Increasing numbers of children attend preschools, and currently about 95 percent of five-year olds, 70 percent of four-year olds and 10 percent of three-year olds attend kindergarten or nursery school. Many older children attend *juku*, or after-school classes, as well. These are private classes in a great variety of subjects, but most usually provide enhancement and reinforcement of subject material as preparation for high school or college entrance examinations.

- Competition for the most prestigious universities is very steep, but still nearly 40 percent of the college-age group manages to attend college or a university.

- Children attend school 240 days a year, compared with 180 in the U.S. Many children spend Sundays studying or being tutored, and vacation classes are also available. Children do not always feel that this is oppressive; younger children often ask their parents to send them to *juku* as a way of being with their friends after school.

- Primary and secondary schools provide what we would call a core curriculum: a required and comprehensive course of study progressing along a logical path. This rich curriculum is offered to all students in all schools across the country. In high school all students take Japanese, English, math, science, and social studies every year, and all also take courses in chemistry, biology, physics, and earth sciences. All high school graduates have had calculus. All of this adds up to the equivalent of an American B.A.

- Computers and other technology do not play much of a role in schools. The calculator is used, but it hasn't replaced mental calculations or—for some—the abacus. There is said to be no national program to develop high-technology skills in children. One third grade math teacher, when asked why she didn't use the school's computers with her students, said "class time is too precious to use machines." We spend much more money on science and technology in schools; the Japanese spend money on teacher training and salaries.

Tradition, ideology, and international competition are not the only forces in Japanese education. Relative homogeneity in the population, an occupational system in which selection and promotion are based on educational credentials, a relatively equal distribution of educational opportunities across the population, and the devotion of families to enhancing the life chances of children through education all contribute. Finally, the school curriculum includes high standards for all kinds of performance and a carefully graded series of expectations for achievement. These factors are more complicated than they appear. For example, "homogeneity" is a kind of cultural choice. Minority groups such as Koreans and the former outcasts exist; they do suffer discrimination, but

Japanese prefer to consider that they don't really exist. And community is emphasized rather than diversity, similarities rather than differences. In a poll taken recently by the Prime Minister's Office, 96 percent of the respondents considered themselves to be middle class. Americans have chosen to emphasize differences in their population; the Japanese have chosen to emphasize cohesion.

Another key factor, perhaps most important in the comparison with the United States, is the position of teachers. In Japan they enjoy respect, high status, job security, and good pay. Teachers are highly qualified. Their mastery of their fields is the major job qualification, and all have at least a bachelor's degree in their specialty. Moreover, they have a high degree of professional involvement as teachers: 74 percent are said to belong to professional teacher organizations where they work together on teaching methods and study plans.

Teachers are hired for life, at starting salaries equivalent to those for college graduates in the corporate world. Salaries rise with seniority promotions, and Japanese teachers see their work as permanent: Teaching is not a waystation on a path to other careers. Teachers work hard at improving their skills and knowledge of a subject, and they attend refresher courses and upgrading programs provided by the Ministry of Education.

Classes are large: The average ratio is 42 students to one teacher. Teachers are responsible for their students' discipline, behavior, and morality, and for their general social adjustment as well as their cognitive development. They are "on duty" after school hours and during vacations and supervise vacation play and study. They visit their students' families at home and are available to parents who have questions and anxieties about their children.

This background—of national consensus, institutional centralization, and financial support—does not alone explain the successes of Japanese education. There are other, less tangible factors derived from cultural conceptions of development and learning, the valued role of maternal support, and psychological factors in Japanese pedagogy, that distinguish it from American schooling. These factors deeply complicate the process of "borrowing" for American education policy makers, and they are what make the Japanese child modern but not Western.

Birth

The Japanese baby is seen to be born with no particular abilities or disabilities, and this *tabula rosa* is seen to be the mother's responsibility. The mother's role is to provide an appropriate environment and support—the motivation and incentive for the child's development. If little is innate and all is possible, what is needed is effort. How the mother rears a child who will be willing to work hard is an important part of the story of the high test scores.

The psychologist William Caudill said that the American mother sees her newborn as a dependent being, needing to be trained to be independent, while the Japanese mother sees the baby as having separated from her, needing to be trained into appropriate dependency. The first step is physical closeness, and the Japanese-invented word "skinship" describes the skin-to-skin closeness that is particularly valued. Babies are almost never left alone in a crib or playpen, and they are always taken with the mother (alternate caretakers are used comparatively infrequently). There are no babysitters as such. Time with the baby is also valued. In studies comparing mothering in the U.S. and Japan, the data indicate that American mothers spend less time than Japanese just being with the child in the same room. Japanese parents prefer to have their baby sleep in the same room; American parents go to what seems to Japanese observers to be great lengths to have the child sleep in a separate room.

American mothers will busily go in and out of a baby's room, doing things perhaps unrelated to the specific care of the child. A Japanese mother will sit quietly by the side of the baby, or even lie down beside a napping infant. The American mother might rub the baby's back until he or she falls asleep, or sing to him but will stop when he or she falls asleep. A Japanese mother will continue to pat, rock, or carry the baby long after he or she has drifted off. One could say that the American sees her role as a set of discrete tasks, such as "getting the baby to sleep," and the Japanese mother sees herself as "being with the baby." So sitting by the sleeping baby is not time wasted, but part of her role. The desk parents buy for a school-aged child also symbolizes this availability. There is a high front and half sides, cutting out distractions and enclosing the workspace in womb-like protection. There is a built-in study light, shelves, a clock, an electric pencil sharpener, and a built-in calculator. A recently popular model had, in addition, a button connecting to a bell in the kitchen to summon mother for help or a snack.

Child-Rearing

While this closeness—what an American psychologist would call "merging"—is important, so is the bridge the mother must provide to the outside world. She gradually exposes the child to the norms of social and institutional settings. The norms of good mothering are set by the *seken*, the community of neighbors, kin, teachers— all those who will measure her and her child. The *seken* is not a group with an active membership, but a kind of "What will the neighbors say?" watchful, normative presence.

Attending to a child's character and predilections, socializing him to the values of society while cementing a special bond, is a time-consuming task and results in the definition of mothering as a full-time job. The relationship prepares the child for other relationships, especially for the importance of appropriate dependency, but part of the mother's task is to make her relationship with her child unlike all others he will encounter. She encourages him to see the difference between the *uchi* (inside) of the home and the *soto* (outside) and reminds him that the outside will have different expectations. Her total, unconditional support of the child may appear to Americans a spoiling sort of indulgence, and it is hard for Americans to see how the child could be motivated to work if he is so cossetted and protected. Sadaharu Oh, the famous baseball player, says in his autobiography that it is through being indulged and nurtured that he was motivated to work hard to overcome his weaknesses on the field and to devise, among other things, his own batting stance, so that time and time again he broke his own records. He says, "*Amae* [positively valued dependency] warms the heart but it also enables you to work twice as hard, to overcome the siren songs of laziness."

We find it hard to understand that the "dependent" situation created by lifetime employment and security could create productive workers. Americans feel that insecurity is a powerful incentive, but in Japan the assurance of security motivates.

The good child, the *ii ko*, is differently conceived in the United States and Japan. Independence and individual self-expression have priority as overt values in American child-rearing. And while the capacity to cooperate appears on American children's report cards, these are never seen to take precedence; cooperation may, in fact, be a second-class skill.

Another difference, in the definition of ability, appears on our children's reports. The phrase, "works to the best of his/her ability" figures often in teachers' reports here. Yet, because we don't know if children's abilities are fixed before birth or if one can infinitely improve oneself, doing "one's best" is hard to define in American folk psychology. One avoids the uncomfortable assessment that a failing child is doing his best. We instead assume that there's better in the child somewhere, and if performance is poor, we may choose to blame environmental factors such as a broken family, illness, or poverty rather than motivation and effort, as do the Japanese. A Japanese child doesn't say, "Well, I did my best" and expect adults to concur. One way of looking at Japanese child development is to look at the words and concepts related to parental goals for their children. A "good child" has the following, frequently invoked characteristics: He is *otonashii* (mild or gentle), *sunao* (compliant, obedient, and cooperative), *akarui* (bright, alert) and *genki* (energetic and spirited). *Sunao* has frequently been translated as "obedient," but it would be more appropriate to use "open-minded," "non-resistant," or "authentic in intent and cooperative in spirit." The English word "obedience" implies to us subordination and lack of self-determination, but *sunao* assumes that what we call compliance (with a negative connotation) is really cooperation, an act of affirmation of the self. A child who is *sunao* has not yielded his personal autonomy for the sake of cooperation; cooperation does not imply giving up the self, but, in fact, implies that working with others is the appropriate setting for expressing and enhancing the self.

One encourages a *sunao* child through the technique, especially used by mothers and elementary school teachers, of *wakaraseru*, or "getting the child to understand." The basic principle of child-rearing seems to be: Never go against the child. *Wakaraseru* is often a long-term process that ultimately makes the mother's goals the child's own, thus producing an authentic cooperation as in *sunao*. The distinction between external, social expectations and the child's own personal goals becomes blurred from this point on. An American might see this manipulation of the child through what we would call "indulgence" as preventing him from having a strong will of his own, but the Japanese mother sees long-term benefits of self-motivated cooperation and real commitment.

Literacy and cognitive development begin very early in Japan. There is even an old tradition of training in the womb, called *taikyo*. Mothers have a real curriculum for their small children. There are counting games for very small babies, songs to help children learn new words, and devices to focus the child's concentration. Parents buy an average of two or three new books per month for their preschoolers, and there are about forty popular monthly activity magazines for preschoolers. The result is that most children can read and write the phonetic syllabary and do simple computations before they enter school, even though nursery schools and kindergartens emphasize play and social behavior, not academic learning.

The Japanese phenomenon of maternal involvement recently surfaced in Riverdale, New York, where many Japanese families live. School teachers and principals there noted that each Japanese family was purchasing two sets of textbooks. On inquiring, they found that the second set was for the mother, who felt she could better coach her child if she studied during the day to keep up with his lessons. These teachers said that Japanese children entering in September with no English ability finished in June at the top of their classes in every subject.

The effort mothers put into their children's examinations has been given a high profile by the Japanese press. This is called the *kyoiku mama* syndrome—the mother highly invested in her children's progress, or "education-minded mother." In contrast to Western theories of achievement, which emphasize individual effort and ability, the Japanese consider academic achievement a product of an interdependent network of cooperative effort and planning. The press emphasizes the negative aspects of maternal involvement with accounts of maternal nervous breakdowns, for example, recently reporting a murder by a mother of a neighbor's child who made too much noise while her child was studying. But the press also feeds the mother's investment by exhorting her to prepare a good work environment for the studying child, subscribe to special exam-preparation magazines, hire tutors, and prepare a nutritious and exam-appropriate diet.

Stereotypes and Realities at School

Among the stereotypes of Japanese education in the American media is the idea that the child experiences heavy competition at school. Americans also commonly assume that Japanese children do well because they work long hours under great pressure to succeed, that their teachers and parents drill them incessantly, and that rote memorization is the primary didactic method. Recent American newspaper and magazine accounts say that there is no individualism and no creativity encouraged in schools. And all of the effort, it is said, is for the economic success of the nation, not for the development of the child. There are a few realities behind these stereotypes: In high school, as opposed to primary and early secondary schools, the study plan does not permit much deviation, and children are not streamed by ability. For the geniuses there may indeed be a problem, for there is little provision for tracking them to their best advantage. The superbright may indeed be disadvantaged.

On the other hand, creativity and innovation are encouraged. But their manifestations may be different from those an American observer would expect. Creativity to an American involves a necessary break with traditional content and methods and implies the creation of a new idea or artifact, at least an independent invention. Whether creativity is in the child, or in the teaching to be transmitted to the child, and how it is to be measured, are questions no one has satisfactorily answered. Why it is emphasized is another question. It is probably related to our theories of progress and the importance we attach to unique accomplishments, to the Henry Fords and Albert Einsteins, to push society and knowledge forward. The fact is, however, that our schools do, if anything, less to encourage creativity than do the Japanese, especially in the arts. In school, Japanese children are given the tools, methods, and practical acquaintance with the media of artistic expression: All learn two instruments, everyone can read music, all are trained in the use of visual arts materials, and electives are offered in other arts after regular school hours. Originality is seen to come after proficiency. It is true, though, that if everyone must be a soloist or composer to be considered creative, then most Japanese are not encouraged to be creative.

The statistical level of pathological symptoms and behavior among school-age children (and their mothers) is, contrasted to that in the U.S., a very low one indeed. The number of problems reported among school-age children in Osaka in one year, for example, is equal to that reported in one day in New York.

But the Japanese public hears about such problems much earlier than we hear about ours because the Japanese are extremely sensitive to them and consider even very small numbers to be predictors and warning signs. The currently well-publicized incidence of *ijime* or bullying (chiefly in middle schools) is said to be the product of high pressure and conformity in schools. Although statistically still low, it is said to predict a moral and intellectual decline. There is extensive controversy over such phenomena, but everyone agrees that schools should have a wide mandate in developing children. The response to bullying and other school problems is to develop increasing controls through *kosoku* (school regulations) which attempt to regulate all aspects of students' lives from the exact length of hair to the color of underpants worn. Where few other resources exist, the development of human resources is of vital importance. Any strain in the population being educated is seen to present risk. Japanese parents are critical and watchful of their schools and are not complacent about their children's successes. There was a telling example of this lack of complacency in a recent comparative study of American and Japanese education. Mothers of elementary school students in Minneapolis and Sendai, roughly comparable cities, were asked to evaluate their children's school experiences. The Minneapolis mothers consistently answered that the schools were fine and that their children were doing well. The Sendai mothers were very critical of their schools and worried that their children were not performing up to their potential. Whose children were, in objective tests, doing better? The Sendai group's, of course, so much better in fact that the poorest performer in the Japanese group was well ahead of the best in the American group.

To return to the stereotype of great interest to American educators: Do the Japanese indeed produce great scholastic achievement in children through drill and rote memorization? Do Japanese teachers emphasize discipline rather than creative thinking?

The high scores Japanese children achieve in math and science are not the product of a rigid, authoritarian classroom. Rather, they are the results of a number of factors. One of these is the important role given to affect in cognitive development in the school. There is a strong relationship between the supportive and nurturant atmosphere of learning and the high performance and achievement outcomes in Japan. The Japanese recognize that a child's commitment to work must be generated through a supportive, positive relationship with teachers and classmates and a positive perspective on his or her own capabilities.

A look at Japanese classrooms will yield some concrete examples. What first strikes the Western observer is the noise and activity level. An American teacher walking into a fourth grade science class in Japan would be horrified: children are all talking at once, leaping and calling for the teacher's attention. The American's response is to wonder, "Who's in control of this room?" But if you could understand the content of the lively chatter, you'd see that all the noise and movement is focused on the work itself. Children are shouting out answers, suggesting methods, exclaiming in excitement over results—not gossiping, teasing, or planning games for recess. The teacher is standing on one side, correcting papers or consulting with individual children. He is not concerned with the noise as long as it is the result of this engagement. He in fact may measure his success by such manifestations. It has been estimated that American teachers spend about 60 percent of class time in organizing, controlling, and disciplining the class; Japanese teachers spend only 10 percent.

Rote memorization and drill are not often part of class activities, and one reason for this is that children spend out-of-school time memorizing so classroom time can be used for discovery and application. Although Japanese children score high on international tests of functional information, they excel by even greater margins in tests of understanding, application, and hypothesis formation, especially in math and science.

A description of one fifth grade math class will reveal some elements of the pedagogy. The teacher presents a general statement about cubing. Before any concrete facts, formulae, or even drawings are displayed, the teacher asks the class to take out their math diaries and spend a few minutes writing down their feelings about and anticipations of this new concept. It is hard to imagine an American math teacher beginning a lesson with an exhortation to examine one's emotional predispositions about cubing.

After that, the teacher asks for conjectures from the children about the surface and volume of a cube and asks for some ideas about formulae for calculation. The teacher asks the class to cluster into its component *han*, or work groups of four or five children each, and gives out a wide variety of materials for measurement and construction. One group leaves the room with large pieces of cardboard to construct a model of a cubic meter. The groups work on solutions to problems set by the teacher and compete with each other to finish first. After a while, the cubic meter group returns, groaning under the bulk of its model, and everyone gasps over its size—there are many comments and guesses about how many children could fit inside. The teacher now sets the whole class a very challenging problem, well over their heads, and gives them the rest of the class time to work on it. The class ends without a solution, but the teacher has made no particular effort to get or give an answer—although she has exhorted them to be energetic. It might be several days before the class gets the answer, but the excitement doesn't flag.

Several points in this description deserve highlighting. First is the combination of attention to feelings and predispositions, provision of facts, and opportunities for discovery. The teacher prefers to focus on process, engagement, commitment, and performance rather than discipline (in the American sense) and product. Second is the *han*: assignments are made to groups, not to individuals (this is also true at the workplace), although individual progress and achievement are closely monitored. Children are supported, praised, and allowed to make mistakes through trial and error within the group. The group is also pitted against other groups. The group's success is each person's triumph, and vice versa.

The point here is that Japanese teachers recognize the role of affect in learning and stress the emotional as well as the intellectual aspects of engagement. To engage the child's commitment and motivate his or her effort is the teacher's primary task. This emphasis is most explicit in elementary and middle schools, but it remains a very strong subcurrent as a prerequisite for the self-discipline children employ in high school.

Our educational rhetoric does invoke "the whole child," does seek "self-expression" and does promote affective engagement in "discovery learning." But Japanese teaching, at least in primary schools, effectively employs a nurturant, engaging, challenging, and sensitive style that surpasses most American attempts. In the cubing class, the spontaneity, excitement, and (to American eyes) "unruly" dedication of the children to the new idea were impressive, as was the teacher's ability to create this positive mood. It could be a cultural difference: Americans tend to separate cognition and affect and then devise means of reintroducing, rather artificially, "feeling" into learning. It is rather like the way canned fruit juices are produced, first denatured by the preserving process and then topped up with chemical vitamins to replace what was lost.

The Workplace

The engagement of the home and school are attempted again at the company or workplace. Just like the first grader entering school as a blank slate, the new recruit in a company develops a new identity as a member of a work team, unit, and company. As in school, melding a group is the first task, and new recruits are often transformed through a special orientation program into well-integrated cohorts over the first few weeks or months. What was learned in college does not give one a skill identity, a technical expertise that is useful in the company. Rather, the company prefers a generalist who can be trained in the company's style and needs. Advanced technical expertise may be acquired through in-service training, or advanced degrees, often overseas under company sponsorship.

What is a good worker? As in school, it is important to be predictable and not to stick out. The famous expression, "The head that sticks up gets lopped off," is an indicator that norms are patrolled. One must spend time with one's colleagues and superiors, and much of this is not what we would call productive, efficient use of time. The goal is to develop trust and understanding, which is seen as the basis for solid and productive work.

Trust is at the heart of work relationships and makes "predictability" more than static conformity. If you have not had a chance to develop such relationships, your work profile is doubtful. People who have been posted overseas, for example, may be seen as unpredictable, since they may have acquired habits of work or style that will differentiate them from their teammates—and they are made to suffer for this. These differences are seen as symbols of the worker's temporary apostasy, his or her absence from the active face-to-face relationships that build trust.

Above all, it is important to have 100 percent attendance. Everyone, men and women, in whatever role or rank, must make a commitment to the things they do and show it by being there. The expression *kao o dasu*—showing your face—is not just a superficial requirement. Working part-time means being at risk. Women who work and mother at the same time are seen as short-changing someone. Further, changing jobs is still problematic, although the numbers of those who do change, usually from a Japanese to a foreign concern, are slightly on the increase. The reverse is rare. Change due to a desire for the fast track is frowned on; patience is still seen as a virtue; perseverance is more important than vaunting ambition.

To sum up some of the characteristics of Japanese society as seen in the family, school, and workplace, we might note first that Japanese see each of these areas as different: Each is a new environment, not at all part of a monolithic institution or experience. The Japanese do not experience a "Japan, Inc." Each has finely tuned measures of identity and performance to be learned, and yet there are constants. For children, wholeheartedness, engagement, and being "available" to learning are important. For students and new employees, working hard, valuing certain kinds of group success, and working as teammates are significant. For men and women in mid-life, the engagement in their children's success and steady commitment in the workplace are crucial. All of these are based on a kind of trust that the group is the best place to realize the self, that the goals of the group are the ones best suited for the individual. Personal value is obtained not through transcending these goals but through fulfilling them. From the American point of view, there are losses in this philosophy that could not be accepted. But from the Japanese point of view, Americans miss much in support, security, respect, and continuity, characteristics of a society based not on the individual but on the community.

A lot has been said about ancient Japanese management skills, samurai asceticism, and transcendent group spirit. But these are stereotypical, formulaic renderings of the more potent idea that culture does inform even the modern school and workplace. And it is important to note that American ideas about family, school, and workplace are similarly pervaded by American culture. The emphasis in the United States on freedom of choice, individualism (however that may be institutionalized), and mobility (among other cultural options) leads Americans to certain family dynamics, patterns of socialization for children, goals for education, and ideal career paths that need to be recognized as "ours" before we identify "theirs" as either exotic or worth emulating.

12

"Spiritual Education" in a Japanese Bank*

Thomas P. Rohlen

Many Japanese companies train their new employees according to a philosophy of "spiritualism," a set of ideas about human psychology and character development that inspired much of the country's pre-war education. "Spiritualism's" debts to the Zen, Confucian, and samurai traditions are quite apparent. It emphasizes social cooperation and responsibility, an acceptance of reality, and perseverance. Its educational methods emphasize specially constructed training experiences. As a case study in the anthropology of education, Japanese company spiritual education points to the value of (1) studying educational processes outside formal school systems; (2) considering native concepts of psychology in analyzing educational processes; (3) finding relationships between educational techniques and techniques found in religious conversion, psychological therapy, and social initiation; and (4) discovering avenues of education that proceed by non-verbal means.

During the last few years Japanese media have given considerable attention to the startling increase of company training programs devoted at least in part to *seishin kyooiku*, a manner of training commonly translated as "spiritual education." As many as

---

*Reprinted, with permission of the publisher, from *American Anthropologist* 75, no. 5 (1973).

one-third of all medium and large Japanese companies may now conduct such programs as part of their regular in-company training.[1] The accounts of these in the media have been impressionistic and generally critical, with journalists in particular labelling company "spiritual education" practices as unwanted and unwarranted echoes of Japan's pre-war educational philosophy, universally condemned in the early post-war period as militaristic and stultifying to individualism and the democratic impulse. This harsh judgment is entirely predictable and not without some validity, but a closer examination of the phenomenon of company *seishin kyooiku* is in order before any reasonable conclusions as to its nature and political implications may be made.[2] Furthermore, spiritualism (*seishin-shugi*) is much more than a sensitive public issue in Japan; it is a key to much that Japanese now regard as traditional and foreigners regard as Japanese in the nation's ongoing cultural pattern. Spiritualism provides a very definite philosophy of socialization and human development, one that underlies such well-known pursuits as flower arranging, judo, and the study of the tea ceremony. At one time it inspired the training of the country's samurai and, more recently, her pre-war youth.[3] Spiritualism offers a perspective by which individual character continues to be widely judged today. Company spiritual education is, in summary, but the most recent manifestation of a very long and still quite vital Japanese orientation to issues of human psychology and education and for this reason the subject is of far greater interest than the matter of resurgent nationalism alone would imply.

In this chapter I wish to describe a company spiritual training program in which I was a participant for its three-month duration in 1969.[4] The full scope of the program is too varied to permit a complete account and consequently only the major activities that are focal events of the instruction and a few themes of training life will be described in detail. The patterns underlying these activities will be discussed as they provide something of a definition of the concept *seishin* and as they indicate the methods by which individual spiritual strength is fostered. Finally, a few observations about the implications of this material for the anthropology of education are presented. In a previous paper (see note 2), I have considered Japanese company training from the point of view of theories about initiation rituals and consequently this topic will not be taken up here.

The training program studied is conducted by a bank located in one of Japan's large regional centers. The bank has 3,000 employees, 2,000 men and 1,000 women. *Seishin* education is given routinely to all men and to many others in the course of their mid-career training. The program described here involved 120 new men, all recent graduates of high schools and universities. It began within several weeks after their graduation and lasted for three months. During that time they lived together in a modern five-story training institute located near the bank's home office. Training sessions lasted between ten and sixteen hours per day, six days a week. The time devoted to *seishin* education was estimated by the training staff to be about one-third of the entire introductory program. The remaining two-thirds is devoted to training new bank members in the numerous technical skills expected of them in their job. This estimate of the division of time between spiritual training and technical training, however, ignores the fact that individual performance in the task of learning banking skills is commonly interpreted according to *seishin* concepts and even many aspects of recreation, such as the songs taught in trainees are, in fact, vehicles for *seishin* messages.

While unquestionably this bank's program varies in many details from the *seishin* training of other companies, the goals and methods involved are essentially the same according to my experience and inquiry. The similarities among all of them are to be found in the underlying patterns and concepts of *seishin kyooiku*. It is the purpose of this paper to clarify and document what these are.

Japanese who have had no personal contact with company spiritual education tend to associate it with the moral education (*seishin kyooiku* or *dootoku kyooiku*)[5] practiced in the public schools before the war. This was essentially education in nationalism and social propriety based in the teaching of parables and reverence for national symbols. In a very much altered form, moral education does survive in the bank's training program, but the morality is considerably altered in content and presentation.

Today, the institution sponsoring the training is the prime focus of morality, whereas before, the nation, in the person of the emperor, was central. Instead of rituals of nationalism, the bank today draws attention primarily to its own symbols. Through such daily actions as singing the bank song, reciting its motto, learning of its history, saluting its flag, being told of the "company spirit," and hearing inspirational messages from its leaders, the trainees are taught pride and respect for their bank. The nation is not ignored, but rather the company stresses the service given to Japan by the bank and urges its trainees to fulfill their responsibilities to the nation through loyalty to their company. It is not uncommon that service to the bank even be characterized as service to the entire world and to world peace, so organic is the model of social life taught by the bank. No matter what the ultimate benefit, however, the message is that the moral man is the man who works hard for his own company. The bank and all other institutions, according to this view, serve as intermediaries between individual intentions to aid the greater society and the actual realization of national well-being. By virtue of its intermediary position, the bank is properly an interpreter and defender of social morality and its practice of moral and spiritual education is done not only for the good of the bank, but also for the entire system.

It is an oversimplification, however, to describe the moral education of the bank exclusively in terms of a narrow focus on loyal role fulfillment. The content of the program includes many elements borrowed from the pool of inspirational stories of other countries. The diary of a missionary's medical work in Vietnam, the pronouncements of President Kennedy, and the opinions of the Ethiopian olympic marathon champion are among the instructional materials drawn from international sources. "Foreigners do this," or "abroad the custom is such and such" are common and powerful arguments in the bank's moral instruction program.

In addition to foreign influence, the bank's program utilizes the prestige of scholarship and science whenever convenient. Writings of famous professors that are consistent with the bank's message are found on the required reading lists and scholars from the regional university lecture occasionally on inspirational topics at the bank's institute.

Yet the overall aim of the moral instruction program is not to "brainwash" or greatly manipulate the thinking of the trainees. This, it is agreed, would be an impossibility. What is intended is that the trainees become familiar with the point of view of the bank, its competitive circumstances, and its intention to contribute to the social good. This moral perspective will hopefully strengthen their will to perform their work properly in the future. In this way, moral education, which is almost exclusively verbal in nature, fits into the spiritual training program in which the emphasis is primarily on learning through experience.

The more dramatic means for teaching the company's values are a series of special training events. The five reported here— zazen, military training, rotoo, a weekend in the country, and an endurance walk—are the most fascinating of a larger group of such activities. They constitute an important part of the introductory training program and find occasional application in mid-career courses. Because individual experience is the key element in these lessons, I have occasionally inserted observations of my own reaction to the events in the course of the following description.

Zen Meditation

During the three months of training, Zen meditation (*zazen*) was practiced on three different occasions.[6] The longest and most thorough of the three sessions took place during the second month of training, when the trainees, in three separate groups, visited a large and well-known Zen temple several hours bus trip from the training institute. This temple, with its many fine buildings and lovely gardens, has long been supported by the leading industries of the area. It has a tradition of being the foremost institution in the region for the training of new Zen priests, and although the number of new priests has diminished somewhat from earlier days, the temple has become extremely busy providing brief Zen training sessions for sports teams, student groups, and business trainees. One priest mentioned that because the calendar for such training was very crowded, requests had to be made long in advance. On arrival the trainees were lined up and marched into the temple to a small room where they deposited their shoes and baggage. They were then conducted to a hall large enough to accommodate the entire group of forty. A priest, the instructor, asked them to sit formally on their knees. Once seated, he informed them of the temple's rules and procedures and explained in detail the special manner of eating meals in a Zen temple. He left and the group sat for some time in silence. When he returned, he brought with him the head priest. The trainees were instructed to bow their heads to the floor, and to stay in that position until the head priest's greeting was ended. For about three minutes, they bowed in this manner while he spoke of the tradition, rigors, and purpose of Zen. When the head priest finished all sat up and silently accompanied him in drinking tea before he left.

The instructor next asked the group to try to sit in the lotus position, and while they struggled with this, he went on to explain the procedures of *zazen*. He emphasized that it was very important to sit up straight. "This will bring one's 'spirit' [*kokoro*] and body together in harmony," he said. "Sit up straight and you won't waver, either in spirit or in body. If you don't waver, you won't go astray or become confused." Next he explained the method of counting breaths, telling them to breathe in and out very slowly, taking as long as possible without becoming uncomfortable. "This serves to preserve the unity of spirit and body. It may be quite helpful for you in your work, since it will teach you the power of spiritual concentration. When you are bothered or worried, you can overcome such interferences and perform more efficiently," he added.

Next the long wooden paddle, the *kyoosaku*, was explained. "You are struck by the *kyoosaku* or more literally given the *kyoosaku* for the purpose of supporting your determination." He then demonstrated how he would walk up and down the room carrying the pole across his shoulder. Stopping before someone he demonstrated how the person was to bring his hands together in a praying position in front of him, bow, and receive two blows across the back between the base of the neck and the top of the shoulder blade. Before assuming the regular *zazen* position, the person was to bow once again to the *kyoosaku*, this time with gratitude.

With the conclusion of the priest's introduction, we underwent two half-hour sessions of Zen meditation. There was no tranquility or concentration, however. Everyone was obviously uncomfortable and throughout the group there was constant movement. The priest walked up and down, stopping frequently to apply the *kyoosaku* to individual backs. The loud "wack, wack" as it struck created considerable anxiety. I tried to concentrate on adjusting my breathing and maintaining the proper count and rhythm, but the noise and motion and the recurring thought that perhaps the priest would stop and strike me made the simple task of mentally counting up to ten over and over very difficult. The more I tried to forget my concern with the progress of the priest the worse my anxiety grew. When I was finally struck by the priest, the pain was inconsequential compared to the relief and physical release I experienced. Afterwards for a few minutes at least I could relax and begin to concentrate. Others told me of having the same response to the *kyoosaku*.

In between the two half-hour sessions, the trainees were instructed to stand and walk in single file around the hall. Keeping their hands in a praying position and their eyes slightly lowered, they were to maintain concentration on breathing and counting as they walked. These brief walking sessions are designed to provide respite from the pain and discomfort of sitting, yet it seemed that just as the circulation in my legs began to return we were instructed to begin another half-hour of painful sitting. The moments when these walking sessions ended were poignantly described as ones of regret and resignation.

After the first full hour of *zazen*, the group was marched single file into the adjoining mess room where all again sat in the lotus position along low, narrow tables. Hymnals were passed out and for five minutes the trainees chanted Buddhist hymns following the lead of the priest. Eating utensils were then passed out, and first soup and then an unappetizing rice gruel were dished out by younger priests running in a squatting position along the line of tables. The recipients were told to bow as the priests passed. Without a word everyone ate these offerings. There was an opportunity for seconds, but most, hungry as they were, refused. Next, hot water was poured and, using it, each cleaned his bowl in turn until only the final one contained warm water and residue. This awful stuff we were told to drink in one gulp. Nothing was left over, and all the utensils were ready for use at the next meal. The entire proceedings had not taken twenty minutes. During the short break after lunch everyone complained bitterly about the food.

With the end of the break we returned to the large hall for another hour and a half of *zazen*. Although tranquility was the goal, most trainees continued to struggle with the uncomfortable sitting position. A few stealthily glanced at their watches to find out how much time remained before the next opportunity to stand and walk around. Yet, most were seriously attempting to breathe and concentrate as the priest instructed. This was the best way to survive the endless discomfort. At the end of this session the priest explained that it was quite natural to feel pain and impatience. Just to learn to sit correctly takes considerable practice and enduring the pain was just the beginning. He repeated that a straight back, counting, the half-opened eyes, and a position of weightlessness for the shoulders are the keys to learning to sit without discomfort. This, he said, was the first step in really learning to concentrate one's spirit.

When the group was told that for the next ninety minutes they were to work silently clearing the gardens and other buildings there was considerable relief. Some went to clean the outhouse and others helped clean up around the kitchen. One detail raked leaves and pulled grass along a path. The priest instructor was unbelievably meticulous in his pursuit of even the smallest weed and leaf, but his example was ignored by many of the trainees who, forgetting their joy at being relieved from the trials of *zazen*, lazily wandered about with rakes over their shoulders.

After work in the garden, the group did another hour of *zazen* and then had dinner exactly on the pattern of the previous meal. From six to seven they were given free time to wander about the temple. Some trainees found a small snack stand in a park adjoining the temple grounds and, against instructions, purchased snacks which they greedily consumed. All agreed the temple food was terrible. Without exception, they observed that all one could possibly think about was enduring each half-hour session until the bell rang and the walking session began. Their discomfort and distraction were so great they said that little or nothing of Zen as a religious experience or as a methodology for anxiety reduction could be appreciated.

From seven until nine that night, the *zazen* practice continued. The temple hall by that time had become quite cold, but there was no relief for the seated trainees. At nine we went to sleep. There was some talk and some illicit eating of food bought at the snack stand, but very soon everyone was asleep.

It was pitch dark and bitterly cold at 3:00 a.m. when the trainees were awakened and brusquely told to get up, to fold up their sleeping gear, and to assume the *zazen* position. Soon after, they were marched to the main hall where, once more sitting, they joined fourteen priests of the temple in an hour long ceremony involving the chanting of prayers, occasional prostrations, and long passages when only the priests chanted. There were no cushions in this hall and the floor was excruciatingly hard. My stomach was empty, and it was very cold. The high point of my difficulties during the two-day session was reached.

Breakfast, served at 5:30, was no different from the two previous meals, and yet many more asked for seconds. By that time some were famished, and the hot soup tasted good on such a cold morning. From six to seven, there was another free period. Most trainees tried to sleep covering themselves with the cushions as best they could. Most were too tired, shocked, and unhappy to talk with one another. I recalled the treatment of prisoners of war a number of times, and found it quite easy to understand the breakdown of morale and social cohesiveness among them. All I wished to do was escape into sleep.

The next hour was spent again sitting and chanting in the main hall of the temple. The head priest gave a half-hour lecture. My outline of his talk, written afterwards, is as follows:

1. A brief history of Zen Buddhism.

2. An explanation of the concept that according to Zen teaching each is to find the answers for his own problems within himself and not from the explanations of others.

3. Temptations, such as the desire to eat, drink, have sex, and be loved, cause people to become confused and disoriented in life.

4. The purpose of Zen is to assist individuals in perfecting (literally "polishing") their own character. This is a process which must last throughout one's life.

5. Self-improvement involves learning to become less selfish and to be of greater benefit to one's company and to others. Improvements in the ability to serve others inevitably mean greater benefit for the individual himself.

6. A company or any group of people working together requires cooperation and good relations. These things can only be attained when people are not selfish.

7. Just as the temple has rules to benefit its priests and guests, so any company has rules that must be supported by its members.

8. Concerning labor-management relations, there should be no strikes, but rather the two parties should work in harmony together to improve production. The profits of this cooperation should be shared alike between both parties.

9. Training of any kind must be painful and difficult for only in this way can the improvements of character be accomplished.

10. He admonished the trainees to be firm of heart and steadfast in spirit. Think for yourself and don't be swayed or silenced by others.

For the rest of the morning we practiced *zazen* for a final time. No one seemed any more comfortable or adapted to the sitting position, and the squirming continued. My legs continued quickly to become numb and often I could not stand in order to walk around at the end of the half-hour sessions. The only consolation during the last two and a half hours was the knowledge that with each minute we were getting nearer the end.

During the ride back there was much comment about the pain, and the terrible food, and how one of the hardest events of the three-month training was passed. While very few of the trainees were impressed by what they had learned of themselves or the nature of Zen experience, many were deeply impressed by the strict discipline and dedication of the younger Zen priests training at the temple. Some indicated that in the future, when they felt depressed or sorry for themselves, they would remember the stern, simple lives of those priests. *Satori* ("enlightenment"), *mushin* ("selflessness"), and other Zen concepts were no more comprehensible after the two days than they had been previously, but the Spartan ways of Zen living had become tangible realities for the trainees.

Visits to Military Bases

The first trip to a Japanese military installation for training came in the second week of the program. The trainees, sixty at a time, went to an army base not far from the city. The purpose, they were told, was to learn to maintain group order. This was the first activity outside of the training institute and the first organized *seishin* event. The young men were noticeably nervous on the bus going to the base. Most of them rode silently looking out the window. After arrival, they were assigned to several barracks and given army fatigues to wear. These were castoff uniforms that gave them an appearance more like guerrillas than members of a regular army.

In the afternoon of the first day, after a lunch in the enlisted men's mess, the trainees were run through an obstacle course and then given the Japanese army physical fitness test. Nothing particularly frightening occurred and people grew more relaxed. During the occasional breaks, there was much joking about being in military uniforms. In particular they took great pleasure in saluting one another. A respectful appreciation for the precision of passing regular army units also developed.

The following morning everyone sat through a two hour program of military history concluded by an explanation of why Japan's Self-Defense Forces needed strengthening. The talk was skillfully presented and illustrated with many anecdotes which the trainees found interesting. While this was obviously propaganda and out of place in a bank's training program, no one seemed offended. Later, the bank's instructors explained that listening to this lecture was one of the conditions for the use of base facilities and the services of the drill sergeants. The director of training in the bank commented that he would much prefer not to use military facilities, but no other source for teaching military drill was available.

The mood on the bus home was in marked contrast to the gloomy atmosphere going out. There was much ebullient yelling back and forth and noisy rubbernecking at girls along the way. Everyone gaily saluted the driver and his assistant as we descended from the bus.

Near the end of the three months, we again went to a military base, this time the former Naval Officer Candidate School at Edajima—"Japan's Annapolis."[7] Today it is still in use as a school for the Self-Defense Force Navy. Some years after the war, a museum for the various personal effects, diaries, reminiscences, and other illustrations of the brief days of Japan's suicide pilots was established on the base. The director of this museum is a man who began collecting these mementos after the war as evidence of the true attitudes and character of the pilots. He has given himself the mission of explaining or reinterpreting the *kamikaze* to a generation of younger Japanese who know very little of their actual lives or character. The day and a half visit to Edajima was made primarily to see the museum and hear the director's explanation.

Our group was prepared for the visit by watching several recent commercial movies that depict the life of midshipmen training there during the war. According to the movies, only the cream of Japan's young men could enter Edajima after having passed the most rigorous academic and physical tests. In one movie it was described as the most difficult school to enter in Japan. The movies emphasized the character strength and camaraderie of the young men, qualities making more tragic the fact that most were destined to die shortly after graduation. Having seen these dramatic portrayals of Edajima, the young bankers were duly impressed with its tradition and its almost sacred quality for prewar generations.

In an hour lecture, the director of the museum told of his impressions of the suicide pilots and the lessons their example might hold for young people in a peaceful, modern Japan. His lecture, entitled "What Is Man's Mission in Life," had a stirring impact on the trainees.

He began by describing the education given at Edajima. In addition to physical and intellectual skill, perfection and alertness were also demanded at all times. Midshipmen arriving at the top of a long flight of stairs might be asked, for example, to say how many steps they had just climbed. Discipline was so strict that many grew to hate their officers and yet they would never complain openly, for to do so was to fail training. Teachers at the school also accepted great personal suffering without complaint, for the spirit of the place was endurance and sacrifice for the nation. Newcomers gradually acquired this spirit and passed it on. The epitome of this was that after 1941, young men coming to Edajima realized that they were in fact volunteering to die. In the classrooms of Edajima, he claimed, there was much discussing of the small possibility Japan had for winning the war. He stressed that preparation to serve one's country up to and including death was not something that began with the suicide pilots. It was the spirit at Edajima long before the war. He told of a pilot of one of the miniature suicide submarines that set off for Hawaii at the time of Pearl Harbor departing with the final words, "We are bound to lose."

Such stories of courage and uprightness continued a while longer and then he observed:

> Nobody wishes to experience unpleasant things, but unpleasant things are part of life and nothing of significance can be achieved without suffering. Today's individualism ignores this fact and easily becomes empty egoism. The men at Edajima had the kinds of individualism and independence that focus on the mission to serve one's country, not on the pursuit of pleasure. The trouble with today's student movement is that they know nothing of the discipline and sacrifice required to change society for the better. Soon enough they are fighting among themselves. There was a young cadet at the academy who, because he opposed a certain rule in the school, sat in the same place for many weeks, fasting and drinking only water to show his opposition. His action was respected by the others because he didn't complain or criticize, but rather demonstrated the sincerity of his objection by personally suffering. How many so-called revolutionaries today are prepared to do that kind of thing?

He told a story about the novelist Kawabata Yasunari. During a visit to a grade school near the end of the war, Kawabata asked the youngsters if there were any in the class willing to die for Japan. One young boy stepped forward and said, "I will." Kawabata asked his reasons with the observation, "If Japan loses, do you think you will be honored?" The little boy replied, "Mister, aren't you being misleading? I know that Japan is going to lose." Kawabata bowed to the little boy.

Through such anecdotes the courage of Japan's wartime youth, particularly those volunteering to become suicide pilots, was presented. Their spiritual strength, not their zealousness or their naivete was emphasized. The kamikaze were Japan's best, the museum director concluded. They were the best informed about Japan's impending defeat, and yet they volunteered to die without even, in most cases, an opportunity to see family or friends a last time. There is a popular song about the fellowship of the suicide pilots, and the fact that they would never again meet at cherry blossom time. The image of these young men taking off on warm spring afternoons is truly a tragic one, and the museum director at the end recalled this scene. Sitting very straight in their chairs, the trainees, to a man, were weeping silently as he finished.

The visit to the museum proper the next day was made in silent interest with none of the trouble-making spirit that the trainees usually brought to their excursions. Once inside, they were allowed to wander about on their own looking at the many rooms of paintings and other mementos of naval history until they reached the rooms containing the story of the suicide pilots. The trainees were deeply affected by the similarity in age between themselves and the young men who died in 1945. They noticed how beautifully written the pilot's diaries were. According to their own statements, it was a moving experience.

Later, after inspecting the base, teams were assigned to row heavy, cumbersome longboats, traditionally part of Edajima training. The difficulties of developing coordination in the crew were stressed. Later, the group climbed a nearby mountain that is climbed at a run every day by cadets of the school. The ascent was made at a jogging pace, and the trainees were amazed to learn that their speed, which they thought to be fast, was twice as slow as the cadet average.

As in the previous visit to an army base, people were extremely courteous and pleasant, and the group did not taste much of the rigors and hierarchy of military life. They were, however, keenly interested in the memories and past glories of the place and they drank up the mood created by the old buildings. It was July and the sunburnt cadets in their summer whites, the ocean breezes, and the pride of the academy combined to create an almost irresistible spell. Without this atmosphere the explanations of courage and purpose might have had less impact, but being at Edajima removed much of the historical distance between the *kamikaze* and the young bankers their age.

Rotoo

For two days during the latter part of the second month of training, the group stayed at a youth center sponsored by the Japanese government. This center, located on a mountainside, overlooks a large agricultural valley and just below is the market town for the area. Early on the morning after arrival the trainees were instructed to go down into the town and find work from the residents. Instructions were to go singly from house to house offering to work without pay. They were to do whatever their host asked of them. It was strongly emphasized that this was not to be a group operation. Each was to go alone and work alone for the entire day. In addition, the trainees were disallowed from making any explanation for themselves or their reasons for volunteering to work. They could offer no more than their name and their willingness to work.

They dressed for the exercise in white, nondescript athletic uniforms, common throughout Japan. Without benefit of a social identify or a reasonable explanation for themselves, the trainees were sent out to make a most unusual request of strangers. Their reliability would not be vouched for by their relationship to a known institution like the bank. They were thus made dependent on the good will of the people they met.

This form of situation, difficult as it would be anywhere, is of particular difficulty in Japan where, as a rule, strangers ignore one another and social intercourse between them is unusual and suspicious. Approached by an unknown person with a request like this the common response would be a hurried and not very polite refusal. People doing *rotoo* in Japanese cities have met refusals perhaps four times out of five. It was with considerable consternation, therefore, that the trainees left for the town below.

At first they wandered about from street to street. Many were reluctant to leave their friends and go alone to the front gate of some house. In the case of some groups, they walked four or five blocks together before anyone mustered the courage to make his first approach to a house, but gradually the groups dispersed. The common experience was to be refused two or three times before finally locating a house or shop where they would be allowed in and given work. All agreed to having been very anxious about the first approach, but found the second and the third easier to make as long as people were polite. An impolite refusal created considerable upset, but was rare. Those who did take them in were regarded as warm and understanding people for whom they were happy to work hard. The common pattern was to volunteer to do things that even the host would not have thought to ask. This was partly to avoid going out again seeking another house and partly from a felt desire to be of help.

Boys who had been raised on farms tended to go to the edge of town seeking familiar work with farming families. The majority found work in various small shops. One helped sell toys and another assisted a mat maker, a third delivered groceries, and another pumped gas. One rather clever young man found work in a small roadhouse by the bus station. He quickly established himself as more than just a dishwasher by showing his skill in mixing cocktails. An instructor happened to notice him working there and was angered by the lack of seriousness with which this trainee regarded the day's exercise. The offender was told he had selected an inappropriate place. Instead of doing service for some respectable family, the young man was busy swapping jokes with the customers and waitresses of a roadhouse. He was sent away from the place and told to find other, more appropriate work. Later he was roundly criticized for taking *rotoo* lightly.

When the group had all returned, a general discussion of the day's experience was held in the auditorium. It was soon apparent that comments from the floor would not be forthcoming, so the instructor in charge had each squad talk over their impressions of the day and discuss the relevance of the *rotoo* experience to the question, "What is the meaning of work?" As usual, a variety of opinions emerged. Some trainees had such an interesting and pleasant time with their hosts that it had not occurred to them to think of their tasks as work. When this was noticed, it was generally observed that enjoyment of work has less to do with the kind of work performed, and more to do with the attitude the person has toward it. The bank's reasons for utilizing *rotoo* centered on establishing precisely this lesson.

The actual intent of *rotoo*, as it is used by some Buddhist temples, is, however, somewhat different. It is used as a method of shocking people out of spiritual lethargy and complacency. The word *rotoo* actually means something like "bewilderment" and refers to the state of insecurity established when the individual is divorced from his comfortable social place and identity. In the course of begging for work, that is, begging for acceptance by others, the subject learns of the superficial nature of much in his daily life. It is expected that his reliance on affiliations, titles, ranks, and a circle of those close to him will be revealed, and, perhaps for the first time, he will begin to ask who he really is. *Rotoo* also provides a unique opportunity for a trusting and compassionate interaction between strangers. After a *rotoo* experience it is unlikely that the person will continue to disregard the humanity of others, no matter how strange they are to him in terms of social relationship. It is hoped that this will foster a greater warmth and spontaneity in the individual.

From the point of view of the bank, however, there are additional purposes for this training, ones that help explain why *rotoo* is included in a training program for new bankers. It has been the experience of many people from the bank that the meaning of work and attitudes toward work have been changed by doing *rotoo*. The anxiety of rejection and isolation mounts with each refusal until finally, when some kindly person takes the individual in and gives him work, a cathartic sense of gratitude for being accepted and allowed to help is created. No matter what the work, even cleaning an out-house, the sense of relief makes the work seem pleasant and satisfying. Work that is normally looked down on is, in this circumstance, enthusiastically welcomed.

After such an experience, it is difficult to deny the assertion that any form of work is intrinsically neither good nor bad, satisfying nor unsatisfying, appropriate nor inappropriate. Pleasure in work, it must be concluded, varies according to the subject's attitude and circumstances. Failure to enjoy one's work is interpreted in the bank as essentially a question of improper attitude, and *rotoo* exemplifies the teaching that any work can be enjoyable with a positive attitude. Since it must assign rather dull and methodical tasks to many of its employees, the bank finds this lesson of obvious value.

Weekend in the Country

One weekend was spent on a small island about an hour's boat ride from the city. The educational purposes for this special session were varied. According to our leaders, we were expected to learn something of self-reliance and the kind of ingenuity engendered by simple, rural living conditions. The weekend's activities were also to provide many opportunities to let off steam and be as boisterous, rowdy, and aggressive as we wished. Several activities designed to teach us a greater appreciation for social inter-dependency and social service were also included. Finally, living together in quarters more cramped and primitive than those at the institute was to be part of our general experience in *shuudan seikatsu* (group living). All of these goals were outlined to us on arrival at the district youth hostel on the island.

The hostel was a large barn-like building of two stories with wooden bunks upstairs and a large open room downstairs. The atmosphere of the hostel was in the boy scout tradition even to the large stone fireplace, and a collection of handicrafts displayed on the walls. The beach was a twenty-minute jog from the place and in the opposite direction on the hillsides were tangerine groves and small vegetable gardens belonging to local farmers.

With the unloading completed we gathered in the main room in our usual squad formations and listened to a short explanation from the head of the training section:

> In the city, in our modern and well-equipped training insti-
> tute, we have no chance to let loose and become rough and
> tumble, so we have come out here to let you express your
> energy and youthfulness. While all of you are bankers and
> therefore are expected to be proper and decorous when work-
> ing as bankers, we want you to have a more aggressive spirit
> burning inside. This weekend will be a chance for you to find
> out just how boisterous and full of fight you can be. So don't
> hold back. Throw yourself into the activities we have planned
> as completely as you can. Finally, we are also going to help
> some farmers in their fields, and we hope that all of you will
> learn and benefit from this experience.

The leader then divided the room into two groups, had them face each other and instructed everyone to yell out in a loud voice, "*washoo, washoo,*" one group alternating with the other. We then began doing squat jumps thrusting our arms high over our heads yelling *washoo.* The two groups alternated and a piston effect was created, one group jumping up and yelling followed by the other. After ten or fifteen minutes of this the room seemed filled with a weird frenzy. The heat, constant rhythmic yelling, and unceasing motion made me feel a bit afraid, as if I had been locked in a boiler room with a monstrous engine. When the exercise ended, and it seemed interminably long, we collapsed with exhaustion. This was our introduction to what the trainers had in mind when they said they wanted us to be full of energy and boisterousness. I was fasci-nated to realized that our training went from the extremes of silent Zen meditation to this mass explosion of energy and noise.

The first morning before dawn the group ran in formation to a wide, empty stretch of beach facing the open sea. A light rain was falling and the wind off the ocean soaked our thin athletic out-fits. After the usual calisthenics we separated into squads arranged in lines facing the wind. Led alternately by each in the squad we screamed commands at the top of our lungs. Most were quite inhibited at first, but eventually all were yelling as loud as

possible. Next we practiced swinging wooden swords up and down
as one would in practicing Japanese fencing. Intersquad sumo
matches, marked by more effort than skill, were the last events
held on the beach before breakfast. The run through the rain back
to the hostel for breakfast seemed particularly long.

During the morning on both days we went off with various
farmers who had agreed to put us to work in their fields. We were
provided with scythes and other farm equipment and under the
farmer's direction we weeded gardens and cut grass under tangerine trees. Some of the trainees worked strenuously while others
loafed. The farmers were not inclined to make the trainees work
harder, and the project was much like other work details we had
experienced, even though it was explained to us as service (*hooshi*)
to the farmers.

When we got back to the hostel that afternoon people were
asked to comment on their experience. The general opinion was
that being directed to go out and help farmers who had obviously
been rounded up by our instructors and persuaded to allow us to
work for them provided very little sense of actual service. Some
said they enjoyed the work, others said they found it inappropriate
to training as bankers. It was agreed that to learn about service to
others the work should be voluntary. The primary lesson for the
city boys had little to do with service; they had learned more about
farmers and their contribution to society.

Incidentally, the president of the bank would like someday to
have all new men spend their entire first year farming together.
He feels the long, arduous agricultural cycle is the best education
in persistent effort and due reward. He has spoken of this on
numerous occasions, and the director of training may have instituted the service to farmers routine as a response to the president's vision.

The second afternoon was spent playing contact sports on the
beach. Stripped to our waists and divided into two teams, we played
several games popular in the old Japanese navy, *kiba gassen* and
boo-taoshi, and then held a sumo wrestling tournament. In the first
game, each side creates a set of mounted warriors with one man
riding on the shoulders of three compatriots. Starting from opposite
sides of the field, the two teams charge and the side that forces the
other's men to the ground first is the winner. The second game
involves the defense of standing poles, one for each team. The object
is to attack and tear down the opponents' pole while preserving
one's own. At each end of the field the attackers assault the other's
defenses by leaping on the group, surrounding the pole, tearing

people away from it, and wrestling with the people who come to reinforce the defenders. Neither of these two games took much over fifteen minutes, but they were fiercely contested and some of the less aggressive trainees were quite evidently frightened to have to fight their fellow trainees. The rest of the afternoon was devoted to a round robin sumo tournament among the squads with contestants from each squad matched by size.

During the time on the island squads were assigned cooking, cleanup, and other chores, and the conditions and organization of life in the hostel followed the usual camp patterns even as far as singing songs around a great bonfire the last night. After the entertainment and singing, the program ended with all standing arm-in-arm in two great circles around the fire swaying back and forth singing the bank's song and the very sentimental song of the *kamikaze* pilots.

Endurance Walk

Ever since the first day, the trainees had heard about the twenty-five mile endurance walk to be held sometime near the end of the training period. The daily morning mile run and the other climbing and hiking activities were explained as preparation for this event. On the morning they were to begin the endurance walk, there seemed to be a high level of anticipation and readiness even among the weaker and less athletic trainees.

The program was simple enough. The trainees were to walk the first nine miles together in a single body. The second nine miles were to be covered with each squad walking as a unit. The last seven miles were to be walked alone and in silence. All twenty-five miles were accomplished by going around and around a large public park in the middle of the city. Each lap was approximately one mile. There were a number of rules established by the instructors. It was forbidden to take any refreshment. During the second stage, each squad was to stay together for the entire nine miles and competition between squads was discouraged. Finally, it was strictly forbidden to talk with others when walking alone during the last stage. The training staff also walked the twenty-five miles going around in the opposite direction. Some dozen or so young men from the bank, recent graduates of previous training programs, were stationed along the route and instructed to offer the trainees cold drinks which, of course, they had to refuse. This was the program and there was no emphasis at all placed on one person finishing ahead of another. Instructions were to take as much time as needed as long as the entire twenty-five miles was completed. The walk began around 7:30 a.m. and finished around 3:00 p.m. There was no time limit and many had not gone the full twenty-five miles, but the collapse from heat prostration of a few led the instructors to call the event off at a point where most had a lap or two remaining.

On the surface, this program was simple enough, but in retrospect it seems to have been skillfully designed to maximize certain lessons related to *seishin*. When we began, the day was fresh and cool and it seemed as though we were beginning a pleasant stroll. Walking together in one large group, everyone conversed, joked, and paid very little attention to the walk itself. The first nine miles seemed to pass quickly and pleasantly, and the severe physical hardship that we had been expecting seemed remote.

Forming up into squad groups at the beginning of the next nine miles we were reminded again not to compete with other squads. But discovering squads close before and behind, the pace began escalating and resulted in an uproarious competition that involved all but a few of the squads. Each time a team would come up from the rear, the team about to be overtaken would quicken its pace, and before long trainees found themselves walking very fast, so fast that those with shorter legs had to run occasionally to keep up. There was much yelling back and forth within each squad, the slower and more tired people crying out for a reduction in speed, the others urging them to greater efforts. A common solution was to put the slowest person at the head of the squad. This not only slowed the faster ones down, but forced the slow ones to make a greater effort. The competing squads were so fast that within four or five miles they had already begun to lap those squads that stayed out of the competition. By the end of the second nine miles the toll on the fast walkers was obvious. Many, besides suffering from stiff legs and blisters, were beginning to have headaches and show evidence of heat prostration. Some lay under a tree by the finish line sucking salt tablets. It was noon by that time and the park baked under the full heat of a mid-June sun.

Any gratification the leading squad found in their victory was soon forgotten. At the finish line, there was no congratulation and no rest. Squads were instructed to break up and continue walking, this time in single file and in silence. Soon a long line of trainees stretched over the entire circumference of the course. Having already covered eighteen miles, the last nine at a grueling pace, most were very tired.

At that point everything was transformed. The excitement and clamor of competition was gone. Each individual, alone in a quiet world, was confronted by the sweep of his own thoughts and feelings as he pushed forward.

My own experience was to become acutely aware of every sort of pain. Great blisters had obviously formed on the soles of my feet; my legs, back, and neck ached; and at times I had a sense of delirium. The thirst I had expected to be so severe seemed insignificant compared to these other afflictions. After accomplishing each lap, instead of feeling encouraged, I plunged into despair over those remaining. My awareness of the world around me, including the spectators in the park and the bank employees tempting us with refreshments, dropped almost to zero. Head down I trudged forward. Each step was literally more painful than the one before. The image of an old prospector lost on the desert kept recurring in my mind. The temptation to stop and lie down for a while in the lush grass was tremendous. Near the end I could do no more than walk for a minute or two and then rest for much longer. The others around me seemed to be doing the same thing. It was hard to be aware of them for very long, however. After a rest, it was difficult to stand and begin again. For some reason it was heartening to discover that six or eight of the trainees had fainted and were prostrate under a shady tree at the finish line where they were receiving some medical attention. I, too, wanted to lie there with them, and yet I felt encouraged by the fact that I had not yet fallen. "I was stronger, I could make it," I thought to myself as I passed by. Other moments brought feverish dreams of somehow sneaking away. I reasoned that no one would notice if I slipped out of the park and returned just when the event was closing. Bushes became places I could hide behind, resting until the group was ready to go home. I kept going, I suppose, because I feared discovery. Although in a feverish state, I was in some sense quite capable of looking objectively at my response to this test of endurance. The content of lectures about *seishin* strength came back to me. I could see that I was spiritually weak, easily tempted, and inclined to quit. Under such stress some aspects of my thoughts were obviously not serving my interest in completing the course. Whatever will power I had arose from pride and an emerging, almost involuntary, belief in the *seishin* approach. If I was to finish, I needed spiritual strength. It angered and amused me to realize how cleverly this exercise had been conceived. I vowed over and over never to get involved in such a situation again, and yet, within days, when the memory of the physical pain had dimmed, I was taking great pride in my accomplishment and viewing my completion of the twenty-five mile course as proof that I could do anything I set my mind to.

These were the most notable activities of the *seishin kyooiku* program during those three months. In addition, there are a number of other aspects to spiritual training that deserve our attention. These efforts are less dramatic and are conducted on a "day in day out" basis.

In order to sponsor an intense group life (*shuudan seikatsu*) for its trainees, the institute staff has devised a number of interesting procedures and episodes. All leadership and direction of daily activities is placed in the hands of the trainees themselves who take turns commanding the various twelve man squads and assuming overall leadership of the entire group. Such things as clean up, kitchen and service details, the morning and evening assemblies, scheduling, and travel are all directed by the young men on a rotation basis. It was expected that a strong appreciation for the burdens of leadership and the need for cooperation would develop under such conditions. The most poignant illustrations of the necessity for order in group living came whenever the entire retinue of 120 travelled as a unit. The value of group discipline and coordination learned during the early sessions of military drill was evident at such times, and waiting at stations and elsewhere the young men enjoyed watching other less orderly groups of young people struggle with the problem of keeping together.

Closely related to the matter of group living is the popular theme of teamwork (*chiimu waaku*). (While this is a borrowed term, it is also translated as "harmony"). The form of organization for most competition is the team, and the regular squads usually serve as the basis for other activities. Studies related to banking, pursuit of hobbies, and other less obviously group oriented pursuits are arranged to require teamwork. While competition between individuals was seldom encouraged, group competition was a major means of motivation throughout the training period. It should be stressed that emphasis on teamwork is so common in Japanese society that none of the young trainees, even those who were critical of other aspects of the program, complained of an overemphasis on subordination of the individual to the group.

Physical conditioning has a definite role in spiritual training. Each morning and evening group exercises were held. On three occasions lectures on physical fitness were delivered, twice by outside specialists. Whenever feasible, the instructors had the trainees hike and even run to their destination. It is not unusual for lectures at the institute to be interrupted by an instructor for the purpose of correcting trainee posture, and the value of good posture, both to health and to mental concentration, is often stressed. Underlying these efforts is the assumption that good physical condition and proper posture are fundamental to the development of spiritual power.

Newcomers who have trouble developing enough skill and speed to pass the bank's standard abacus test find that practicing the abacus is an exercise with strong *seishin* overtones. The practice required is long and tedious, and there are no shortcuts to developing speed. Practice is left entirely up to the individual trainees, but the instructors watch their response to this situation with great interest. Those that do not practice or who give up easily are privately cautioned in *seishin* terms and encouraged to try harder. The moral that dogged persistence will solve the problem is one that lies at the heart of *seishin* oriented thought. Practicing the abacus, like many other aspects of the overall training program, is not officially described as part of spiritual training, but because of the wide applicability of its principles, *seishin* philosophy influences it and most other training activities.

Discussion

As already mentioned, *seishin kyooiku* is commonly translated as "spiritual education," but the meaning of "spiritual" in this case is far from clear to non-Japanese. Certainly, the education described above is quite different than, say, the "spiritual education" of Christian churches. For Japanese the concept *seishin* is sufficiently general and vague to allow many interpretations and variations,[8] yet underlying the diversity are common patterns of thought and practice which may be described.

If we begin by using experience as the groundwork for our explication of Japanese "spiritualism," then perhaps for Westerners it would be useful to keep in mind the parallels between the activities described above and the practices of such quasi-educational organizations in the West as summer camps, Sunday schools, sports teams, boy scouts, and military training. These all claim special qualities and abilities in the socialization of both adults and youth which formal public education, according to the claims, cannot or will not offer. We have no overreaching word for the special kind of education these institutions offer in common, but it is not too difficult to appreciate certain similarities underlying all of them.

In Japan, training in social membership and the cultivation of the individual (*shuuyoo* and *kyooyoo*) have for centuries been very serious enterprises regarded as imperative to the creation of an orderly society, individual character, and personal fulfillment. In the Chinese tradition the properly organized state is believed to depend on leadership by men of outstanding character, and the Japanese, especially during the Tokugawa period (1600–1868), have also emphasized this perspective. In China, personal development was primarily the concern of the scholar-official and activities and disciplines of a scholarly nature were accordingly emphasized, whereas in Tokugawa Japan, the pursuit of the same basic goals was strongly flavored by the fact that the Japanese elite was largely military in outlook and experience. In both China and Japan the social benefit of such training was seldom separated from the acknowledged benefits to the individual, and various arts and military skills, such as judo and the tea cult in Japan, were appreciated as important paths of spiritual growth. A point to note is that unlike in the West, there arose no distinctions encouraging the separation of the individual and the social or the sacred and the secular in education.

After the Meiji restoration of 1868, the responsibility for spiritual education in Japan shifted from local governments, private academies, and commercial enterprises to the new national educational system. Until defeat in 1945 the government pursued a policy of spiritual education for the masses based on a combination of the teachings and methods of Confucian China, the samurai heritage, and the morality of the Tokugawa merchants. What the West has long attempted to accomplish through religious schools, youth organizations, and sports, the Japanese chose to institutionalize in the public school program proper, a fact the reformers of the American occupation hardly appreciated in their enthusiasm to root out the "totalitarian," "nationalistic," and "militaristic" strains in Japanese education. According to spokesmen for companies now practicing *seishin kyooiku*, this approach was for Japanese synonymous with education in good citizenship, and when it was purged from the school system, an educational vacuum was created. Company spiritual training, they explain, is but an attempt to reinstate conventional and necessary socialization practices which, for political reasons, the government has been reluctant to revive. Does spiritual education mark a revival of Japanese militarism? Companies assert they are experimenting with this form of education for the more immediate reason that they wish to produce more highly socialized and effective employees. The fact that spiritual education has deep historical connections with the Japanese military tradition serves to color spiritual training, they say, but it does not mean that it is militaristic in the usual sense of the term. Spiritual training is primarily the product of a reaction against both the loosening of social ties in contemporary Japan and the Western influence that is blamed for this trend.

How may we define the term *seishin*? If the frame of reference is a very general one contrasting physical and mental, the concept *seishin* would most likely be placed in the mental column. Attitudes, will power, concentration, and many other "mental" qualities are important aspects of spiritual power. Yet this kind of distinction obscures more than it clarifies, for the physical/mental distinction is not central to the concept. It is true that the "mind over matter," and "power of positive thought" philosophies approach the meaning of *seishin*, but there are differences. In the case of traditional Japanese thought, the mind/body duality (which does exist in Japanese expressions such as *nikutaiteki* "physical or corporal") is overridden by the concept *kokoro*, important in Zen and in many traditional forms of education. *Kokoro*, translated "heart" or "spirit," represents the broad area of individual psychosomatic unity. The state of an individual's *kokoro* may be composed or disturbed, and there are numerous terms for both of these. Composure implies that both the mind and the body operate properly, efficiently, and in harmony; in the state of disturbance, the mind and body are accordingly upset, undependable, and involved in an adverse way with one another. Both of these states may be distinguished as to degree. Learning to achieve composure is one goal of *seishin* training, and a composed *kokoro* is regarded as a major source of *seishin* strength.

Many lessons in bank training are specifically aimed at teaching the trainees how to attain composure, or at least to awaken in them a greater awareness of the inter-relationship of the physical and mental aspects of disturbance. Zen meditation and the emphasis on posture are two outstanding examples. Yet, composure is not an end in itself so much as it is a basis for more effective individual action. The standard by which spiritual strength (*seishinryoku*) is measured is performance. The outward manifestations of strength are such things as the ability to endure trouble and pain, a coolness in the face of threat, patience, dependability, persistence, self-reliance, and intense personal motivation; qualities we would associate with "strong personal character." Yet

spiritual strength is not measured by performance, no matter how
spectacular, that results solely from cleverness or physical power,
although these qualities are often interpreted as products of spiritual strength.

Illustrations of *seishin* strength hinge on difficulties that test
a man's will, particularly his will to carry on in some social purpose.[9] Most often these difficulties are "psychological" (actually
psychosomatic) in nature. They include fear, disillusionment, bore-
dom, loneliness, and failure, as well as the more obvious problems
of physical pain and the temptations of easy reward. Any form of
stress that tempts a person to resign his effort or to escape a problem is relevant as a test. Similarly, any quality that helps the individual pass such tests is part of his spiritual strength. For this
reason verbal education in morality can be regarded as contributing directly to spiritual power, if it provides conviction and
strengthens the individual's resolve to carry on.

Education for spiritual strength uses artificially created tests
to build up staying power for life's actual tests. The most dramatic
examples in the bank's training program are the endurance walk
and *zazen*. The designs for tests are usually quite well considered,
for there are a number of factors governing their success as educational devices. First they can be neither so easy that they are not
really tests, nor so hard that they cannot be passed. Secondly, the
experience of passing them must reveal to the individual both the
process of temptation and the methods of dispelling it. That is, the
trainee must be prepared to experience the test in *seishin* terms,
and this often requires considerable teaching, in the normal sense,
before the event.

The test must also be of some relevance to the trials of real
life either by virtue of imitation or analogy. An endurance walk
may not seem very relevant to work in a bank, but the instructors
pointed out that the temptation to take a forbidden drink of water
"which costs nothing" is like the temptation to steal from one's own
bank. An analogy was also made between the arduousness of sitting in *zazen* and the problem of maintaining concentration during
mundane clerking in the bank.

No matter what form of test is devised for training purposes,
the key element in the whole process is the experience of emotional
wavering and the "spiritual" struggle within the individual to carry
on until the test is completed. Passing any *seishin* test is not a matter of scoring high, or coming in ahead of others. Competition is
within self, and success is marked by completion of the ordeal.
Enduring one test to its conclusion will make completion of subse-

quent, similar tests less difficult, it is assumed. During the moments of greatest wavering, the individual experiences his own individual weaknesses with heightened awareness and on the basis of this self-knowledge, he is enabled to proceed to overcome such weakness and prepare to endure even greater tests in the future.

According to *seishin* thought, "incorrect" attitudes are often the source of personal difficulty.[10] What is meant by attitudes in this instance is not opinions, such as political opinions, but rather the issue is the person's general attitude toward things around him to which he must personally respond. For example, the bank's purpose in using *rotoo* is to teach a better attitude toward work, one that is positive and enthusiastic. With such an attitude, according to *seishin* theory, the individual could better enjoy working as well as work better. The basis of a proper attitude, in this meaning of the term, begins with acceptance of necessity and responsibility. Instead of fighting life's requirements, such as work, the most satisfactory attitude is to acknowledge and accept necessary difficulties. To regret or attempt to avoid them only leads to frustration, disappointment, and upset. The dimension accepting/resisting, which is consistently important throughout Japanese life, is the key to evaluating the "correctness" of a person's attitudes, and judgments depend less on verbal expression than on other actions. Complaining, criticizing, arguing, and other forms of resistance constitute examples of the kinds of actions that evidence improper attitudes. Ready acceptance of unpleasant or difficult tasks, on the other hand, illustrate a man's correct attitude. Those who complained during training, for example, were asked to reconsider their attitude.

While *seishin kyooiku* seeks to sponsor an accepting attitude[11] toward all of life's necessities, greatest attention is paid to developing the proper attitude toward social responsibilities.[12] The requirements of a social system and the interdependent quality of society, both of which make the diligent performance of every role important, are taught as the basic facts of life. The necessity that individual responsibility to the role assigned by the system be accepted and fulfilled follows from this fact. In the bank's training, improper attitudes toward tasks and exercises were frequently pointed out by the training staff, and much of the morally oriented lectures and reading focused on teaching acceptance of the necessities of social life. One such reality, international economic competition, was an ever-present theme in these discussions.

While social realities are underlined, individual requirements, other than the most elementary necessities, are ignored or treated as unimportant. It is a firm principle that individual needs and desires are properly challenged and controlled as part of the program to develop spiritual strength, and there are numerous historical cases in which the coincidence of a desire to demonstrate spiritual strength on the part of the trainees have resulted in endurance tests causing serious injury and even death in extreme cases. In the post-war period the training activities of student outing clubs have produced the only examples of how a *seishin* orientation can produce tragic results when the limits of physical endurance are ignored.

For any person, the correct and most satisfying goals according to *seishin* thought are fulfillment of his social role and achievement in his chosen personal pursuit. These goals are assumed to be self-evident. The spiritually strong man is by definition a contributor to society. He excels in cooperation and service to others because he has mastered the art of self-discipline. The bank's training program strongly emphasizes social values such as cooperation, yet these are regarded by the training staff as rudimentary lessons that, once learned, allow the individual to graduate to more independent kinds of spiritual development. Training to social necessities is also stressed because of its immediate relevance to the trainee's transition from being a student to membership in the bank, and because it is felt that today's young people are not learning in the public school system to subordinate themselves to the group. Executives of the bank state that socialization should not be of such concern to companies; it is more appropriately carried on in the family and the school, but as already mentioned, they feel these other institutions, particularly the new "progressive" schools, have failed to perform this function adequately.

A few more characteristics of the *seishin* approach to education should be noted briefly:

1. In *seishin* education, emphasis is placed on non-verbal forms of behavior. A well-behaved but silent class, for example, is not necessarily an indication of lethargy, stupidity, or the failure of the teacher. It is likely to be interpreted as evidence that students are well disciplined, receptive, and respectful. In some instances, a *seishin* orientation may take a skeptical view of verbal logic and its forms of understanding, favoring experiences as the basis of knowledge instead.

2. Rather than viewing difficulties and hardships the students face as barriers to education and therefore things to be overcome by better facilities or improved methods of instruction, *seishin*

based education is liable to regard problems in the educational situation as valuable assets to the training process itself. They are tests and therefore useful. Environmental problems are viewed as opportunities rather than as the source of failure.

3. A knowledge of self and self-reflection (*jikaku* and *hansei*) are stressed in *seishin* training and the blame for difficulties or failure, individual or social, will be placed most heavily on spiritual weakness rather than on a lack of knowledge or inadequacy of social organization. The *seishin* approach to social betterment gives precedence to spiritual reform over social reform. Schools are viewed as instruments of change and improvement, but their influence should be over individual character rather than over the shape of society.

4. Rather than encouraging students to consider themselves as different from one another and thus sponsoring individualistic thought and creativity, *seishin* education sponsors outward conformity to teachers' examples and group standards. Nonconformity is viewed as disruptive of group unity and a sign of individual character weakness. It is thought that conformity is made from conviction, not dullness, and that to conform to the group is difficult, rather than easy.

5. *Seishin* education aims to help the individual achieve contentment through the development of an ordered and stable psyche free from confusion and frustration. This is to be attained through the gradual conquest of *waga* or *ga* (one's primitive self, or id in Freudian terms). The phrase expressing this process, *waga o korosu* (literally "kill the self"), is a common expression related to the *seishin* approach.

6. Whenever possible in *seishin* education, competition is organized along group rather than individual lines and many events have no obvious competitive quality. This is not because competition hurts feelings, but because it disrupts group unity and because the real competition takes place within each individual.

7. The unchanging nature of spiritual problems and their solutions is a basic assumption of the *seishin* approach. Teachers, parents, and senior students are, by virtue of greater experience and training, spiritually more advanced and therefore worthy of respect and authority. Age does not become a sign of out-datedness, and intergenerational continuity and concord in the unchanging pursuit of spiritual strength is encouraged.

I would, in conclusion, like to offer a few observations on the significance of this material to the emerging field of the anthropology of education.

1. The bank example represents a kind of education which to date has received very little attention. It is not centered in a school system; it involves adults; it is not universal for the society; and it is operated by a kind of institution that in other societies may conduct little or no education at all. Such conditions would hardly attract the attention of anthropologists about to study education, and yet, at least in Japan, such forms of education are quite significant. It is my impression that educational anthropologists have devoted relatively far too much attention to studies of schooling, schools, and school systems and not enough to religious education, sports training, military indoctrination, and the countless other ways societies seek to improve and integrate their members.

2. The manner in which *seishin* concepts regarding human psychology and the methods of *seishin* education interlock indicates that the cross-cultural study of education must take cognizance of the culture's "common sense" psychology in analyzing the intent and methods of any educational endeavor. That is, there is a broad area of overlap between concepts of education and those of psychology in any situation, and the educational anthropologist dealing with a non-Western educational system should be prepared to inquire deeply into the psychological understandings of the people involved. One benefit of a greater attention to ethnopsychology in education would be a greater clarification of how our own native psychology influences the manner in which we pursue educational goals.

3. The similarity between the bank's program and processes and methods found in certain Japanese forms of psychiatric therapy, Zen training, religious rituals of individual reform, and practices of therapy for criminals in Japan illustrates a simple lesson, namely, that educational efforts which seek some kind of character change or improvement are perhaps best studied within a single theoretical framework, one that will also adequately account for other kinds of psychological transformations. At various points in the training reported here, for example, anxiety or deprivation was artificially intensified and then reduced, creating a strong sense of relief and catharsis which served to strengthen certain intended directions of change in a

trainee's view of himself and of his relationship with society. The parallels between education and such processes as initiation, therapy, and conversion would deserve more attention.

4. Whether the bank's program is to be labelled education, initiation, socialization, conversion, or therapy is not, however, a profitable question to ask, except as it illustrates the pitfalls of viewing education as equivalent with schooling. There is a strong academic inclination to understand education as verbal instruction leading to improved storage and manipulation of symbolic information. This is what explicitly happens in schools between teachers and students. Yet learning and maturation may be sponsored by many means, not just verbal instruction. *Seishin kyooiku* emphasizes experience and the development of spiritual strength. There are, no doubt, many other valued avenues of human growth which are as unlike Japanese spiritual education as they are unlike classroom instruction. The use of various hallucinogenic drugs to educate religious initiates and train practitioners is one widespread example.

Just as the study of kinship began to make notable headway only after considerable skepticism arose about the ethnocentricity of the concerns and impulses which originally gave it momentum, so the anthropology of education could benefit from a reexamination of its implicit understanding of education.

SECTION IV

Management and Marketing in Japan

The specific context of Japanese behavior that has thrown Japanese and Americans into frequent interaction with each other is the subject of Section IV. The remarkable success of Japanese business has naturally led to a broad interest in knowledge about "how they do it." The American company's desire for—or necessity of—entering into commercial relationship with Japanese companies has made the availability of accurate descriptions of Japanese business practices both urgent and essential. Everything that occurs within the Japanese organization is a reflection of Japanese culture. Thus, even though many of the selections in this and subsequent sections do not address the link between culture and behavior as explicitly as the articles in earlier sections, viewing these selections from the perspective of the framework presented in the Introduction will continue to be useful.

In "A Guide to Japanese Business Practices," Mayumi Otsubo surveys the whole range of behaviors that Americans will confront when seeking business relationships with the Japanese. The Japanese, as we have seen in the previous sections, are very concerned with observing proper form in all situations. Every business encounter in Japan begins with the ritual of exchanging business cards, and as in everything else, there are prescribed ways of conducting this ritual. The most important function of the business card is the determination of relative rank. Otsubo follows the foreign visitor through all the phases of his or her interaction with the Japanese: the bow, the guest room, gift-exchange, and so on. Another aspect of Japanese business organization that is often perplexing to Americans is job titles, and the organizational power associated with them. Otsubo reveals the working of the differentia-

tion principle that underlies job titles: "It is expected that you are called by title regardless of time, occasion, or place," even in bars and restaurants. One's rank at work carries over into all other interpersonal contexts. The primacy of the organization over the individual is also revealed in the Japanese tendency to identify themselves as members of XYZ company instead of by profession.

The collectivity orientation of the Japanese is responsible for the uniquely Japanese way of making decisions: proposals are circulated to all employees who may be affected by the proposal. The process is time consuming, but failure to follow it would increase the risk of disturbance of harmony.

Whereas Otsubo discusses this consensus style of decision making, in the next selection the focus is on the motivation that lies at the back of such decision making. In "Strategic Planning in Japan," Milton C. Lauenstein reveals that strategic planning and decision making in Japanese companies is driven by the overriding objective of the well-being of the employees. Japanese executives pay close attention to factors that affect prestige, like market share rather than profitability, because in Japanese society the company's prestige reflects upon the prestige or status of its employees. Lauenstein also points out that the policy of lifetime employment allows Japanese companies to focus on the long-term, but also requires very careful selection procedures. We see here the corporate consequences of the Japanese preference for stability and continuity.

Japanese attitudes toward women at work reflect the strong cultural support for a sharp sex role differentiation. Attitude surveys indicate that a majority of Japanese, both men and women, continue to believe that women should devote their best energies to raising the children, and men should dedicate themselves to their careers. Nonetheless, more Japanese women than ever before are working, and attitudes are changing. Paul Lansing and Kathryn Ready note in "Hiring Women Managers in Japan: An Alternative for Foreign Employers" that, although full-time employment for women is becoming more common, Japanese employers of Japanese women still do not consider women to be managerial material. Even when a woman declares her intention to pursue a full-time career, her chances of being promoted to a managerial position are slim. At the same time, foreign employers in Japan find it difficult to attract well-qualified men. Lansing and Ready hit upon the intriguing suggestion that foreign employers actively pursue the strategy of hiring young Japanese women for managerial positions. The authors review the legal aspects of women at work and the statistics on the labor force participation of women in Japan. They next examine the cultural pressures on Japanese women and conclude that, with adequate attention to the sensitivities of the Japanese people, the alternative of hiring Japanese women for managerial careers could be very beneficial for foreign employers in Japan.

In the next selection in this section, Tomasz Mroczkowski and Masao Hanaoka look at the future of the Japanese style of human resources management. In "Continuity and Change in Japanese Management," Mroczkowski and Hanaoka note that businesses in Japan, as in other countries, face an environment much different from what they encountered when the current system of management was developed in 1945. Under the pressure of this changed environment, Japanese managers are slowly but surely modifying their managerial practices. For example, the need to lower labor costs comes into conflict with the policy of lifetime employment. One response to this problem being attempted by some Japanese companies is inter-company personnel leasing. Another major problem facing Japanese managers emerges from changes in attitudes toward work. Young people are less willing than their fathers to devote their whole life to their organizations, and talented youngsters are unwilling to wait the requisite number of years before they are given opportunities to utilize their special talents. The pressure of international competition is also forcing managers to encourage independence, ambition, and creativity. In response, merit- and performance-based evaluation and reward systems are increasingly being grafted on to the traditional promotion by seniority policies. All these changes are unlikely to radically alter the traditional management system, which the authors believe will be retained, but modified to make it more flexible. This is consistent with our suggestion that organizational policies in Japan are deeply rooted in culture, and thus not likely to change rapidly or radically.

Politicians may engage in "tough negotiations" and trade missions may fly back and forth from the United States to Japan, but in the final analysis America's trade imbalance will ease only to the extent that American companies are able to get their products to Japanese consumers and convince them to buy American products. This requires better understanding of Japanese consumers as well as a more thorough knowledge of the marketing and distribution system in Japan. The next two selections in this section address these vital issues.

In "Market Research the Japanese Way" Johny K. Johansson and Ikujiro Nonaka quote a Japanese executive who expresses a not uncommon sentiment among Japanese businessmen: "Why do Americans do so much marketing research? You can find out what you need by travelling around and visiting the retailers who carry your product." Johansson and Nonaka report that Japanese companies do use the tools and techniques popular in the United States, but they trust their instincts first. The Japanese tend to utilize two kinds of marketing data. Soft data is obtained from visits to dealers and retailers, and hard data is generated from company records of shipments, inventories, and sales. Even when attitude surveys are conducted, the goal is to obtain data about the experience of actual consumers of the product, and not about the attitudes of the general public.

We find these marketing practices to be consistent with the cultural tendencies identified in the Introduction. Zen engendered distrust of the overly rational and the consequent development of intuition noted by Durlabhji in his article in Section I is directly relevant to Johansson and Nonaka's discussion. The overall impression of a press-the-flesh or human contact approach to obtaining marketing data, compared to the more scientific, "dry" approach popular in the United States seems to be exactly what one would expect from the more affectively oriented Japanese.

One of the major areas of trade conflict between the United States and Japan is related to the complex, multi-layered distribution system in Japan. Japan has more wholesalers and retailers per capita than any other industrialized country. Reportedly, wholesalers and retailers show little enthusiasm for the products of foreign suppliers even when the terms are more attractive than those of the local manufacturers. The primacy of long-standing relationships over pecuniary considerations means that suppliers who have established channels of distribution have a tremendous advantage over newcomers. Continuation of an old relationship, even if less profitable, is preferred over change to a new supplier. Shortage of storage space has led to a practice of tiny inventories and frequent resupply. Manufacturers in Japan provide an incredible array of services to their retailers, and readily accept returns of any unsold merchandise. Even if a foreign supplier can overcome all these obstacles to gaining a foothold in the Japanese market, competition from a local manufacturer can endanger whatever success has been achieved, since the Japanese will allegedly abandon a foreign supplier if a comparable local source comes along. All these features conspire to make marketing in Japan a nightmare for foreign companies.

In "Distribution in Japan: Problems and Changes," Michael R. Czinkota provides a thorough overview of the Japanese distribution system. Czinkota maintains that many of the complaints about the Japanese distribution system ignore changes that have occurred over the last two decades. His review of these changes leads him to an optimistic assessment of the prospects for foreign marketers.

13

A Guide to Japanese Business Practices*

Mayumi Otsubo

When Meeting the Japanese

The Business Card

Japanese business greetings usually begin with the exchanging of
business cards. This is a ceremony Japanese business people
observe regardless of occasion or place whenever they meet a business person or are introduced to someone. They exchange business
cards on the street, in a commuter bus, or even a bar. When going
to Japan on business, you are always expected to give your business card to a person you meet and you should accept his business
card with thanks. You would have to do so even if you never plan
to see this person again. It is simply what is done.

The business card is the identification or credential of almost
anyone in business in Japan. The business card is often accepted
by large restaurant or store managers as if it was a credit card. Of
course, you would have to work for a reputable and creditable corporation and must be in a well-regarded position in that company.

The Bow

When a Japanese greets his customer, visitor, superior, or fellow worker, he bows by bending his body forward. This is called the *ojigi*. Most Japanese perform the *ojigi* only when greeting another Japanese. When a Japanese greets a Chinese, a Korean, an American, or a person from another country, he usually does not bow but extends his hand for a handshake. The Japanese observe the *ojigi* even when they greet fellow Japanese in foreign countries. Some combine the traditional *ojigi* with the handshake when they meet a fellow countryman on a street in Los Angeles or New York.

In the *ojigi* greeting, they do not bow just once, but three or four times or even more before they start verbal greetings. Japanese etiquette calls for *ojigi* in greeting regardless of time and place. The deeper the bow, done gracefully and slowly, the more courteous it is. It is no wonder that in Japan one sometimes comes up against a sudden congestion on a busy street or in a crowded public transport.

When the Western businessman visits the office of a sizeable company in Japan, he will be greeted with handshakes instead of *ojigi*. He will most likely be led to a guest room instead of the private office of the executive he is calling on.

The Guest Room

Company visitors are usually not invited to the office of the person on whom they are calling. The higher the position of the caller, the less the chance of being invited into the office, because it is considered informal and sometimes even impolite to ask a caller into the office or to come up to one's desk.

The office layout of Japanese companies contains guest rooms or drawing rooms where visitors are normally received. They serve the same function as the private offices in large American and European corporations. It is here that the caller discusses business with management personnel or negotiates with department heads.

The guest room is sometimes a place for serious negotiations. On such occasions, the foreign businessman finds that he is faced not only by his Japanese counterpart, but also by his subordinates and other staff members who seem little related to the subject under discussion. This one-against-many situation may seem intimidating. However, it is not true that the Japanese intention is to overwhelm the other party by attending a meeting in numbers.

All the people attending are there because they want to familiarize themselves with the subject as it relates to their particular functions. They listen to the conversation very carefully so that they may be able, if later required, to provide information, advice or comments, or to coordinate matters. The Japanese tend to move and act in a group, particularly when they are dealing with a very serious matter. But the Western businessman invariably feels that Japanese meetings are loaded with irrelevant people, which for them is time-consuming and costly.

Actually, this format saves a great deal of time and energy which otherwise would be needed to explain the contents of the conversation to the staff or related people of other departments for necessary coordination. Japanese management also believes that this format gives their employees an opportunity to meet more people and to participate in the negotiation process. This participation not only motivates the employees, but also creates a better understanding of and consensus on the subject, thus fostering cooperation with employees.

There are also practical reasons why Japanese call in groups of two or more on a foreign businessman. It may be that they are working together and that the younger one is being trained. It may be that the subordinate is taken along in order to save the time and energy to transmit to him later what transpired at the meeting. The subordinate needs to know because he is the one who will do the follow-up work. It may be that it is to prevent misunderstanding arising from discussing the subject in a foreign language. They can compare notes later to see whether they understood things correctly. In addition, they could analyze problems from different angles.

The Gift-Giving Custom

While it is not a mandatory custom, it is true that a Japanese usually carries a small gift with him when calling on a person for the first time. A well-chosen gift might serve as a conversation opener. Some people take a gift as a small token of thanks for the opportunity given him to meet the person or for the time he is spending for him. Some hope that the gift will act as a reminder when they need to call again to follow up on the matter discussed in the first meeting. Japanese people consider the gift as a lubricant in human relations.

Whatever the reason given for taking a small gift on a first visit, there is no denying that the intention is to gain the goodwill of the person visited. Yet, it can safely be said that normally there is no taint of bribery in this type of gift giving. A gift of this nature is a sort of business calling card and should not be taken seriously unless the object presented is of extraordinary or exorbitant value.

What then is exorbitant? It is very difficult to define what would be exorbitant as a calling gift. From the receiver's side, the definition might be "an object of such high value that one feels an obligation if he accepts it." In other words, the gift must not make the receiver feel obligated.

What does a Japanese do if he is presented with an exorbitant gift, which he could not reject at the time but which might later be construed as a bribe? He simply returns the gift by mail or delivers to the giver a present of equivalent value immediately. It is considered that this cancels out the original gift and releases one from any future obligations.

Some Japanese are always giving things as a token of thanks or as a gesture of friendship or goodwill. Many people present a gift to persons they visit after returning from an extended trip. This type of gift is called *omiyage*. People often give *omiyage* when they visit customers, friends, fellow workers, or even their boss. They bring an *omiyage* especially when they visit acquaintances in a distant place. If an Osaka businessman visits a customer in Tokyo after a long interval, he will most probably take along an *omiyage*. As an extension of this practice, Japanese business people visiting their customers, associates, friends, or professionals in other countries invariably take along some sort of *omiyage*.

The Japanese love to give gifts. They seem to be giving them all the time. If a Japanese should present you with a gift, just accept it with a "thank-you" (*arigato*, in Japanese) and you need not feel any embarrassment or obligation (unless it is something extravagantly expensive). When you receive a gift from a Japanese, you may open it in front of that person. However, when you present a gift to a Japanese, do not expect the recipient to open it immediately in front of you. It is simply a Japanese custom not to do so.

There are two periods in the year when business corporations give gifts. One is at the year-end and the other is at the end of the first half-year. The year-end one is called *oseibo* and it covers approximately the period from the end of November to the end of December. The other one is called *ochugen* and it covers the period from the end of June to the middle of July. During these two periods, companies send gifts to their customers or to those with whom they have business relations. The gifts are to express thanks for patronage or for favors received. Not only businessmen but also ordinary Japanese give gifts during these two periods—to friends, teachers, relatives, and others to whom they feel indebted in some way or another.

The items presented are inexpensive, ordinary things such as beer, *saké*, whiskey, sugar, canned goods, cookies, soap, towels, and shirts. A trip to any Tokyo department store during the *oseibo* or *ochugen* period will reveal at once what kinds of items serve as gifts. The stores set aside a large space to display suggested gift items and shopping consultants are present to suggest what is best for your gift-giving budget.

Corporate Titles and Organization

The titles in a Japanese business organization are often confusing to American and European people. At the top management level, there are a few positions which are a hodge-podge of British and American titles. The highest titles in the Japanese corporation are chairman, vice-chairman, president, vice-president, senior managing director, and director.

The chairman is the chairman of the board of directors, but the position is often only symbolic and the chairman might not even be the chief executive officer of the company. The title of chairman is often given to a semi-retired president or is simply an honorary title. There is a tendency among many active and large corporations for the chairman to hold the authority and power to represent the corporation and act as its chief executive officer.

Strictly speaking, there are no such titles or positions in Japanese corporations as chief executive officer or chief operating officer, which are typical of U.S. corporations. Japanese business law requires the appointment of a "representative officer" who has authority to represent the corporation. There can be more than one representative officer. However, there is no legal requirement to appoint a chairman or a president in a corporation. The titles "president" and "chairman" are products of business custom or a matter of convenience. When you meet a Japanese executive and receive his business card, read his title carefully. If his title reads "representative director and president" or "representative director and chairman" or even "representative director and senior managing director," he is the most powerful man in the organization. His authority equals that of the chief executive officer in a U.S. corporation.

"President" as a title is not easily translated into Japanese as there are a variety of names for the head of an organization. The president of a bank in Japan is not called a president, but the name *todori* is translated as president when it is printed on his English business card. Recently, a woman was introduced in a Japanese newspaper and her title was translated as vice *todori* of a U.S. bank, even though she was just a manager of a small research department in the bank. It is often puzzling for Japanese to find so many vice-presidents in American financial institutions. Practically every branch manager of a U.S. bank is a vice-president. Some U.S. banks have more than 100 vice-presidents and some New York advertising agencies have 50 vice-presidents. This is not so in Japan. The vice-president is the person who is most influential next to the president. I am under the impression that most of the vice-presidents in U.S. corporations—except for very large traditional corporations—are very much victims of status inflation. They are usually equivalent to the manager of a large department of a Japanese corporation as far as their authority and power are concerned.

In U.S. corporations, the real power and authority rest with the executive vice-president or senior vice-president, as opposed to all the other vice-presidents. However, there are no such vice-presidents in Japanese corporations. Instead, there is a senior managing director or executive director, although these positions are not necessarily equal to the executive vice-president. Most possibly, the Japanese vice-president is equal to the executive vice-president in U.S. corporations.

"Director" is a very tricky title. In Japanese business practice, the title of "director" usually indicates a member of the board of directors who also performs some executive function at the operating level. In the United States, the title "director" is often a fancy name given to a certain office holder such as financial director or public relations director.

Japanese business law requires that installation of an auditor at the top management level. This is not the internal auditor, but what we call a statutory auditor who is considered to be the representative of shareholders independent from the board of directors and acts as a watchdog to see to it that the corporation does not commit any illegalities. In addition, this auditor audits the books from the viewpoint of shareholders in cooperation with certified public accountants.

You rarely find an outsider on the board of directors in a Japanese corporation. Most of the directors are nominated from among the employees of the corporation. The first step on the ladder of promotion to the top management of a corporation is the nomination for board membership and the next step would be the shareholders' approval. If you are successful, you would be appointed as a plain director. As "director" is one of the most desired titles sought by the working people, the management tends to reserve as many director's positions for employees as possible. Therefore, there is hardly any room left to accept outside directors. Thus, in a strict sense, capital and management are not separated in most cases.

One of the most startling aspects of this system is the fact that many of the directors—or sometimes even the president—have had experience as officers in the labor unions. Some have even served as the president of the union with which they now have to negotiate. Some people claim that this is one reason why there is so much cooperative spirit and atmosphere between labor and management (although there are, in some cases, hostile labor-management relations such as is often found in American labor-management relations).

As an American, when do you feel the value of your title in daily life? You feel it when you use it in your business letter or on a document or when you present your business card. In Japan, you feel your title whenever you have a conversation with your boss, fellow workers, subordinates, or even customers. For example, suppose a Mr. Ichiro Nakayama works for the marketing department as manager and you are his subordinate. You never call him "Ichiro" or "Mr. Nakayama." You are supposed to call him "Manager Mr. Nakayama" ("Nakayama *bucho*" in Japanese) or just "manager" ("*bucho*"). It is very impersonal by American standards. Sometimes people even address him as *bucho-san* ("Mr. Manager"). You can call your associates by name, but only rarely. If you are not a manager and you want to call the attention of one of your associates, you can call him by name (such as "Tanaka-san") if he too is not a manager.

The Japanese are very status conscious. They expect to be called by their title. Even among top management, it is expected that you are called by title regardless of time, occasion, or place—whether in a bar, train, airplane, restaurant, or even geisha party. You feel the value of the title in Japan whenever you talk with someone. Calling each other by title is a deeply rooted practice among Japanese business people.

In the middle management of Japanese corporations, there are four categories of manager.

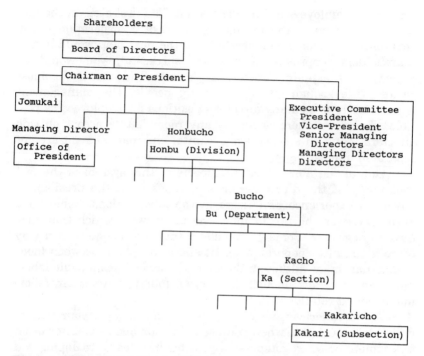

Figure 13.1 Model Strata of Japanese Corporations

- The highest ranking manager is called *honbucho,* or general manager, and is in charge of several departments.

- The *bucho,* or department head, usually reports to the *honbucho* and is in charge of several sections.

- The *kacho,* or section head, reports to the *bucho* and is in charge of several subsections.

- The *kakaricho,* or subsection head, is considered to be the counterpart of the supervisor in America.

Japanese business practice is to translate *honbu* as division, *bu* as department, *ka* as section, and *kakari* as subsection or unit. *Cho* means head in English, so *honbucho* means division head. [These are shown in Figure 13.1.]

Nevertheless, there are wide variations in translation. Quite a few new organization units have been invented besides these formal and traditional ones. These are called office, group, room, chamber, center, and unit. These creations have been made partly to satisfy the desire of status seekers. Some of them are called variously leader, in-charge, or head. Some of them are given the title "manager," but it is a nominal title and some of them have no subordinates or even a secretary.

What's Your Profession

Suppose someone asks you about your profession, how would you answer? You would probably say that you are an engineer, a programmer, an economist, or an accountant. Most Japanese people would answer differently. They would say that they are working for Sony, or Honda, or Canon and they would never mention their occupation. If you insist on knowing what he does in his company, he may then say that he works in the research and development department or in the accounting department. However, he would never say that he is a scientist, economist, or accountant. In their minds, most Japanese workers are not so sure whether they are working in their own profession or working just for their company. Probably, most Japanese workers would be unable to answer a questionnaire asking them to indicate their profession. They would usually indicate only that they are a company person or a salaried person (in Japanized English, a "salary man").

There are quite a few people with a specialist title (such as researcher, advisor, senior system engineer) which are sometimes called *susha* (in-charge). Some specialist titles are nominal titles given to a semi-retired person or to a person on the waiting list for some future assignment. Some specialist titles are given to ambitious workers in lieu of the title of *kacho* because of the lack of adequate positions for promotion. These specialist titles are not only confusing, but also are often not good enough to satisfy the ego of ambitious status seekers. Generally speaking, specialist titles are not accepted as having status value in Japanese society since they do not indicate a rank in the organization. Thus, many corporations tend to indicate the rank or grade of the specialist title and people in business tend to call the specialist by rank—for example, "*Kacho* Otani" instead of "Economist Otani."

Many people in Japanese corporations are often transferred between unrelated jobs or departments without giving enough consideration to specific requirements in knowledge, skill, and experience. A person working in a sales department could be transferred to the personnel department, or a person working in the research section may be transferred to the accounting department. Such transfers happen often and easily in Japan but not in the U.S. Most people given the title of specialist in Japanese corporations are not specialist in the Western concept, but rather are generalists.

Some of the organizational units in Japanese corporations need some explanation as they are rather unique:

- *General Affairs*—The general affairs section or department handles miscellaneous functions which are independent of each other but are not large enough to set up a separate and independent organization. As the functions and authority of such organizations vary from company to company, nobody can judge the activities of the general affairs section by its name alone. Some of the heads of such sections are very influential. They might even be a member of the board. The head of the general affairs department may supervise office management, custodial services, shareholder affairs, training, transportation (company cars), and office supplies. In some companies, he might even handle public affairs, accounting, and hiring. Some general affairs sections act as a staff section under the direct control of the branch manager. In such cases, the head of general affairs handles almost all of the corporate functions of this area on behalf of the corporate headquarters.

- *The Office of the President*—The office of the president is a unique institution found in many Japanese corporations. In most cases, the office of the president handles the so-called general staff activities. The head of the office of the president is the chief of staff and usually reports to the president and chairman and other board members, advising them on many important corporate strategic matters. Often, the head of such an office is a member of the board.

- *The Liaison Department*—Originally, the liaison department of many Japanese corporations handled international matters and government relations. Many of the international functions were separated and became independent as many Japanese corporations became internationalized. The liaison department of many international corporations is now called international relations or the international business section and handles international negotiation, licensing, joint ventures, and international meetings (but not exporting and importing).

- *The Legal Department*—You will rarely find a legal department in Japanese corporations. This does not mean, however, that there are no such functions. Legal matters are handled by the secretary section in Japanese corporations. The secretary section, or "secretariat," is not a secretarial pool, but rather an organizational unit which serves the needs of top management and handles corporate documents and seals in legal matters. Also, if you would like to meet with one of the top executives of a Japanese corporation, you would contact this section for an appointment.

While you sometimes do find a legal department in a Japanese corporation, you would not find a person with the title of "general counsel." It is very rare to meet a head of a legal department with the title "attorney at law" in a Japanese corporation. Since a lawyer is allowed only to handle legal matters in court and to give legal advice officially, the legal department, if there is one, usually takes care of legal business for the company through outside lawyers. Many corporations in Japan hire outside lawyers in an advisory capacity.

· *The Controller*—In a strict sense, in most Japanese corporation there is no controller such as you would find in an American corporation. Financial activities in Japanese corporations are usually grouped as financing and accounting or financial accounting and control.

· *The Personnel Department*—The personnel department of Japanese corporations is very similar to those in United States corporations, but its influence upon management and workers is much greater than in the United States. The functions of the personnel department in most Japanese corporations are fundamentally service and advice, but their recommendations on personnel policies relating to promotion, transfer, and salary are very influential. In particular, workers are very concerned with the moves of the personnel department. The personnel department in many major Japanese corporations is larger in staff than in their American counterparts. It is usually headed by a managing director or a director at least. It is the personnel department, in most cases, which creates status inflation. If you need a good fancy title, just visit this department. They might create one for you if you are eligible.

Decision Making

Many Americans feel that Japanese business people take too long to decide and attribute this to status inflation and the resulting

complexity in the organizational structure of Japanese corporations. In contrast, others say that American business people sometimes make hasty decisions on important matters without giving
much consideration to the long-term consequences. To understand
these attitudes, we need to examine the decision-making process
typical of Japanese organizations.

The board of directors is, of course, the highest decision-making body in the Japanese corporation. In some companies, the
board meets once or twice a month, but the typical corporation
holds a formal board meeting once every three or four months. In
order to supplement the board meeting, many major companies set
up *jomukai*, which translates as "meeting of the managing directors." This meeting is usually held once a week or once every two
weeks. After listening to the advice and discussion of the participating members of the problems brought into this meeting, the
president makes the final decision. In reality, these meetings are
even more important than the formal board meetings. Many large
organizations tend to set up still other meetings to reduce the load
of the *jomukai* and to separate higher policy matters from the
agenda of *jomukai*. Some companies call this meeting the "executive committee" after the American practice. The Japanese executive committee usually consists of the chairman, president, and
vice-president and occasionally some senior managing directors.
This meeting handles corporate policy matters of a higher level
and meets less frequently than *jomukai*.

In conducting these meetings, items are presented for discussion and for approval or decision by the president. Most of the time
they are in written form called *ringisho*. A *ringisho* can be originated at any level of the organization and will go through various
organizational units for review or comment before it reaches the
final decision point. This journey sometimes takes a week or two,
depending upon the scope of the problem the *ringisho* carries. The
matter described in the *ringisho* can be decided by a department
head or managing director in charge of the specific matter without
submitting it to the *jomukai* or executive committee. It all depends
upon the nature and scope of the matter to be approved. Most corporations provide authority schedules so that people can locate the
appropriate decision point easily.

The *ringisho* is a useful instrument in the sense that it
assures participation of related departments or sections in a subject matter. As it goes through channels, comments and review are
attached to the *ringisho*. By the time it reaches the decision point,
all the pros and cons have been attached and the decision is made

much more easily. This process assures that the matter is well screened and coordinated before a decision is made and helps to create consensus in the organization. However, it also tends to delay decision making and invites conservatism in the organization. People tend to be overly cautious when they know their *ringisho* will be scrutinized by various people. This is particularly true when the *ringisho* is initiated in the lower levels of the organization in what is called the bottom-up process.

Many people are under the impression that the Japanese decision-making process is always bottom-up, that higher management waits for *ringisho* to work their way up for approval and thus management tends to forget to initiate its own policies. However, this does not describe the whole picture, particularly in the case of small firms and progressive companies where corporate general staffs are well organized and work together with their top management. In such corporations, quite a few policy matters are initiated by top management and are brought into a meeting for discussion in order to form a corporate consensus. After the decision is made, the policies or instructions are directed to various departments for execution.

In any case, the *ringisho* is used as an instrument to show the record of approval and to transmit the decision to related departments. It is also used as a corporate record. This formality serves to protect the continuity of corporate policies as well as to give the opportunity to participate in the decision-making process.

Similar formality is also used in many American corporations. In many cases, when matters are circulated among various departments for coordination and review, people participating in the specific matter usually put their initial on it in order to indicate their approval. On other documents, Europeans as well as Americans place their signature or initials on it as a sign of approval. Japanese, however, use a *hanko*, or individual seal, instead of a signature or initial. Practically every adult Japanese has his or her own *hanko*, which usually shows the surname in character or *kanji*. The *hanko* is made of wood, ivory, animal bone, plastic, or stone. Whenever and wherever a formal signature is required, the *hanko* is used. Business persons place their *hanko* on many papers, including *ringisho*. Sometimes, the *ringisho* looks like a showcase of the *hanko* of the executives of the corporation. Some people try to use their signature or initial instead of the *hanko* but meet a lot of resistance. This is particularly true when a document is being submitted to the government—they insist on the use of *hanko*. *Hanko* can be purchased at a stationers store or at special *hanko* stores. In cases where strict identification is required, a certified *hanko* authenticated by a local government agency is used. Japanese never use the *hanko* when engaging in business in other countries. However, Americans engaging in business in Japan would do well to have not only their business cards printed in Japanese but also have their own *hanko* made.

Business Meetings

Many of my American friends tell me that they have the impression that Japanese business people love to spend many hours in meetings and conferences. One of them even suggested jokingly that in the interest of accuracy the word "conference" should be added to Japanese corporate names, as in "XYZ Products and Conference, Inc." Many American and European business people believe that the Japanese spend a great many hours in meetings in order to arrive at a consensus. Some American scholars have labeled the form of Japanese business management as "management by consensus." Do Japanese really love meetings and conferences as much as Americans believe they do?

According to a survey conducted in 1981 by the Japan Management Association, a typical Japanese manager spends 10 hours and 11 minutes a day in business activities. Out of this total, he spends 1 hour and 40 minutes for conferences and 2 hours and 18 minutes for meetings. (The distribution of the rest of his time is 1 hour and 38 minutes for reading documents and reference material; 1 hour and 50 minutes for writing and compiling documents and reports; 38 minutes for thinking; 26 minutes for visiting; and 1 hour and 46 minutes for meals, rest, and other.) These figures reveal that Japanese mangers spend 3 hours and 58 minutes a day, or 39 percent of their total business hours, for conferences and meetings. A breakdown showed that executives at the highest level spend 42.8 percent and department heads spend 42 percent of their time for conferences and meetings. Thus, the higher the post, the more time spent for conferences and meetings.

Not having comparative statistics for American and European managers, I leave the reader to judge whether Japanese actually spend more time in conferences and meetings. However, to evaluate the importance of such conferences and meetings, I would like to describe how they operate.

There is a difference between the conference and the meeting.

In translating the Japanese terminology used in the study, I have used "conference" for the Japanese work *kaigi* and "meeting" for *uchi-awase*. The *uchi-awase* is a kind of informal meeting of a very limited number of personnel, say between a boss and a few of his subordinates or even between two persons. It could even be called a "consultation."

The Ceremonial Kaigi

Kaigi, the conference, is more or less a formal type of meeting participated in by several people. The *kaigi* is usually held in a conference room in an atmosphere of formality and perhaps some stiffness. The *jomukai* (the executive committee meeting) is a typical example of *kaigi*. Usually, the *kaigi* is carefully prearranged and scheduled. There will be an agenda which may be the presentation of a business report, a problem, a project, or a discussion of policies or long-range plans. Some *kaigi* are held to conform to the law requiring certain matters be decided through a formal process.

Most *kaigi* are very superficial and often held simply as a formality or stepping stone for moving on to the next stage of something or just to make a certain decision formal. Some people say that the *kaigi* is just a ceremony in Japanese business. Most of the attending persons know that important matters are decided or negotiated unofficially before they are brought into the *kaigi*. Most participants seldom discuss the pros and cons of the matter presented nor do they express themselves. They just sit still and listen to a discussion between a few members. They speak up only when requested to do so. It is a very quiet affair compared with American conferences. There is seldom any argument, debate, or planning at *kaigi*. This is more likely at conferences of the higher levels of management. When do they discuss matter more seriously? When do they put their heads together to solve problems and exchange ideas and information openly? It is at the *uchi-awase* meeting.

Real Business at the Uchi-awase

At the *uchi-awase*, people vigorously discuss problems and scrutinize projects and ideas. Matters to be presented to the higher level of management will be more thoroughly discussed, screened, and coordinated among the *uchi-awase* participants. At the *uchi-*

awase, a boss explains his ideas, instructions, or policies to subordinates and they make counterproposals if requested and provide first-hand information to assist the boss in making judgments. The *uchi-awase* is also held between personnel of different departments or divisions and with outsiders such as suppliers, vendors, agencies, or research and consulting firms.

The *uchi-awase* is often held at informal places—at the boss's desk or at a small table in an open space in the middle of the office. Sometimes, it is held in a small guest room or in an unoccupied office. The most informal *uchi-awase* is a chat in a nearby coffee shop. Many Japanese business people often escape from their office and visit a nearby coffee shop during office hours and spend hours chatting with their associates over a cup of coffee or tea—they are usually engaging in informal *uchi-awase* often as a prelude to more serious *uchi-awase* to follow back at the workplace.

The Coffee Shop

The Japanese coffee shop is known as the *kissaten*. It is not like most American coffee shops. The *kissaten* serves coffee, tea, soft drinks, and cakes, but they do not offer meals. It is a place only for chatting over coffee or tea and meeting people.

Some progressive Japanese companies operate *kissaten* within their own premises in order to encourage employees to chat over coffee and thereby improve communication. For example, an internationally known automobile manufacturer has a very sophisticated *kissaten* appointed with imported furniture which is normally found only in high-ranking executives offices. The company encourages its employees to visit this tearoom for relaxation and *uchi-awase*.

Japanese executives at the top management level prefer to hold *uchi-awase* not at *kissaten* but at a *ryotei*, which is a very exclusive and highly sophisticated Japanese restaurant where alcoholic beverages are served. The *ryotei* also offer dinner and entertainment. *Uchi-awase* at a *ryotei* often combine business and entertainment. This type of *uchi-awase* is very sophisticated and usually concerns a delicate matter, often of a political nature. It is very expensive and executives pay US$200-300 per person for *uchi-awase* at a *ryotei*. Such use of *ryotei* is, of course, limited to the top-level people and its exorbitant charge is considered as the cost of communication—particularly when the *uchi-awase* is for *nemawashi*.

Nemawashi

The *nemawashi* is a type of *uchi-awase* through which executives brief their associates on their ideas, problems, or projects before they are discussed at a formal *kaigi*. As mentioned, most Japanese know that important matters are decided or negotiated unofficially before they are present in a *kaigi*. The unofficial agreement is engineered through this process called *nemawashi*. *Nemawashi* is the groundwork for an important *kaigi* in order to make sure that there will be unanimous agreement at the formal *kaigi*. The origin of the term *nemawashi* is the process of planting a tree. When a big tree is to be moved from one place to another, the gardener first digs around its roots and turns them around a bundle. *Ne* means "root" and *mawashi* means "turning around."

The Office Layout

When you enter a large Japanese office, you will usually see small clusters of people here and there. In all likelihood, they are having *uchi-awase*. Japanese offices are laid out in such a way that *uchi-awase* can be held conveniently at any time. The boss's desk is located where he can easily call his subordinates or staff over for a quick *uchi-awase*, which could be just as easily suspended or interrupted if the need arises. The typical Japanese office layout is very flat and open. There are hardly any independent rooms or enclosures. It is called the large room system. If a person stands at his desk, he can see at a glance his associates, subordinates, or boss. Often, he is close enough to be able to overhear the conversation between his boss and someone else. There is hardly any privacy in this system, but each member of the staff can keep up with what's going on in the office just by being a bit attentive. The working environment is laid out so as to promote *uchi-awase* and teamwork.

It is my impression that American managers are very particular about the size and interior furnishing of their own office room. An individual office is a status symbol of the American executive. Executives of large American corporations take it for granted that they will be provided with an individual office room consonant with their title. A typical American office consists of partitioned sections and independent rooms for managers and specialists. Such a layout is rare in Japanese corporations. Among my acquaintances is the advertising executive of a large beverage manufacturer with a multi-billion yen sales. He has no office of his own. He occupies just one of many desks in a spacious room. His desk is alongside that of the assistant manager. The only thing that distinguishes his space in the office is that his desk is slightly larger than the rest and his chair has an armrest. Surprisingly, he is not only the advertising manager but also a member of the board of directors of the firm. However, when an executive rises as high as managing director or president, he usually gets an independent and individual office of his own.

Another noticeable feature of a Japanese office layout is the large number of small conference rooms and guest rooms where the staff meet visitors or customers. These rooms are, of course, also used for *uchi-awase*.

The *uchi-awase* should not be categorized simply as a meeting or conference. The *uchi-awase* is a vital part of the Japanese business institution and is how corporate employees work together as a team. *Uchi-awase* makes business dynamic and the participants more creative. Although it may appear to my American friends that the Japanese people love conferences and meetings, *kaigi*, *uchi-awase*, and *nemawashi* are the essence of what makes the Japanese group-oriented participative management process work.

14

Strategic Planning in Japan*

Milton C. Lauenstein

The American business community has recognized the importance of strategy as a determinant of corporate success. Academics, consultants, and executives themselves have studied the subject in depth and have written extensively on it. Any corporation with pretensions of being well managed has installed a strategic planning procedure to improve its prospects of long-term success.

The Japanese have noted the development of strategic thinking in the United States and are interested in it. Just as they did with American quality control methods a quarter-century ago, they are studying U.S. methods of strategic management. They are reading U.S. books and articles, sending young managers to U.S. business schools, and organizing delegations of executives to visit this country specifically to learn how U.S. corporations approach strategic planning.

In light of the success of Japanese corporations in competition with those in the United States, this may seem ironic. The Japanese are widely credited with exhibiting unusual strategic skills. Why then are they studying American methods? Are they in

---

*Reprinted with permission from the Fall 1985 *Journal of Business Strategy*. Copyright © by Warren, Gorham, and Lamont, Inc., 210 South Street, Boston, MA 02111. All rights reserved.

fact superior in strategic management? How do Japanese firms handle strategic planning now? How well do their methods work? Are there things U.S. managers can learn from the way Japanese companies do their long-term planning?

Intrigued with these questions, the author went to Japan and learned firsthand how they do strategic planning and how well it works. This article reports the findings.

The author talked with planning executives in ten Japanese companies, and discussed the subject with Dr. James C. Abegglen and Dr. Noritake Kobayashi, leading authorities on Japanese business.

While there are obvious similarities, Japanese strategic planning procedures differ from those in the United States in both spirit and method. In some ways their approach is less sophisticated. They indeed have something to learn from this country. But American businessmen have something to learn from them, too. The Japanese approach to planning reflects certain ways to thinking and cultural values which are different from those in the United States.

Japanese Attitudes

According to many writers, strategic planning should begin with a definition of objectives. A company should determine the relative importance of possible goals, such as growth, profitability, stock value, technological innovation, social responsibility and other factors.

Japanese executives profess not to think in these terms. They consider all of these objectives as a part of an integrated whole, rather than as separable ends. But if one objective can be said to outrank the others in Japan, it is the well-being of the employees.

Japanese firms are more like a family than firms in the United States. Employees of larger companies normally stay with the same corporation until retirement. They say that of the two major choices each young Japanese man must make, his wife and his employers, the latter is the more important. In such a situation, executives feel a deep sense of responsibility to their fellow workers. Managers in several companies said that they considered growth, profits, and other economic goals to be important primarily for insuring the welfare of the employee group.

This attitude has important strategic implications. Because of the lifetime employment practice, hiring decisions are crucial. Japanese companies must look ten to twenty years ahead to determine this year's hiring profile. Because of the relative immobility of personnel, it is vital that the Japanese firms hire a mix of skills which will be appropriate for the activities they will pursue over the long term. The young professionals recruited this year must also yield the top management group of a quarter-century or so from now.

Another result of the family feeling and sense of responsibility for employee welfare is that terminating or selling an operation is almost unthinkable. Getting into the wrong business ultimately results in a long, painful period of shrinkage, reducing the work force only by attrition and transfers. To a Japanese company, entering a new business is something like getting tattooed; before deciding to proceed, one had better be sure it's something one will want to live with for a long time.

Prestige

Prestige is important in Japan. The prestige of one's company is important to one's own status. Company size, growth rate, and technical achievements tend to be more important determinants of prestige than profitability. Thus those objectives tend to receive a lot of attention in Japan.

Japanese tend to guide their actions more by the practical requirements of a specific situation than by abstract rationalizations. They prefer to approach business situations on a case-by-case basis rather than to commit to follow predetermined principles. For this reason, the Japanese have been jokingly called "unprincipled people." The situation of a Japanese firm tends to represent the natural result of continuous experimentation, rather than the result of a carefully devised "grand strategy."

Japanese executives are less concerned than Americans with return on investment. This is partly because Japanese companies have found it so easy to borrow from supportive banks. Moreover, Japanese middle managers are not concerned with finance, which is a private domain of top management and the bankers.

A primary objective of Japanese planning is to identify new fields to enter or new product opportunities to exploit. Immediate financial progress is of lesser importance.

The Japanese executives are more oriented to qualitative than quantitative strategic thinking. They express skepticism about anyone's ability to forecast the future in specific terms. Many feel that five years is too long a time for meaningful plans. While some of the firms calculate internal rate of return as part of their evaluation of investment proposals, none seems to give much weight to it. They are sensitive to the possibility that unforeseen developments can completely upset their plans, as has happened in the past.

Competition

The Japanese are skeptical, too, about the possibility of developing a sustainable competitive advantage. Their approach is almost uniformly to identify a promising area in which to invest, to find a way to achieve some temporary advantage on the basis of which to establish themselves in the market, and then to rely on unremitting effort to make further progress. Over and again, executives expressed their conviction that any competitive advantage they may gain (except for economy of scale) will be transient. They are convinced that competitors will quickly duplicate any edge they may get in product or process design. They do put weight on the desirability of being number one in a field. Yet even the manufacturer of Seiko watches is skeptical of the value of its leadership in its own field, and is looking to other areas for its growth.

While the Japanese often attack national markets one by one, their strategic orientation is worldwide. Exports are vital to Japan because they must pay to import nearly all of their raw materials.

While Japanese companies have shown remarkable skill in segmenting markets for *operational* purposes such as advertising, distribution, and product line planning, their *strategic* thinking is aimed at broad, general market areas. There is little effort to measure return on capital by market segment. And they make no effort to determine differences in cost to serve various customer groups.

The Japanese practice of reaching decisions through consensus has a pervasive effect on their approach to strategic management. In the long series of conversations which takes place during planning, executives consider a wide range of possible developments. They think of the implications of various possibilities as they work toward agreement as to how best to proceed. Managers from all phases of operations participate in these deliberations. In this informal, unsystematic, and time-consuming way, Japanese companies manage to consider a wide range of possibilities and viewpoints as they approach major decisions. Once made, decisions are well understood and have wide support, since all interested parties participate in deliberations.

Sophisticated quantitative analytical techniques play a minor role at best in such a decision-making procedure. None of the companies the author interviewed reported using computer modeling, simulation, or "decision support systems" in strategic planning. The Japanese approach to strategic issues was softer, more qualitative, and sometimes almost spiritual. In contrast, their planning was precise and thorough. The notion of building a distinctive competence to win a competitive advantage in carefully defined market segments seems to be foreign to Japanese thinking.

Long-Term Vision

One of the primary responsibilities of a Japanese chief executive is to articulate a vision of the nature of the firm, the direction it will pursue, and its long-term goals. A company's character is embodied in the feelings of mutual responsibility and respect between company and employee, in its spirit, and in how its people related to one another and work together. Its direction and long-term goals are expressed in terms of markets, growth, technologies, products, and industry position. Japanese chief executives focus more on defining these issues and less on making operating decision than do American CEOs.

In Japan, important decisions require consensus. In the strategy area, however, the degree of participation in decision-making depends on the situation and on the personality of the CEO. In some firms, the CEO makes the strategic decisions. In others, he focuses more on creating an environment in which the executive group can determine the directions the company will pursue. In any case, he will go over these issues with his board of directors, which is also his senior executive staff. They discuss the company and its relation with a changing world, formally and informally. From time to time, the CEO articulates and promulgates a new or modified vision of the company's long-term future, as changes in circumstances require.

These policy statements by the CEO are extremely important in Japanese corporations. They represent the official policy of the firm, which all of the employees are expected to support. Such fundamental pronouncements are especially important to employees because their careers depend on their company's long-term progress. Lifetime employment and the practice of articulating a long-term vision of the enterprise combine to focus much more attention on the distant future than is common in America.

Bold Objectives

Often the objectives announced by the CEO are quite bold. For example, in 1980, Dr. Ichiro Hattori of Hattori Seiko was concerned about his company's dependence on the increasingly competitive watch business. He likened the dominance of watches in his firm to Mount Fuji, towering above everything around it. Continuing the analogy with mountains, he told his people that by 1990, he wanted the corporation to be more like Yatsugatake, a famous eight-peaked mountain in central Japan. By 1984, the company had already defined and was active in five or six businesses, including microcomputers, computer peripherals, and robots. All of these technologies stemmed from the watch business.

NEC, founded in 1899, was once a rather lethargic manufacturer of telephone equipment. Under Dr. Koji Kobayashi, it has adopted the slogan, "C and C," meaning "computers and communications," to define a more dynamic economic role. It features its C and C concept not only in communications to employees, but in reports to shareholders and in advertising.

With this concept, it has become one of Japan's outstanding companies. It is a leader in some growth areas; one example is optical fiber communication equipment. It is also by far the largest manufacturer of personal computers in Japan, with nearly half of the market.

A clear definition of a company's business helps it focus on achieving its objectives and avoiding costly diffusion of effort. The thinking of Japanese executives is shaped by the company's vision of the future. They have a clear idea of what business they are in. For example, executives at Toyota told the authors that they would never consider making a Cadillac. "Toyota is in the business of making *small* cars," they explained. Even so, they have a clear-cut goal of raising their percentage of the worldwide auto market from 8 percent to 10 percent.

Japanese companies tend to confine their business to related activities. When they have ventured too far from what they do best, they have often had troubles, as Toyota did with its foray into housing. Consequently, the chief executive usually expresses a more concrete concept of his company's role than American company slogans such as "Look to the leader" (Bank of America), "We work for America" (Internorth), or "Addressing society's major unmet needs as profitable business opportunities" (Control Data).

The Japanese practice of having the CEO articulate and promulgate a vision of the company's long-term direction contributes to that country's economic effectiveness. Employees understand clearly where the company is headed and work together to get there. Management sees what capabilities and resources will be needed in the long run and takes steps to develop them. Firms make fewer costly excursions into unrelated businesses. By focusing on their areas of greatest competence, companies are less likely to miss attractive opportunities close to home.

A Lack of Capital Allocation

The lack of more specific guidelines for capital allocation leads to waste. Toyota's policy of focusing on only one part of the automobile market, small cars, is unusual. More often, Japanese companies engage in entire industries. They make little use of financial standards such as return on capital when evaluating investment opportunities. As a result, they often enter segments of a broad market for which they are not well equipped and which may detract from their progress in their prime areas.

Shiseido, Japan's leading cosmetics producer, has had a fine reputation for costly, upscale products. It began pushing an inexpensive line, aimed at a younger customer group which is less affluent. It also opened a new distribution channel: convenience stores. This irritated its traditional outlets. When Shiseido made these moves to broaden its business, its image blurred, and market share and profitability began to decline.

NEC, which has achieved outstanding progress in computers and communications, continues to invest in products in which it has much less reason to expect success. In home electronics, for example, it competes head-to-head with Matsushita, a company much stronger in that field. NEC has little hope of doing well there. It would probably achieve better results by concentrating more narrowly on its C and C concept, where its greatest strengths lie. Computers and communications provide plenty of room for growth. But of course abandoning a business is very difficult to do in Japan.

The Japanese approach to strategic decision-making often results in companies running with the herd and investing in activities in which they have little prospect of earning an attractive return. Their concern about the possibility of a competitor getting ahead of them exacerbates this problem. Thus, when pocket calculators became popular, scores of Japanese companies began making them. Only four appear to have made a real success of that business. More recently, a horde of companies has flocked to enter the robotics field. Even though many of these companies, such as Hattori Seiko, have some applicable technology in the field, only a few will succeed. The many failures represent a needless waste of national resources.

The corporate vision articulated by a Japanese CEO is effective in developing an integrated long-term program. It would be even more effective, however, if it provided clearer guidelines for selecting specific market segments to address and if it provided criteria by which to evaluate specific proposals.

Intermediate-Term Planning

Progressive Japanese companies perform formal intermediate-term planning exercises. For some, it is a new activity. A few are still modifying their procedures and looking for an effective method. Nevertheless, they follow a generally similar pattern.

The term of the plan is most often three or five years, with more companies using three than five. A survey reported in *Toyo Keizaiin*, February, 1984, indicated that three-year plans outnumbered five-year plans in Japan by almost two to one. Even those which do five-year planning expressed skepticism about the significance of the figures for the last two years. Some do the planning each year while others develop a new plan only when the old one is about to terminate; that is, once every three or five years.

The preparation of the plan is characterized by extensive and intensive personal interactions among executives at different levels and in different departments. The resultant plan reflects the views of both line and staff. It incorporates both the broad, general perspective of top management and the detailed knowledge of operating executives about specific situations.

The coordination of the planning operation is usually assigned to a planning department. Before the formal activity begins, planning staff members talk with managers at different levels to get their views. Naturally, the plan must conform to the CEO's long-term vision of the company's future. After enough discussion to reconcile divergent views, the planning staff prepares an initial rough draft of the intermediate-term plans. The various departments are assigned the task of fleshing out the document with detailed implementation programs.

The broad plans may specify such things as the amount of cost reduction or sales increase to be achieved by each division. The operating executives have the task of determining how they will achieve their assigned objectives.

Resolving Problems

Inevitably there are problems. Some departments have difficulty determining how they can meet the plan's objectives. Others want to strive to achieve more and to have the needed resources provided. The planning staff works with operating managers to resolve these problems. They arrange meetings with senior executives as needed to address knotty issues. Ultimately, consensus is reached and a formal plan is adopted and approved by the board.

Scheduling of the Japanese planning process is exemplified by the Sony procedure. Overall policy setting is done by top management in November through January, prior to the formal planning operation. During this period, the planning department facilitates an extensive exchange of information and views between operations and the corporate office.

In March, the corporate planning staff begins the process of preparing the intermediate-term corporate plan in consultation with operating executives. In mid-April, planning in the divisions begins. For a time, the corporate and divisional planning operations proceed simultaneously, with extensive interaction between them. The corporate plan is completed in May and the division plans, which must conform to the corporate projections, are finished by the end of June. Finally, during the summer, operating budgets are prepared.

Japanese vs. American Planning Procedures

The Japanese planning procedures differ from the American in several respects. There is more interaction between executives at different levels and between line and staff. At the same time, the Japanese approach is more "top down" in nature than the American. The plans must implement the long-term vision of the company articulated by the CEO. Division plans must conform to the corporate plan, which is completed first.

In America, the process more often begins with divisions proposing their plans first. They are then combined and modified by the corporate office. But with a "bottom-up" approach, it is much more difficult to achieve a really coherent, integrated forward program.

Even in Japan, there may be sharp differences of opinion. But once the plan is adopted, it enjoys a greater degree of acceptance and support than is common in the United States. Executives feel a strong commitment to achieving or surpassing what is projected.

Professional hiring occupies a more prominent position in Japanese planning than it does in the United States. The number hired each year by each company tends not to vary much, although, depending on the long-term vision, the composition may. Some companies have a policy of not expanding the size of the total executive staff, expecting to increase management productivity as the company grows. Or, a company that does not expect to grow may hire only half as many new executives as retire each year. This policy, too, represents a commitment to improving executive productivity.

Planning executives appear to work more effectively with line managers than in the United States. Because of the Japanese practice of rotating executives through a wide variety of assignments, the planners typically have had significant operating experience. They understand operating problems and are better equipped to work with line executives in reconciling differences than are bright young American MBAs who have not had operating responsibility.

In addition to the corporate intermediate-term plan, operating units prepare other specific plans, such as a plan to build a new plant. Such plans may extend over a longer period of time than the corporate plan, especially when the latter is for only three years or is not done annually. This presents no special problems. Those parts of the specific plans which take place during the intermediate-term plans are incorporated in them. The balance simply extends beyond.

As is often true in the United States, the intermediate-term plan helps shape the annual budget. In principle, the budget must conform to the plan, although in unusual circumstances the board may approve specific deviations. Budgeting is done meticulously. Normally, the budget is revised before the second half of the year, so that in essence many Japanese companies run on six-month budgets.

In effect, then, the intermediate-term plan serves as a bridge between the CEO's long-term vision and the operating budget, which affects day-to-day activities and decisions. Its effectiveness stems from the nature and extent of interactions between executives in different parts of the organization. In facilitating these interactions and the flow of information, planning staff members play a vital role rather more effectively than their typical American counterparts.

Implications

Strategic planning effectiveness affects the economic performance of corporations and of national economies. When companies misallocate resources and invest in activities for which they are not well suited, both they and their countries suffer. When they focus their efforts on businesses in which they are best qualified, and continue to enhance their ability to do a better job for their customers, everyone benefits. The relative performance of the American and Japanese economies will depend to a considerable extent on how well executives in each country allocate capital to activities in which they can reasonably expect to excel.

The Japanese strategic management approach appears to be superior to the U.S. approach in two respects. The Japanese articulate a clearer vision of what the company is and where it is headed. This helps to integrate plans of operating units into a more coherent whole. It also serves to focus the efforts of the management team on working together toward a shared objective. Second, the Japanese procedures provide for more extensive interaction between staff and line executives, and between the corporate office and lower-level operating managers. The resulting plans appear to reflect a better balance between conceptual (staff) and practical (line) considerations.

American CEOs often resist being constrained by a clearly defined long-term vision of where the company is headed. As a result, employees are less certain about how best to prepare for the long term. Moreover, because of the greater mobility of American managers, they are less concerned about their companies' long-term futures.

This contributes to two competitive disadvantages for American firms. One is an excessive preoccupation with near-term performance which results in short-sighted decisions. The second is uncertainly, vacillation, and, frequently, ill-advised investment in areas for which a company is not well equipped to compete in the long run. Unless American top managers, perhaps as the result of some urging by the directors, establish a clearer vision of where their companies are headed, this country's industry will continue to labor under a serious handicap.

The top-down Japanese planning system, with its extensive provision for interaction, is better suited to developing a coherent and effective overall corporate strategy than the American approach. The line experience of planning staff members also adds to their effectiveness. These aspects of Japanese experience are ones American executives would do well to emulate.

Conversely, there are some aspects of strategic planning in which the United States enjoys potential advantages over the Japanese. Americans are more comfortable with and skilled at using business principles and financial standards as criteria against which to evaluate investment proposals. Americans have more developed concepts of strategic management. The United States has a much more extensive infrastructure, such as business schools and consulting firms, for developing and disseminating effective methods of strategic management. U.S. executives are more skilled at applying techniques such as internal rate of return or net present value to help guide investment decisions.

As yet, these skills have done little to advance American industrial effectiveness. Like the Japanese, Americans tend to use a shotgun approach and attack broad markets. They fail to focus on carefully defined business segments in which they have a better chance to build a competitive edge. Americans are sometimes too willing to accept a mechanistic approach to strategic decision-making, such as simply comparing a projected internal rate of return to the established hurdle rate. U.S. executives must pay more attention to qualitative criteria, such as what additional opportunities are likely to result from an investment and how it relates to other corporate moves in the longer-term picture.

U.S. businessmen must be concerned about the possibility that the Japanese may learn to beat them at their own strategic planning game. The Japanese did it in quality control, where they applied American methods to outperform U.S. companies. They are now studying U.S. strategic planning methods and concepts. And in their newly changed economic circumstances, they have a pressing need to become more discriminating in the way they select areas in which to invest.

After World War II, there was an enormous deferred demand for products of all types in Japan. Beyond their domestic market, there was a world market the Japanese were not yet serving. They had an intelligent and disciplined work force. They had access to a wealth of foreign technology on favorable terms. Japanese financial and governmental institutions were dedicated to helping to rebuild industry. Under these circumstances, a Japanese company could attack almost any market with good prospects of success, first at home, then abroad.

Now, Japan has essentially exhausted its low-cost foreign sources of new technology. To continue to progress, Japan is now having to invest in its own research. Japanese labor is no longer cheap. There are no more new foreign markets: The Japanese have already established themselves throughout the world. And they are meeting resistance to the growth of their exports to many countries.

Japanese companies are continuing to seek growth by entering new businesses. Now, however, with fewer new technologies and new markets to tap, good opportunities are harder to find. Many of the fields Japanese companies are now entering are already crowded. Even within the small group of companies the authors visited, there were several cases of one invading another's turf. Such beggar-thy-neighbor investments will be much less productive for the Japanese than building new industries as they did over the past thirty-five years. Japanese companies need better methods for identifying and evaluating specific business opportunities in which they can expect an investment to yield an attractive return. Without such methods, they will squander much of their capital on duplicating facilities which already exist.

It is natural that they are seeking answers by studying American strategic management techniques. They will have difficulty translating them into a Japanese context. But the Japanese have proven themselves resourceful in adopting foreign practices to their own needs in the past. The Japanese government is helping to channel investment into areas in which it will do the most good. If Japanese private industry finds ways to improve its strategic planning and methods of resource allocation, it may well continue to make faster economic progress than other industrialized nations.

The United States enjoys important economic advantages over Japan, such as more natural resources, capital, public facilities (roads, sanitation, etc.), and business support systems (business schools, consultants, continuing education). It has developed more advanced analytical techniques for evaluating investment alternatives. Like Japan, it has an able labor force. If American industry can find ways to take a longer-term, more effective strategic approach to resource allocation, it should be able to outperform even the Japanese.

15

Hiring Women Managers in Japan: An Alternative for Foreign Employers*

Paul Lansing and Kathryn Ready

Foreign business persons in Japan complain of the difficulty in attracting well-qualified Japanese to the employ of foreign multinational corporations. In spite of such allurements as greater salary and more holiday time, deep cultural reasons aid in explaining why bright, young Japanese managers refuse to work for foreign multinational corporations. The employment relationship in Japan for managers is different from most foreign concerns and, given a choice, the Japanese employee will choose to work for a Japanese firm.

Traditionally, the reasons for this choice center on the perceived responsibilities of the parties to an employment situation—employees promise complete allegiance to the employer, which means they will not seek employment elsewhere or strike the employer (except for the ceremonial spring *shunto*) in exchange for the employer's promise of lifetime employment and the provision of amenities such as housing allowances and recreational facilities. In addition, Japanese workers have indicated a preference to work with and among Japanese rather than *gaijin* (foreigners), which accentuates employment difficulties for foreign concerns.

In order for foreign firms to remedy this shortage of male Japanese labor, we propose that foreign concerns actively pursue an alternative—the employment of young Japanese *women* for managerial positions. Japanese women constitute a rising proportion of college graduates trained in managerial work, and Japanese firms are reluctant to hire them even if they may be better qualified than male graduates. In our view, this leaves a large untapped pool of well-qualified people who may be willing to forego traditional prejudices about foreign firms if they are given the opportunity to demonstrate their abilities.

This article explores problems foreign firms can expect to encounter in hiring women employees. The relevance of career management in developing training programs for women will aid in their transition to a new "career woman" employee as opposed to traditional part-time employee.

Legal Aspects

Traditionally, women were discriminated against in the workplace because their work life was short. The cultural expectation was that women would work only until their marriage at approximately age 24. If she continued to work after marriage, it would be a severe loss of face to the husband because it meant that he could not afford to support his wife. Female employees who did not marry generally faced a mandatory retirement age at about 28. Due to these culturally imposed restrictions, employers made no effort to train female employees for jobs beyond making tea or greeting customers.

The Japanese Constitution and the Labor Standards Law of 1947 eliminated the legal barriers to sexual equality in employment in Japan. The law provided regulations about equal pay, working hours, night work, menstruation leave, maternity leave, holidays, employment of minors, dangerous work, restrictions on underground work, and so on. It was so protective that the regulations over time have worked against the principle of equality.[1] Women employees cost firms money. Overtime work for women was restricted to 2 hours per day, 6 hours per week, or 150 hours per year. Night work was normally prohibited for women between the hours of 10 p.m. and 5 a.m. This meant that firms employing women in positions that demanded longer hours were disadvantaged in comparison with firms that employed males.

In 1966, the first judicial decision was handed down declaring the system of compulsory retirement upon marriage to be unconstitutional and nullifying the dismissal based thereon. Since then about forty judicial decisions have been made nullifying such discriminatory dismissals on the ground of unconstitutionality.[2] The Supreme Court ruled in March of 1981 that special protection for women is not inconsistent with equality since women need special protection owing to the fact that they are handicapped by their physical characteristics and biological function.

On April 1, 1986, the newly legislated Equal Employment Opportunity Law went into effect in Japan. Motivation for the enactment was to enable Japan to ratify the United Nations sponsored Convention on the Elimination of All Forms of Discrimination Against Women, which required Japanese legislation ensuring sexual equality in the workplace. The new legislation also amended existing provisions of the labor standards law concerning women.

Because of a conflict between labor groups (which maintained that all provisions of the law must be of a prohibitive nature accompanied by penalties) and management groups (which maintained that company policies should not be affected by the law), the Equal Employment Opportunity law contains provisions prohibiting certain actions and other provisions merely calling for the "making of efforts" in other areas. Concerning employment, the law prohibits employers' discriminatory treatment toward women workers in new employee education and training, in welfare benefits for workers, and in retirement and dismissal policies. However, the law only asks employers to "make efforts" to treat women workers equally with men in recruitment, hiring, position assignments, and promotion.

Amendments to the Labor Standards law relax restrictions and protective provisions regarding female employment. Under the new amendments, female executives and professionals will have no restriction on overtime, or holiday and Sunday work. Restrictions on late night work will be lifted for executive and professional women. The new law does not clearly state what constitutes a professional job, but physicians, reporters, computer engineers, researchers, and designers are expected to be included.

The easing of restrictions on overtime or late night work for women workers is a benefit for professionally oriented women (resulting in opportunities for promotion and advancement) but not for the majority of women who work in clerical jobs or in the service sector. In fact, most women are skeptical or indifferent toward the new legislation since even the prohibitive sections impose no penalties on violators.

For the first time, female professional employees may legally use their education in the workplace without the previous restrictions imposed on them. While Japanese firms will likely be reluctant to "make efforts" to treat women workers equally, there is now an opportunity for foreign employers to take advantage of the new legislation and actively seek out female university graduates for professional positions.

Women in the Japanese Labor Market

Labor Force Participation

Women in the Japanese labor market have typically been referred to as part-time workers. Workers classified in this group may work as many days or as many hours as full-time workers, yet in terms of annual income, a full-time employee earns as much as two part-time employees. Part-time work is particularly popular for women due to the absence of any other type of employment for which they are qualified.[3]

Labor force participation for women has been increasing during the last ten years (see Table 15.1). In 1985, approximately 71.9 percent of the women in their early twenties (20–24) were looking for and finding full-time or part-time salaried employment. The largest growth has come in the 25- to 34-year-old group which has increased from 43.2 percent in 1975 to 52.2 percent in 1985. This trend is important because it indicates that over one-half of women in this age group are choosing to remain in the work force during their childbearing years. Similar trends are evident in all other age categories.

The percentage of women entering employment after graduating from colleges and universities has increased steadily (see Table 15.2). In 1960, only 10.6 percent of women graduating entered employment compared to 89.4 percent of men. In 1985, 23.2 percent of women compared to 76.8 percent of men were gainfully employed upon graduation. Despite the increase in female employment, statistics still indicate that fewer than one in four women enter employment after graduating from colleges and universities. The low percentage of women employed means that

Table 15.1 Japanese Labor Force Participation Rate in 1975 and 1985 for Males and Females

AGE	MALES		FEMALES	
	1975	1985	1975	1985
20–24	76.1	70.0	66.2	71.9
25–34	97.6	96.5	43.2	52.2
35–44	97.8	97.4	56.9	63.7
45–54	96.5	96.1	59.8	64.6
65+	44.4	37.0	15.3	15.5

Source: Research and Statistics Division, Minister's Secretariat, Ministry of Education, *Japan Statistical Yearbook*, 1986, p. 71.

Table 15.2 Percentage of Male and Female Total Graduates from Colleges and Universities Entering Employment

YEAR	TOTAL GRADUATES ENTERING EMPLOYMENT	% MALE	% FEMALE
1960	99,541	89.4	10.6
1965	135,321	87.1	12.9
1970	187,691	84.5	15.5
1975	232,558	81.8	18.2
1980	285,056	78.4	21.6
1982	293,279	78.2	21.8
1983	281,888	77.8	22.2
1984	285,369	77.4	22.6
1985	288,272	76.8	23.2

Source: Research and Statistics Division, Minister's Secretariat, Ministry of Education, *Japan Statistical Yearbook*, 1986, p. 663.

many qualified women are being turned away from organizations. In 1985, 23.8 percent of all women graduating were without a job (see Table 15.3). Males without jobs represented only 12.5 percent of the total male graduates. This is particularly devastating for women because they constitute only 25 percent of all college and university graduates.[4]

Table 15.3 Status of College and University Graduates
by Sex in 1985

	TOTAL GRADUATES* 366,382	MALES 274,958 (75%)	FEMALES 91,424 (25%)
Further Education	21,985	19,338	2,757
	(6.0%)	(7.0%)	(3.0%)
Employed	228,272	221,394	66,878
	(78.7%)	(80.5%)	(73.2%)
Without Occupation	56,054	34,377	21,777
and Other	(15.3%)	(12.5%)	(23.8%)
Further Education	71	59	12
while Employed	(0%)	(0%)	(0%)

*Clinical Trainees (including Probationers) excluded from totals.

Source: Research and Statistics Division, Minister's Secretariat, Ministry
of Education, in *Japan Statistical Yearbook*, 1986, p. 663.

As the normal age of women graduating from college was
twenty-two, three years' service was about all employers expected
of them. If college-educated women worked too many years, they
would accumulate seniority and commensurately higher annual
salary; but, lacking training, they would be regarded as an unnecessary expense item to the firm despite their education. In addition, due to women's liberal arts backgrounds, which is the common education received in universities, college-educated women
are very competitive with each other for opportunities in prestigious corporations, mass media, education, and government. Since
there are few positions available, they accept positions for less
money in order to work, thus cheapening their own value.[5]

Over the years, statistics have been used by Japanese firms
to paint a rather dismal picture for continued employability of
women. Organizations illustrate the need for retaining women as
part-time employees because they argue the typical Japanese
female will begin work in an organization upon graduation from
school, retire for marriage or childbirth, and then, when the children have reached the age of junior or senior high school, she will
seek employment again. Between the ages of 23 and 28, 26 percent
of working women quit their jobs. At the age of about 35, married
women once more begin to work outside the home. By the time
they reach 40, the rate of working married women to the total

married women population rises to 64 percent; 38 percent regular employees and 26 percent part-timers.[6]

Japanese working women have stereotypically been young, unmarried, and short-term workers, but an examination of age, marital status, and length of service indicates a change in the profile of the Japanese working woman. The average age of women workers has risen from 23.8 years in 1949 to 34.9 in 1980.[7] This has led to a lengthening of the term of service with one employer (3.2 years in 1950 to 6.2 years in 1979 compared with 10.8 for men) and a growing proportion of married women working outside the home. In 1979, 67 percent of married Japanese women, including those widowed or divorced, worked outside the home.[8] According to the Labor Ministry's report on female labor, released in October 1984, 33 percent of the female wage earners were employed in clerical work, 22 percent in manufacturing, 14 percent in professional jobs, and 12 percent in sales work. Only 1 percent of all women workers are in supervisory or managerial posts (compared with 8.1 percent of men), representing a mere 6.9 percent of all supervisory and managerial personnel.[9]

In absolute terms, the largest growth industry for men and women in Japan from 1975–1985 has been non-agricultural (see Table 15.4). Women are joining the work force in larger numbers than previously, which is evidenced by the 18 percent increase over all industries during 1975 to 1985 compared to only a 7.1 percent increase for males. The total increase during this period has been 11.2 percent. The largest growth areas for women are fisheries, construction, finance, non-agricultural, wholesale and retail trade, drinking places, and manufacturing. The average growth rate for women is considerably larger than the overall average total growth rate in all of these industries (except finance, where the growth rate is approximately the same). However, this isn't the total picture. It is necessary to examine the percentage change in women given the total percentage change in each industry to determine the impact of women's employment relative to changes in industry employment. The change in the percentage of women employed in each industry is given in Table 15.5.

The data in Table 15.5 have been obtained from the employment data in Table 15.4 and indicate that women are increasing their relative size in all industries except agriculture, forestry, and electric, gas, heat, and water. Women as a total percentage of the work force by industry increased from 37.4 percent in 1975 to 39.7 percent in 1985. Women have made the greatest strides in the fishing industry, increasing from 18.6 percent of the total work force in 1975 to 28.9 percent in 1985.

Table 15.4   Change in Growth Rate from 1975–1985 by Industry

	TOTAL		MALES		FEMALES		MALE %
INDUSTRY	1975	1985	1975	1985	1975	1985	CHANGE
Agriculture and Forestry	618	464	295	233	323	231	-21.0
Non-Agricultural	4605	5343	2975	3270	1630	2072	10.0
Fisheries	43	45	35	32	8	13	-8.6
Mining	16	9	15	7	1	1	-53.3
Construction	479	530	420	454	59	76	8.1
Manufacturing	1346	1453	871	879	475	574	.9
Wholesale and Retail Trade and Drinking Places	1127	1318	619	693	508	625	12.0
Finance, Insurance, and Real Estate	170	217	94	119	76	97	26.6
Transport and Communication	332	343	291	299	40	44	2.7
Electric, Gas, Heat, and Water	32	33	26	29	4	4	11.5
Total	5223	5807	3270	3503	1953	2304	7.1

(IN 10,000 PERSONS)

Source: Research and Statistics Division, Minister's Secretariat, Ministry of Education in *Japan Statistical Yearbook*, 1986, p. 72.

Further analysis is needed to determine which occupations have experienced employment changes. Despite the fact that women are increasing across industries, it is necessary to determine if this has affected the types of jobs women are entering. Increased employment figures for women across industries does not necessarily indicate increased responsibilities and occupational upgrading.

A second analysis is needed to ascertain the change in female composition by occupation. Women have experienced the largest growth in laborers, professional and technical, clerical, govern-

Table 15.5 Percent Change in Female Composition Rate by Industry 1975–1985

INDUSTRY	1975	1985
Agriculture and Forestry	52.3	49.8
Non-Agricultural	35.4	38.8
Fisheries	18.6	28.9
Mining	6.3	11.1
Construction	12.3	14.3
Manufacturing	35.3	39.5
Wholesale and Retail Trade and Drinking Places	45.1	47.4
Finance, Insurance, and Real Estate	44.7	44.7
Transport and Communication	12.0	12.8
Electric, Gas, Heat, and Water	12.5	12.1
Total	37.4	39.7

ment, and managers and officials occupations (see Table 15.6). This means that from 1975 to 1985 women's employment figures increased more rapidly in the occupations that had undergone growth than in other occupations that employed females. Again, a more complete analysis is necessary to determine the change in overall female composition rate across occupations. These data are obtained from the employment data in Table 15.6. The percentage change in women, controlling for the total percentage change of each occupation, is presented in Table 15.7.

The data in Table 15.7 indicate that women are gaining position in the clerical and laborer occupations. In clerical positions, the percentage of women employed has increased from 50.6 percent in 1975 to 55.6 percent in 1985. Women employed as laborers have experienced an increase from 35.1 percent in 1975 to 44.3 percent in 1985. Smaller gains have been achieved in service, government, managers and officials, sales, and craftsman occupations. Women are entering the work force in greater numbers but are still concentrated in traditional, less-prestigious occupations with small gains being made in managers and officials occupations.

Table 15.6   Change in Growth Rate from 1975–1985 by Occupation

OCCUPATION	TOTAL		MALES		FEMALES		MALE % CHANGE
(IN 10,000 PERSONS)	1975	1985	1975	1985	1975	1985	
Service	855	1173	430	578	425	595	34.4
Government	196	199	165	164	31	35	-0.6
Professional and Technical	364	538	207	293	156	245	41.5
Managers and Officials	206	211	195	197	11	14	1.0
Clerical and Related	820	1021	405	453	415	568	11.9
Sales	738	861	457	537	282	324	32.6
Farmers, Lumbermen, and Fishermen	654	502	326	261	329	241	-19.9
Mining	9	4	9	4	0	0	-55.5
Transport and Communication	237	227	219	216	17	11	-1.4
Craftsman and Production Process	1508	1689	1142	1171	437	517	2.5
Laborers	148	230	95	128	52	102	34.7
Protective Service	457	501	207	228	250	273	10.1

Source: Research and Statistics Division, Minister's Secretariat, Ministry of Education, *Japan Statistical Yearbook*, 1986, p. 73.

The high concentration of women in a limited number of industries and occupations—i.e., the segregation of women in the labor market—persists in spite of the rapid overall increase of women workers. A significant part of this market segregation can be attributed to the lack of equal opportunities and discriminatory practices in employment, based on prejudices against women's aptitude and working ability.[10] In spite of the constitutional guarantee of equality of the sexes and the 1986 EEO law, women workers suffer, in many cases, from discriminatory practices in recruitment, assignment, wages, in-service education and training, upgrading, and promotion.

Table 15.7 Percent Change in Composition Rate of Females by Occupation 1975-1985

OCCUPATION	1975	1985
Service	49.7	50.7
Government	15.8	17.6
Professional and Technical	42.9	45.5
Managers and Officials	5.3	6.6
Clerical and Related	50.6	55.6
Sales	38.2	37.6
Farmers, Lumbermen, and Fishermen	50.3	48.0
Mining	—	—
Transport and Communication	7.1	4.8
Craftsman and Production Process	27.7	30.6
Laborers	35.1	44.3
Protective Services	54.7	54.5

Wage Disparity

If women succeed in getting a job, they are paid lower wages than men and will fall further behind over the years. Men's wages increase more with age: In 1981, the 50- to 54-year-old high school educated male with 1 to 2 years of firm tenure had a monthly wage that was 56 percent higher than that of a similarly educated 18- to 19-year-old. Among women, a worker aged 50 to 54 received only 17 percent more than her younger counterpart.[11] Wage dispersion among employees graduated from lower school levels is smaller, but becomes greater for graduates from four-year universities. Compared with male employees with the same years of service, the wages of female employees aged 40–44 are lower by 26 percent for junior high school graduates, 29 percent for senior high school graduates, and 35 percent for university graduates.[12]

Remuneration consists of a basic wage, various allowances, a semiannual bonus, and a number of fringe benefits. The basic wage depends upon the employee's education, age, and job abilities. Past work experience is taken into consideration to some extent when determining the salary of a newly hired middle-aged man. However, a woman in a comparable situation is treated as though she has no past work experience and receives exactly the same starting salary as an 18-year-old female high school graduate. This results in the majority of "older" women being transformed into a group willing to work whenever required due to the unavailability of full-time work.[13]

Japan's wage system is based on seniority and work responsibilities. Women's lower wages can be attributed to shorter service periods resulting from marriage and home affairs, and to women's lower status and less onerous duties at work. In addition, women tend to work in small factories and industries where wages are low and fringe benefits almost nonexistent.[14]

Wages and salaries are paid every month. A bonus is paid twice a year—about two month's wages in summer and about three month's wages in December. The bonus is related partially to the profit of the company and is usually a fixed amount. It is usually paid as a straight multiple of monthly wage, without any reflections of merit.[15] While extensively used by all Japanese employers, the bonus tends to be relatively larger in the larger firms, while smaller firms compete for labor on the basis of regular monthly wages and therefore must emphasize wages as opposed to bonuses. Japanese employees also receive an annual increase which is based on years of service to the firm, new job abilities, and merit, as well as a general increase in the base wage.[16]

Training Differences

In employment contexts, women still suffer discrimination in compensation and opportunities for advancement. The seniority and lifetime-employment systems impede the chance of success for women to rise to equal status with men in the corporation. Many firms fail to accord women the opportunities to gain promotion to managerial positions. The seniority system discriminates against short-term employees, who typically have been female, and discriminates against educated women as candidates for future management positions. More importantly, even after getting a job, women are excluded from in-company rotation and company training programs which are necessary prerequisites for advancement. As male employees become older, they develop as specialists; but female employees are forced to remain in low-level positions due to their lack of training.[17]

New employees are trained predominately by lectures and

on-the-job training. On-the-job training is the most emphasized and is conducted with planned instruction by the supervisors and job rotation. Under the promotion by length of service system, the employees are not in competition with one another and the supervisors are willing to pass on the necessary skills. The training women receive is minimal, with emphasis placed on receptionist activities, including how to greet customers and how to bow. Special attention is placed on the correct procedure in answering phone calls and on the use of polite language. For women, technical information and material for advancement in a profession are limited,[18] whereas men receive managerial training in the company's centers to improve conceptual and human skills.[19]

For college-educated women, it has been *assumed* that they will not work their entire adult lives and thus will not desire to move from place to place in job progression—the normal procedure in Japan. Employers considered them expensive due to the emphasis placed on seniority and training. Businesses invest money in college graduates during their first two years of service for training and indoctrination and only begin to balance these costs with increased productivity during the third year.[20]

Cultural Pressures Encountered by Japanese Women

Despite the fact that women in the Japanese work force have in the past traditionally been considered part-timers with a short worklife expectancy, cultural pressures have influenced women's decisions to return to work. As the number of divorces has been increasing in Japan, women have sought to return to the work force earlier than they had previously.[21] Japanese women generally take care of the children after a divorce as custody goes to the mother in about 80 percent of the cases. The judge makes his decision based on two factors—age and economic condition. If the child is under ten years of age, mothers tend to get custody; if the child is older than ten, and especially if the child expresses a preference to be with his father, the father may get custody. Statistics show that 167,300 families have a single father compared to 718,000 families with a single mother.[22]

The divorce agreement generally includes only one lump-sum settlement payment, which averages 1 to 5 million yen ($4,176–20,833).[23] There is usually no alimony in Japan, although the settlement is occasionally paid out monthly until a fixed sum is reached. Child support is minimal, and 78 percent of men do not keep up the payments.[24] Divorce represents a severe financial burden for women because even if they wish to return to the work force, virtually no child-care facilities are available. Japanese women are also responsible for the care of elderly parents who are no longer capable of caring for themselves, which presents an added financial burden to the unemployed single mother.

A woman's most important job is the education of the children at home and at school. Getting into the best high school increases the chances of getting into the best university, which means getting the best possible job four years later. Cultural norms dictate that mothers spend a good deal of time with their children in order to achieve this goal. Higher education is the key to social mobility and status. When applying for a job, the name of the university is more important than the student's grades. University names like Todai, Keio, Waseda, Kyodai open doors to the best jobs in the larger firms. Firms such as Mitsubishi, Mitsui, Sumitomo, Japan Air Lines, Fujitsu, or Hitachi are known to offer the best pay, the best hours, and the best fringe benefits in Japan.[25]

Utilizing Women in Japanese Firms

Human resource management in Japanese firms is developed under a strategy of internalizing the labor market. It aims to recruit, allocate, and utilize its own human resources, relying on outside labor markets as little as possible. This strategy leads to employment relations and human resource management with a long-term perspective. It also operates within an "extended internal labor market," whereby the management of a parent company transfers and re-allocates its personnel within a group of related companies.[26]

Due to this long-term philosophy, Japanese firms encounter a major problem with employing women. They cannot distinguish "career women" from short-term employees. Male graduates are sought after by government offices and businesses, whereas female graduates are basically ignored. Frequently, men look down upon their female colleagues due to cultural biases. Women are not usually put on the promotion track unless they insist on it. In fact, according to a Ministry of Labor survey, more than half the companies (52 percent) do not give female employees any chance at promotions. They claim that the job women do is of an auxiliary nature, the length of service is short, and they have little or no supervisory capability.[27] This means that a large supply of talented females are not considered for employment by any major Japanese firms.

It is our assertion, however, that circumstances in Japan have changed sufficiently for a re-examination of the potential place of women managers within Japanese society. We have reviewed the new legal status granted to women through the enactment of the Equal Employment Opportunity Law and determined that increasing numbers of women are entering the work force in a number of industries. As the number of female university graduates increases, meaningful employment needs to be made available for them to take advantage of their educational abilities. To do otherwise would only waste the expense of educating them and frustrate those who may want to seriously pursue a business career.

On the other hand, we recognize that Japanese society demands that women fulfill certain family and social obligations that are at odds with the demands of a business career. In Japan, the ordained role of women is to put marriage and family before all other obligations, much as the role of women in America thirty years ago. In addition, Japanese business requires long working hours which often includes after-work social contact with customers and associates, a business custom that would make most Japanese men uncomfortable if it were to include Japanese women.

Since the idea of women working as business managers in Japan is a relatively new idea, it is unclear how many Japanese women would truly want to make the necessary sacrifices to become business managers. However, in view of the increasing number of female university graduates, one must assume that some small number of Japanese women want to pursue a more meaningful role than pouring tea for three years before marriage. It is to these women that the new equal opportunity law was directed and it is for them that we think that employers in Japan need to re-evaluate their employment practices.

Recognizing the conflict between family obligations and work obligations for women in Japan, and the historical reticence of Japanese firms to employ women in managerial roles in Japan, we think it a good opportunity for foreign companies to consider hiring those women who are serious about a managerial career. Perhaps this can best be accomplished by beginning with new female university graduates. In Japan, by law, all hiring of university seniors commences on the first day of October before graduation (although many Japanese firms disregard this law, especially for graduates of imperial universities). Many female graduates have better grades than their male counterparts but are only considered for interviews after the men have completed theirs—this being because of the Japanese firms' reluctance to hire females. Foreign firms are at a disadvantage in attempting to hire these graduates because of the Japanese preference to work with a Japanese firm that understands their expectations of the employment arrangement.

However, if foreign firms were willing to actively pursue female graduates, they would be able to obtain the best students available. Foreign firms would have to impress upon the women graduates that the firm's expectation is that female employees need not retire upon marriage and, more importantly, would be encouraged to continue their employment. Women in these firms would receive the same training and promotional opportunities that was available to men. Perhaps most importantly, the firm would have to demonstrate that the employment responsibilities in the Japanese context are understood by the firm. If this could be accomplished, foreign firms could end up hiring the best and brightest of the Japanese graduating class.

In following this strategy, it is apparent that certain foreign firms would be at an advantage over others. Since Japanese business practices put so much emphasis on personal relations with customers and clients, and since most Japanese men would feel uncomfortable dealing with Japanese women, foreign firms that would be able to offer employment with little or no customer contact would have an advantage in hiring prospective female managers. Therefore, jobs not involving sales might be a logical position to place female managers. For example, IBM Japan has recently commenced the hiring of female university graduates in their software division. Foreign banks and publishing companies have hired some Japanese women managers who are fluent in English to manage their foreign accounts and deal with foreign clients.

In fact, any job that is technology-directed and requires little contact with Japanese customers would be a very suitable opportunity for a prospective female manager. Other examples would be language schools, entertainment firms, brokerage houses, airlines, and shipping firms. Interestingly, as the Japanese economy changes from an emphasis on production to an emphasis on technology, more managerial opportunities for females should be available.

Once the initial hire has been accomplished, individual firms would have to devise means of maintaining their employees and advancing their career objectives. Training programs are needed internally for women in order to develop managerial talent. Many highly skilled women are unaware of what career opportunities exist within firms. Even if she aspires to a particular position, she may not know the "path" that she should take to get there. Cultural norms in Japan have precluded women from the opportunity to advance vertically in the organization.

Career management could be utilized by foreign firms in Japan to effectively utilize Japanese "career" women and involve them in their career development. A wide variety of career planning activities have become common practice in business organizations.[28] Career development is a sequence of educational, personal, and vocational experiences in which a person plans, directs, and participates in during his or her working life. The organization is involved in structuring the activities that direct the flow of the individual into, through, and ultimately out of the institution.[29] This organizational perspective, commonly known as career management, encompasses a planned program of recruitment and placement of new personnel, performance and potential evaluation, design of effective internal career systems, and a blend of positional experiences with on- and off-the-job training assignments.

Career path planning is the process of documenting possible patterns of job movement (both laterally and vertically) that an employee might follow within the organizational hierarchy. The development of career paths requires three steps: defining work activities, identifying skill and knowledge requirements, and establishing job families.[30] Work activities and skill knowledge requirements are used to identify groups of jobs with similar requirements (job families), which are subsequently used to outline career paths. The importance of career planning for Japanese firms is the involvement of women with management in the process. While it is true that Japanese males experience a considerable amount of cross training, this training—which is essential for upward mobility—currently does not exist for women.

The key to successful implementation of career-planning programs is to involve Japanese women in the process. Societal norms assume that the Japanese male will remain with the organization and the Japanese female will leave after a relatively short tenure. However, if firms were to modify their promotional policies and practices to create an open rather than a closed male-dominated internal labor market, Japanese firms could experience a knowledgeable and capable female work force that has previously been overlooked.

Even with the best of intentions, foreign firms should be prepared for the high risk that many new female employees may still choose to retire upon marriage or pregnancy. After all, the societal pressures are great and the choice to break with tradition is a difficult one. Until Japanese male attitudes change in regard to women, the employer must contemplate the possible retirement of the newly trained female manager. However, in spite of the risk, the potential benefit is great and foreign firms are uniquely positioned to take advantage of the new opportunity for women in Japan.

Conclusion

There is an increasing pool of college-educated women in Japan who, if given the opportunity, are prepared to take on managerial positions in Japanese business. Due to the difficulties foreign concerns face in hiring Japanese male graduates in Japan, it seems appropriate that foreign firms seriously consider a managerial strategy to encourage qualified female employees as a means of obtaining local managers in Japan. The legal environment has created a labor force that is ripe for change. Innovative firms stand to gain by taking actions to accord women equal opportunities in recruitment, hiring, and promotion. This extends beyond the "make efforts" dictum of the new Equal Employment Opportunity law. While this strategy is not without risk, the potential return seems well worth the risk.

16

Continuity and Change
in Japanese Management*

Tomasz Mroczkowski and Masao Hanaoka

The relationship between tradition and change in Japan has always been complicated by the fact that change itself is a tradition

—Edward Seidensticker

For Japan, the era of competing on the basis of being the low-cost imitator of the West and of using exports to stimulate its domestic economy came to a dramatic end with the rise of the yen. Japanese companies reacted by shifting the competitive battleground to a different plane. They have moved up-market to compete on the basis of quality, innovation and product leadership while defending their cost structures against NICs and Western competitors by rapid automation. They have also sped up the process of multinationalization, moving lower value-added production offshore and locating production facilities close to consumer markets in Europe and the United States.

This strategy has required accelerated restructuring of the Japanese economy, including dramatic shifts in employment. It has also required that the Japanese management system be modified to make it more efficient. One of the most important changes is that the "new" management system will have to encroach upon the traditional practices of lifetime employment and seniority-based wages.

Recent economic results indicate that after the shock of the high yen the Japanese economy has pulled off another "miracle"; and those in the West who saw an end to Japanese competitiveness have been proven wrong again. In 1987, Japanese industrial output was 4 percent higher than in the previous year. The profits of Japanese manufacturers grew by 25-30 percent in fiscal 1987 (after falling by 29 percent in 1986) and investment in new plants and machinery grew by a total of 33 percent in real terms in 1984–86.

Remarkably, Japanese manufacturing wage costs have been kept in check. After adding in productivity growth, Japanese firms now have lower unit wage costs than they did a year ago (while West Germany's have leapt by almost 5 percent). Japan has achieved all this while adjusting the size of its work force, shifting manpower out of sunset industries and into new industries and the service sector, and also moving production offshore. This remarkable achievement could not have been possible without major changes in Japanese companies' employment and reward systems—changes that many Western observers believed would be so disruptive and difficult that they would take a much longer time to implement.

This article assesses the magnitude and direction of the changes in the employment and promotion systems inside Japanese companies. An evaluation of these changes is crucial to understanding Japan's competitive strategy for the 1990s.

The Romantic Myth of Japanese Management

Almost all of the many books and articles on Japanese management published in the West have been written by non-Japanese observers. Frequently, these analyses have been used for the purpose of criticizing the shortcomings and failures of Western management. This practice has contributed to the creation of the myth of Japanese management. Until recently, this myth has gone largely unchallenged, especially in the United States.

The system of manpower management developed in the sixties and seventies that has served Japan so well is currently undergoing a gradual transformation. Even before economic and demographic conditions made it obvious, perceptive Japanese observers pointed out the inherent weaknesses of "Japanese management":

- The system of lifetime commitment and groupism encouraged employee dependency and suppressed individual creativity.

- The employment system discriminated against non-lifelong employees (temporary employees, women, part-timers, seasonal laborers and employees hired midway through their careers) and prevented the formation of a free horizontal labor market.

- The seniority-based system of rewards created a promotion gridlock for middle management and especially for the younger outstanding employee.[1]

Japanese executives have long been aware of the disadvantages of their system but believed these were outweighed by its strengths. However, by the mid-1980s many companies found themselves unable to fully maintain the "old system." The search for a new Japanese management system was assumed with a great deal of urgency.

Continuous Evolution and the Crisis of Japanese Management

In order to understand how it was possible to effect major changes in Japanese manpower management relatively smoothly and effectively, it is important to realize that Japanese management practices have never been static but rather have evolved through continual adjustments to new economic, social, and competitive priorities.

Prior to World War II, Japanese industry used a rigid form of status promotion (*shikaku-seido*). Employees were divided into *shokuin* (white collar) and *koin* (blue collar) workers, with simple seniority promotion ladders within each category and no possibility of upward mobility for *koin* workers into the *shokuin* category. After the end of World War II, during the American occupation, a number of important changes occurred. A labor standards law was introduced and labor union growth occurred. The U.S. Army introduced management training programs, and wage systems were changed as the old employee status classification system collapsed.

An attempt was made to introduce an American-style job classification system. While this attempt largely failed, companies, to varying degrees, began using ability and skills instead of seniority alone as a basis for job grade assignment.

During the 1950s and 1960s, Japan experienced labor shortages due to very rapid industrial expansion. Many of the familiar features of "Japanese management" were broadly introduced at that time: By the mid-sixties more than 70 percent of companies used employee suggestion schemes and almost a third used regular employee morale surveys. Companies used core groups of lifetime employees who were promoted using systems of grade ladders within integrated functions. Because of the labor shortages, part-time employment of women outside the lifetime system became widespread. The actual number of hours worked was reduced while efforts were made to prolong the retirement age from 55 to 60.

Japanese management scholars regard the seventies as marking a "peak" in the development of the practices which the world learned to regard as "Japanese management." However, in the seventies there were also a number of factors that demanded modifications in Japanese personnel management practices. Economic growth rates were, on average, only half that of the previous decade. With broad introduction of automation, Japanese companies began hiring significantly fewer recruits into entry-level positions. Over the years, this caused the average age of employees moving up the seniority ladder to increase, putting pressure on average wage costs. Real opportunities for advancement became increasingly limited, and attempts to boost sagging morale brought a proliferation of new titles empty of substance.

Japanese management reacted to these problems by increasing flexibility in the employment and reward systems. Temporary transfers of surplus employees and flex-time systems were introduced. Systems of "specialist" or "expert" posts with grades similar to those for managers were created to provide ways of promoting staff workers who had already reached the highest grade and for whom managerial positions were unavailable. Efforts were made to decrease the importance of seniority as the major condition for pay raises and introduce merit components into wage and bonus systems.[2]

The early eighties saw the sharp rise in the value of the dollar, making Japanese goods very competitive in the United States. The Japanese experienced an export boom which allowed them to postpone some of the inevitable changes in their economic policies.[3] The sharp rise of the yen in 1985 suddenly put enormous pressures on many Japanese companies. To remain competitive they had to control costs, innovate, restructure, and often move offshore. In 1986, Japan's exports declined by 15.9 percent and the profits of Japanese companies also declined dramatically. Because of the strong yen, the number of bankruptcies shot up (since May 1986, more than sixty companies have gone bankrupt every month) and unemployment increased.[4] Capital productivity has been decreasing in Japan in the past few years. While total factor productivity in Japan grew more rapidly than in other countries in the 1960s and 1970s, in the 1980s the growth rate leveled off. Japanese productivity specialists forecast that under these conditions it will be very difficult to continue to make the kind of productivity improvements that Japanese companies made in the past.[5] The Japanese have reached a watershed in their economic policies.

By the mid-1980s, the entire system of Japanese management faced three major challenges:

• Japanese companies have mainly relied on the variable bonus and flexible benefits to control their wage costs. After the dramatic rise in the value of the yen, the problem of cost containment became much more difficult. Average wages in Korea and Taiwan are now respectively eight times and six times lower than in Japan. The challenge many Japanese companies face is how to reduce labor costs, cut capacity, and restructure without resorting to massive layoffs.

• The second major challenge Japanese management faces is how to continue to *motivate* employees and managers in a new environment in which the system of evaluation and rewards, as well as employee attitudes and expectations, is changing.

• The third challenge for Japanese management is how to redesign employment relationships in a way that would blend the advantages of the older system of dependence on the company with the necessity to promote employee self-reliance, initiative, and creativity.

The Emergence of a New Management Paradigm

Restructuring: Methods of Employment and Wage Control

For many Japanese companies, especially those in mature industries, the most immediate problem is how to achieve significant reductions in employment levels as they reduce capacity and modernize. For example, over the next three years the three biggest Japanese steel companies plan to shed 40,000 jobs without firing anyone.

This process is being carefully monitored by the Japanese Labor Ministry as well as by the Japanese Confederation of Labor, which compiled a survey of how Japanese companies carried out employment cuts and what methods they intended to use for future reductions (see Tables 16.1 and 16.2). The tables reveal the lengths to which Japanese companies will go to avoid layoffs. All companies rely on hiring freezes and to a lesser extent on elimination of overtime. Both of these approaches are also commonly used in the West. What is peculiarly Japanese is the extensive use of job rotation and employee reassignments. In the case of larger companies (over 1,000 employees), almost half report using this as a major method of employment restructuring. Although part-time workers are indeed often laid off, firings and layoffs of full-time employees are reported by less than 10 percent of the companies surveyed (with the exception of the very small companies). Interestingly, in their plans for the future, the companies intend to continue the same policies by putting even greater emphasis on job-rotation. Layoffs of full-time employees will continue to be rare.

Some of the methods used by Japanese management to control wage and salary costs differ even more from Western practices. Wage, salary, and bonus reductions are shared by all groups in the enterprise: directors and managers as well as employees. Even when temporary or permanent layoffs *are* used, they do not have the same implications for employees as similar practices in the West. Japanese companies widely use inter-company manpower leasing and transfer. The system is run by company groups called *igyoshu koryu*[6] and is organized on a territorial basis with local government and Chamber of Commerce support. According to a 1987 survey by the NHK (*Nippon Hoso Kyokai*, Japan Broadcasting Corporation), there are 471 local centers in which 17,000 Japanese companies participate. These centers exchange information on manpower surpluses and shortages and arrange for temporary or permanent transfers between the participating companies. They may also engage in joint new business/new product development. In effect, this system extends the lifetime employment principles while maintaining flexibility and economic rationality.

According to some Japanese manpower policy experts, Japanese companies will be moving toward more flexibility in their employment and wage policies. International and domestic compe-

Table 16.1 1986 Employee Reduction
(in number of companies and percent of total responses)

	SIZE OF COMPANY (BY NUMBER OF EMPLOYEES)					ALL COM-PANIES
	1–99	100–299	300–999	1000–2999	3000+	
Methods of Employment Control						
Hiring freeze	54	48	57	23	21	203
	36.5%	30.8%	42.5%	54.8%	51.2%	39.0%
Part-time workers terminated	36	24	22	10	14	106
	24.3%	15.4	16.4%	23.8%	34.1%	20.3%
No overtime	23	19	21	8	6	77
	15.5%	12.2%	15.7%	19.0%	14.6%	14.8%
Shortening of working day	11	12	7	2	0	32
	7.4%	7.7%	5.2%	4.8%	0%	6.1%
Job rotation	29	34	30	17	19	129
	19.6%	21.8%	22.4%	40.5%	46.3%	24.8%
Temporary lay-offs	2	2	0	1	2	7
	1.4%	1.3%	0%	2.4%	4.9%	1.3%
Planned employee reductions	9	3	5	2	3	22
	6.1%	1.9%	3.7%	4.8%	7.3%	4.2%
Employees fired	23	12	8	3	3	49
	15.5%	7.7%	6.0%	7.1%	7.3%	9.4%
Other	8	12	4	3	4	31
	5.4%	7.7%	3.0%	7.1%	9.8%	6.0%
Methods of Wage Control						
Overtime pay eliminated	46	66	64	23	22	221
	31.1%	42.3%	47.8%	54.8%	53.7%	42.4%
Director's/manager's pay reduced	45	32	31	6	9	123
	30.4%	20.5%	23.1%	14.3%	22.0%	23.6%
Postpone increases or reduce basic pay	55	44	38	12	13	162
	37.2%	28.2%	28.4%	28.6%	31.7%	31.1%
Director's bonus reduced	62	44	45	9	10	170
	41.9%	28.2%	33.6%	21.4%	24.4%	32.6%
General bonus reduced	56	45	39	11	9	160
	37.8%	28.8%	29.1%	26.2%	22.0%	30.7%
Other	6	3	8	2	3	22
	4.1%	1.9%	6.0%	4.8%	7.3%	4.2%
Total Number of Companies:	148	156	134	42	41	521

Source: Susumu KoyoChousei, Ministry of Labor Employment *Rationalization Survey*, 1986.

Table 16.2 Future Reduction Forecast
(in number of companies and percent of total responses)

	SIZE OF COMPANY (BY NUMBER OF EMPLOYEES)					ALL COM-PANIES
	1–99	100–299	300–999	1000–2999	3000+	
Methods of Employment Control						
Hiring freeze	57	60	57	22	15	211
	34.8%	36.8%	40.4%	51.2%	34.1%	38.0%
Part-time workers terminated	46	37	25	8	12	128
	28.0%	22.7%	17.7%	18.6%	27.3%	23.1%
No overtime	42	28	26	7	7	110
	25.6%	17.2%	18.4%	16.3%	15.9%	19.8%
Shortening of working day	23	12	12	4	1	52
	14.0%	7.4%	8.5%	9.3%	2.3%	9.4%
Job rotation	38	37	40	17	27	159
	23.2%	22.7%	8.4%	39.5%	61.4%	28.6%
Temporary lay-offs	7	4	4	1	3	19
	4.3%	2.5%	2.8%	2.3%	6.8%	3.4%
Planned employee reductions	10	7	6	4	2	29
	6.1%	4.3%	4.3%	9.3%	4.5%	5.2%
Employees fired	20	8	9	2	2	41
	12.1%	4.9%	6.4%	4.7%	4.5%	7.4%
Other	6	9	5	4	7	31
	3.7%	5.5%	3.5%	9.3%	15.9%	5.6%
Methods of Wage Control						
Overtime pay eliminated	69	77	72	23	21	262
	42.1%	47.2%	51.1%	53.5%	47.7%	47.2%
Director's/manager's pay reduced	45	28	29	8	10	120
	27.4%	17.2%	20.6%	18.6%	22.7%	21.6%
Postpone increases or reduce basic pay	70	55	28	6	13	172
	42.7%	33.7%	19.9%	14.0%	29.5%	31.0%
Director's bonus reduced	74	49	43	8	8	182
	45.1%	30.1%	30.5%	18.6%	18.2%	32.8%
General bonus reduced	85	70	56	12	15	238
	51.8%	42.9%	39.7%	27.9%	34.1%	42.9%
Other	7	5	3	2	3	20
	4.3%	3.1%	2.1%	4.7%	6.8%	3.6%
Total Number of Companies:	164	163	141	43	44	555

Source: Susumu KoyoChousei, Ministry of Labor Employment *Rationalization Survey*, 1986.

Table 16.3   Relative Contributions of Seniority and Merit
Factors to Pay Raises

	SENIORITY	ABILITY (MERIT)
1978	57.9%	42.1%
1983	54.4	45.6
1984	49.0	51.0
1987	46.0	54.0

Source: Romu Gyosei Kenkyujo (July 8–September 11, 1987); 1,900
Japanese companies surveyed.

tition may ultimately force companies to begin treating a larger
portion of labor costs as variable costs rather than as fixed costs.[7]

The New Motivational System:
Performance-Based Evaluation and Rewards

The Changing Importance of Seniority

It is broadly believed that the principle of seniority governs the
Japanese system of motivating employees, rewarding loyalty, and
maintaining group harmony. In fact, the pure seniority principle
has been systematically eroding in Japan, as evidenced by results
of surveys carried out in Japanese companies by the Romu Gyosei
Kenkyujo (a private research foundation). In the decade between
1978 and 1987, according to the personnel departments of the surveyed companies, the contribution of the seniority factor to pay
raises systematically declined from an average of 57.9 percent to
46 percent while the contribution of the performance factor
increased from 42.1 percent to 54 percent (see Table 16.3).
Low economic growth rates, which result in fewer recruits being
hired, have made it uneconomical for companies to continue to pay
ever higher wages to an increasing proportion of their senior
employees. Japanese companies have reacted to this situation by
remodeling the motivational system. While the retirement age in
Japan has been extended, many companies are using various forms
of early retirement incentives. Often, employees are finding their
wage increases capped at age 40–45. In fact, in many companies
average pay may drop by as much as 20 percent after age fifty.

In order to gauge the magnitude of change taking place in the motivation systems employed by Japanese companies, it is necessary to understand the relationships between seniority and the other factors that affect employee promotion. However important, seniority has never been the only factor determining a wage or salary in a Japanese company. Assignment of an individual to a wage/salary grade depended largely on education and job-related skills. In inter-grade promotions, both of these factors also played an important part. In the process of annual within-grade raises and bonus awards, however, it is general company performance which is the important factor in the increment negotiations. Under the traditional system the final outcome in terms of a wage increment would typically incorporate a combination of the negotiated raise and seniority. The raise formula would thus look like this:

individual base wage/salary within grade x negotiated % raise ("up rate") +
distribution by length of service years (expressed in yen not as a %) = raise

Loyalty to the company and peer pressure were judged to be sufficiently strong to motivate employees. The outstanding employee was not singled out for immediate large rewards but was kept motivated by interesting assignments, training opportunities, and eventual promotion to a higher grade or managerial position ahead of his peers.

According to a study performed by the authors at the Institute of Business Research at Daito Bunka University, this system has been undergoing substantial modifications. The personnel managers from thirty large and medium-sized companies representing a cross-section of Japanese manufacturing and service sectors were surveyed and they felt without exception that the old seniority system could not be maintained without substantial change. On the other hand, only a handful of the managers wanted to abolish it completely. The majority of companies were planning and implementing gradual modification of the system allowing them to keep some of its most useful features. Modifications usually started with the introduction of merit evaluation into the promotion/reward process.

Performance Appraisal Japanese Style

The *Shikaku* (position title) classification system is used to form the basis of grading, promotion, wage, and bonus decisions in

Japanese companies. This gradually has been giving way to performance appraisal and merit rating systems. Rather than replacing the old system with a new one, Japanese companies grafted performance evaluation onto the old system by incorporating it as a factor in the formulas used for pay increment calculation. In companies which have embraced the individual merit rating system, the formula would typically look as follows:

individual base salary/wage x average "up rate" within each grade (%) x
individual merit rating x seniority coefficient = raise

The actual impact of performance evaluations on pay varies from company to company and also depends on the position and grade of the employee. According to a 1985 study by the Japan Personnel Policy Research Institute, 35 percent of managerial bonus awards depended on the performance appraisal component, while for clerks this rate was only 22 percent.[8] Individual performance appraisal results can account for anywhere from 20 percent to 50 percent of the pay increment. The higher percentage is found in those companies that have pursued change most aggressively, including companies under Western management and joint-venture operations.

The Japanese concepts of performance and achievement are not the same as in the West and the relative importance of different components and ways of measuring and weighing them are different. The concept of personnel evaluation most widely used in Japan is the merit rating (*jinji koka*). This concept is based on educational attainment and job ability factors such as communication skills, cooperativeness, and sense of responsibility. *Jinji koka* is being gradually replaced by performance evaluation based on work results. The Japanese concept of performance (*gyo seki*) is distinct from the Western concept and includes not only the achievement of actual results, but the expenditure of good faith effort. New performance evaluation systems are currently being introduced in 75 percent of Japanese companies.[9]

Individual achievement based rewards are likely to continue to grow in importance in the motivational systems in Japanese companies. One of the factors contributing to the problems of motivating Japanese employees is the erosion of labor unions. At one time, 56 percent of the labor force belonged to unions. As the Japanese economy matured, labor union membership declined and union participation rates have now fallen below 28 percent.[10] As Japan moves out of the smokestack industries and becomes a "service" economy, further declines in union membership are expected to occur. Company and work-group loyalties are being replaced by individualism.

The trend away from seniority and toward individual performance-based pay has been documented in a survey carried out by the Social and Economic Congress of Japan which asked management and labor unions about changes in the factors that will determine Japanese wages by the year 2000 (see Table 16.4).

Redesigning the Employment Relationships

While maintaining considerable continuity with past practices, the system of lifetime employment is undergoing change. A 1984 survey conducted by the prime minister's office found that nearly half of all Japanese between the ages of twenty and twenty-nine expressed a preference for an "employment changing" job environment to the assurance of lifetime employment. In another survey conducted by a large job placement firm, a quarter of the college graduates interviewed had already changed jobs at least once.[11]

Most Japanese employers feel that it is advantageous to maintain the lifetime employment principle even if only in a modified form. Only a minority feel that the idea has outlived its usefulness. Most employers feel they must maintain lifetime employment for core employees in order to attract recruits of sufficient calibre. However, the group of "core" employees who enjoy lifetime employment can be quite small (it is only 10 percent in the fast-food industry).

While most companies have postponed the retirement age (as noted earlier), employees are now obliged to consider whether they will continue to stay with the company after the age of 40 or 45 or face the possibility of being transferred to affiliated companies. Companies are also using "specialist" positions for senior employees who are either being retired from managerial posts or are not considered promotable to managerial ranks.

The lifetime employment system is also being modified through increased use of diversified hiring methods. The routine hiring of school graduates is being more and more frequently supplemented by the hiring of contract employees and part-timers.[12] Hiring on the basis of skills for a specific, narrowly defined job opening is growing. For example, in 1988 Niko Shoken (Nikko Security Co., Ltd.) started recruiting foreign exchange traders at high salaries on a contract basis. These employees in principle

Table 16.4 Emphasized Factors of Wage System Around in 2000

(IN PERCENT)

	MANAGEMENT			LABOR UNION			NEUTRAL			TOTAL		
	+*	NC	−	+	NC	−	+	NC	−	+	NC	−
Age	6.7	21.0	69.0	15.5	26.1	57.1	5.5	21.9	71.6	8.8	22.7	66.4
Service years	6.7	28.6	61.9	11.2	33.5	55.3	3.3	32.8	62.3	6.9	31.4	60.1
Educational background	5.7	17.6	73.8	10.6	18.6	70.2	4.4	19.7	76.0	6.7	18.6	73.5
Experience years	25.7	49.5	21.4	33.5	44.7	22.4	23.5	51.9	20.8	23.7	48.9	21.5
Job, occupational category	80.0	15.7	0.5	82.6	13.7	1.9	77.0	19.1	2.7	79.8	16.2	1.6
Ability for achievement	91.0	4.8	1.0	84.5	9.3	5.0	86.9	10.9	0.5	87.7	8.1	2.0
Amount of work done	50.0	35.7	11.0	34.2	42.2	21.1	38.3	48.1	13.1	41.5	41.7	14.6
Family size	2.4	45.7	47.1	7.5	47.8	44.1	7.7	49.7	40.4	5.6	47.7	44.0

Source: Takao Watanabe, *Demystifying Japanese Management* (Tokyo: Gakuseisha Publishing Co., 1937), p. 195.

*+ = Inrease
NC = No Change
− = Decrease

Table 16.5 The Prospect of Worker's Mobility
in Future Japanese Society

	MANAGEMENT	LABOR	NEUTRAL	TOTAL POLLED
It will increase remarkably	3.2%	2.2%	3.3%	2.9%
It will increase a bit more or less	69.4	59.0	66.9	65.4
Unchanged	17.2	19.4	9.9	15.4
It will decrease a bit	0.6	1.5	0.6	0.9
It will decrease remarkably	0.6	—	—	0.2
No answer	8.9	17.9	19.2	15.2

Source: Takao Watanabe, *Demystifying Japanese Management* (Tokyo: Gakuseisha Publishing Co., 1987), p. 185.

cannot transfer to the lifetime employment track and if their performance is below expectations their salaries may be cut or they may be fired. Similarly, Sumitomo Trust Bank has been hiring security traders and economic analysts on a contract basis. As Mr. Osamu Sakurai, president of the Bank, put it: "Under the lifetime employment system we could not offer appropriately high salaries to obtain top talent. Nor could we hire on a short-term basis."[13] With these new hiring practices, labor mobility is rising and is expected to continue to increase gradually in the future (see Table 16.5). Mobility among Japanese managers and professionals is also increasing. According to a study performed by Nippon Manpower, a Japanese human resource development company, 75 percent of those surveyed declared that they would entertain a lucrative offer from a headhunter.[14]

While Japanese management clearly wants to continue to tap the advantages of lifetime employment for selected employee groups, there is growing evidence that a partial horizontal labor market is emerging rapidly. For years, Japanese employees demonstrated a preference for security over risk and opportunity. This attitude began to change after the oil shocks. Japanese employees realized that they could not place all their reliance on their companies and that they would have to start relying on themselves. Today, the latest catch word among personnel specialists in Japan is "employee self-reliance." It is not only that the attitudes and expectations of employees—especially younger employees—are changing, but the companies themselves are creating programs designed to promote new attitudes of self-reliance. Career development programs have been among the most popular new personnel systems adopted by Japanese companies in the past few years.[15] Today, companies like Toshiba and Yamaha use extensive career counseling to help employees develop new skills and attitudes that would enable them to survive in a horizontal labor market.

The Multi-Track Employment System

As they gradually redesign the employment and reward system in their companies, Japanese managers are trying to maintain the advantages of group harmony, employee loyalty, and cooperation (based on the lifetime employment principle) while both eliminating the burdens of employment hypertrophy and enhancing flexibility by shifting more of the risk on a greater proportion of employees. At the same time, for many companies which base their strategies on product leadership and innovations, stimulating employee initiative and creativity is a high priority.

The way Japanese management hopes to reconcile these conflicting goals is through the creation of a multi-track employment system. Employees hired for "life" enter the general track and can be moved horizontally (job rotation) as well as vertically (grade promotion). In the past, vertical promotion was often restricted by rules governing the minimum and standard "staying years" within one grade—effectively ensuring promotion by seniority. As companies relax those rules, more rapid promotion becomes possible. As job rotation and the hiring of specialists becomes more common, it becomes possible for a relatively junior employee to achieve a high grade. As companies choose to limit the percentage of lifetime employees, they expand hiring into the restricted tracks—which may include hiring more women, part-timers, and specialists.

As specific expertise becomes increasingly more important and seniority increasingly less, promotion grades become defined more precisely in terms of specific tasks rather than experience, general educational attainment, and general skills. Expanded flexibility can then also be applied at the higher (managerial) levels. However, promotion into these higher grades does not have to mean a managerial post. A variety of specialist positions offering high pay can be made available, which would allow for moving less-able managers into specialist positions and more-able specialists into management positions. A separate "subtrack" can be created for the failed or non-promotable. This is the well-known *taigu shoku* or "window job" track.

Compared with the grade systems that were used in the sixties and seventies, the systems emerging today offer more flexibility and more options to personnel management. Hiring methods have diversified. Today, Japanese personnel departments use headhunters to fill managerial and specialist technical positions, they lease groups of needed employees from manpower agencies, they entertain "walk in" offers from candidates, and they write a variety of contracts with employees on restricted tracks—including, to a greater extent, foreigners.[16] This is indeed a far cry from the standard practices in the past of relying primarily on school and university graduates. The flexibility of the system is being continually expanded. Many high-tech companies are diversifying grade denominations and promotion rules within particular tracks—especially research and development—to stimulate employee initiative and creativity.

Conclusion

Many of the critical practices on which the Japanese company bases its functioning depend on the principles of lifetime employment, company loyalty, and employee commitment. The Japanese will make every effort to maintain these principles in the foreseeable future. The changes going on in employment practices and employee motivation are not designed to destroy the old system but to increase its flexibility. This is very much in keeping with the traditional Japanese approach to change; however fast and deep it is, continuity with the uniquely Japanese "essence" must be maintained. The new Japanese management paradigm will certainly be different, yet like the modern Japanese home which usually retains a Japanese style room among Western style rooms and furniture, the Japanese company will retain a core of Japanese practices.

Western assessments of Japanese capabilities tend to oscillate between total awe and serious underestimation. The difficulties in changing to a new management system should not be underestimated. Japanese company presidents find that responsibility for decisions that have to be made rapidly is being transferred to them, that they have to act boldly and quickly, and that often there is no time for gradual consensus building. Popular

Japanese magazines have noted a large number of company presidents who have died in office during the past eighteen months or so, blaming their untimely deaths on the pressures of diversifying, building offshore plans, cutting costs, and laying off employees.[17]

The Japanese have handled profound change in the past very well (during the Meiji era and after World War II). This suggests that they are in a good position to overcome the obstacles and difficulties. Research on the introduction of robotics and flexible manufacturing systems in Japanese and Western companies show the Japanese to have superior capabilities in effective implementation of new manufacturing technology.[18] The Japanese appear very well positioned for the age in which competitive survival will depend on the ability of human groups to manage very rapid change. After the strains and difficulties of the current transformation, Japanese companies are likely to emerge in the 1990s as even more formidable competitors than ever before.

17

Market Research the Japanese Way*

Johny K. Johansson and Ikujiro Nonaka

When Sony researched the market for a lightweight portable cassette player, results showed that consumers wouldn't buy a tape recorder that didn't record. Company chairman Akio Morita decided to introduce the Walkman anyway, and the rest is history. Today it's one of Sony's most successful products.

Morita's disdain for large-scale consumer surveys and other scientific research tools isn't unique in Japan. Matsushita, Toyota, and other well-known Japanese consumer goods companies are just as skeptical about the Western style of market research. Occasionally, the Japanese do conduct consumer attitude surveys, but most executives don't base their marketing decisions on them or on other popular techniques. As the head of Matsushita's videocassette recorder division once said, "Why do Americans do so much marketing research? You can find out what you need by traveling around and visiting the retailers who carry your product."

Hands on Research

Of course, Japanese corporations want accurate and useful information about their markets as much as U.S. and European companies do. They just go about it differently. Japanese executives put much more faith in information they get directly from wholesalers and retailers in the distribution channels. Moreover, they track what's happening among channel members on a monthly, weekly, and sometimes even daily basis.

Japanese-style market research relies heavily on two kinds of information: "soft data" obtained from visits to dealers and other channel members, and "hard data" about shipments, inventory levels, and retail sales. Japanese managers believe that these data better reflect the behavior and intentions of flesh-and-blood consumers.

Japanese companies want information that is context specific rather than context free—that is, data directly relevant to consumer attitudes about the product, or to the way buyers have used or will use specific products, rather than research results that are too remote from actual consumer behavior to be useful. When Japanese companies do conduct surveys, they interview consumers who have actually bought or used a product. They do not scrutinize an undifferentiated mass public to learn about general attitudes and values. When Toyota wanted to learn what Americans preferred to small, imported cars, for example, the company asked owners and others who had driven the car what they liked of disliked about the Volkswagen Beetle.

Soft-Data Gathering

Senior as well as middle-level Japanese managers get involved in gathering soft data because they see the information as critical both for market entry and for maintaining good relationships later. Though impressionistic, such hands-on data give the managers a distinctive feel for the market—something they believe surveys or quantitative research methods can't supply. Talks with dealers yield realistic, context-specific information about competitors' as well as their own market performance.

A good example is Canon's decision on a new U.S. distribution strategy. In the early 1970s, the company's senior management became concerned about U.S. camera sales. Other product lines were doing well, but camera sales had lost ground to the chief competitor, Minolta. Canon finally decided it needed its own sales subsidiary because its distributor, Bell and Howell, wouldn't give additional support for the Canon line. Senior managers didn't use a broad survey of consumers or retailers to make this decision. They sent three managers to the United States to look into the problem and changed strategies based on their observations.

Canon's head of the U.S. team himself spent almost six weeks in 1972 visiting camera stores and other retail outlets across the United States. From talks with store owners, Tatehiro Tsuruta learned that U.S. dealers weren't giving Canon much support because their sales forces were too small. He also found out what kinds of cameras and promotional support would get them excited about the company's line.

This soft-data approach appears to lack the methodological rigor of scientific market research, but it is by no means haphazard or careless. In fact, Tsuruta's results were more meaningful because he actually observed how consumers behaved in the stores and how salespeople responded. On entering a store, Tsuruta would act as if he were just a customer browsing around. He would note how the cameras were displayed and how the store clerks served customers. Then by simply asking "What cameras do you stock?" he could assess whether the dealer was enthusiastic or indifferent about the Canon line. He could also determine how knowledgeable people were about camera features.

Tsuruta would then identify himself and invite the store manager to lunch to discuss cameras and whatever else happened to be on the dealer's mind. The payoff was more than just market research. He was building lasting relationships with the dealers— an important competitive advantage.

When Tsuruta visited drugstores and other discount outlets that Minolta favored he could see that these markets wouldn't work for Canon. Customers got poor service—in part because salespeople knew little about the products they were selling. The mass merchandisers' heavy price competition also made it difficult to project a quality image.

Tsuruta's research decided Canon's distribution strategy: sell exclusively through specialty dealers serving an upscale, high-quality niche just below Nikon's targeted segment. The successful introduction of Canon's AE-1 camera in 1976 proved the strategy right.

Canon is by no means unique among Japanese companies in the sales and distribution problems it experienced in the United States or in the means it used to remedy them. A group of managers

Honda sent to the United States in 1965 learned to their surprise that few dealers there stocked and serviced motorcycles exclusively. Company executives realized they would have to develop their own dealer network. Sony entered the U.S. radio and TV market in the late 1950s and almost immediately decided to establish its own U.S. distributor so it could be sure to get adequate sales support.

This soft-data approach is popular even after a Japanese company has penetrated the market. Frequent visits to people in the distribution channel help manufacturers resolve problems before they escalate and damage sales or relationships. Isao Makino, president of Toyota's U.S. sales subsidiary from 1975 to 1983—a period of great gains in market share—used to visit every Toyota dealer in the United States at least once a year. "I found," he said, "that out of the ten complaints from each dealer, you could attribute about five or six to simple misunderstandings, another two or three could be solved on the spot, and only one or two needed further work."

Hard-Data Gathering

When Japanese managers want hard data to compare their products to competitors', they look at inventory, sales, and other information that show the items' actual movement through the channels. Then they visit channel members at both the retail and wholesale levels to analyze sales and distribution coverage reports, monthly product movement records (weekly for some key stores), plant-to-wholesaler shipment figures, and syndicated turnover and shipment statistics on competitors.

Japanese managers routinely monitor their markets at home and abroad this way. Consider how Matsushita dealt with the weak performance of its Panasonic line distributor in South Africa. The sales figures he reported were reasonable, but he couldn't produce reliable data on sales and shares for the various types of stores or on inventory levels in the distribution chain.

In early 1982, three managers from the company's household electronics division paid a call on the South African distributor. Then they dropped in on the distributor's retail stores and wholesale facilities. Customarily, after exchanging greetings and presenting a token gift from headquarters, they got right down to business. They asked to see inventory, shipment, and sales records as part of a complete store audit covering Matsushita and competitive products. Six weeks later, after analyzing all the data, they gave the incredulous distributor a complete picture of Panasonic's product movement and market share through the entire South African channel. They also told the distributor what figures he should collect and report to the home office in the future.

Monitoring the Channels

Japanese managers try to track changing customer tastes closely and quickly. Their "one step at a time" management style for decision making also applies to how they approach marketing. After analyzing both hard and soft data on their channels, they make small, incremental changes in product features, packaging, and promotional efforts. Awareness of what is happening in the channels on a weekly or even daily basis gives them a deep and focused understanding of the marketplace and enables them to fine-tune their marketing rapidly—thereby protecting their competitive edge. This skill is especially important in the highly competitive packaged goods and consumer durable goods markets.

Kao Corporation, which dominates the detergent and soap market in Japan, illustrates this tight channel monitoring and incremental changes in marketing strategies. Kao executives analyze point-of-sales data weekly and wholesale inventory and sales statistics monthly.

The company occasionally uses consumer surveys and other quantitative research tools, but executives never base marketing decisions primarily on the information from them. These findings merely trigger more thorough audits of the channels using both soft- and hard-data gathering. If a survey or household panel study, for example, shows a sudden change in brand preferences or in family purchase patterns, Kao will send a high-level management team out to the stores. The group will spend one day at each store just observing customer behavior. The next day the team will talk to the store owner or manager to learn what kinds of support will move the products better. They will also ask if the dealer needs help stocking shelves or if special promotions would help.

Such tight channel monitoring has paid off handsomely for Kao, among others. When Procter and Gamble introduced disposable diapers in Japan in the mid-1970s, it immediately took 90 percent of this new and growing market. Lured by the big sales and earnings potential, Uni Charm, Kao, and other Japanese manufacturers created their own lines. With tight channel monitoring, the Japanese could quickly change product features to better suit consumer tastes, and by 1984 P and G's market share had plummeted to an anemic 8 percent.

One factor that frustrates U.S. and other Western corporations' efforts to enter Japanese distribution channels is their lack of knowledge about distributor expectations, which limits their ability to respond to consumer tastes. The handicapped Westerners can't refine their marketing quickly enough in Japan to parry competitors' moves.

Tight channel monitoring also improves operations and cost control. Kao and other Japanese companies would never be caught with the kind of inventory pileups that Warner Communications' Atari subsidiary found itself saddled with in 1983. A six-month lag in reports from retailers led to disastrous inventory of TV game cassettes.

Strong Vertical Integration

Japanese companies exert considerably more control over their distribution channels than do most U.S. and European corporations. Toyota has been more successful than Nissan in the Japanese market because of its stronger distribution network. In many cases, this control is nearly absolute because the manufacturer actually owns the distributors or has sufficient market power to dominate the channel. Shiseido, for example, a cosmetics manufacturer, has a strong market presence in Japan. It sells through a network of independent stores that use company-trained salespeople and reserve exclusive shelf space for the company's brands. In Japan, a consumer's choice of store often dictates what brand he or she will buy.

Such strong vertical integration affects the kind and quality of market research information Japanese managers can gather. They can shift some research tasks to the dealers, for example. It is not unusual for store employees to survey Japanese households by mail or phone, interview people when they come into a store, or even visit customers' homes for a talk.

Japanese salespeople change jobs less often than U.S. and European retail employees, so they are in a better position to develop expertise about customers and competitors. Moreover, stores tend to remain in the same locations. When Matsushita wants information on its Japanese customers, it goes to its 4,000 retail stores to find out.

Generalist Managers

Few Japanese managers at all corporate levels have received a formal business eduction; it is still something of a novelty in Japan. Other than Keio Business School, only a few business institutes exist there, and those offer continuing education programs more often than degree options.

That is one reason why marketing is not yet a specialized business profession in Japan—and hence one of several reasons why Japanese companies have not adopted Western-style market research. But even if formal training in marketing did exist, Japanese executives would probably consider the marketing function too important to leave to mid-level specialists.

Honda is a case in point. When it picked Kihachiro Kawashima to head its U.S. sales organization, the company chose a domestic sales expert who knew very little about the United States. Kawashima ascribes his ultimate success in America to three principles: "Be real, be close to the action, and be localized." What made the difference for Honda in the United States was the senior managers' decision to spend up to 50 percent of their time visiting and talking with distributors and dealers—the people who knew what U.S. customers really wanted. The ultimate goal of this hands-on, close-to-the-customer approach is to generate a better understanding of customer desires and behavior. The Japanese do not see marketing as something like engineering or finance that can be taught in school. Sensitivity to customers' desires is learned through hard work and experience.

Consensus Decision Making

In contrast to Western practice, Japanese executives do not give managers sole responsibility for a research area. They conduct research and make decisions by consensus, and they lean toward their intuitive judgment. Rarely do Japanese executives call in an outside professional, and when they do, they often disregard the consultant's report if it goes against their instincts about the best course of action. When Kozo Ohsone, the executive in charge of developing Sony's portable, compact Discman, heard that the company's marketing people were thinking about commissioning a research study he told them not to waste their money.

Lack of Diversification

Tight channel monitoring is also closely associated with the more specialized nature of Japanese industry. Most Japanese corporations have only one or a few related product lines, so managers and employees at all levels can learn more easily what is needed to succeed in the business. This specialization fosters an inductive, bottom-up approach to business planning and problem solving, whereas U.S. and European managements favor more deductive, top-down planning methods. Many large, diversified American corporations have to depend on Western-style market research because they lack the experience and knowledge to sell effectively in multiple industries. But outside marketing consultants and the battery of survey and other research tools they offer cannot fully substitute for intimate knowledge of distribution channels and customer tastes.

But Will It Be Enough?

General Electric's chief, John F. Welch, put it this way, "The Japanese have got the American consumer's number." Hands-on market research has given Japanese companies solid beachheads in the United States and other countries. Especially in mature industries like consumer goods, where customer preferences are so well understood, incremental adjustments in product features or promotional tactics may be all that is needed to have a competitive product.

Japanese-style research is starting to catch on in the United States and in other Western countries. Western executives are trying to get close to the customer and fine-tune product lines and marketing practices after listening carefully to what customers and distributors tell them. But this practice is still the exception in the West.

Ironically, just as some American and European executives are adopting a hands-on approach, a few Japanese companies are asking if their market research style can sustain their competitive edge over the long run—especially in the global marketplace. Some Canon executives, for example, are coming around to the view that surveys and other more scientific methods may be necessary as the company begins to look for ways to diversify.

Why are both sides changing like this? Increasing internationalization of both industries and business practices is doubtless one important reason. Global marketing is leading to a blending of managerial cultures and practices for all countries. Japanese executives are now thinking they may need some Western practices to keep their overseas footholds.

Consider, for example, the problem that Shiseido experienced in the U.S. market. Because it followed the Japanese tradition of sending in executives and managers from the home country, rather than hiring foreign nationals to fill top overseas posts, the company made no headway in the United States for ten years. No one at Shiseido headquarters understood that its cosmetics had to be introduced first into the high-status New York City stores before they could be sold successfully elsewhere. Only after hiring an experienced American cosmetics executive did Shiseido finally get its U.S. marketing effort on the right track.

Japanese corporations' reluctance to hire non-Japanese executives reflects a kind of provincialism that now poses hazards in an era of global markets. Their approach to market research could reinforce this parochialism because it focuses management attention on products and markets that the company already knows well—rather than on potential markets and industries. In their intensive channel monitoring, Japanese business leaders may see only narrow paths and miss the big picture.

Japanese executives today may need a broader perspective than they have taken in the past. Concentration on step-by-step marketing changes may keep them from spotting the social and economic trends that can throw seemingly unshakable industries into upheaval—precisely the changes that large-scale surveys and other Western-style methods uncover very effectively. As bulging surplus cash reserves and global marketing pressures push big Japanese corporations to diversity, more Japanese managers may begin to consider the potential advantages of Western-style market research.

18

Distribution in Japan: Problems and Changes*

Michael R. Czinkota

The large and growing Japanese trade surplus with the United States (as well as with most of the other industrialized nations of the world) has led many business, government, and academic leaders, both in the United States and abroad, to accuse Japan of maintaining barriers to the entry of foreign goods. Many of these accusations focus on the Japanese distribution system, which is perceived by a number of analysts to be Japan's primary non-tariff barrier to trade.[1] Studies of the Japanese market that deal with the importation of products refer extensively to the country's complex and highly unique distribution system. The multilayered channel structure, the fact that wholesalers ("*tonya*") keep on selling to each other, and the atomistic competition among retailers are frequently mentioned. As one report by the Office of the United States Trade Representative noted, Japan has a vast distribution network "with more wholesalers and retailers per capita than any of the advanced industrial nations."[2] Western observers often refer to Japan's traditional distribution system as "mysterious, complex, archaic, old fashioned, stubborn, inefficient and anachronistic."[3] As

*Reprinted with the permission of the *Columbia Journal of World Business* 20 (Fall 1985). Copyright 1985.

a result, it is frequently believed that "the manner in which the Japanese channels of distribution are structured and managed presents one of the major reasons for the apparent failure of foreign firms to establish major market participation in Japan."[4]

Often, however, the Japanese distribution system continues to be perceived today as it was twenty years ago. Only infrequently are changes and the current dynamism of the system taken into account and reported. It is the purpose of this chapter to review the major facets of the Japanese distribution system, and to highlight the changes taking place. By better understanding shifts in the wholesaling as well as the retailing sector, firms can better prepare for successful market entry into Japan. Policy-makers, in turn, are provided with information about changes already taking place and future changes needed and worth negotiating for.

This chapter represents the findings of a small scale exploratory study. Apart from the customary literature review, the results are based on facts and opinions gathered during a series of in-depth interviews in Japan and the United States with ninety-seven individuals from fifty-one public and private sector institutions. The individuals interviewed included corporate executives, government officials from a variety of bureaus and departments, consultants, academics, and journalists.

Major Features of the Japanese Distribution System

This section will highlight major unique features of the Japanese distribution system. It will briefly trace the underlying reasons for their development, then comment on their effects on the importation of products.

Number of Actors

One major feature of the Japanese distribution system is the overwhelming number of companies that participate in it. For example, in spite of its much smaller geographic expansion and population, Japan has about the same number of wholesalers as the U. S. Most of these firms have nine employees or less.[5] Only 5.6 percent of Japanese wholesalers have thirty or more employees.[6]

The ratio of wholesale to retail sales in Japan is more than double that in the United States, which indicates the more frequent interaction between wholesalers in Japan than between wholesalers in the United States.[7] Japanese wholesalers sell their goods twice as frequently to other wholesalers as do their counterparts in the United States. Such frequent interaction will, of course, drive up the price of products due to the necessity of every intermediary adding some mark-up.

Japan has also only 10 percent fewer retailers than does the United States. Firms are small (having an average of only 3.6 employees), and their sales are less than half that in the U. S.[8] As a result, many of these firms possess a small capital base which permits for only limited flexibility in terms of inventory size and expansion.

Due to this vast number of participants in the distributive process, it is very difficult to find avenues with reach them all. Also, direct distribution to them is often prohibitively expensive. This is particularly true if market penetration is sought outside the urban centers.

Purpose of the Distribution System

In the United States, the primary function of intermediaries is seen as improving the efficiency of the distribution system. As the principle of channel geometry has demonstrated, intermediaries are useful economically only if the services and functions they provide are cheaper than the cost of direct distribution. This underlying axiom does not hold true for Japan. Social aims which go beyond pure economics contribute to the continued existence and expansion of smaller channel members. Japanese society has come to accept a degree of tolerated inefficiency within its distribution system to maintain employment and income flows. According to a study by Arthur D. Little, Inc., retailing has come to serve to some extent as a "form of social welfare system."[9] Since Japanese employees are paid a lump sum at retirement rather than an ongoing pension, this payment is often seen by the recipient as an opportunity to set up one's own shop in order to be independent and to derive a steady income. In addition, the Japanese distribution system is used to "absorbing labor during economic downturns in lieu of a more extensive unemployment insurance system."[10]

Both of these factors contribute to the development of small retailers with a small capital base and limited managerial talent. However, given these social aims of the distribution system, the argument of economics alone is often insufficient to effect a restructuring on the macro as well as the micro level. Foreign firms entering the Japanese market must therefore accept the existence of some of this inefficiency in spite of the theoretical possibility of substantial streamlining of the distribution process.

Physical Constraints of Channel Members

Geographic constraints have made space a very valuable commodity in Japan. Due to their low level of capitalization, most channel members suffer from substantial lack of storage space. As a result, only small quantities are purchased, and very liberal return privileges exist within the system's channels, extending not only to damaged merchandise but also to merchandise that does not sell easily. While the handling of these returns can be costly, it does permit channel members to carry out a push policy without encountering channel resistance.

The small order size has led to a requirement for frequent replenishments. Even in instances when sophisticated sales forecasting systems are used, immediate channel response to short-term orders is expected.

As a result, factors such as short lead time and secure supplies can often outweigh price competitiveness. Suppliers, particularly those from abroad, are frequently chosen on the basis of order responsiveness. In certain product categories, this responsiveness simply cannot be provided competitively from abroad. For example, many retailers expect delivery time for out of stock products to be less than six hours. In order to provide such short lead times, suppliers need to be located in close vicinity to their customers, a strategy which is very difficult to incorporate into an export philosophy by a foreign firm.

Interaction Among Channel Members

One major characteristic of this interaction is the close organizational ties between channel members. The distribution system is often marked by the "*keiretsu*" relationship, in which producers, distributors, and retailers are all financially linked with each other, either directly or through a banker or trading company. Even management linkage is sometimes possible.[11] As a result, members of the family tend to prefer sourcing from each other to sourcing from the outside. Not only does this phenomenon make it difficult to break into the system, it also continues to haunt the successful firm. For example, while the possibility of selling a unique product is quite high, it must be kept in mind that, once a member of the *keiretsu* begins producing a similar product, other *keiretsu* firms may shift their orders to the new producer, leaving the innovator out in the cold. Since the lag time between innovation and imitation is shrinking continuously, this problem increases in significance for innovators.

This familial sourcing relationship is also marked by close financial ties. Due to the small capital base of many channel members, the role of promissory notes is quite large. Trade credit is liberally extended and delayed payments are readily accepted. In addition, an elaborate system of rebates to channel members is in place. Rebates are provided for channel cooperation, market expansion and channel innovation.[12] Since small retailers in particular are often highly dependent on financing and rebates, any new firm planning to work with them needs to make provisions to accommodate these needs.

Close ties among channel members, however, do not necessarily have to result from business interdependence and financial dependence alone. The Japanese distribution system also relies heavily upon personal relationships which are built through frequent visits and elaborate courtesies. The maintenance of these relationships is often far more important than the sales level of a certain product or short-term profitability, and includes the occasional provision of money to "send the son to school," frequent exchanges of gifts, friendly discussions, and very little direct pressure to sell. Time is, of course, the key to building such relationships, and precisely the one variable which foreign firms in particular cannot benefit from in their initial market penetration efforts. Only a continuous market presence combined with great cultural sensitivity will enable them to start building such relationships.

Active involvement in product and business development is also a major feature of the distribution system. Manufacturers, wholesalers, and retailers interact quite closely and frequently in regard to new product development and product introduction. Successful product introduction needs to be followed up continuously through further product improvements so that channel members see the commitment of the product manufacturers to the product line. Lack of innovation is often seen as a lack of commitment which translates into weak relationships. While local presence is ideal for an importer to obtain input from the channel members, close interaction can also be fostered through frequent visits by both sides. However, regardless of the number of visits, innovation and continuous product refinement is a must in order to demonstrate commitment to the other channel members and to maintain their continued cooperation.

Sales support is another major characteristic of the interaction among channel members. Apart from traditional dealer aids, wholesalers, for example, are expected to supply a substantial number of personnel to retailers to support their product sales. Such support staff often work in the retail store (wearing store uniforms) but are paid for by the wholesaler. The rationale behind this practice is the belief that it is in the interest of the wholesaler and manufacturer to have their own employees selling their products since they are better able to explain the products to the customers than retailer employed personnel. Also expected are thorough product specific sales training and extensive after sale service. Since these dimensions comprise one of the main competitive fields among channel members, foreign suppliers need to ensure that such service and training backup is provided with the product in order to maintain channel goodwill.

Interaction with Consumers

Japanese channel members also work very closely with consumers. One major facet of this interaction is the strong emphasis on quality, form, and presentation. Most channel members insist on carrying only highest quality products and do not tolerate even slight defects and deviations. Much attention is also paid to packaging and wrapping. Sometimes, the cost of packaging may even exceed the value of the product sold.

Retailers also take pride in offering integrated selling systems. For example, product classes are grouped together in similar areas and are enriched by usage demonstrations and supplemental information.

Japanese retailers take on a major counseling role toward their customers, sometimes even going as far as organizing their customers into purchasing clubs. There, retailers register consumers as members of the club and record their purchases. This mechanism permits the retailers to keep sales records and to provide customers with incentives to buy by rewarding them with a bonus once given purchase quantities are reached during the year.

For the foreign firm, this close interaction with consumers again requires proper preparation of the channel members for its products. It also necessitates planning for a "proper fit" of one's products within the palate of a channel member's product offering. Without proper research and closeness to the market, however, this is difficult to achieve.

Changes in the Japanese Distribution System

Over the past decades, the economy of Japan has made significant strides toward a quantitative maturation. Translating this development into a better quality of life has—to some extent—been made the onus of the distribution system. Perhaps this mission is formulated most clearly by the director of the Industrial Policy Bureau of the Ministry of International Trade and Industry (MITI) who stated, "as consumer needs diversify with an emphasis on quality rather than on quantity, it becomes increasingly important for the distribution system to meet these needs."[13]

It is the purpose of this section to explore how responsive the distribution system has been to the changes in the Japanese economy, and what the shifts in the distribution strategies and the emergence of new participants in the distributive process mean to foreign firms. Even though it has been argued "that little distributive change has occurred (in Japan) and that improvement in this sector will take a great deal of time," such changes do occur.[14] In a typical Japanese fashion, they are not coming about with fanfare, but are taking place rather subtly. Nevertheless, they have profound long-term implications for both the Japanese firm as well as the importer.

Increased Distribution Integration

The past decade has seen an increase in vertical integration efforts by channel members. Many wholesalers are joining forces or are becoming integrated with manufacturers and other wholesalers.[15] One emerging trend is the formation of manufacturer-wholesalers who produce some merchandise but subcontract out the major part of their production. In addition to manufacturers absorbing wholesalers, wholesalers have also integrated smaller manufacturers into their operations and begun integration into the retail sector. Furthermore, large wholesalers have begun to consolidate their activities with those of their secondary or tertiary partners in order to retain their market positions.

This integration can pose both problems and opportunities for foreign firms. One major problem is the fact that integrated wholesalers and manufacturers are more likely to buy from each other than from foreign firms, therefore making penetration more difficult. By the same token, however, wholesalers who grow stronger and larger through integration are able to establish more international linkages, import more, and conduct more direct activities than smaller wholesalers.

The Evolution of Chain Stores

The formation of chain stores has become increasingly common in Japan, particularly in the convenience store sector. Since 1977, chain stores have experienced an average annual growth rate of 32 percent. Total sales of the thirty-three leading chain stores amounted to $3.4 billion in 1982.[16] Seven-Eleven, the largest convenience store chain in Japan, had 2,000 stores by the end of February, 1984, with 350–400 more outlets expected to open every year. These stores are typically located in residential areas, carry only goods needed daily, and are open long hours. In most instances, the stores are owned by an individual on a franchise or volunteer membership basis. The chain management provides owners with training in stocking and management techniques. As a result, 1,800 out of 3,000 stock-keeping units have been replaced by different merchandise in a six month time span in response to consumer needs.[17]

MITI's Industrial Policy Bureau sees the future for smaller retailers mainly in the organization of small stores into voluntary and franchised chains. MITI is apparently willing to lend its support to such developments, since one of its officials stated that "the organization of small retailers is...important as they represent the greater part of the Japanese retail industry."[18]

These emerging chain stores can become valuable allies to importers; based on past practices, their willingness to change the composition of merchandise is quite high. In addition, a centralized purchasing function can provide for large-sized orders which would be otherwise difficult to obtain. Finally, centralized distribution can provide many service functions which would be difficult for a foreign supplier to deliver.

The Emergence of Self-Service Stores

Even though most traditional Japanese stores have suffered a constant decline in their market share in the past decade, self-service stores have enjoyed rapid real growth. In 1979, self-service stores had a national market share of about 15 percent, compared to just over 5 percent in 1966.[19] This rapid growth indicates the increased acceptance of the self-service concept among consumers. The implications of this change are that goods marketed through self-service outlets need to be self-explanatory in nature and familiar to the buyer. Therefore, for new products, firms wishing to use these self-service outlets need to exert a pull strategy, in addition to the traditional Japanese requirements of a push strategy, in order to work with the channel members.

Cash and Carry Wholesaling

One newly emerging type of channel member which operates very much contrary to the established notions of the Japanese distribution system is the cash and carry wholesaler. These firms, whose primary competitive tool is price, aim at those channel members who do not need financing, delivery, or service. Frequently their main customers are the very small retailers who come every day to purchase products in small quantities. Cash and carry wholesalers refuse to accept returns from retailers and instead suggest that slow selling merchandise be discounted. They do not develop personal relationships and grant no rebates, bonuses, or special payments.

These cash and carry wholesalers are similarly unconventional in their dealings with manufacturers. Again, no personal relationships are developed. These firms deal with many small manufacturers and select suppliers purely on the basis of product and price competitiveness. Although this method of doing business results in low prices to the end purchaser, such wholesalers often cannot sell national brand merchandise, since many large and well-known manufacturers are unwilling to sell to them for fear of disturbing their well-established channel relations. However, in spite of this handicap, these firms do quite well, based mainly on their high annual inventory turnover, which is often a multiple of that of traditional wholesalers.

Due to their lack of allegiance to any specific manufacturer and their primary focus on price and product, these cash and carry wholesalers have the potential to become good partners of foreign manufacturers.

Increase of Non-Store Retailing

Two major types of non-store retailing activities on the increase are mail-order retailing and new retail experimentation. While mail-order retailing has existed in Japan for some time, its international expansion is a novelty. For example, Matsuzakaya, a Nagoya department store, has had a mail-order relationship with a German mail-order firm, Quelle, for years. Customers of Matsuzakaya were able to select Quelle products from a catalog in Japan. Matsuzakaya then checked the availability of such a selection via air mail. Once availability was confirmed, the customer paid and the merchandise was shipped from Germany. To cut down on the lag time between merchandise selection and receipt, Matsuzakaya is currently in the process of establishing a direct satellite link with Quelle. Customer catalog selections will now be transmitted directly to Quelle via computer terminals located in the store in Japan. Merchandise can then be shipped immediately after a check for availability via the on-line system. Thus, the total order lag-time is reduced to two weeks, a facet which makes the mail-order process much more desirable for Japanese customers.[20]

For importers willing to participate in the cost of such on-line ordering systems, new opportunities can be opened up in the mail-order sector. These opportunities are to be found both with current Japanese mail-order firms and firms which can be attracted to the mail-order concept, as well as with the Japanese consumer.

In the area of retail innovation, one particular project should be briefly mentioned. With the support of the Ministry of International Trade and Industry, a two-way interactive cable television system is being developed. This project, which was initiated in 1976, permits the two-way transmission of both voice and picture and allows individuals to request the showing of specific video tapes on their television sets. The program currently experiments with providing retail functions. Large companies are given time slots to explain products and to interact with viewers. A tele-shopping program is also offered in which viewers can examine merchandise and obtain price information. While this live program is enjoyed by the viewers, it has not been very enthusiastically received by retailers and has not yet fully resolved the settlement problem as to how customers pay for their orders.

Although the program is operative, it faces big future challenges in the areas of initial investment cost, consumer resistance to costly system purchases and transmission technology constraints. At the same time, given sufficient acceptance and developmental progress, this avenue of retailing directly to the consumers could provide major opportunities for foreign firms, particularly since this direct distribution would make companies independent from established channel structures.

Restrictions in Department Store Growth

While so far the changes enumerated have all presented new opportunities for foreign firms, one major negative trend is also visible. Currently, most imported consumer products in Japan are sold through department stores. This fact is the result of the greater financial capabilities of such stores, their broader international orientation and the composition of their clientele. However, the growth of these stores has been radically curtailed. In the past decade, the so-called "large store law" has increasingly restricted the development of larger sized stores. The Ministry of International Trade and Industry and local councils (which need to agree to the opening of new department stores) have imposed many unreasonable restraints and burdens on corporations planning to open such stores. The rationale behind this restriction is the desire to aid small and medium sized stores which run the danger of being run out of business by an increase in department stores.

For the foreign firm attempting to sell consumer products to Japan, this restriction on department store growth presents a major danger because it reduces the growth in the availability of potential major outlets. However, it must be stated that these restrictive measures are being implemented mainly for domestic Japanese policy reasons rather than for purposes of restricting the importation of products.

Major shifts are also occurring in the performance of the physical distribution function in Japan. These are taking place in the area of transportation, warehousing, and information processing.

Changes in the Transportation Function

Due to increased urban congestion, channel members are faced with a growing inability to provide competitive delivery service. More and more transportation companies are being formed exclusively for order consolidation purposes. Alone or in cooperation with channel members, such transportation firms can achieve major transport economies; transportation cost savings average about 30 percent and are sometimes as high as 60 percent. The use of consolidation is growing rapidly among channel members because non-users are suffering severely from the competitive advantage of the low transportation cost of users. Turning over the delivery function to outside companies changes the activities of many channel members substantially. Instead of focusing mainly

on delivery services, they are now increasingly concentrating on
the providing of financing, break-bulk and assortment services.

For the foreign firm, this trend toward order consolidation
offers the opportunity of cooperation with the newly emerging
transportation companies. Many of them are not tied to any specific channel members and can provide an important complementary ingredient for competitive distribution in Japan.

The Emergences of Distribution Centers

Recognizing the increasing problems of congestion, in the late
1960s the Japanese government began to legislate distribution
improvements. These legislative efforts resulted in government
sponsored joint ventures between small firms, large warehouse
companies, and terminals that were designed to create more modern storage and warehouse facilities. In the meantime, manufacturers themselves have begun to join forces to form distribution
centers. These newly formed centers contain distribution ware-
houses, display space, office buildings, and much valued parking
space. These warehouse buildings offer efficient space utilization,
direct truck access, and fully climatized and largely automated
warehousing space. The administration of these centers provides
maintenance, security and common facilities. As a result, tenants
need to worry only about their own business.

Although participation in these newly created distribution
centers is quite expensive, they can offer new opportunities to foreign firms. Rather than having to rent a multiplicity of depots in
each city, one centralized location can now be sufficient. Warehousing also becomes easier due to the distribution center's administrative support, and inventories can be kept more efficiently. Due
to the high inventory requirements in Japan, savings in this sector
can have a major impact on a corporation's profits.

Improvements in Distribution Information

Major emphasis is placed by the distribution channel members
and by the Japanese government on improvements in the area of
information processing within the distribution system. As a MITI
representative noted,

> The distribution system is increasingly being required to
> meet consumer needs more effectively in a maturing indus-

trial society. It must serve not only as a pipeline through which goods flow from producers to consumers, but also as a relay point allowing the information to flow between the two. The information function of the distribution system is expected to increase as the advanced information society develops. In other words, the importance of the distribution system as a relay point for the flow of producer-consumer information will increase as the Japanese economy matures and handles more information.[21]

This increased emphasis on information is apparent when one notes that the distribution system accounts for 43 percent of all computers used in all industries in the country.[22]

One application of this information emphasis is the increased installation of Point of Sale (POS) systems by retailers. This computerized cash register system collects information on all items sold in the store and is used for research, merchandising, and planning. By encouraging consumers to use store credit cards, which are encoded with socio-economic customer data, the POS system can identify consumer segments that purchase certain products, preferred size of product package, and the time of day the products are purchased. Unlike in the United States, Japanese privacy laws do not restrict such information flows. The system is used also for shopping basket analysis, customer traffic analysis and merchandise layout experimentation. Furthermore, it permits more precise demand forecasting, better inventory planning, reduced cash register error, and better personnel utilization.

The use of the POS system reduces the need for employees. However, rather than resulting in layoffs, the freed up employees are used to foster more direct contact with customers, providing them with more information and services. As a consequence, new product introduction is eased, product differentiation is enhanced, and a shift in product mix toward products with high explanatory needs is made possible.

For foreign firms, this information revolution presents numerous opportunities. First of all, market research can be more easily conducted and results more quickly obtained. Secondly, improved information flow can reduce the need for flexible inventory size. Thirdly, countering the trend toward self-explanatory merchandise which occurs through the increased acceptance of the self-service concept, more complicated products can be introduced due to the greater availability of sales personnel.

Conclusions and Perspectives

The Japanese distribution system is undergoing change as a reflection of the shifts occurring in the Japanese economic environment. Facing substantial changes in demand and an increasing unwillingness to pay high prices, channel members have to adjust to remain in business. The current Japanese distribution system serves its markets and in most instances serves it well. In cases in which the system is inefficient, changes are coming about. If these changes appear to be slow, it must be kept in mind that change by consensus is always likely to be gradual. However, such changes may sometimes result in distribution configurations in which the process has outpaced the structure, but such situations reflect only a delay in the inevitable.

The thrust for change needs to continue, both on the side of Japan as well as on the part of firms planning to enter the Japanese market. Japanese policy makers need to continue and strengthen their market-opening efforts and carefully weigh the effects of domestic policies on the importation of foreign products. Encouragement should be provided to the development of new distribution channels, the emergence of new channel members, and the use of new distribution processes. The current large store legislation should be seriously reconsidered due to its substantial negative impact on foreign consumer product importation. Finally, some attention should be paid to consumption patterns within the Japanese society, and demand stimulation with concurrent plans for price reductions should be seriously considered.

In turn, prospective importers to Japan should keep in mind the existing Japanese distribution system, with all its constraints. If they wish to work within the system, they must adapt their business practices to it. However, foreign firms should not remain stuck in the perception of Japanese distribution channels formed twenty years ago; rather, they should take advantage of the system's recognized changes. The current saturation of the Japanese home with physical products and the increased desire for innovation and services present unique opportunities. Foreign firms need to work with newly emerging intermediaries and cooperate with the innovators in the distribution process. Armed with the knowledge about changes and opportunities, they need to make a renewed effort to enter the large and potentially very profitable Japanese market.

SECTION V

Manufacturing: The Japanese Approach

Among the most remarkable achievements of the Japanese are the powerful innovations they have made in a production management system originally imported essentially from the United States. The image of the Japanese as imitators of the West began to erode rapidly when details of Toyota's just-in-time production system became available in the late 1970s. Since then, innumerable books have been published detailing various other production management concepts developed by the Japanese. Many American companies have investigated these innovations and implemented them in their local operations.

In this section, we have included chapters describing some of the less familiar of these innovations. Michael A. Cusumano argues in "Manufacturing Innovation: Lessons from the Japanese Auto Industry" that the performance of Japanese firms in auto production is rooted in innovations in technology and management. Cusumano suggests that these methods are potentially applicable to American firms, but must first be understood. He reviews the history of these innovations and finds that the economic imperatives facing Japanese manufacturers created the conditions in which these innovations emerged. In addition to just-in-time, Cusumano examines the drive for process simplicity and the strategy of subcontracting whenever possible. Cusumano believes that these three elements are the keys to understanding the source of the higher productivity in Japanese automobile manufacturing. While noting that these concepts do not depend on any peculiarities in the Japanese personality for their success, he does observe that they require "considerable cooperation among managers, workers, and suppliers." He lists a number of requirements for American automobile companies to successfully implement these innovations.

Another feature of Japanese manufacturing that is often mentioned in the popular literature is the practice of depending on a single supplier for even critical raw materials or components. Business orthodoxy in the United States stridently warns against depending on a single supplier, and thus American executives are frequently astonished by the Japanese practice. Faced with a practice radically different from the American way, they are tempted to see in it another of those "secrets" of Japanese business success.

In "The Myth of the Cooperative Single Source," John Ramsay warns against a simplistic understanding of this practice and especially against a blind attempt by American companies to duplicate under American conditions something that is so culture bound. Ramsay finds this practice rooted in the peculiarities of the Japanese social environment, in the now familiar "web of debt and obligation" that we have seen to be a pervasive feature of Japanese society. Complex intercompany connections based on such ties of debt and obligation are an ancient tradition in Japan, and only the Confucian ethic of benevolence prevents the stronger parties in these networks from exploiting the weaker. Such exploitation is not completely absent in Japan, and this is why Ramsay finds the suggestion that these single sources are cooperative out of a sense of goodwill to be a "myth." Ramsay concludes with a warning that the dangers of cultural misrepresentation cannot be overemphasized.

The last selection in this section deals with a new dimension in the analysis of Japanese manufacturing: the substantially different role accounting plays in Japan. In the United States, the function of managerial or cost accounting is to rationally allocate direct and indirect costs to each unit of production. As Toshiro Hiromoto explains in "Another Hidden Edge—Japanese Management Accounting," Japanese companies do not seem to use management accounting to obtain information on cost, variances, and profits. Instead, accounting is designed to motivate employees to seek cost reduction. Hiromoto explains this difference in detail and explains the organizational implications and strategic foundations of Japanese management accounting.

19

Manufacturing Innovation: Lessons from the Japanese Auto Industry*

Michael A. Cusumano

Several studies published in the 1980s indicated that Japanese firms, led by Toyota, have achieved the highest levels of manufacturing efficiency in the world automobile industry. Physical productivity, which reflects the "throughput" speed for completing products and the amount of labor required, has been significantly higher than in most U.S. plants (although differences vary by company and U.S. firms have made improvements in recent years).[1] Japanese auto producers have also demonstrated rates of inventory turnover (sales divided by work-in-process and finished goods, or the cost of goods sold divided by work-in-process) several times those of U.S. firms.[2] (Inventory turnover is a useful measure of efficiency, since it reflects how well firms manufacture to meet market needs rather than production schedules. It also reflects how effectively they reduce the number of parts and semifinished goods; these add to operating costs and often cover up inefficient practices or process errors.)

*Reprinted from "Manufacturing Innovation: Lessons from the Japanese Auto Industry," by Michael A. Cusumano, *Sloan Management Review* (Fall 1988): 29–39, by permission of the publisher.

High productivity and other aspects of process efficiency, such as rapid inventory turnover, help solve a problem as old as mass production itself: that the conventional factory tends to produce huge lots of standardized components, while consumer markets demand a variety of products at low prices. Looking for the reasons Japanese companies have managed this problem so well, many authors cite the contribution of Japanese workers and Japanese culture. However, the performance of Japanese firms in auto production depends not on the employment of Japanese workers but on Japanese innovations in technology and management. Perhaps the most important innovations challenged fundamental assumptions about mass production. These consisted of revisions in American and European equipment, production techniques, and labor and supplier policies introduced primarily in the 1950s and 1960s, when total Japanese manufacturing volumes and volumes per model were extremely low by U.S. (or European) standards.

While Japanese "good practices" are potentially applicable to any market, U.S. and other non-Japanese managers must first *understand* and then consider adapting some of these techniques. This chapter is meant to promote that understanding by summarizing some of the major findings from a five-year study on the Japanese automobile industry focusing on Nissan and Toyota.[3] A major objective of this study was to explain Japanese innovations in production management by exploring the reasoning behind them as well as their evolution over time, while simultaneously documenting observable improvements in productivity and inventory levels. The concluding section of this chapter suggests what managers might learn by examining not only the nature of Japanese competition, but the potential role of manufacturing as a source of competitive advantage.

Historical Myths and Realities

Automobile mass production began in the United States with Ford achieving volumes of over 2 million per year for one model during the 1920s. Some observers of Japan have assumed, as a result, that Japanese firms copied U.S. manufacturing equipment and techniques and then benefitted from workers with better education and more cooperative attitudes. Indeed, various authors have suggested that superior performance in manufacturing is linked to the unique characteristics of Japanese employees. However, if the performance of Japanese firms in the automobile industry depends primarily on the unique characteristics of Japanese employees in Japan, then one would expect Japanese auto plants in the United States to perform no better than factories run by U.S. companies.

This is not the case. Japanese-run automobile plants located in Tennessee (Nissan), Ohio (Honda), and California (the Toyota-GM MUMMI joint venture) have demonstrated higher levels of productivity and quality, and nearly equivalent process flexibility (the ability to assemble a number of distinct models on the same lines without reducing productivity or quality) compared with U.S. factories and Japanese plants in Japan.[4]

In addition, not all Japanese automakers copied and imported American or European equipment and production-management techniques. Those who preferred in-house experimentation created opportunities for learning, as well as innovation and improvement. During the 1930s and 1950s Nissan, Isuzu, Mitsubishi, and Hino assembled European and American vehicles under license, largely using conventional mass-production technology developed in the United States. These models accounted for 30 percent of Japanese car production from 1953 to 1959.[5] But the largest postwar Japanese producer, Toyota, deliberately avoided copying foreign models or techniques and focused on developing a more efficient production system uniquely tailored to the needs of the Japanese market. Toyota adopted *innovation in production management* as an integral part of its competitive strategy and then spent the 1950s and 1960s making this strategy work.

Thus Toyota, and then other Japanese automakers, did not simply implement conventional mass-production processes more effectively; they made critical changes in U.S. procedures and concepts. Their creativity led to greater flexibility in equipment and labor, lower in-process inventories and higher overall turnover rates, more attention to process quality, and, ultimately, higher levels of productivity. Furthermore, during the 1960s and 1970s, rather than copying United States or European practices, Japanese automakers such as Hino, Daihatsu, Mazda, and Nissan copied production techniques introduced at Toyota in the 1950s and 1960s.

Others have suggested that superior performance can be linked to management emphasis on long-term growth in market shares, which leads to large production volumes and accumulation of experience.[6] (This thesis is frequently presented by the Boston Consulting Group to account for the performance of Japanese firms in a number of manufacturing industries.) Instead, efficient manufacturing, and gradually improved designs, might *themselves* have

Table 19.1 Vehicle Productivity Adjusted for Vertical Integration, Capacity Utilization, and Labor Hour Differences, 1965–1983

FY	GM, FORD, CHRYSLER[a]	NISSAN	TOYOTA
1965	1.0	0.9	1.5
1970	1.0	1.9	2.4
1975	1.0	1.7	2.6
1979	1.0	2.0	2.7
1983[b]	1.0	1.9	2.2
1985[c]	1.0	1.9	2.2

Relative Scale (U.S. = 1.0)

Notes: [a]This column averages figures for GM, Ford, and Chrysler based on worldwide data.

[b]The 1983 figures for GM and Ford, but not for Chrysler, assumed the vertical integration levels of 1979.

[c]Estimate.

Source: Derived from annual reports. For additional explanation of these data, see M. A. Cusumano, *The Japanese Automobile Industry: Technology and Management at Nissan and Toyota* (Cambridge, Mass.: Council on East Asian Studies/Harvard University Press, 1985), pp. 196–200. Unless noted otherwise, annual reports for Nissan and Toyota refer to the Japanese-language equivalents of the 10-K reports (*yuka shoken hokokusho*).

led to higher sales and higher market shares. In fact, Toyota and Nissan, the top producers in the Japanese auto industry, appear to have matched or surpassed U.S. productivity levels by the late 1960s though annual production levels were far below those of their counterparts in the United States at the time (see Table 19.1).

Finally, some link high Japanese productivity to higher levels of capital investment per worker. Even avoiding the use of exchange rates and using purchasing power parity data for capital equipment, in 1983 workers at Nissan and Toyota had two to two and a half times as many fixed assets (plant, property, and equipment) as their counterparts at GM, Ford, and Chrysler. This suggests that Japanese workers were twice as productive because of investment levels that were twice as high.

But a historical perspective leads to a different conclusion. When Toyota and Nissan matched and then doubled U.S. productivity levels in the 1960s, capital stocks per employee and per vehicle produced were comparable to U.S. firms. Furthermore, the amount of fixed assets required to produce one vehicle by the late 1970s and early 1980s was roughly equivalent in Japan and in the United States. Only because "throughput" per worker per year was twice as high in Japan did workers at Nissan and Toyota show twice as many fixed assets each. In other words, Japanese automakers required half as many workers to produce a single car, and these fewer workers used as much capital to do it as U.S. workers. Since capital productivity was not higher in Japan than in the United States, it had to be other factors, not simply greater investment, that led to higher productivity.[7]

The Need to Produce Efficiently at Low Volumes

An examination of Toyota and Nissan in the years after World War II reveals an overriding concern with "small-lot" production. In order to become more efficient than U.S. automakers, manufacturers needed to produce a wider variety of models at extremely low volumes relative to the United States or Europe; they also needed to keep their costs low, since they faced a rising number of competitors. This contradicted the mass-production philosophy pioneered by U.S. auto producers, which attempted to lower costs by minimizing product diversity and maximizing economies of scale, and which Japanese manufacturers imitated before and during World War II.

During the war, Japanese automakers used American-style mass-production equipment and techniques for trucks, since they produced these models in relatively large runs (compared to passenger cars) and with few changes. For example, it was possible to machine or stamp thousands of identical components, as U.S. manufacturers did for much higher volumes, and store the excess for future months. The protected market that existed in Japan from 1936 to 1945 and then from 1953 until the mid-1970s ensured high prices, permitting this expensive use of equipment.

Nissan's history illustrates this strategy. In the mid-1930s, Nissan entered into an agreement with Graham-Paige (which sold out to Dodge before World War II) and bought specialized and expensive American machine tools and stamping presses to produce the U.S. company's standard-size truck. A dozen high-salaried American engineers came to Japan for two years and set up operations. Nissan then sold nearly all its output, at rather high profit margins, to the Japanese army until 1945 and continued to make the same truck and engine, with only minor changes, until the late 1950s.

After World War II, when the military market disappeared (except for some truck sales to the U.S. armed forces), Nissan, Toyota, and other Japanese automakers had to make the transition from trucks and buses (about 95 percent of production in 1950) to passenger cars. (Car production at the leading Japanese automakers rose from merely 5 percent of output in 1950 to about 65 percent by 1970.) Passenger vehicles also came to require more equipment and options, as well as a variety of styles and more frequent model changes, especially as the Japanese companies improved their vehicles incrementally. Nissan and Toyota, for example, went from producing only two basic models each circa 1950—one standard-size truck and one small truck, which were fitted with a car body to create a passenger vehicle—to several models each by the end of the 1950s.

In 1950 Japanese auto production consisted of 31,597 cars and trucks—little more than one day's output for the U.S. auto industry. Four local companies—Nissan, Toyota, Isuzu, and Hino—shared the market. Believing that such low volumes per model would perpetuate high costs and make it difficult for Japan to compete in international markets, Japan's Ministry of International Trade and Industry (MITI) adopted two major policies. The most successful was to help domestic auto producers cover their high costs by limiting imports to about 1 percent of the Japanese market following the postwar U.S. occupation. Prices for Japanese-made vehicles still dropped between the early 1950s and 1970s, since six more companies—Mitsubishi, Honda, Mazda, Daihatsu, Suzuki, and Prince (which merged with Nissan in 1966)—entered the field by the early 1960s. However, since the domestic market grew faster than supply, each company made a significant profit.

Another policy, which was largely a failure, was an attempt to "rationalize" the auto industry by encouraging mergers and specialization. Right after World War II, MITI tried to convince firms to abandon passenger car production. Again during the 1960s, MITI wanted to reduce the number of producers competing in the industry to raise scale economies for any one manufacturer. But most company executives saw great potential in the auto industry and repeatedly refused to bow to the wishes of government planners.

An additional incentive to increase productivity and reduce costs was the Japanese automakers' desires (beginning in the late 1950s) to expand car sales beyond the limits of the small domestic market. However, because of high prices (which did not match international levels until the late 1960s) and problems in some design features and components, exports were still only about 20 percent of total production as late as 1970, and did not exceed 50 percent of output until 1977.[8]

Departing from U.S. Practices

In the lean years following World War II, Japanese managers were not sure how to accommodate these changing market needs and the potential export requirements of low-cost, high-quality vehicles. Not surprisingly, many Japanese managers, especially at Nissan, first believed that the best way to compete in automobile manufacturing was to continue to copy as closely as possible the best techniques perfected at Ford, GM, and other mass producers.[9]

The U.S. model for mass production involved a set of techniques and concepts that assumed the following practices were most efficient: high levels of worker and equipment specialization; extensive automation; long production runs on hugh machines requiring long setup times; large manufacturing scales with buffer stocks to keep the expensive machines and specialized workers constantly active; and the "push" concept of production control. (The push concept involved manufacturing and delivering components according to a master schedule, which was designed to keep machines running and components coming in despite problems that might develop at a few stations or suppliers.)

To inspect all the components made in huge lots required too many inspectors, so companies adopted statistical sampling techniques to test a few parts and determine if any entire lot met an "acceptable quality level," even though this meant some defectives would pass through the system at every stage. U.S. automakers also tried to bring in-house as much of components production and assembly as possible, to ensure acceptable levels of price, quality, and supply.

Increasingly, however, Japanese managers, led by Toyota's Taiichi Ohno, realized that the best way to manufacture in volumes far smaller than were common in the United States or even Europe was to increase the "flexibility" and utilization of the key elements in their manufacturing systems—equipment, workers, and suppliers. They also sought to lower, as much as possible, investment needed for in-house personnel, factory or warehousing space, and variable costs such as in-process or finished-goods inventories. While individual Japanese automakers made these changes with varying degrees of success and in different years, all pursued three basic policies.

Just-in-Time Manufacturing

Before 1950 at Toyota and in the mid-1950s at Nissan, managers introduced the "just-in-time" (JIT) concept for in-house production (or assembly) and deliveries of components. This required several departures from U.S. practices. Faster setup times for machine tools and stamping presses (techniques first written about in the United States and incorporated in American equipment such as Danly stamping presses) meant that each piece of equipment could be used for different models or components without long waiting times. Tighter synchronization between subassembly production, parts deliveries, and final assembly increased equipment utilization and reduced in-process inventories, while mixed scheduling of different components or models on single machines or assembly lines avoided specialized but under-utilized equipment and workers. Finally, broader job specifications allowed managers to get by with less workers through shifting people to different jobs as needed at any given moment.

These modifications appear to have resulted in higher productivity as workers learned how to operate several different machines simultaneously, and did much of their own machine maintenance, janitorial work, and inspection, especially in times of slow demand. The discipline imposed by the just-in-time pace, reduced buffer stocks of extra components, and the small-lot production philosophy also tended to improve quality. Because workers could no longer rely on extra parts or rework piles if they made mistakes, they paid more attention to what they were doing. Since they made only a few parts at a time for the stations immediately ahead of them, rather than large lots to store in inventory for weeks or months, more rapid throughput on the line also led to rapid "feedback" between stations regarding process problems or defects. Small lots thus seem to have improved learning rates and reduced defectives, both of which resulted in higher yields—another boost to productivity.

Temporary Reduction of Process Complexity

A second policy was to reduce unnecessary complexity in product designs and manufacturing processes. Nissan and Toyota accomplished this by standardizing components across different car and truck lines, eliminating wasteful "annual model changes" and limiting the number of options available to customers. Until recent years, some Japanese automakers offered models in only two combinations—standard and deluxe. Some export models still come with prepackaged options.

The increasing flexibility of assembly lines and small-lot production, on the other hand, made it possible to introduce gradually a greater variety of models, options, and variations for different export markets—with little or no decrease in productivity. Nissan and Toyota actually doubled the number of models they were offering between the mid-1960s and 1980s and dramatically improved product sophistication and overall quality, while maintaining high rates of productivity. This observation—that, with the type of production techniques pioneered in Japan, there need not be any "tradeoffs" between productivity and quality—has recently been confirmed in an MIT survey of major auto assembly plants in Japan, the United States, and Europe.[10]

Vertical "De-integration"

The third policy involved decreasing levels of in-house vertical integration between component production and final assembly, while building up networks of lower-wage subsidiaries (and other subcontractors). Toyota began establishing a network of suppliers in the late 1930s and founded all its major subsidiaries during the 1940s. While Nissan took longer to set up a supplier network, by the end of the 1970s Japan's leading auto firms demonstrated levels of "group integration" (with groups defined by the percentage of total costs they accounted for in-house plus payments to subsidiaries in which Nissan or Toyota held a minimum 20 percent equity share) that were far higher than the most integrated U.S. auto producer, General Motors (see Table 19.2). This made it possible to achieve many of the benefits of vertical integration without the higher personnel or other costs that formal integration would have required.

For example, in 1983, for each small car Nissan and Toyota produced, their subsidiaries accounted for about 50 percent of manufacturing and other operating costs. These subsidiaries, furthermore, paid wages equal to merely 80 percent of those received by Toyota and Nissan workers. But, while wages were lower at subsidiaries, productivity gains were not. By working with these

Table 19.2 Company and Group Integration, U.S.–Japan, 1965–1983

(%)

| FY | NISSAN | | TOYOTA | | GM | FORD | CHRYSLER |
	IN-HOUSE	GROUP	IN-HOUSE	GROUP	IN-HOUSE	IN-HOUSE	IN-HOUSE
1965	32	54	41	74	50	36	36
1970	29	52	35	66	49	39	36
1975	22	50	30	73	45	36	36[a]
1979	26	70	29	74	43	36	32
1980	26	73	29	76	—	—	34
1981	26	71	28	75	—	—	31
1982	26	75	26	70	—	—	34
1983	26	78	26	73	—	—	28

Notes: [a]Estimate, assuming that the level of payments to suppliers (as a percentage of sales) in 1975 equaled the average for 1974 (64.1%) and 1976 (64.3%), since Chrysler did not publish this figure in 1975.

In-house vertical integration is defined as internal manufacturing and other operating costs divided by sales minus operating profits. Group vertical integration is defined as internal operating costs plus operating costs paid to affiliates (20% equity minimum) divided by sales minus operating profits.

Table 19.2 (*Continued*)

Since the Japanese and U.S. firms do not publish comparable data, I employed the following methodology and assumptions to construct the table above. For Nissan and Toyota (including Toyota Motor Sales), I multiplied the percentage of manufacturing costs for small cars not subcontracted by total manufacturing costs listed in the *yuka shoken hokokusho* (Japanese 10-K reports), added other operating expenses incurred in-house (executive and other non-manufacturing employee compensation, retirement and severance payments, and depreciation), and divided by sales minus operating profits. For group integration, I added operating costs paid to affiliates, listed in the notes to the balance sheets in the Japanese reports, to in-house costs. For the U.S. firms, I subtracted payments to suppliers from sales minus operating profits and divided by sales minus operating profits. GM and Ford stopped publishing data on payments to suppliers after 1979, so I could not calculate their levels of integration for 1980–1983.

The Japanese figures are estimates, therefore, assuming that the percentages Nissan and Toyota published regarding subcontracting are accurate, and that total subcontracting was roughly equal to that for small cars.

Source: Reprinted from M.A. Cusumano, *The Japanese Automobile Industry: Technology and Management at Nissan and Toyota* (Cambridge, Mass.: Council on East Asian Studies/Harvard University Press, 1985), by permission of the publishers. Derived from annual reports. For additional explanation of this data, see ibid., pp. 187–191.

companies to improve their production systems as well as the quality of their components or assembly services, value-added productivity tripled between 1960 and 1983. This was a rate of increase slightly faster than the improvements registered at Nissan and Toyota in this same period.

Toyota: The Process Innovator

Toyota's history is critical to understanding these developments, because its managers and workers pioneered the techniques now associated with Japanese manufacturing in general.

By importing what was essentially a Dodge truck, Nissan went quickly into "mass production" in the mid-1930s and turned out a vehicle comparable to U.S. models—while establishing a predilection for American manufacturing equipment and practices that managers carried through to the 1980s. Toyota, however, could not afford to buy American blueprints, equipment, and assistance when they began in the 1930s.[11] Instead, founder Kiichiro Toyoda designed his first vehicle by copying a Ford chassis, a Chevrolet engine, and a Chrysler DeSoto body—combining the "best" features of each U.S. manufacturer. The first truck broke down on the way to the showroom, portending a series of technical problems in Toyota vehicles that took more than a decade to overcome.[12]

Realizing they would need to improve vehicles frequently, Toyota's objectives were to cultivate in-house design skills and to set up an inexpensive production system for low volumes. (Since their early vehicles were unreliable, the Japanese military would not buy all Toyota's output, in contrast to Nissan's.)

To solve its unique problems, Toyota bought universal machine tools and small stamping presses that were affordable and easily adaptable to model changes. This was the beginning of the "flexibility" in the Toyota production system that helped the company improve its designs before 1945 and then, after World War II, introduce numerous new models for the domestic and export markets quickly and cheaply. Again, unlike Nissan, Isuzu, Hino, and Mitsubishi, during the 1950s Toyota chose not to become affiliated with a European or U.S. auto producer and preferred to deemphasize automation.

Taiichi Ohno, who rose to executive vice president before retiring in 1978, had joined Toyota in 1943, having worked previously for a loom-machinery producer. He had no experience in automobiles and no predilection for U.S. methods. Benefiting from the versatile equipment first purchased in the 1930s, Ohno gradually introduced a series of interrelated innovations in manufacturing that complemented and rivaled the achievements of Frederick Taylor and Henry Ford. Between 1948 and the mid-1960s, Ohno initiated a virtual "revolution" that would change the way production managers around the world viewed optimal inventory levels and many of the most basic concepts of production management.[13]

1948

Ohno instituted a "pull" system in the machining shop for engines, asking each worker to move back to the previous station to retrieve work-in-process, just at the necessary time in the amount needed only for immediate processing. He first read about the idea of a pull system in a Japanese newspaper that described this practice in the U.S. aircraft industry during World War II and in U.S. supermarkets. This contrasted with the traditional "push" systems used at Nissan and other automakers in the United States, Japan, and Europe, where components and information signalling production flowed according to a schedule, whether or not stations were ready to receive the components.

The push system was not well suited to small-lot production and tended to build up in-process inventories whenever stations fell behind, due to machinery breakdowns or other factors, or when sales fell and production schedules were not revised downward. Toyota management wanted to control in-process and finished-goods inventories because of large financial losses associated with post-war inflation and the collapse of the military market.

1949

The pull system in the machining shop allowed Toyota to end the intermediate stockpiling of engines.

Ohno also made workers in the machining shop operate several machines each, rather than specialize (as did auto workers at Nissan as well as at U.S. and European companies), because demand was low and there was not enough work to keep all machines operating constantly. This procedural change seemed to improve worker productivity.

Ohno then asked production workers to conduct their own inspections. This improved quality *on the line* and raised worker output by cutting down on nonproductive inspection staff.

1950

Toyota extended the pull concept to marketing through the policy, prompted by financial difficulties and demanded by company bankers, of limiting production to orders received by Toyota Motor Sales from dealers.

Toyota synchronized engine and transmission machining with final assembly, to reduce further in-process inventories.

Indicator lights introduced on the engine lines alerted supervisors to problems.

1953

Ohno introduced an early *"kanban"* system into the machining shop, using the exchange of paper tags to signal processing operations or parts production. The Japanese called this the "supermarket method," since it mimicked the practice in U.S. supermarkets where customers went to stores to buy what they wanted when they wanted it, rather than store goods, while the supermarket replaced items on shelves as it sold them.

To simplify manufacturing, procurement, and conveyance Toyota also instituted a standardization program for car and truck components.

1955

Toyota synchronized its body and final assembly shops to eliminate more in-process inventories.

Controls introduced on parts deliveries further cut inventories.

Toyota started to mix the loading of components in small lots for machine tools and to mix model runs on final assembly lines to raise equipment utilization as well as lower inventories.

Line-stop buttons introduced on assembly lines gave workers authority to halt production if they noticed defects or if other problems arose.

1957

Indicator lights installed on all production lines alerted supervisors outside the machining shop to problems.

1959

A control system for internal and in-house-to-outside conveyances again cut in-process inventories and waiting time.

1961

Toyota introduced the *kanban* system to some outside parts suppliers.

1962

Toyota then extended the *kanban* system to all in-house shops, placing the entire company on a small-lot, pull system.

Foolproof devices added to machine tools helped prevent defects and overproduction.

As an example of rapid setup, Toyota lowered stamping-press changeover times for dies from two or three hours in previous years to fifteen minutes, through techniques such as automating as much of the process as possible, doing preparations for the changeover while machines were running, and training teams to specialize in setup. Rapid setups increased equipment utilization and made small-lot production more economical, as well as helped reduce in-process inventories by cutting lead times.

1963

Managers were now asking workers to operate an average of five machines each, compared with three to four since 1949, two in 1947, and one in previous years. This seemed to raise labor productivity further.

1965

Toyota extended the *kanban* system to all outside parts deliveries, further reducing in-process inventories.

1971

Toyota cut die setup times for stamping presses to three minutes and adopted the practice of moving workers to different positions on assembly lines as needed.

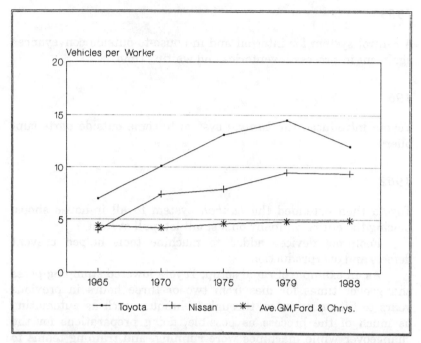

Figure 19.1 Vehicles Productivity Adjusted for Vertical Integration, Capacity Utilization, and Labor Hour Differences, 1965–1983

Source: Derived from annual reports. Unless otherwise noted, annual reports for Nissan and Toyota refer to the Japanese-language equivalents of the 10–K reports (*yuka shoken hokokusho*). Adapted from *The Japanese Automobile Industry: Technology and Management at Nissan and Toyota.* M. A. Cusumano (Cambridge, Mass.: Council on East Asian Studies/Harvard University Press, 1985). By permission of the publisher.

1973

Toyota allowed suppliers to deliver directly to assembly lines, fully linking them with its in-house parts conveyance system.

Improvements in Productivity and Inventory Levels

These measures corresponded to impressive improvements in productivity and inventory turnover. Vehicles manufactured per worker per year tripled at Toyota between 1955 and 1957 and then

Table 19.3 Unadjusted Vehicles per Worker at Toyota, Nissan, GM, and Ford, 1955–1964 and Selected Years

FY	TOYOTA	NISSAN	GM	FORD
1955	4	3	8	12
1956	8	6	7	10
1957	13	7	6	10
1958	12	8	6	9
1959	14	9	7	11
1960	15	12	8	12
1961	16	14	7	11
1962	16	15	9	11
1963	19	17	9	12
1964	20	18	9	12
■	■	■	■	■
1970	38	30	8	12
1980	56	41	10	10
1983	58	42	11	15
1985	60	42	11	15

Source: Annual reports.

rose another 60 percent by 1964. Even making adjustments for vertical integration, capacity utilization, and labor hour differences, Toyota appears to have passed the productivity levels at GM, Ford, and Chrysler by 1965 (see Table 19.1). While Nissan did not adopt the *kanban* or pull system, and focused on improving its levels of automation, at roughly the same time as Toyota it also worked at reducing setup times, improving in-house synchronization, and controlling parts deliveries. Gross productivity levels at Nissan increased fivefold between 1955 and 1964 and doubled between 1965 and 1970 (adjusting for vertical integration, capacity utilization, and labor hours). In contrast, productivity at U.S. automakers stagnated between the mid-1950s and the early 1980s (see Table 19.3 and Figure 19.1).

Equally remarkable advances can be seen in inventory levels. In the mid-1950s Toyota, Nissan, GM, Ford, and Chrysler all had relatively low turnover rates (total inventories divided into sales). In 1950, Toyota turned over its inventory merely three times, and in 1955 merely eight times—worse than U.S. firms. Only with better synchronization, mixed runs in parts production and assembly, and experiments with *kanban* and the pull system did turnover rates increase significantly. They rose again between 1962 and 1963 when Toyota adopted the *kanban* system for all in-house shops, and in 1965 and 1966 when Toyota brought suppliers onto the *kanban* system. Nor was rapid turnover the result of rapid increases in sales. Even when production volume fell 8 percent in 1974 following the first oil shock, Toyota maintained a turnover level of twenty-one times—twice as high as U.S. firms and Nissan. In addition, the company continued to improve in this area, with turnover rates reaching thirty-eight times in 1985 and 1986.

In the late 1960s Toyota began teaching its production system to major subsidiaries and affiliates such as Hino and Daihatsu. These efforts helped produce significant rises in turnover (as well as productivity) at nearly all firms in the Toyota group. Companies affiliated with Nissan followed, as did Mazda, in the mid-1970s. But not all Japanese auto companies have been able to implement just-in-time systems as effectively as Toyota. Nissan, as well as Honda, Fuji Heavy Industries (Subaru), and Isuzu have turnover rates comparable to GM, Ford, and Chrysler.

Nissan has trailed Toyota in inventory turnover for several reasons. One is that its factories and suppliers are more dispersed than Toyota's. Since the 1930s, Nissan has also been more committed to automation and specialized equipment than Toyota, and in the 1960s it introduced a computerized push system for production control resembling "Materials Requirement Planning" (MRP) systems common in the United States. Nissan thus manufactures automobiles according to a computer-generated schedule that is directly tied to market demand and does not adjust almost instantaneously to changes in shop conditions or at suppliers, as in Toyota's *kanban* system. The result is that managers prefer to keep larger buffer inventories on hand "just in case" there are disruptions in the supply system or inaccurate computer information.

Yet, like Toyota, to accommodate product diversity at small volumes and to reduce warehousing requirements in Tokyo and Yokohama, in the 1950s and early 1960s Nissan began modifying machine tools to get more rapid setup times and began requiring more frequent parts deliveries. These practices brought Nissan to a level of inventory turnover faster than it did U.S. firms (although U.S. companies also have the disadvantage of even more geographically dispersed production and supply operations). In the late 1970s Nissan also began experimenting with *kanban* for outside suppliers located more than twenty minutes from its factories (nearer suppliers are connected by on-line terminals). Only then did the company increase the rates of inventory turnover it had achieved by the mid-1960s. (U.S. companies made no progress in this area between the 1950s and the early 1980s—until they began experimenting with a limited just-in-time concept around 1982.)

It should be noted that Honda, as well as NUMMI in California, simulates some effects of just-in-time production by keeping parts away from production lines and in warehousing areas and delivering components to assembly only as they are needed. These stocks still add to aggregate inventory costs and do not necessarily improve overall turnover, but keeping them off the assembly lines appears to maintain greater discipline in process and quality control.[14] It also appears that Honda has been able to achieve substantial profits with productivity and inventory turnover levels below the industry leaders because its designs are received very favorably by customers.

The successful transfer of Japanese manufacturing techniques to U.S.-based plants demonstrates clearly that Japanese workers are not necessary to implement these practices. However, Toyota-style techniques do require considerable cooperation among managers, workers, and suppliers. During the main development period in the 1950s, Japanese managers reflected with great concern on U.S. companies' labor difficulties in the 1930s and then *planned* how to ensure more cooperation from the workers and how to reduce personnel costs.

Japanese managers, again led by Ohno, accomplished their goals through a combination of persuasion and collaboration with workers and officials from government and industry. They undercut industrial unions and set up company unions dominated by white-collar workers; frequently promoted union officials to management positions to increase the likelihood that union leaders would cooperate; fired large numbers of workers after World War II and then offered "lifetime" employment to select groups of employees in return for their cooperation; reduced the number of job categories to only a few, so that they could move workers to different positions easily and expand worker job routines; and used subcontractors highly dependent on the final assemblers to produce 70 percent or more of the components (by cost) of each Japanese car.

What Have We Learned?

The history of Japan's auto industry is a story of American lapses as well as Japanese innovations. These innovations involved a spectrum of changes in conventional production management, broadly conceived. Toyota was the most radical, while most other Japanese automakers, typified by Nissan, incorporated less extensive modifications of U.S. practices and equipment. Two concluding thoughts seem relevant for managers of any country in any setting.

Manufacturing Innovation Can Lead to Competitive Advantage

An obvious point is that innovation in manufacturing can lead to competitive advantage. While a company might compete equally or more effectively through high quality or innovative designs, or customer service and advertising , customers must see a substantial advantage in products or services. This means that a company competing in the broader marketplace, rather than in specialized segments such as luxury goods, cannot afford to fall too far behind productivity leaders. If competitors offer even comparable products at lower prices, catching up in manufacturing efficiency *and* reestablishing an edge in product design may prove inordinately difficult. If competitors offer superior products at lower prices, then less efficient companies will certainly encounter trouble in the marketplace and may require manipulation of the market—government-guaranteed loans or import quotas—to survive.

This is what happened in the automobile industry: Relying on a series of process innovations pioneered at Toyota in response to the small but highly competitive Japanese market, Japanese companies equaled their U.S. and European competitors first in physical productivity. Then they continued improving their manufacturing processes, along with product designs and subcontractor operations. The result was that by 1980 U.S. and many European companies lagged so far behind in productivity and quality that they were no longer competitive. U.S. firms also cut back on design programs that might have led to more popular smaller cars and procured less costly components, with the result that the variety and overall reliability of U.S. vehicles suffered. But the major story is that Japanese firms consistently introduced highly reliable and increasingly stylish products at low prices, leaving only a few premium European producers with a defensive market niche.

Improvement Must Be an Incremental, Continual, Integrated Effort

There is a tradition in manufacturing dating from Adam Smith, but epitomized in Frederick Taylor and his principles of "scientific management," that calls for managers to analyze and freeze a process, divide it into small pieces, then dictate to workers and suppliers their "piece" in the process. While management might introduce automated equipment or even radically new procedures, there is not much room on the manufacturing floor for creativity, innovation, or incremental improvement. Nor is there any recognition that workers and suppliers might participate more fully, for example, by inspecting their own work and maintaining their own equipment, operating more machines, or delivering supplies in smaller quantities but more frequently.

To a large degree Toyota and Taiichi Ohno built upon Taylor's work in process analysis and Ford's efforts to create an integrated, smoothly running mass-production system. But Toyota and other Japanese companies introduced a fundamental concept: *continual* rather than one-time improvement, achieved through successive process refinements and a greater integration of workers and suppliers into the production system.

To understand what happened in Japan it is important to understand the U.S. automobile industry. By the early 1960s, American managers viewed automobile manufacturing as a stable or "mature" technology, assuming certain limits to productivity, minimum efficient scales of productions, unit costs, quality, and the ability of workers and suppliers to cooperate (or be coerced) and to contribute to improving production operations. The "American paradigm"—characterized by large production runs, push-type scheduling, high levels of automation and worker specialization, and large numbers of inspectors using statistical sampling—dominated the thinking and the goals of U.S. (as well as many European) managers.

There was nothing particularly wrong with this approach to manufacturing. It proved to be remarkably effective for high-volume production of a limited number of models. But market conditions and financial constraints in Japan after World War II presented an opportunity for Toyota and other Japanese auto producers to challenge convention and become equally or more efficient at far lower volumes.

Critical to the Japanese success in auto manufacturing was that managers such as Toyota's Ohno did not accept U.S. practices as the only viable way to produce automobiles and did not believe that U.S. firms had reached their limits in capital and worker productivity, quality, or inventory turnover. There was nothing mysterious or miraculous about what Toyota and other Japanese automakers accomplished in manufacturing. They responded to specific market conditions, creatively applying techniques first developed in the United States in new ways. Ultimately, by seeking a better solution to a fundamental problem, the Japanese set new standards of efficiency and started a revolution in manufacturing theory and practice that has yet to end. While companies and management-labor relations have evolved differently in the United States, the unique quality of Japanese workers in Japan can no longer be used as an excuse in the United States for a lack of efficiency, innovation, and improvement in manufacturing.

20

The Myth of the Cooperative Single Source*

John Ramsay

Introduction

The flood of Japanese goods that engulfed the West in the seventies and early eighties was accompanied by waves of "new" management practices. Many of these novel techniques have since been revealed as cleverly implemented versions of ideas originating in the West in earlier decades. Reinventing the wheel is one fault that cannot be laid at the door of Japanese management, and their skill at translating other peoples' good ideas into successful working practices is enviable and beyond dispute. However, among the revitalized old ideas were a handful of genuinely novel approaches to business problems. Perhaps none was more startling, yet less noticed, than the large Japanese corporations' habit of developing long-term, cooperative, single-source relationships with their suppliers.

This is a truly remarkable feat. Conventional Western wisdom suggests that the use of single sources is a high risk strategy

*Reprinted with permission from the publisher, the National Association of Purchasing Management, "The Myth of the Cooperative Single Source," by John Ramsay, *Journal of Purchasing and Materials Management* 26, no. 1 (Winter 1990).

that severely restricts a buyer's freedom of action and thus the power and ability to influence his or her company's profits. Western sourcing strategies tend to be openly adversarial in nature, relying on multiple sources to provide an insurance policy against supply interruptions, and to allow the buyer to develop power through competitive pressure. Power through competition is at the heart of the Western approach. Power struggles are the accepted mechanism whereby buyer and supplier try to control their respective profit levels.

The Japanese have apparently developed a trading system that dispenses with the need for competition or the manipulation of power entirely. Mutual benefit through cooperation seems to be at the heart of their system. Financial prosperity without competition seems to be the promise they extend. How have they achieved this? Can a fundamentally uncompetitive technique really be effective? With manufacturing industry allocating an average of 60 percent of total costs to purchased materials and services, a technique as radical and spectacularly successful as this Japanese innovation deserves close attention.

The Issues

Much of our understanding of Japanese management practice comes from reports of the behavior of Japanese auto companies. Nissan and Honda, in particular, have been held up as examples of the benefits that can be achieved through long-term deals with suppliers. In purchasing circles this information has filtered through a variety of different channels and has colored opinions to such an extent that the traditional competitive Western approach to sourcing has taken on an old fashioned, wasteful, inefficient and primitive image. The perceived Japanese image is one of successful long-term, single-source, egalitarian, power-sharing relationships between equals. If this image is accurate, then the abandonment of current Western practice is well justified. However, evidence concerning the accuracy of the image is ambiguous.

The Japanese auto manufacturers, for example, do indeed have a large number of single sources with whom they have long-term arrangements. Direct discussion with the staff of such suppliers confirms the way in which the security offered by long-term joint forward planning between customer and supplier drastically reduces the degree of competition in the market. Fear of competitors is not high on the list of corporate anxieties found in single-sourced Japanese car company suppliers. Nevertheless, few of these deals can truly be described as egalitarian power-sharing contracts between equals:

> Each major Japanese enterprise swims in the economy like a shark with its cloud of pilot fish, surrounded by subcontractors, sub-subcontractors, sub-sub-subcontractors, and so on down the line.[1]
>
> The result is that every large firm is the center of a constellation of small and medium firms which are, in greater or lesser degree, dependent on it for business.[2]

The fact of the matter is that the large Japanese corporations have made a specialty of developing small suppliers. Indeed, the Japanese are masters of the home-working method of manufacture:

> Historically, much of the manufacturing activity in Japan has been accomplished by cottage industries, which supplied a retail and distribution system that was also dominated by petty firms. This situation eventually led to the formation of trading companies that were able to sell the petty firm's merchandise outside of the respective home districts. This general practice continues even today. The ten largest Japanese trading company clusters account for half of Japan's economic activity.[3]

The situation is indeed little changed today; there may even be an increase in the practice of using small suppliers. While discussing the structure of one section of the Japanese weaving industry that used to be dominated by a few large mills, Dore comments:

> By 1980, however, the picture had changed. The large mills had closed. The integrated firms had retreated, as far as direct production was concerned, to their original base in spinning. Most of them were still either alone or in collaboration with a trading company, producing their own brand cloth, dyed and finished. But they were doing so through the coordination of the activities of a large number of family enterprises.[4]

It would appear that, similar to most other economies, the familiar 80/20 rule has applied to the degree of Japanese industrial concentration. As a result, the majority of Japanese firms are small businesses subcontracting to much larger organizations. It likely is also true that the proportion of home workers, one-person businesses, and small family enterprises is markedly higher than in developed Western economies. It is impossible to avoid drawing the conclusion that significant numbers of single-sourced Japanese suppliers inevitably find themselves in a potentially extremely weak bargaining position with respect to their much larger customers. In financial terms alone, any contract made between such companies can hardly be described as a "deal between equals."

In the West this kind of situation typically leads to the exploitation of the weaker party by the stronger, but it may well be that certain aspects of Japanese personal and business culture have a restraining influence on the behavior of the dominant partners in these trading relationships. Dore, in particular, highlights one aspect of Japanese business dealings that is conspicuously absent from many Western relationships. He distinguishes between "spot contracting" (the Western norm) and "obligational contracting" (the Japanese pattern) emphasizing: "the explicit encouragement, and actual prevalence, in the Japanese economy of what one might call moralized trading relationships of mutual goodwill.... The stability of the relationship is the key. Both sides recognize an obligation to try to maintain it."[5]

Despite (or possibly because of) this inhibiting, moralizing culture influence, the large corporations have successfully developed a unique market structure that acts to reduce or neutralize any nascent power that the larger suppliers in the market may be tempted to develop and wield. In describing the development of the *Sogo Shosha* (the giant Japanese trading company clusters, such as Mitsubishi, Mitsui, and Sumitomo), Cusumano observes that their typical structure has been built around: "A holding company extended over a network of subsidiaries and affiliates through the linkages of intercorporate stockholdings, interlocking directorates, management help, personnel transfers, and bank credit."[6]

This practice of building complex intercompany connections and controls is an ancient Japanese tradition with a history stretching back to the eighteenth century and beyond. The net effect of this practice has been to further concentrate power in the hands of the large dominant trading oligopolies. Most Western companies would find the temptation to use this kind of power to further their own interests impossible to resist. There is some evidence that Japanese companies have been similarly corrupted:

There is a segment of public opinion in Japan that views the *Sogo Shosha* very negatively, as the ruthless oppressor of small business. There is no question that the *Sogo Shosha* are able to exert tremendous pressures on the small businesses over whom they loom so large. Often these pressures are to reduce price, delay payment, or otherwise squeeze net resources out of a business relationship. In a declining business, the *Sogo Shosha* is allocating economic pain, not economic gain, and this is always a poorly received role in any situation.[7]

Again, in discussing the Japanese automotive industry and the application of obligational contracting, Dore points out that: "Here again, the obligations of the relationship are unequal; the subcontractor has to show more earnest good will, more 'sincerity,' to keep its orders than the parent company to keep its supplies" and later:

> Benevolence all too easily shades into exploitation when the divorce option—the option of breaking off the relationship—is more costlessly available to one party than to the other. There is even an officially sponsored Association for the Promotion of the Modernization of Trading Relations in the Textile Industry in Japan that urges the use of written rather than verbal contracts in these relationships. [The association] is devoted to strengthening mutual constraints on what it calls the abuse—but our economic textbooks would presumably call the legitimate full use—of market power.[8]

It would appear that the Japanese business veneer of courtesy, tolerance, and good will may occasionally conceal an interior of considerable ruthlessness. And we may tentatively conclude that although Japanese trading relationships have been offered up as shining examples of the cooperative ideal, in practice the balance of power in many, if not most, of these relationships is heavily weighted in the buyer's favor. Large sections of Japanese industry rest on a foundation of very low cost, subcontracted cottage or "home" labor. Individual home workers and small family businesses form the backbone of many Japanese supplier networks. Moreover, although the foundation is overlaid with a layer of larger, potentially more powerful companies, the long-developed complex of intercompany control mechanisms serves to retain power in the hands of the big buyers. The true nature of Japanese "supplier networks," with their boards of "tame" directors and financial dependence on their customers, is in sharp contrast to the Western archetype of independent suppliers free to discard customers as and when the opportunity arises.

Indeed, in some sections of the Japanese economy this process of supplier emasculation is so far advanced that many of these companies are not "suppliers" as we use and understand the word. They are more like off-site workshops of the main buying plant. The great advantage of this arrangement for the buyer is that in periods of downturn, orders to these "suppliers" can be turned off, and the work brought back in-house without any of the expense and inconvenience associated with reducing activity within the parent plant itself. When times are good, subcontractors are treated as parts of the main company—like partners. When times get bad, they are magically transformed into simple suppliers toward whom the company, despite the cultural constraints of obligational contracting, has no real commitment. It is little wonder, then, that many single sources fail to strike fear into the hearts of some Japanese buyers.

Conclusion

It is undoubtedly true that the Japanese trading system is anticompetitive, but it can hardly be described as egalitarian. In light of these facts, the current rash of Western business fads for win-win negotiating, profit partnerships (and the latest, "value adding partnerships"[9]), and sundry other expressions of the cooperative approach may appear to be a trifle foolhardy. Cooperation may be bursting out all over, helped along by the desire to have some of the Japanese success rub off on us, but the dangers of cultural misinterpretation cannot be overemphasized. Even when Dore begins to describe the apparently familiar role of gift giving in business, it is the strangeness of the Japanese approach rather than the similarities with Western behavior that leaves the most lasting impression: "What are entirely traditional, however, are first, the basic pattern of treating trading relations as particularistic personal relations; second, the values and sentiments which sustain the obligations involved; and third, such things as the pattern of midsummer and year-end gift exchange which symbolizes recognition of these obligations."[10]

When we in the West come to regard the practice of suppliers giving and customers receiving Christmas gifts without the slightest suspicion that it is little more than an expression of low-level corruption, it will be safe to adopt single-sourcing strategies. Until that day, we would be well advised to remember that the differences between Japanese and Western business cultures far outweigh the similarities, and to think twice before relinquishing power and entrusting our future to strangers. If you feel compelled to follow the Japanese example, then imitate their practice of developing single sources only when the source is at a serious power disadvantage. Remember, commercial xenophobia may be good for your financial health.

21

Another Hidden Edge—
Japanese Management Accounting*

Toshiro Hiromoto

Much has been written about why Japanese manufacturers continue to outperform their U.S. competitors in cost, quality, and on-time delivery. Most experts point to practices like just-in-time production, total quality control, and the aggressive use of flexible manufacturing technologies. One area that has received less attention, but that I believe contributes mightily to Japanese competitiveness, is how many companies' management accounting systems reinforce a top-to-bottom commitment to process and product innovation.

I have studied management accounting systems at Japanese companies in several major industries including automobiles, computers, consumer electronics, and semiconductors. Although practices varied greatly, several related patterns did emerge. These patterns differentiate certain aspects of Japanese management accounting from established practices in the United States.

Like their U.S. counterparts, Japanese companies must value inventory for tax purposes and financial statements. But the Japanese do not let these accounting procedures determine how

*Copyright 1988 by the President and Fellows of Harvard College; all rights reserved. From *Harvard Business Review* (July–August 1988).

they measure and control organizational activities. Japanese companies tend to use their management control systems to support and reinforce their manufacturing strategies. A more direct link therefore exists between management accounting practices and corporate goals.

Japanese companies seem to use accounting systems more to motivate employees to act in accordance with long-term manufacturing strategies than to provide senior management with precise data on cost, variances, and profits. Accounting plays more of an "influencing" role than an "informing" role. For example, high-level Japanese managers seem to worry less about whether an overhead allocation system reflects the precise demands each product makes on corporate resources than about how the system affects the cost-reduction priorities of middle managers and shop-floor workers. As a result, they sometimes use allocation techniques that executives in the United States might dismiss as simplistic or even misguided.

Accounting in Japan also reflects and reinforces an overriding commitment to market-driven management. When estimating costs on new products, for example, many companies make it a point not to rely completely on prevailing engineering standards. Instead, they establish target costs usually well below currently achievable costs, which are based on standard technologies and processes. Managers then set benchmarks to measure incremental progress toward meeting the target cost objectives.

Several companies I studied also de-emphasize standard cost systems for monitoring factory performance. In general, Japanese management accounting does not stress optimizing within existing constraints. Rather, it encourages employees to make continual improvements by tightening those constraints.

The following cases highlight some of the differences between management accounting in Japan and the United States. My intention is to be suggestive, not definitive. Not all Japanese companies use the techniques I describe, and some U.S. companies have adopted approaches similar to what I have seen in Japan.

Allocating Overhead

American executives have been barraged with criticism about how long-accepted techniques for allocating manufacturing overhead can distort product costs and paint a flawed picture of the profitability of manufacturing operations. Accounting experts challenge direct labor hours as an overhead allocation base since direct labor represents only a small percentage of total costs in most manufacturing environments. They argue that a logical and causal relationship should exist between the overhead burden and the assignment of costs to individual products. They believe that an allocation system should capture as precisely as possible the reality of shop-floor costs.

Japanese companies are certainly aware of this perspective, but many of the companies I examined do not seem to share it. Consider the practices of the Hitachi division that operates the world's largest factory devoted exclusively to videocassette recorders. The Hitachi VCR plant is highly automated yet continues to use direct labor as the basis for allocating manufacturing overhead. Overhead allocation doesn't reflect the actual production process in the factory's automated environment. When I asked the accountants whether that policy might lead to bad decisions, they responded with an emphatic no. Hitachi, like many large Japanese manufacturers, is convinced that reducing direct labor is essential for ongoing cost improvement. The company is committed to aggressive automation to promote long-term competitiveness. Allocating overhead based on direct labor creates the desired strong pro-automation incentives throughout the organization.

The perspective offered by Hitachi managers seems to be shared by their counterparts at many other companies. It is more important, they argue, to have an overhead allocation system (and other aspects of management accounting) that motivates employees to work in harmony with the company's long-term goals than to pinpoint production costs. Japanese managers want their accounting systems to help create a competitive future, not quantify the performance of their organizations at this moment.

Another Hitachi factory (this one in the refrigeration and air-conditioning equipment sector) employs an overhead allocation technique, based on the number of parts in product models, to influence its engineers' design decisions. Japanese companies have long known what more and more U.S. companies are now recognizing—that the number of parts in a product, especially custom parts, directly relates to the amount of overhead. Manufacturing costs increase with the complexity of the production process, as measured, for example, by the range of products built in a factory or the number of parts per product. In plants assembling diverse products, reducing the number of parts and promoting the use of standard parts across product lines can lower costs dramatically.

Using standard parts can also lower materials costs, insofar as it creates possibilities for more aggressive volume buying. Yet

on a product-by-product basis, many cost systems fail to recognize
these economies.

Consider a factory building several different products. The
products all use one or both of two parts, A and B, which the factory buys in roughly equal amounts. Most of the products use both
parts. The unit cost of part A is $7, of part B, $10. Part B has more
capabilities than part A; in fact, B can replace A. If the factory
doubles its purchases of part B, it qualifies for a discounted $8 unit
price. For products that incorporate both parts, substituting B for
A makes sense to qualify for the discount. (The total parts cost is
$17 using A and B, $16 using Bs only.) Part B, in other words,
should become a standard part for the factory. But departments
building products that use only part A may be reluctant to accept
the substitute part B because even discounted, the cost of B
exceeds that of A.

This factory needs an accounting system that motivates
departments to look beyond their parochial interests for the sake
of enterprise-level cost reduction. Hitachi has adopted such an
approach by adding overhead surcharges to products that use non-
standard parts. The more custom parts in a product, the higher
the overhead charge.

Accounting for Market-Driven Design

By the time a new product enters the manufacturing stage, opportunities to economize significantly are limited. As the Hitachi
refrigerator example suggests, Japanese companies have long recognized that the design stage holds the greatest promise for supporting low-cost production. Many U.S. manufacturers, including
Texas Instruments, Hewlett-Packard, and Ford, are also making
competitive strides in this area. But certain Japanese companies
have taken the process even further. They do not simply design
products to make better use of technologies and work flows; they
design and build products that will meet the price required for
market success—whether or not that price is supported by current
manufacturing practices. Their management accounting systems
incorporate this commitment.

Daihatsu Motor Company, a medium-sized automobile producer that has yet to enter the U.S. market, provides a good example of market-driven accounting practices. It installed the *genka
kikaku* product development system in its factories soon after affil-

iating with Toyota, which pioneered the approach. The *genka kikaku* process at Daihatsu usually lasts three years, at which time the new car goes into production. The process begins when the *shusa* (the product manager responsible for a new car from planning through sales) instructs the functional departments to submit the features and performance specifications that they believe the car should include. The *shusa* then makes recommendations to the senior managers, who issue a development order.

Next comes cost estimation. Management does not simply turn over the development order to the accountants and ask what it would cost to build the car based on existing engineering standards. Rather, Daihatsu establishes a target selling price based on what it believes the market will accept and specifies a target profit margin that reflects the company's strategic plans and financial projections. The difference between these two figures represents the "allowable cost" per car.

In practice, this target cost is far below what realistically can be attained. So each department calculates an "accumulated cost" based on current technologies and practices—that is, the standard cost achievable with no innovation. Finally, management establishes a target cost that represents a middle ground between these two estimates. This adjusted price-profit margin cost becomes the goal toward which everyone works.

At the design stage, engineers working on different parts of the car interact frequently with the various players (purchasing, shop-floor supervisors, parts suppliers) who will implement the final design. As the design process unfolds, the participants compare estimated costs with the target. The variances are fed back to the product developers, and the cycle repeats: design proposals, cost estimates, variance calculations, value engineering analysis to include desired features at the lowest possible cost, and redesign. The cycle ends with the approval of a final design that meets the target cost.

A similar dynamic operates at the production stage, where Daihatsu uses complementary approaches to manage costs: total plant cost management and *dai-atari kanri*, or per-unit cost management.

Reports based on total plant cost management are prepared for senior executives and plant managers. The studies compare budgeted costs with actual costs for an entire factory. Reports generated by the *dai-atari kanri* system are intended for managers at specific workstations. Comparisons between budgeted and actual costs are made only for "variable" charges, which include some cost, like tools, that do not vary strictly with short-term output. Put simply, items subject to *dai-atari kanri* include all costs that can be reduced through workers' continual efforts and process improvement activities—that is, controllable costs.

In production, as in the design stage, Daihatsu does not take a static approach to cost management. During the first year of production for a new car, the budgeted cost reflects targets set during the *genka kikaku* process. The cost is a starting point, however, not an ultimate goal; over the course of the year, it is tightened monthly by a cost-reduction rate based on short-term profit objectives. In subsequent years, the actual cost of the previous period becomes the starting point for further tightening, thereby creating a cost-reduction dynamic for as long as the model remains in production.

Good-Bye to Standard Costs

The market-driven philosophy at Daihatsu and other Japanese companies helps to explain why standard cost systems are not used as widely in Japan as they are in the United States. Standard costs reflect an engineering mind-set and technology-driven management. The goal is to minimize variances between budgeted and actual costs—to perform as closely as possible to best available practice. Market-driven management, on the other hand, emphasizes doing what it takes to achieve a desired performance level under market conditions. How efficiently a company should be able to build a product is less important to the Japanese than how efficiently it must be able to build it for maximum marketplace success.

Many Japanese companies that have used standard cost systems seem to be moving beyond them. NEC, the diversified electronics giant, designed and installed its standard cost system in the 1950s. The company still uses standard cost reports as a factory management tool and continues to train new employees in the system. But NEC recognizes that it has reached a strategic turning point and it is adjusting its management accounting policies accordingly.

NEC installed its standard cost system when it was supplying a stable product range (mostly telephones and exchanges) at stable prices to a large and stable customer, Nippon Telegraph and Telephone (NTT). Today NEC produces a vast array of products subject to rapid obsolescence and technological change. Its product line poses severe challenges to the standard cost system. The cost standards cannot be revised quickly enough for many products, so variance reports are increasingly open to question. (NEC revises its cost standards every six months, and even then only for a subset of products.) As a result, the company is relying more heavily on departmental budgets than product-by-product variances from standard costs. As with Daihatsu, targets are based on market demands and planned profit levels, and are tightened over time.

The U.S. subsidiary of a major Japanese electronics company takes this budgeting approach even further. Its production and marketing departments operate as separate profit centers. These departments interact to establish internal transfer prices for products. The transfer price is a negotiated percentage of the market price. Under this method, market prices critically influence departmental performance, since market prices are the basis for determining transfer prices. Both the production and marketing functions are encouraged to respond to market demand and competitive trends rather than focus solely on internal indicators.

The company recently extended this approach to its sales department, which is separate from marketing. Selling costs used to be allocated to individual products under a standard cost approach. Now the sales department operates as a profit center and negotiates commission levels with the marketing department. Through the cost system these commissions are then assigned to products. Thus the marketing department can make product decisions without accepting selling expenses as given, which increases pressure on the sales force to operate as efficiently as possible.

Accounting and Strategy

The accounting practices I have described do not necessarily represent Japanese practices as a whole. They do, however, point to a central principle that seems to guide management accounting in Japan—that accounting policies should be subservient to corporate strategy, not independent of it. Japanese manufacturing strategy places high premiums on quality and timely delivery in addition to low-cost production. Thus companies make extensive use, certainly more than many of their U.S. competitors, of nonfinancial measures to evaluate factory performance. The reason is straightforward: If a management accounting system measures only cost, employees tend to focus on cost exclusively.

I have encountered many practices designed to capture the nonfinancial dimensions of factory performance. One Japanese automaker wanted to motivate its managers and employees to reduce throughput time in assembly operations. It recognized that direct labor hours measure costs, not the actual time required to build and ship a car. So for time-management purposes, the company has replaced direct labor hours with a variable called managed hours per unit. In addition to direct labor, this new measure incorporates the time required for nonproductive activities like equipment maintenance and product repairs.

In an effort to improve machine and equipment efficiency, many companies are emphasizing preventive and corrective maintenance over breakdown maintenance. (Corrective maintenance means redesigning equipment to reduce failures and facilitate routine maintenance.) This emphasis goes beyond exhorting shop-floor personnel to pay more attention to their machines. Companies regularly measure rates of unexpected equipment failures, ratios of preventive and corrective maintenance to total maintenance, and other variables that track machine performance. These results are widely distributed and evaluated during small group discussions in the factory.

For companies to maintain competitive advantage, employees must be continually innovative. This requires motivation. A product designer must be motivated to play a significant role in cost reduction. Shop-floor workers and supervisors must constantly strive to improve efficiency beyond what "best practice" currently dictates. The Japanese have demonstrated that management accounting can play a significant role in integrating the innovative efforts of employees with the company's long-term strategies and goals.

NOTES

Foreword

1. Michael A. Cusumano, *Japan's Software Factories: A Challenge to U.S. Management* (New York: Oxford University Press, 1991).

Introduction

1. In "Professor Heinman on Religion and Economics," *Journal of Political Economy* (1948).

Chapter 1

1. Y. Sakudo, *Showa-Kyoho no Keiei* [Management in the Showa-Kyoho Period] (Tokyo, 1978) Chapter 1, Diamondo-sha.

2. *Gesellschaft* refers to an association of individuals bound together only by contractual obligations, in contrast to *gemeinschaft*, in which they are bound together by mutual affection and sentiment.

Chapter 3

An earlier, abridged version of this chapter was read before the Conference on Confucianism and Modernization, August 17–19, 1986, Taipei, Taiwan. It also appeared as *"Jukyo Bunka Ken Ron No Ichi Kou Satsu—'Wakon Yousai' to 'Chutai Saiyo' no Wakareme"* [An Inquiry into the Theory of "The Confucian Cultural Area"—The Difference Between "Japanese Spirit, Western Learning," and "Applying Western Technology Within the

Structure of Chinese Learning"], *Sei Kai* (December 1986) (published by Iwanami Shinsio), pp. 136–149.

1. For writings on the life of Shibusawa, see his *Ama yo gatari* [Conversations on Rainy Nights] (Tokyo: Iwanami Bunko, 1984). T. Tsuchiya, *Shibusawa Eiichi den* [The Biography of Shibusawa Eiichi] (Tokyo: Kaizoshia, 1931, latest ed., Toyo Shoka, Tokyo, 1955). K. Rohan, *Shibusawa Eiichi den* [The Biography of Shibusawa Eiichi] (Tokyo: Iwanami Shinsio, 1986).

2. The latest edition of *The Analects and Abacus* was published by Kokushio Kankokai in 1985. *Rango kogi* was incorporated into *Kou Dan Shia Gakujutsu Bunko* [Kuo Dan Shia Encyclopedia], published by Kou Dan Shia in 1975.

3. *The Analects and Abacus*, ibid., pp. 1–2.

4. Y. Irobe, "Rango to dento Nihon" [The Analects and Traditional Japan], *Yomigaeru Rongo* [The Analects Resurrected], (Tokyo: Tokuma Shoten, 1981).

5. *The Analects and Abacus*, pp. 2–3.

6. T. Tsuchiya, *Shibusawa Eiichi den*, pp. 188–189.

7. E. Shibusawa, *Shibusawa Eiichi zen shu* [The Complete Works of Shibusawa Eiichi], vol. 1 (Tokyo: Heibon Shia, 1930), pp. 222–224.

8. *The Analects and Abacus*, pp. 102–105.

9. Irobe, "Rongo to dento Nihon."

10. Y. Chio, *Meicho—sono hito to ji dai—Seienhiyakuwa*, [The Author and Times of a Celebrated Work—*Seienhiyabuwa*] *Economisuto* [The Economist] (published by the newspaper Mainichi), July 6, 1965, p. 77.

11. See J. Kato, *Nihon kyoiku shiso shi kenkyu—Wakon Yousai setsu* [An Inquiry into the Evolution of Japanese Educational Principles—Wakon Yousai] (Tokyo: Bai Fu Kan, 1926), pp. 316–346.

12. See M. Nakajima, *Nijiu ichi seki wa Nihon, Taiwan, Kankoku da* [The Twenty-First Century Belongs to Japan, Taiwan, and South Korea] (Tokyo: Dai Ichi Kikaku Shu Tsu Pan, 1986).

Chapter 4

1. D. T. Suzuki, *Zen and Japanese Culture* (Princeton, N.J.: Princeton University Press, 1959), p. 140.

2. F. Tonnies, *Fundamental Concepts of Sociology*, trans. C. P. Loomis (New York: American Book Co., 1940).

3. S. Durlabhji, "Primary Relations and Social Organization: A Theoretical and Empirical Investigation." Unpublished doctoral dissertation, Michigan State University, East Lansing, 1981.

4. C. H. Cooley, *Social Organization: A Study of the Larger Mind* (New York: Schocken Books, 1962).

5. O. W. Ritchie, and M. R. Koller, *Sociology of Childhood* (New York: Appleton-Century-Crofts, 1964). R. Warren, *The Community in America* (Chicago: Rand McNally, 1972). A. Maslow, *Motivation and Personality* (New York: Harper, 1954).

6. Suzuki, *Zen and Japanese Culture*, p. 53.

7. R. Tsunoda, W. T. Bary, and D. Keene, *Sources of Japanese Tradition*, Vol. 1 (New York: Columbia University Press, 1958).

8. Ibid., p. 48.

9. Ibid., p. 54.

10. J. G. Abegglen, *The Japanese Factory: Aspects of Its Social Organization* (Glencoe, Ill.: The Free Press, 1958).

11. E. Durkheim, *The Division of Labor in Society*, trans. G. Simpson (New York: The Free Press, 1933).

12. Abegglen, *The Japanese Factory*, p. 11.

13. J. G. Abegglen, *Management and Worker* (Tokyo: Sophia University, 1973), p. 68.

14. C. Nakane, *Japanese Society* (Berkeley: University of California Press, 1970), p. 3.

15. W. G. Ouchi, and J. B. Johnson, "Types of Organizational Control and Their Relationship to Emotional Well-Being," *Administrative Sciences Quaterly* 23, no. 2 (1978): 310.

16. T. J. Peters, and R. H. Waterman Jr., *In Search of Excellence: Lessons from America's Best-Run Companies* (New York: Warner Books, 1982).

17. B. DeMente, *The Japanese Way of Doing Business* (Englewood Cliffs, N.J.: Prentice-Hall, 1981), p. 16.

18. Nakane, *Japanese Society*, p. 80.

19. H. Dumoulin, *A History of Zen Buddhism*, trans. from the German by Paul Peachey (New York: Pantheon Books, 1963), p. 63.

20. Ibid., p. 61.

21. Suzuki, *Zen and Japanese Culture*, p. 21.

22. Ibid., p. 100.

23. Ibid., p. 197.

24. T. Ken, "Japan's Matrix of Nature, Culture, and Technology," *Management Review* 74, no. 5 (1985): 42.

25. T. P. Rohlen, *For Harmony and Strength* (Berkeley: University of California Press, 1974), p. 204.

26. Ibid.

27. R. C. Christopher, *The Japanese Mind* (London: Pan Books, 1984), p. 23.

28. W. G. Ouchi, *Theory Z: How American Business Can Meet the Japanese Challenge* (Reading, Mass.: Addison Wesley, 1981).

29. R. T. Pascale, and A. G. Athos, *The Art of Japanese Management: Applications for American Executives* (New York: Simon & Schuster, 1981).

30. M. Mushashi, *The Book of Five Rings: The Real Art of Japanese Management* (New York: Bantam Books, 1982), p. 67.

31. J. A. Reeder, "When West Meets East: Cultural Aspects of Doing Business in Asia," *Business Horizons* 30, no. 1 (1987): 70; emphasis added.

32. Ouchi, *Theory Z*.

33. Ibid., p. 61.

34. Pascale, and Athos, *The Art of Japanese Management*, p. 50.

35. Ibid.

36. Ibid.

Chapter 5

1. Additional findings on Japanese and American behavior will be found in D. C. Barnlund, *Public and Private Self in Japan and United States* (Tokyo: Simul Press; and Yarmouth, Me.: Intercultural Press, 1975). D. C. Barnlund, *Communicative Styles of Japanese and Americans: Images and Realities* (Belmont, Calif.: Wadsworth, 1989).

Chapter 7

1. In most statistics, figures for expenditure of gifts are included in the category of "social expenses" (*kosai hi*) along with expenditures for

entertaining guests. Data published by the Japanese government show that figures in this category range from about 1 percent to 3 percent of the total household expenditure, the percentage increasing as the income level rises. R. P. Dore's *City Life in Japan* is probably the only publication to provide a separate category for gift items in the analysis of household expenditures in Japan. His table shows seventeen households in Tokyo, spending 0.8 percent to 19.4 percent of the total household expenditure on gifts. (Dore's definition of "total household expenditure" is, however, slightly different from that of the government.) Unfortunately Dore's sample does not reflect a larger population of which it is a part, since the sample was not randomly selected.

2. Japan, National Commission for UNESCO, *Japan: Its Land, People and Culture* (Tokyo: Author, 1958), p. 950. K. Sakurada, *Noshi* [The Symbolic Attachment to a Formal Gift], in *Nihon shakai minzoku jiten* [Dictionary of Japanese Ethnography and Folklore], ed. N. M. Kyokai, vol. 3, (Tokyo, 1954). K. Segawa, *Nihonjin no ishokuju* [The Food, Clothing, and Shelter of the Japanese] (Tokyo, 1964), p. 245. K. Yanagita, *Shokumotsu to shinzo* [Food and Heart] (Tokyo and Osaka, 1940), pp. 249–274.

3. E. Ishida, "Unfinished but Enduring: Yanagita Kunio's Folklore Studies," *Japan Quarterly* 10 (1963): 35–42.

4. I wish to express my gratitude to the Center for Japanese Studies, University of Michigan, for providing financial aid in carrying out interviews on gift-giving with Japanese nationals resident in Ann Arbor in 1965–1966. I wish to thank Mr. Makio Matsuzono for conducting the interviews and making initial analysis of the data. Thanks are also due Professor Takashi Nakano, who served as a teacher, consultant, and informant for the writer.

5. For an overall discussion of old beliefs surrounding food and food production and consumption, see Segawa, *Nihonjin no ishokuju,* pp. 208–246.

6. *Minzokugaku jiten* [Dictionary of Ethnology] (Tokyo: Ethnological Research Institute, 1951), pp. 418–419.

7. K. Sugiura, *"Minkan-shindo no hanshi* [Folk Religion]," in *Nihon mizokugaku kenkyu* [Studies in Japanese Folklore], ed. K. Yanagita (Tokyo, 1935), pp. 128–132. K. Yanagita, *Shokumotsu to shinzo* [Food and Heart] (Tokyo and Osaka, 1940), p. 249–274. T. Wakamori, *Nihon minzoku-ron* [Japanese Folklore] (Tokyo, 1947), pp. 199–200.

8. G. De Vos and H. Wagatsuma, *Japan's Invisible Race* (Berkeley and Los Angeles, 1966), pp. 370–372.

9. Ibid., pp. 370–371.

10. Y. Shiibashi, *"Amazake to Kisetsu* [Sweet Rice-Wine and Seasons]," *Minkan densho* 8 (1942): 21–23.

11. T. Mogami, *"Koeki no hanashi* [Trade]," in *Nihon minzokugaku kenkyu* [Studies in Japanese Folklore], ed. K. Yanagita (Tokyo, 1935). T. Wakamori, *"Shako to kyoyo* [Social Interaction and Cultural Sophistication]," *Minkan densho* 10 (1944): 447–448.

12. I. Kurata, *"Toshidama ko* [The New Year's Gift]," *Minkan densho* 8 (1943): 497–502.

13. Sakurada, *Noshi,* in *Nihon shakai minzoku jiten,* vol. 3.

14. E. Norbeck, "Yakudoshi: A Japanese Complex of Supernatural Beliefs," *Southwestern Journal of Anthropology* 11 (1955): 105–120.

15. J. Embree, *Suye Mura: A Japanese Village* (Chicago, 1939), p. 104. Wakamori, *"Shako to kyoyo,"* pp. 447–448.

16. Yanagita, *Shokumotsu to shinzo,* pp. 101–129.

17. This token gift does not cancel the debt created by the gift brought. It simply symbolizes the good wishes of the receiver, who is in effect saying through the token return gift, "Please accept the supernatural power inherent in me which I hope will help you in some way." To reciprocate the gift and cancel the debt, the receiver must let some time elapse and then return a gift of appropriate value. A sick patient generally cancels his gift-debt by holding a feast when he recovers, to which he invites all those who paid him a visit during his illness.

18. Segawa, *Nihonjin no ishokuju,* p. 228.

19. T. Oomachi, *"Kankon-sosai no hanashi* [Ceremonies for Initiation, Marriage, Funeral, and Ancestors]," in *Nihon minzokugaku kenkyu* [Studies in Japanese Folklore].

20. The social framework of gift-giving, especially in relation to the concept of reciprocity, has been discussed in my paper, "Gift giving and Social Reciprocity in Japan: An Exploratory Statement," *France/Asie* 21 (1966/1967): 161–168.

21. M. Mauss, *The Gift: Forms and Functions of Exchange in Archaic Societies* (Glencoe, Ill., 1954).

22. T. Furukawa, *"Giri* [Social Obligation]," in *Nihon shakai minzoku jiten* [Dictionary of Japanese Ethnography and Folklore], vol. 1, p. 291. Y. Mori, *"Mura no kosai to giri* [Social Interaction and Obligations Among Villagers]," in *Sanson-seikatsu no kenkyu* [Life in Mountain Villages], ed K. Yanagita (Tokyo, 1937), p. 162. Wakamori, *Nihon minzokuron,* p. 198. Wakamori, *Rekishi to minzoku* [History and Folklore] (Tokyo, 1951). Wakamori, *Nihonjin no kosai* [Social Interaction Among Japanese] (Tokyo, 1953). *Minzokugaku jiten* [Dictionary of Ethnology], p. 164.

23. R. P. Dore, *City Life in Japan* (Berkeley and Los Angeles, 1958), pp. 260–262.

24. Incidentally, *koden*, which is now given in cash (hence the translation "incense money") and is used to supplement the cost of the funeral, originated as an offering of the new crop of rice to the dead. See I. Kurata, *"Koden no konjaku* [The Funerary Gift: Past and Present]," *Minkan densho* 10 (1944): 457–463.

25. Dore, *City Life in Japan,* pp. 258–262.

26. Ibid., pp. 387–389.

27. Wakamori, *Nihon minzoku-ron,* p. 198. M. Takagi, *Nihonjin no seikatsu-shinri* [Japanese Psychology of Daily Life] (Tokyo and Osaka, 1954).

28. Dore, *City Life in Japan,* p. 262.

29. R. K. Merton, *Social Theory and Social Structure* (Glencoe, Ill., 1949), pp. 125–150.

30. W. Caudill, and L. T. Doi, "Interrelations of Psychiatry, Culture and Emotion in Japan," *Man's Image in Medicine and Anthropology,* ed. I. Gladston (New York, 1963). W. Caudill and D. W. Plath, "Who Sleeps by Whom? Parent-Child Involvement in Urban Japanese Families," *Psychiatry* 29 (1966): 344–366. W. Caudill and H. A. Scarr, "Japanese Value Orientations and Culture Change," *Ethnology* 1 (1962): 53–91; reprinted in *Japanese Culture and Behavior: Selected Readings,* ed. T. S. Lebra and W. P. Lebra (Honolulu, 1974).

31. L. A. White, *The Evolution of Culture* (New York, 1959).

32. R. Benedict, *The Chrysanthemum and the Sword: Patterns of Japanese Culture* (Boston, 1946, reprinted 1961). Furukawa, *"Giri* [Social Obligation]," in *Nihon shakai minzoku jiten,* vol. 1.

33. I. Nakayama, *Nihon no kindaika* [Japan's Modernization] (Tokyo, 1965), pp. 86–87.

Chapter 9

1. Dan F. Henderson, *Foreign Enterprise in Japan: Laws and Policies* (Tokyo: Tuttle, 1975), p. 98.

2. On the workings of the Japanese state bureaucracy, see Chalmers Johnson, *MITI and the Japanese Miracle* (Stanford, Calif.: Stanford University Press, 1982), Chapter 2.

3. See John Creighton Campbell, *Contemporary Japanese Budget Politics* (Berkeley: University of California Press, 1977), Chapter 5.

4. On rural poverty in prewar Japan, see Mikiso Hane, *Peasants, Rebels, and Outcasts: The Underside of Modern Japan* (New York: Pantheon, 1982).

5. Gianni Fodella, "Economic Performance in Japan and Italy," in *Japan's Economy in a Comparative Perspective*, ed. G. Fodella (Tenterden, England: Paul Norbury, 1983), p. 26.

6. For current trends in Japanese administrative law, see "Symposium on the Oil Cartel Case," Japanese-American Society for Legal Issues, *Law in Japan: An Annual* 15 (1982): 1–101.

7. For a fairly comprehensive example, see Steven Schlosstein, *Trade War: Greed, Power, and Industrial Policy on Opposite Sides of the Pacific* (New York: Congdon and Weed, 1984).

8. See Fodella, "Economic Performance in Japan and Italy," p. 1–2; Alexander Eckstein, ed., *Comparison of Economic Systems* (Berkeley: University of California Press, 1971); Gregory Grossman, *Economic Systems* (Englewood Cliffs, N.J.: Prentice-Hall, 1967); and Raymond Aron, *The Industrial Society* (New York: Simon and Schuster, 1967).

9. Hugh Patrick, "Japanese High-Tech Industrial Policy in Broader Context," unpublished paper for the Conference on Japanese High-Tech Industrial Policy in Comparative Perspective, sponsored by the Committee on Japanese Economic Studies, New York, March 17–19, 1984, p. 25.

10. See Harry L. Cook, "Scope and Method in Economics," paper presented to the annual meeting of the Western Economics Association, Las Vegas, June 27, 1984.

11. For further discussion of what makes Japan different from the Anglo-American countries and a comparison between modern Japan and medieval Venice as examples of "trading nations," see Chalmers Johnson, "*La Serenissima* of the East," *Asian and African Studies* (Journal of the Israel Oriental Society) 18 (March, 1984): 57–73.

12. For further analytical details, see C. Johnson, ed., *The Industrial Policy Debate* (San Francisco: Institute for Contemporary Studies, 1984), pp. 3–26, 235–244.

13. "MITI Guides Biotech Industry," *Japan Times Weekly* (August 11, 1984), p. 11.

14. See Ministry of International Trade and Industry, *Background Information: White Paper on Small and Medium Enterprises in Japan, 1983*, MITI publication BI–52 (Tokyo: MITI, 1983); Paula Doe, "Benchaa Boomu: Japanese for Venture Capital," *Electronic Business* (January 1984): 98–100; *Japan Economic Journal* (July 19, 1983) (on the JDB); "The Technopolis Plan: Recent Developments," *News from MITI*, NR–289 84–5 (March 6, 1984); and Yoshimitsu Kuribayashi, "Japan's Venture

Businesses Forge Ahead," *International House of Japan Bulletin* 4 (Summer 1984): 2–3.

15. Andrea Boltho, "Italian and Japanese Postwar Growth: Some Similarities and Differences," in *Japan's Economy in a Comparative Perspective*, p. 54.

16. *Japan Economic Journal* (June 26, 1984), p. 26.

17. Japan's policies and institutions for dealing with declining industries have not been thoroughly analyzed in English. For a good study of one industry, see Richard J. Samuels, "The Industrial Destructuring of the Japanese Aluminum Industry," *Pacific Affairs* 56 (Fall 1983): 495–509. In Japanese, the most important source is Tsusho Sangyo-sho Sangyo Seisaku Kyoku (MITI, Industrial Policy Bureau), ed., *Sankoho no kaisetsu* [Explanation of the Special Measures Law for the Stabilization of Designated Recessed Industries], May 1983 (Tokyo: Tsusho Sangyo Chosa Kai, 1983).

18. The Industrial Structure Council is MITI's blue-ribbon, permanently in-session forum for discussing and coordinating its policies with the private sector.

Chapter 10

1. T. Hanami, and Y. Fukase, *Shugyokisoku no riron to Jitsumu* [The Theory and Practice of Works Rules] (Tokyo: Japan Institute of Labor, 1980).

2. Ministry of Labor, *Rodoshyo shirabe* [Survey by the Ministry of Labor] (Tokyo: Author, 1981).

3. Japan Institute of Labor, *80 nendai no rodokumiaikatsudo ni kansuru jittai chosa* [Survey on the State of the Trade Union Movement in the 1980s] (Tokyo: Author, 1982).

4. Prime Minister's Office, *Jigyosho tokei chosa* [Survey of Establishments] (Tokyo: Author, 1986).

5. For details of collective bargaining, see T. Shirai; "Recent Trends in Collective Bargaining in Japan," *International Labor Review*, no. 3 (1984): 307–318.

6. Ministry of Labor, *Rosi komyunikeishon chosa* [Survey on Labor-Management Communication] (Tokyo: Author, 1984).

7. See T. Inagami, *Labor-Management Communication at the Workshop Level* (Tokyo: Japan Institute of Labor, 1983).

8. Ministry of Labor, *Rodokumiai kiso chosa* [Basic Survey of Trade Unions] (Tokyo: Author, 1987).

Chapter 12

1. This is my estimate based on (1) correspondence with the Industrial Training Association of Japan concerning the number of their members practicing *seishin kyooiku*, (2) reports reaching me or the bank about other company training programs, and (3) mention in magazines, newspapers, and on television of the increase of *seishin kyooiku* in companies.

2. The material on company *seishin kyooiku* of a descriptive nature in Japanese includes articles in S. Nakamura's *Noryoku kaihastu keikaku* [A Plan for the Development of Ability], the special issue entitled "Seishin Kyooiku Tokushuu" of the magazine *Sangyoo Kunren* (1969), and my articles in *Kyoiku to Igaku* (17 [1969]), and in *Sangyo Kunren* (16 [1970]). In English, there is only my article in the *Journal of Asian and African Studies* 5 (1970), reprinted in *Japanese Culture and Behavior*, ed. T. S. Lebra and W. P. Lebra (1970), for descriptive information. There are, however, a large number of books in English that describe educational methods in Japan that come under the broad heading of *seishin kyooiku*. They include the writing on sports training, Zen, and pre-war education. Of special interest is H. Minami's 1953 *Nihohjin no Shinri* [The Psychology of the Japanese] for his discussion of wartime spiritualism. Ruth Benedict also discusses training and discipline in her analysis of Japanese character in *The Chrysanthemum and the Sword*.

3. See, for example, I. Nitobe's *Bushido: The Soul of Japan*; Benedict, ibid.; D. T. Suzuki's *Zen and Japanese Culture*; and Minami, ibid. Unfortunately, explanations of Japanese arts and sports in English seldom mention the *seishin* foundations or much of their methodology.

4. This study of the company's training program was part of a general study of the ideology and social organization of the bank which has been reported in my Ph. D. Dissertation, "The Organization and Ideology of A Japanese Bank: An Ethnographic Study of a Modern Organization," University of Pennsylvania, 1971.

5. For an account of this, see R. K. Hall's *Shushin: The Ethics of a Defeated Nation*.

6. P. Kapleau, in his classic *Three Pillars of Zen*, offers a thorough account of the procedures and philosophy of *rinzai* Zen, the same sect as the temple visited by the trainees. D. T. Suzuki described something of the life in a Zen temple where training is conducted in *The Training of the Zen Buddhist Monk*.

7. J. Toland mentions the Edajima tradition as it affected Japanese military spirit during World War II in *The Rising Sun: The Decline and Fall of the Japanese Empire 1936–1945.*

8. The term *seishin* has many applications, including *seishin no ai* (platonic love), *seishin bunseki* (psychoanalysis), *seishin kagaku* (mental science), and *dokuritsu seishin* (the spirit of independence). Many of these are Japanese translations of foreign concepts and perhaps it is not correct to argue for a single meaning for the word, yet, once the broad, inclusive perspective of human psychology at the foundation of the *seishin* concept is grasped the differences among the various applications recede in significance. My understanding is that *seishin* is a universal, human quality. Its character, strength, and development are relative to such factors as culture, education, experience, and the individual.

9. Many of the most commonly encountered values about personality, such as expressed by *nintai* (fortitude), *gaman* (patience), *shimboo* (endurance), *gambaru* (tenacity), and the like point to this form of behavior. Of course, loyalty is hardly meaningful without the ingredient of persistence.

10. Here I have in mind the expressions *kokoro-gamae, taido, kokoro no mochikata,* and *mono no kangaekata,* all of which translate as attitude.

11. To receive or accept in a *sunao* manner. *Sunao* is translated as gentle, obedient, and honest.

12. In the case of bank training, *sekinin* (responsibility) is frequently used, but the concepts *on* (beneficence), *giri* (obligation), and *gimu* (duty), emphasized by Benedict (1946) are seldom heard. My impression, however, is that *sekinin* is often used to support the same behavioral patterns that *gimu* and *giri* allegedly supported in the pre-war company situation.

Chapter 15

1. Dorothy Robins-Mowry, *The Hidden Sun* (Boulder, Colo.: Westview Press, 1983), p. 107.

2. Tomako Nakanishi, "Equality or Protection? Protective Legislation for Women in Japan," *International Labour Review* 122, no. 5 (September–October 1983): 613.

3. "Industrial Japan '82," *Far Eastern Economic Review* (December 3, 1982): 90.

4. Keiei to Jinji Kanri, No. 217, February 1980.

5. Robins-Mowry, *The Hidden Sun*, p. 173.

6. Hiroshi Takeuchi, "Working Women in Business Corporations— The Management Viewpoint," *Japan Quarterly* 229, no. 3 (July–September 1982): 319.

7. Robins-Mowry, *The Hidden Sun*, p. 168.

8. Ibid., p. 169.

9. Nakanishi, "Equality or Protection?" p. 609.

10. Ibid., p. 610.

11. Robert Evans, Jr., "Pay Differentials: The Case of Japan," *Monthly Labor Review* (October 1984): 26.

12. Takeuchi, "Working Women in Business Corporations," p. 321.

13. "Industrial Japan '82," p. 90.

14. Robins-Mowry, *The Hidden Sun*, p. 169.

15. "Personnel Management System," *Japanese Economic Studies* 13, no. 1–2 (Fall–Winter 1984–1985): 187.

16. Evans, "Pay Differentials," p. 24.

17. Mariko Bando Sugahara, "When Women Change Jobs," *Japan Quarterly* 33, no. 2 (April–June 1986): 181.

18. Jon Woronoff, *Japan's Wasted Workers* (Totawa, N.J.: Allanheld, Osum and Co., 1983), p. 118.

19. "Personnel Management System," p. 181.

20. Robins-Mowry, *The Hidden Sun*, p. 173.

21. Takako Sodei, "The Fatherless Family," *Japan Quarterly* 32, no. 1 (January–March 1985): 77.

22. Jane Condon, *A Half Step Behind* (New York: Dodd, Mead and Co., 1985), p. 56.

23. Ministry of Health and Welfare, *Survey of Single Mother Families* (May 1984).

24. Condon, *A Half Step Behind*, p. 49.

25. Ibid., p. 121.

26. Hideo Ishida, "Transferability of Japanese Human Resource Management Abroad," *Human Resource Management* 25, no. 1 (Spring 1986): 117.

27. Woronoff, *Japan's Wasted Workers*, p. 119.

28. T. Gutteridge and F. L. Otte, *Organizational Career Development: State of Practices* (Washington, D.C.: ASTD Press, 1983); J. W. Walker and T. G. Gutterridge, *Career Planning Practices: An AMA Survey Report* (New York: ASMACOM, 1979).

29. Andrew F. Sikula and John F. McKenna, "Individuals Must Take Charge of Career Development," *Personnel Administrator* (October 1983): 92.

30. J. W. Walker, "Let's Get Realistic About Career Paths," *Human Resources Management* 55 (Fall 1976): 2–7.

Chapter 16

1. Kunio Odaka, "Japanese Management: A Forward Looking Analysis," *Asian Productivity Organization* (Tokyo, 1986).

2. Masao Hanaoka, *Nihon no Romukanri* [Personnel Management in Japan], 2d ed. (Tokyo: Hakuto Shobo, 1987).

3. Peter F. Drucker, "Japan's Choices," *Foreign Affairs* (1987).

4. Ministry of Foreign Affairs, "Background Statistics on the Japanese Economy," *Japan* (May 1987).

5. Takao Watanabe, *Demystifying Japanese Management* (Tokyo: Gakuseisha Publishing Co., 1987).

6. *Igyoshu Koryu* are groups or networks of small and medium-sized enterprises organized to exchange technical information, promote management development, and engage in manpower exchange.

7. Hanaoka, *Nihon no Romukanri*.

8. *Nippon Jinji Gyosei Kenkyujo* [Japan Personnel Policy Research Institute] survey (February 8, 1985).

9. *Nihonteki Koyokanko no Henka to Tenbo* [Ministry of Labor Research Center] (Tokyo: Author, 1987).

10. "All That's Left," *The Economist* (November 28, 1987).

11. Robert C. Christopher, *Second to None: American Companies in Japan* (New York: Crown Publishers, 1986).

12. "Japanese Research Organizations Tap Foreign Technical Talent," *Nikkei High Tech Report* (April 13, 1987).

13. *Nihon Keizai Shinbun* (February 15, 1988).

14. Tomasz Mrocakowski, and Masao Hanaoka, "Japan's Managers Merit More Attention," *Asian Wall Street Journal* (October 29, 1987).

15. Masao Hanoaka, "Setting up a Hypothesis of the Characteristics of Personnel Management," Institute of Business Research, Daito Bunka University, 1986.

16. "Japanese Research Organizations Tap Foreign Technical Talent."

17. Bernard Wysocki, "In Japan, Breaking Step Is Hard to Do," *The Wall Street Journal* (December 14, 1987).

18. Ramchandran Jaikumar, "Postindustrial Manufacturing," *Harvard Business Review* (November–December 1986).

Chapter 18

1. Raymond J. Ahern, "Market Access in Japan: The U.S. Experience," *Congressional Research Service*, Report #85–37E (February 14, 1985).

2. "Japanese Barriers to U.S. Trade and Recent Japanese Government Trade Initiatives," Washington, D.C.: Office of the U.S. Trade Representative (November, 1982), p. 71.

3. Mitsuaki Shimaguchi and William Lazer, "Japanese Distribution Channels: Invisible Barriers to Market Entry," *MSU Business Topics* 27, no. 1 (Winter 1979): 51.

4. Randolph E. Ross, "Understanding the Japanese Distribution System: An Explanatory Framework," *European Journal of Marketing* 17, no. 1 (1983): 12.

5. Yoshi Tsurumi, "Managing Consumer and Industrial Systems in Japan," *Sloan Management Review* (Fall 1982): 42.

6. *Commercial Census*, Ministry of International Trade and Industry, 1979.

7. *Statistics of Commerce*, Ministry of International Trade and Industry, 1981; and *Statistical Abstracts of the United States, 1984* (Washington, D.C.: U.S. Dept. of Commerce, 1984).

8. *Statistics of Commerce*, ibid.

9. Arthur D. Little, Inc., "Strategies for Alleviating Recurring Bilateral Trade Problems Between Japan and the United States," in *The*

Japanese Non-Tariff Trade Barriers Issue: American Views and Implications for Japan–U.S. Relations, Report to the Japanese National Institute for Research Advancement (May, 1979), pp. iv, 249.

10. Chalmers Johnson, "The Internationalization of the Japanese Economy," *California Management Review*, no. 25 (Spring 1983): 19.

11. "Japanese Barriers to U.S. Trade," p. 72.

12. Shimaguchi and Lazer, "Japanese Distribution Channels," pp. 57–58.

13. Keiichi Konaga, "Future of Japan's Distribution Industry," *Dentsu Japan Marketing/Advertising* (Spring 1984): 1.

14. Ross, "Understanding the Japanese Distribution System," p. 12.

15. William Lazer, Shoji Musata and Hiroshi Kosaka, "Japanese Marketing: Towards a Better Understanding," *Journal of Marketing* 49, no. 2 (Spring 1985): 79.

16. William Lazer, Shoji Musata and Hiroshi Kosaka, "In the Convenience Store Sector, Strategic Management Is a Must," *Japan Times* (December 1983).

17. Hitomi Sekikawa, "Seven-Eleven Japan Develops About 2,000 Stores," Distribution Code Center (The Distribution Systems Research Institute, mimeo, February 1984), p. 1.

18. Konaga, "Future of Japan's Distribution Industry," p. 3.

19. Dodwell Marketing Consultants, *The Structure of the Japanese Retail Distribution Industry 1981/1982* (Tokyo: Author, 1981), p. 17.

20. Kyodo News Release [Tokyo] (March 1984).

21. Konaga, "Future of Japan's Distribution Industry," p. 1.

22. Ibid., p. 2.

Chapter 19

1. J. E. Harbour, "Comparison and Analysis of Automotive Manufacturing Productivity in the Japanese and North American Automotive Industry for the Manufacture of Subcompact and Compact Cars" (Berkly, Mich.: Harbour and Associates, 1981). National Academy of Engineering, *The Competitive Status of the U.S. Auto Industry* (Washington, D.C.: National Research Council, 1982). W. J. Abernathy, et al., *Industrial Renaissance* (New York: Basic Books, 1983). M. S. Flynn, "Comparison of

U.S.–Japan Production Costs: An Assessment," *Automobiles and the Future: Competition, Cooperation, and Change*, ed. R. E. Cole (Ann Arbor: Center for Japanese Studies, University of Michigan, 1983). M. A. Cusumano, *The Japanese Automobile Industry: Technology and Management at Nissan and Toyota* (Cambridge, Mass.: Council on East Asian Studies/Harvard University Press, 1985). A. Aizcorbe, et al., "Cost Competitiveness of the U.S. Automobile Industry," *Blind Intersection: Policy and the Automotive Industry*, ed. C. Winston (Washington, D.C.: Brookings Institution, 1987). J. F. Krafcik, "Comparative Analysis of Performance Indicators at World Auto Assembly Plants," Master's Thesis, MIT Sloan School of Management, Cambridge, Mass., 1988. M. B. Lieberman, "Learning, Productivity, and U.S.–Japan Industrial Competitiveness," *Managing International Manufacturing*, ed. K. Ferdows (Amsterdam: North Holland-Elsevier, 1988).

2. Cusumano, ibid.; National Academy of Engineering, ibid.

3. Cusumano, ibid.

4. J. F. Krafcik, "Learning from NUMMI," unpublished manuscript, MIT International Motor Vehicle Program, Cambridge, Mass., 1986. J. F. Krafcik, "Comparative Analysis of Performance Indicators at World Auto Assembly Plants," Master's Thesis, MIT Sloan School of Management, Cambridge, Mass., 1988.

5. Amagai Shogo, *Nihon jidosha kogyo no shiteki tenkai* [The Historical Development of the Japanese Automobile Industry] (Tokyo: Aki Shobo, 1982). Japan Automobile Manufactures Association, *Nihon no jidosha kogyo* [The Japanese Automobile Industry], Annual Report, Tokyo.

6. E. F. Vogel, *Japan as Number One* (Cambridge, Mass.: Harvard University Press, 1979). T. Pepper et al., *The Competition: Dealing with Japan* (New York: Praeger, 1985). J. C. Abegglen and G. Stalk, Jr., *Kaisha: The Japanese Corporation* (New York: Basic Books, 1985). C. Johnson, *MITI and the Japanese Miracle: The Growth of Industrial Policy* (Stanford, Calif.: Stanford University Press, 1982).

7. My thanks to Kim Clark of the Harvard Business School for helping me interpret these numbers from an economist's point of view.

8. Iwakoshi Tadahiro, *Jidosha kogyo ron* [A Discussion of the Automobile Industry] (Tokyo: University of Tokyo Press, 1969). (For international price comparisons by former Nissan president).

9. This comment is based on interviews with former Nissan managers Okumura Shoji, Sasaki Sadamichi, Kawazoe Soichi, Katayama Yutaka, Maeda Riichi (May 1982), and Matsuzaki Shiro (July 1982).

10. Krafcik's data confirms that the Japanese assembly plants with

the highest levels of productivity also tend to have the highest levels of quality (fewest defects reported by customers) and are highly flexible, measured by the number of distinct underbodies produced per assembly line. See Krafcik, "Comparative Analysis of Performance Indicators."

11. *Nihon jidosha kogyo shi kojutsu kiroku shu* [Recordings of Oral Interviews on the History of the Japanese Auto Industry], vol. 2 (Tokyo: Jidosha Kogyo Shinko Kai [Automobile Promotion Association], 1975). Aikawa Yoshisuke, *Watakushi no rirekisho* [My Career], vol. 24, (Tokyo: Nihon Deizai Shimbunsha, 1965). *Nissan jidosha sanjunen shi* [A Thirty-Year History of Nissan Motor] (Tokyo: Nissan Motor Company, 1964). Interviews with former Nissan managers Katayama, Sasaki, Okumura, and Matsuzaki.

12. *Toyota jidosha sanju-nen shi* [A Thirty-Year History of Toyota] (Nagoya: Toyota Motor Company, 1967). Okumura Shoji, *Jidosha kogyo no hatten dankai to kozo* [The Development Stages and Structure of the Automobile Industry], Gendai Nihon sangyo koza [Series on Contemporary Japanese Industry], ed. Arisawa Hiromi (Tokyo: Iwanami Shoten, 1960). Shotaro Kamiya, *My Life with Toyota* (Nagoya: Toyota Motor Sales, 1976). Morikawa Hidemasa, "Toyoda Kiichiro," *Nihon no kigyoka* [Japanese Entrepreneurs], vol. 3, ed. Morikawa Hidemasa et al. (Tokyo: Yuhikaku Shinso, 1978).

13. Ohno Taiichi, *Toyota seisan boshiki* [The Toyota Production System] (Tokyo: Daiyamondo, 1978). My interview with Ohno (March 18, 1983); and *Toyota jidosha sanhju-nen shi.*

14. On NUMMI and Honda, see Krafcik, "Learning from NUMMI." Haruo Shimada and J. P. MacDuffie, "Industrial Relations and 'Humanware': An Analysis of Japanese Investments in the U.S.," working paper 1855–88, MIT Sloan School of Management and MIT International Motor Vehicle Program, 1986.

Chapter 20

1. W. Kendall, "Why Japanese Workers Work," *Management Today* (January 1984).

2. G. C. Allen, *The Japanese Economy* (London: Weidenfeld and Nicholson, 1981).

3. A. S. Baillie, "Sub-Contracting Based on Integrated Standards: The Japanese Approach," *Journal of Purchasing and Materials Management* (Spring 1986).

4. R. Dore, *Taking Japan Seriously* (Atlantic Highlands, N.J.: Athlone Press, 1987).

5. Ibid.

6. M. A. Cusamano, *The Japanese Automobile Industry* (Cambridge, Mass.: Harvard University Press, 1985).

7. M. Y. Yoshino and T. B. Lifsan, *The Invisible Link—Japan's Sogo Shosha and the Organization of Trade* (Cambridge, Mass.: MIT Press, 1986).

8. Dore, *Taking Japan Seriously.*

9. R. Johnston and P. R. Lawrence, "Beyond Vertical Integration— The Rise of the Value-Adding Partnership," *Harvard Business Review* (July–August 1988).

10. Dore, *Taking Japan Seriously.*

GLOSSARY AND INDEX OF JAPANESE WORDS AND PHRASES

genkan	entrance	127
genki	energetic, spirited	175
giri	indebtedness	103, 113–17, 119–20
giri-gatai	responsible, trustworthy	115
guinomi	type of saké cup	130
gyo seki	performance	281
haiku	17-syllable poem	68
han	work groups	179
hanko	seal	234
hansei	self-reflection	211
haragei	"belly" language	106
hiragana	Japanese phonetic alphabet	41
honbu	division	228
honbucho	general manager	228
honne	true feelings	107
hooshi	service	200
igyoshu koryu	company groups for manpower exchange	276
ii ko	good child	174
ijime	bullying	177
jen	compassion	61
jibun	self-awareness	106
jikaku	self	211
jinji koka	merit rating	281
jizo	roadside Shinto shrines	111
jokyuu	restaurant service personnel	129
jomukai	executive committee meeting	232, 235
juku	after school classes	170
ka	section	228
kacho	section head	228
kaigi	conference	235
kaisha	my company	63
kakari	subsection	228
kakaricho	subsection head	228

nikutaiteki	physical or corporal	207
ningen kankei	network of relationships	104
ninjo	empathy	106, 116
Noh	dance form	33
noshi	decoration	109
o-bon	festival	114, 116
ochazuke	rice preparation	125
ochugen	gift-giving season	224
okamisan	restaurant service personnel	129
omiyage	type of gift	224
omote	front	106
on	obligations	103, 114
oosetsuma	reception room	127
oseibo	gift-giving season	224
otonashii	mild or gentle	175
otshidama	type of gift	112
raiu	thundershowers	34
ringi	decision making process	24, 232
ringisho	document used for ringi	232
rotoo	training exercise	195–98
ryooriya	Japanese style restaurant	128
ryootei	Japanese style restaurant	123, 128, 236
saké	rice wine	130–32
samidare	early summer rain	34
samurai	warrior class	68–69, 183
satori	enlightenment	191
seishin kyooiku	spiritual education	70, 183–213
seishin-shugi	spiritualism	184
seishinryoku	spiritual strength	207
seken	reference group	174
seppuku	ritual suicide	68
shikaku	position title	280
shikaku-seido	status promotion	273
shikon shosai	scholarly spirit, commercial talent	47

CONTRIBUTORS

Dean C. BARNLUND is Professor of Speech Communications, San Francisco State University, San Francisco, California.

Harumi BEFU is Professor in the Department of Anthropology, Stanford University, Stanford, California.

Michael A. CUSUMANO is Mitsubishi Career Development Associate Professor of Management in the School of Management, Massachusetts Institute of Technology, Cambridge, Massachusetts.

Michael R. CZINKOTA is Professor in the School of Business, Georgetown University, Washington, D.C.

Subhash G. DURLABHJI is Associate Professor in the Division of Business, Northwestern State University, Natchitoches, Louisiana.

Edward T. HALL is Emeritus Professor of Anthropology at Northwestern University. He is the author of the best-selling *The Silent Language* and seven other books on intercultural communication. His most recent book *An Anthropology of Everyday Life* was published by Doubleday/Anchor in 1992.

Mildred Reed HALL is an author and partner in Edward T. Hall Associates, consultants in intercultural communication, and resides in Santa Fe, New Mexico.

Masao HANAOKA is Professor of Management at Daito Bunki University, Tokyo, Japan.

Toshiro HIROMOTO is Professor in the Graduate School of Commerce, Hitotsubashi University, Kunitachi, Tokyo, Japan.

Johny K. JOHANSSON is the McCrane-Shaker Professor of International Business and Marketing in the School of Business Administration, Georgetown University, Washington, D.C.

Chalmers JOHNSON is Professor in the Graduate School of International Relations and Pacific Studies, University of California, San Diego, in La Jolla, California.

Tobioka KEN is Director of the Modern Human Science Institute in Tokyo, Japan, and is a systems engineering specialist who undertakes research projects commissioned by government agencies, serving also as a consultant for private corporations.

Paul LANSING is Professor in the Department of Business Administration at the University of Illinois, Champaign-Urbana.

Milton C. LAUENSTEIN is Chairman of the Board of Telequip Corporation, Hollis, New Hampshire.

Norton E. MARKS is Professor of Marketing, Department of Marketing, at California State University, San Bernadino, California.

Tomasz MROCZKOWSKI is Professor of International Business in Kogod College of Business Administration at The American University, Washington, D.C.

Ikujiro NONAKA is at the Institute for Business Research, Hitotsubashi University, Kunitachi, Tokyo, Japan.

Kunio ODAKA is with the Asian Productivity Organization, Minatu-ku, Tokyo, Japan.

Toshiaki OHTA resides in Sapporo, Japan.

Mayumi OTSUBO is with the Bridgestone Tire Company, Chuo-ku, Tokyo, Japan.

John RAMSAY is Senior Lecturer in Purchasing, Economics, and Negotiation at the Management Center of the Staffordshire Polytechnic, England.

Kathryn J. READY is Associate Professor in the Department of Business Administration, University of Wisconsin, Eau Claire.

Scott ROACH is in the Division of Business, Northwestern State University, Natchitoches, Louisiana.

Thomas P. ROHLEN is Professor in the School of Education and Senior Fellow, Institute for International Studies, Stanford University, Stanford, California.

Merry I. WHITE is Associate Professor of Sociology, Boston University, and Associate in Research at the Edwin O. Reischauer Institute of Japanese Studies, Harvard University.

INDEX